The
Dissidence of Dissent
The Monthly Repository
1806-1838

The
Dissidence of Dissent
The Monthly Repository, 1806-1838

Under the Editorship of Robert Aspland,
W. J. Fox, R. H. Horne, & Leigh Hunt

With a Chapter on
Religious Periodicals, 1700-1825

By
Francis E. Mineka

OCTAGON BOOKS

A DIVISION OF FARRAR, STRAUS AND GIROUX

New York   1972

Copyright, 1944, by The University of North Carolina Press

Reprinted 1972
by special arrangement with The University of North Carolina Press

OCTAGON BOOKS
A Division of Farrar, Straus & Giroux, Inc.
19 Union Square West
New York, N. Y. 10003

Library of Congress Cataloging in Publication Data

Mineka, Francis Edward, 1907-
    The dissidence of dissent; the Monthly repository,
    1806-1838.
    Originally presented as the author's thesis, Columbia, 1943.
    Bibliography: p.
        1. The Monthly repository. 2. Dissenters, Religious—Eng-
        land. 3 Religion—Periodicals—Bibliography. 4. Theology
        —Periodicals—Bibliography. 5. Fox, William Johnson,
        1786-1864. I. Title.
PN5130.M6M5   1972   052   72-159215
ISBN 0-374-95770-3

Manufactured by Braun-Brumfield, Inc.
Ann Arbor, Michigan

Printed in the United States of America

To
My Father and Mother

Preface

MONCURE D. CONWAY, prominent liberal American preacher who spent the chief years of his ministry in London, wrote in 1894 in his *Centenary History of the South Place Society:* "In the *Monthly Repository* . . . you will find a better history than anywhere else of the progress of English thought and reform during the first twenty years of this chapel." Conway later refers to the *Repository* as the best work of reference for "anyone who would study the intellectual progress of England sixty years ago."

In the present study I have attempted to trace the development of this now little known periodical from the years of its publication as the miscellaneous journal of the Unitarian movement (1806-1831), through its transformation under the editorship of William Johnson Fox (1828-1836) into a liberal magazine of political, social, and literary significance, to its demise in the hands of Richard Hengist Horne (1836-1837) and of Leigh Hunt (1837-1838). I have given especial emphasis to the period of the editorship of Fox, a leading reformer of his day and friend of Browning, Forster, Macready, John Stuart Mill, and Harriet Martineau; for under Fox, the *Repository* broke away from its moorings in the Unitarian controversy to sail the wider seas of political and social reform.

The circulation of the periodical was never large, at least in comparison with that of the great reviews, the *Edinburgh* and the *Quarterly,* or of the popular magazines, like *Blackwood's* and *Fraser's,* or of the larger denominational periodicals, like the *Baptist* and *Methodist* magazines; but it led the way in the advocacy of reforms that took the long years of the nineteenth century to complete. During its best years, the period immediately preceding the reign of Victoria, the *Repository* published the early work of now well known writers such as Mill, Browning, and Harriet Martineau, and of lesser figures such as R. H. Horne, Charles Reece Pemberton, Emily Taylor, and Thomas Wade. It was the first periodical to give recognition to the genius of Browning, and one of the earliest to hail Tennyson. In religion, the *Repository* was a leader in the breaking down of dogmatism, in the modern critical study of the Bible in England, and in the removal of legal disabilities of Dissenters and freethinkers.

Little study has thus far been made of religious periodical literature in England; in fact, it is only within recent years that there has been much study even of the outstanding secular reviews and magazines. The reason for the almost complete neglect of the religious periodicals is not far to seek. Many were short-lived; many existed chiefly for the defense of some religious dogma that has now disappeared into the modern limbo reserved for doctrinal controversy; most of them are dull reading, today at least. Perhaps only a professional theologian can be expected to follow in all its ramifications the tortuous course of eighteenth- and nineteenth-century theological warfare. The modern reader is appalled by the seemingly endless and often fruitless debates over minor doctrinal points. Nevertheless, religious periodicals do offer a fruitful if hitherto largely neglected field of investigation for the social and the literary historian. Though usually of little importance as literature, these publications are often of genuine significance as a record of both the clerical and the lay mind and as an index to tastes in popular reading. Since to date there seems to have been no comprehensive study of English religious journalism, I have included an introductory survey of religious periodicals from 1700 to 1825.

Although I have provided a bibliography of works consulted, I should here like to acknowledge my important debts to certain writers. My chief source has been, of course, the close to 30,000 pages of the *Repository* itself and innumerable pages of eighteenth- and early nineteenth-century periodicals, but I am also considerably indebted to pioneer workers in the field of English periodicals. To the compilers of the British Museum *Catalogue*, of the *Union List of Serials*, and the *Times Tercentenary Handlist*, and to R. S. Crane and F. B. Kaye for their *Census of British Newspapers and Periodicals, 1620-1800*, every student of periodical literature owes a lasting debt. Walter Graham's *English Literary Periodicals* and George L. Nesbitt's *Benthamite Reviewing* have been the two modern studies to which I have had most frequent occasion to refer. I am also grateful to James M. McCrimmon, who has generously granted me permission to make use of some hitherto unpublished information concerning John Stuart Mill's contributions to periodicals.

Unitarianism has been fortunate in its historians, and to three of them in particular I am indebted: to the late Alexander Gordon for much biographical information; to Raymond V. Holt for his *Unitarian Contribution to Social Progress in England;* and to Herbert McLachlan for his survey of Unitarian periodicals in his *Unitarian Movement in the Religious Life of England* and for several of his other studies. The chief source for the career of W. J. Fox continues to be the *Life* by Richard Garnett, which it has been necessary to correct or supplement only occasionally.

It is a pleasure also to record more personal obligations incurred during my research. As a former member of the faculty of my Alma Mater, Hamilton College, I owe many debts to friends and colleagues there: to Librarian Emeritus Joseph D. Ibbotson, who first encouraged me to undertake this study and secured materials for me; to his successor Dr. Lewis F. Stieg, who has cheerfully supplied many of my needs; to Professor John M. Moore, who located a file of the *Repository* for me; to Professor Frank H. Ristine, whose encouragement and helpful advice over a long period of time have been unfailing and generous; and to Professor George L. Nesbitt, who by his own study of the *Westminster Review* led the way for me and by his criticism of the manuscript in its final stages made several important contributions. I would also acknowledge my thanks to the Trustees of Hamilton College for two generous leaves of absence which made possible the completion of my work.

My debts at Columbia are also many: to the Trustees of the University for an appointment in 1941-1942 as University Fellow in English and Comparative Literature; to the Columbia Library for many services; and to Professors Oscar James Campbell, Susanne Howe Nobbe, Frank A. Patterson, William Haller, Marjorie Nicolson, Roger Sherman Loomis, William York Tindall, and Herbert Schneider for reading and criticizing my manuscript. Greatest of my debts, however, is to Professor Emery Neff, under whose guidance the study has been completed. Professor Neff's encouragement, his wide knowledge of nineteenth-century literature, and his helpful criticism have always been available to me, and for them I am deeply grateful.

To libraries and librarians other than those already mentioned I owe thanks for many courtesies and much assistance: to the British Museum for the manuscript identification of authors of the second series of the *Repository;* to Dr. Williams' Library in London for the typescript of Crabb Robinson's Diary and for other materials on the history of Dissent; to the library of the State University of Iowa for Leigh Hunt's identification of authors in the final volumes of the magazine; and to the libraries of Oberlin and Tufts colleges, of Yale, Harvard, Chicago, Cornell, Colgate, North-western, and Texas universities, of Union, Colgate-Rochester, and Princeton theological seminaries; and to the Enoch Pratt Free Library, the New York Public Library, and the Library of Congress, for the use of various items in their periodical collections.

Last of all, I would acknowledge the unfailing encouragement and assistance in countless ways that my wife has given me. Without her help, the task would have been immeasurably greater and far less rewarding. It is her first book, too.

F.E.M.

The University of Texas
June 24, 1943

Contents

Introduction

1: "A Sect Every Where Spoken Against"

Our present situation, and that of the Dissenters in general, calls in a particular manner for the exercise of Christian principles. The cause of the Dissenters may now be said to be, what Christianity itself was, and long continued to be, viz. "a sect every where spoken against." We are exposed to insult and outrage, though not to avowed persecution, on this account. . . .[1]

THE SCENE IS the Gravel Pit Meeting House in Hackney, near London; the date, March 30, 1794; the speaker, Joseph Priestley; the occasion, his farewell address to his congregation before embarking for America, there to spend his last years in exile from his native England for the expression of his radical religious and political views. The room is crowded, not alone with members of the Gravel Pit congregation, but with visitors from London, curious to see this man who three years earlier had been driven from Birmingham, where his home and his property had been destroyed by a raging mob led, some of his adherents say, by a clergyman of the Established Church. Perhaps the visitors hope to hear a wicked diatribe against Church and King, for it has been rumored that George III has privately approved the mob's treatment of Dr. Priestley and his friends; but if the visitors expect Socinian, Jacobinical fulminations, they are disappointed, for Priestley's sermon breathes charity and tolerance. There is none of the extravagant rhetoric which five years earlier marked that famous sermon of Dr. Priestley's friend and predecessor at the Gravel Pit, Dr. Richard Price, before the Society for Commemorating the Revolution in Great Britain, which Mr. Burke had belabored in his *Reflections on the Revolution in France;* here are to be

[1] Joseph Priestley, *The Use of Christianity, Especially in Difficult Times*, p. 7.

heard none of Dr. Price's resounding phrases of "the dominion of kings changed for the dominion of laws, and the
dominion of priests giving way to the dominion of reason
and conscience," or of the "blaze that lays despotism in
ashes, and warms and illuminates Europe."[2]

Priestley does, it is true, express his faith in the ultimate
triumph of liberal ideas in religion and government, but
he expresses that faith, in his hesitant, at times stammering
delivery, with moderation and candor. He alludes with
pride to the fact that, though Unitarians in all ages and
all nations have been repressed by civil magistrates and by
established religion, they have continued to gain ground,
and of late more rapidly than ever before. He appeals for
the dominance of reason and reflection over dogma and
blind faith. "Men cannot embrace as sacred truth anything
at which their common sense revolts. Nor can that be considered as a truth of revealed religion, which is contrary to
the most obvious and acknowledged truths of natural religion."[3] The great increase in unbelief has arisen only because Christianity has not purified itself by the light of
reason from its corruptions and abuses.

One week after this final avowal of his faith in rational
principles in religion, in Unitarianism, Priestley set sail for
America, where he eventually settled in the home state of
his departed friend, Benjamin Franklin, and lived there the
last ten years of his life. But, though gone from England,
he continued to be regarded as the chief apostle of Unitarianism; as such he was attacked alike by Churchmen and
orthodox Dissenters—and perhaps even more vigorously by
the latter, for orthodox Dissent felt ever compelled to ward
off suspicion of heresy.

The fight against Unitarianism united in opposition

[2] Richard Price, *A Discourse on the Love of Our Country, November 4, 1789*,
pp. 49-50.
[3] Priestley, *op. cit.*, pp. 25-26.

groups as dissimilar as the Anglicans, the Methodists, and the Roman Catholics. Unitarians continued to regard themselves, often almost with pride it seems, as "a sect every where spoken against." Their religion was criticized as cold, unfeeling, a thing of head instead of heart, even in a day when *enthusiasm* in religion was still something of a social stigma. They were accused of undermining the government as well as the Church, for the Anglicans at least chose to regard Church and State as having a common foundation. Unitarians were linked with Deists, blasphemers, scoffers, though common justice was compelled to admit that among their ranks were some of the most intelligent, God-fearing citizens of their day. Some of the orthodox denied them even the name of Christian,[4] and until 1813 they were legally, though not in practice, subject to prosecution for blasphemy in denying the doctrine of the Trinity.

The origins of the Unitarian movement are even more involved and intricate than the many doctrinal battles which it provoked, but some brief account is necessary as a basis for understanding the ideas and principles of the periodical which is the immediate subject of concern in this study. If the present writer fails to make completely clear the development of the movement, he will not be the first so to fail; even apologists of the Established Church have been known to fall into error or heresy themselves in their attempts to unravel or refute Socinian or Unitarian doctrines. When in the late seventeenth century the Dean of St. Paul's, Dr. William Sherlock, in attempting to defend the doctrine of the Trinity from the assaults of the Unitarian tracts, proceeded to divide the Trinity into three distinct entities, he himself was promptly accused by the prominent preacher, Dr. Robert South, of advocating another heresy—Tritheism. Dr. South's refutation in turn was also labeled as heresy, for, in

[4] In the United States today the Federal Council of Churches of Christ does not admit the Unitarians.

explaining the Trinity as a belief in three aspects or modes of one God, he had lapsed into what was known as Sabellianism. At length the King was prevailed upon to order the clergy to abstain from unusual explanations of the doctrine; it was felt to be safer to let the Trinity be regarded as an unexplainable mystery![5]

William Hazlitt once said, "It would be in vain to strew the flowers of poetry round the borders of the Unitarian controversy."[6] Certainly Hazlitt knew what he was talking about, for his father, the Reverend William Hazlitt, was a Unitarian preacher, both in England and America, and an eager and devoted partaker in the controversy.[7] There is no intention on the part of the present writer to strew flowers of any kind about the movement, but he does feel that its significance has sometimes been underestimated.

Though we are here almost solely concerned with Unitarianism as it developed in England, it must be remembered that the movement was in origin not purely English. The name itself seems to have originated in Hungary about the middle of the sixteenth century, but differences in the interpretation of the concept of the Trinity had caused controversy ever since the time of Arius, who died in 336, and for whom the Arian heresy is named. Not until the time of the Reformation, however, did the anti-Trinitarians, in their attempt to restore Christianity to what they considered its lost purity, again become important enough to warrant the use of stern repressive measures against them. Then so rapidly for a time did the movement spread that Protestants even more than Catholics became alarmed. It was John

---

[5] Henry Gow, *The Unitarians*, pp. 34-35.

[6] "On the Tendency of Sects," *Works*, I, 51.

[7] Cf. Hazlitt's tribute to his father in "On Court Influence," *Works*, III, 265-66. The younger Hazlitt's first literary production, written at the age of thirteen, was a letter to the *Shrewsbury Chronicle* on the Birmingham riots of July 14, 1791, which drove Priestley from his home. See P. P. Howe, *William Hazlitt*, p. 12.

Calvin who bore the responsibility for burning Michael Servetus at the stake in Geneva in 1553; years earlier Servetus had published his heretical *De Trinitatis Erroribus*, in which he had declared the doctrine to be unscriptural and the product of the Greek sophists.

Anti-Trinitarianism first definitely took root in Poland and achieved toleration there for nearly a century. The heresy had appeared there as early as 1539; the arrival in 1579 of the Italian, Faustus Socinus (1539-1604), led to the establishment of a new type of Unitarianism, henceforth known as Socinianism. The *Racovian Catechism*, published in Poland in 1605, is largely an expression of the views of Socinus, which, unlike those of modern Unitarians, did not stress the human nature of Christ and permitted him to be worshipped. Socinus was more concerned with the doctrines relating to original sin, eternal punishment, and the atonement; in his rejection of these lay the great difference between Socinianism and Calvinism. Perhaps his greatest contribution was his emphasis upon the use of critical reason in examining Scriptural doctrines; among the orthodox, *Socinian* eventually became an opprobrious epithet to describe anyone who had the temerity to apply critical reason to Revelation. Later English Unitarians always rejected the name "Socinian" so frequently hurled at them as a term of reproach, though actually, on the doctrine of the Trinity, they were more heretical than the real Socinians.

Protestant immigrants from the Low Countries during the reign of Henry VIII seem to have been the first to bring anti-Trinitarianism to England. Between 1548 and 1612 at least eight persons were burned at the stake for the avowal of such beliefs; two executions resulted from the overbold dedication to James I of a Latin translation of the *Racovian Catechism* in 1609, and the publication itself was formally burned in 1614. Although at this time there was no defined movement, the law sought the suppression of even isolated cases of Unitarianism. In 1640 the importation, printing, or circulation of Socinian books was prohibited by a canon of the Church of England; ministers were forbidden to preach the heretical doctrines, and laymen who held such views were to be excommunicated.

But it was not the Anglicans alone who held Socinianism in detestation: Independents and Presbyterians alike agreed in this. In 1648, with the Presbyterians in power, Parliament decreed that the denial of the Trinity should be a capital crime; by the strange reversals of time, it is to these seventeenth-century Presbyterians that some of the oldest Unitarian societies in England trace their ancestry. Cromwell was more tolerant; he refused to apply the extreme law in the case of Paul Best (1590?-1657) and John Biddle (1615-1662), though both men suffered long imprisonment. An English translation of the *Racovian Catechism,* published at Amsterdam in 1652, led the Council of State to order John Owen, Vice-Chancellor of Oxford, to issue a reply, which appeared three years later as *Vindiciae Evangelicae.* Owen declared that the Socinian poison had infected almost every corner of England.

Biddle has sometimes been called the "father" of English Unitarianism, though there is little direct connection between the seventeenth-century movement and that of the late eighteenth century. He was a graduate, not of Cambridge, whence came so many of the radical Puritan divines, but of Oxford. Imprisonment and exile did not prevent the increase of his followers, and from 1652 to 1654 he presided over a Socinian conventicle in London. The Act of Uniformity and Biddle's death in 1662 checked the growth of the movement, however, though the tendency persisted. The chief source of the heresy at this time, strangely enough, was the study of the Bible, which the Puritans so vigorously recommended and required; Biddle himself claimed to have reached his conclusions by reading the Bible before he encountered the teachings of Socinus. John Milton, though he was acquainted with some of the Socinian literature, arrived at the so-called Arian position in theology by his study of the Sacred Text. James Martineau, leading nineteenth-century Unitarian thinker, has said: "The earlier Unitarians, notwithstanding their repute of rationalism, drew their doctrines out of the Scriptures, much to their own surprise, and did not import it into them."[8]

Neither the anti-Trinitarians nor the Catholics were given relief by the Toleration Act of 1689, but Socinian ferment was at work within the Established Church itself. Unitarianism about this time underwent what has sometimes been called its "Tractarian" period, though the analogy with the nineteenth-century movement in the Church is not altogether complete. Thomas Firmin (1632-1697), a well-to-do merchant and philanthropist, an Anglican and yet a follower of Biddle, promoted the publication of a series of Unitarian tracts, chiefly by members of the Establishment, designed to inject more liberal doctrines into the theology of the Church. One of the most important of the tracts was *A Brief History of the Unitarians, called also Socinians* (1687), by the Reverend Stephen Nye, an Anglican clergyman. Though no important secessions occurred as a result of this tractarian activity, a long controversy was provoked within the Church, in the course of which defense of the Trinity sometimes led to other heresies.

In the early years of the eighteenth century a movement in theology somewhat less radical than Unitarianism, labeled by its opponents as "Arian," had considerable vogue within Anglican bounds. For a time Arian or semi-Arian views, which attributed a sort of "quasi-divinity" to Christ

[8] G. Bonet-Maury, *Early Sources of English Unitarian Christianity*, Introduction (by James Martineau), p. xii.

(i.e., that his nature was essentially subordinate to that of God), seemed more likely to prevail, both in the Church and among certain Dissenters, than did Unitarian views, which insisted upon the simple humanity of Christ. Arianism rather than Unitarianism dominated the rationalist theology for at least the first half of the century. In 1712 Dr. Samuel Clarke, Rector of St. James's, Westminster, published *The Scripture Doctrine of the Trinity,* which aroused much attention, particularly among the Dissenters. The volume contained the Scripture texts which bore on the Trinity, statements of the doctrine, and discussion of relevant passages in the liturgy of the Church. Protected by its formularies, the Church was able to withstand or absorb the controversy and nothing of lasting consequence came of it.

But in the Dissenting churches, protected by no articles, rationalism made deeper inroads. Crucial in the development of the rationalistic movement was the Salters' Hall controversy of 1719. At Exeter, James Peirce, a Dissenting minister, had been publicly accused of spreading Arian views. Advice was sought from the association of ministers of the Three Denominations in London. At a gathering of over one hundred Presbyterian, Baptist, and Independent ministers held at Salters' Hall Meeting House, an attempt was made to impose a declaration of belief in the doctrine of the Trinity, which was to be attached to "Advices" to be sent to the Exeter churches. The attempt failed by four votes, or as the chairman of the meeting announced, "The Bible has it by four votes." This failure to adopt something approaching a creed should not be interpreted as meaning that a majority at this time held anti-Trinitarian views; it was rather evidence of the determination of the Protestant Dissenters not to impose creeds or any checks upon the development of thought, and of a desire to maintain the principle of allowing individual congregations freedom. The vote was a verdict on the side of liberty as opposed to uniformity.

From this time on may be noted in the three chief Dissenting sects the growth of the rationalistic movement which was to culminate in the Unitarianism of the latter half of the century. In the Presbyterian group, oddly enough, the development became most marked; oddly, because in the seventeenth century the Presbyterian had been the most rigidly orthodox of the three denominations, and in some respects more conservative than the Established Church itself. By the end of the eighteenth century, English (not Scottish) Presbyterianism had become almost completely identified with Unitarianism.

In the excellent study *Religion and Learning,* which traces the development in English Presbyterian thought from 1662 to 1800, Olive M. Griffiths clearly establishes that "the general trend of the development resulted from their knowledge of the contemporary movements in science and philosophy, epistemology and psychology."[9] It must be remembered that the Presbyterians were deeply shocked by their ejection as a result of the Act of Uniformity in 1662. Before that, they had wanted, not separation from the Church, but establishment for themselves; they had sought to abolish the episcopacy and establish their own form of ecclesiastical government, resembling that of Scotland. Under the Long Parliament they had opposed the principle of toleration of sects as inconsistent with their ideas of a true church. The Presbyterians had opposed the execution of Charles I and had worked for the return of his son in 1660, hoping for more favor than they had received under Cromwell. But they mistook their man; Charles II soon made it evident that he did not consider Presbyterianism "the religion of a

[9] O. M. Griffiths, *Religion and Learning,* p. 3.

gentleman." As a result of the Act of Uniformity, "the two thousand" English ministers on St. Bartholomew's Day, 1662, became Dissenters. The Presbyterians among these were worse off than they had been under Cromwell, for they were now quite cut off from the Church.

The ejected ministers were by no means infected with Unitarianism; in some ways they were more orthodox in their theology than some of those who subscribed according to the Act and remained within the Anglican communion. The great majority of them, like Richard Baxter, hoped for eventual reinclusion in the Church; they revered the Church and sought only correction of what they regarded as her errors. By the time of the Toleration Act (1689), however, the Nonconformists began to lose hope of inclusion; they began to build chapels of their own and to educate a new generation of clergy to replace their aging ministers. Most of the new chapels were built with "open," or non-doctrinal, trusts: no creeds were specified, and the chapels were simply dedicated to "the worship of Almighty God." Since no subscription to articles or creed was required and since no central organization existed to ensure uniformity, opportunities arose for the development of changing ideas.

Excluded from the universities of Oxford and Cambridge by the requirement of subscription to the articles of the Church (Cambridge admitted Dissenters but granted no degrees without subscription), the Nonconformists developed independent academies at home and patronized Scottish and foreign universities, especially Edinburgh and Glasgow, Leyden and Utrecht. In the Dissenting academies at home, the emphasis upon natural science and upon the principle of the sufficiency of the Scriptures in the elucidation of Christian doctrine, led to the progress of independent, free inquiry. John Taylor (1694-1761), divinity tutor at Warrington Academy, urged his students to "assent to no principle or sentiment, by me taught or advanced, but only so far as it shall appear to you to be supported or justified by proper evidence from Revelation or the reason of things." His students were told to keep their minds always open to evidence and to assert for themselves "and freely allow to others the inalienable rights of judgment and conscience."[10] Those English students who pursued their higher education in the Dutch universities found their Calvinism being modified by the more liberal foreign theologians.

At home other influences were at work, not the least of which was John Locke. Locke had endeared himself to Nonconformists by his defense of toleration; behind the scenes he had helped draw up the Toleration Act of 1689, and his first *Letter concerning Toleration* (published anonymously that same year) had set up that principle as "the chief characteristical mark of the true church."[11] Throughout the century Locke remained the idol of the Dissenters. His *Essay concerning Human Understanding* (1690), long used as a text in the Dissenting academies, by its attack on innate ideas of God, undoubtedly strengthened the cause of rational inquiry into sacred truth: "I doubt not but to show that a man, by the right use of his natural abilities, may, without any innate principles, attain a knowledge of God, and other things that concern him."[12] Reason rather than authority should be regarded as the basis of truth. In his *Vindication of the Reasonableness of Christianity* (1695) and its two supplementary letters, Locke argued not only for the impartial use of reason in examining the Scriptures but also for a reduction of the essentials of Christian doctrine to a recognition of the Messiahship of Jesus, virtually the Socinian position.

[10] *Monthly Repository*, VIII (1813), 89.   [11] Locke, *Works*, II, 232.
[12] *Essay concerning Human Understanding*, Bk. I, ch. 4, sec. 12.

Convince but men of the mission of Jesus Christ, make them but see the truth, simplicity, and reasonableness of what he himself taught, and required to be believed by his followers; and you need not doubt, but, being once fully persuaded by his doctrine, and the advantages which all Christians agree are received by him, such converts will not lay by the Scriptures, but by a constant reading and study of them, get all the light they can from this divine revelation, and nourish themselves up in the words of faith, and of good doctrine.[13]

Though his views were held suspect by the orthodox of his own day (one of the anti-Trinitarian tracts published by Firmin was attributed to him), complete evidence was lacking as to the extent of his heretical views until the publication, long after his death, of his *Commonplace Book* (1829).[14]

In summary, it may be said that the predominant influence on Presbyterian thinking from the late seventeenth through the eighteenth century, like the spirit of the age, was rationalistic. The reverence for authority which had marked earlier Presbyterianism was breaking down; the discoveries in science, in medicine and psychology particularly, led to increased respect for human reason in investigating both sacred and profane truth. The earlier Presbyterian acceptance of the Reformation doctrines of original sin, the total depravity of man, and the atonement, became more and more modified, both through the influence of Polish and Dutch theologians and through the English and Scottish philosophers' development of the theory of the natural goodness of man. Increasingly, Presbyterians asserted the right of individuals to employ reason in the interpretation of Scripture and insisted that the Bible, not the

[13] Locke, *Works,* II, 546.

[14] See Herbert McLachlan, *The Religious Opinions of Milton, Locke, and Newton.* For an examination of the important effect of Locke's thought on the social and political philosophy of the Dissenters, see Anthony Lincoln, *Some Political and Social Ideas of English Dissent, 1763-1800.*

opinions of the Fathers, was the basis of the Protestant religion.

These ideas found one outlet of expression in the so-called Arian movement. Critical examination of the Bible had led to the conclusion that there was little support for the doctrine of the Trinity as it was set forth in either the Athanasian Creed or the Westminster Catechism. There was much evidence to show that Christ was subordinate to the Father. But though subordinate to the Father, Christ could be worshipped, the Arians believed, as the Great Mediator. These Presbyterian Arians drew much of their doctrine from Samuel Clarke and William Whiston, both of the Anglican communion. The Arian movement never became popular, however, perhaps chiefly because its theology was so complicated. Arianism remained largely in the background of the thought of the clergy, in both Presbyterian and Established churches. Its chief strongholds were in the west and southwest of England. More important than the relatively limited number of converts it won was its effect upon the growth of tolerance. Tests, creeds, formularies became increasingly suspect. So much refining upon the doctrines of the Trinity had led eventually to the belief that the doctrine was too complicated for ordinary mortals to comprehend and that it could therefore scarcely be regarded as an essential article of faith. By the middle of the century, though the Arian party was small, even the orthodox wing had become half reconciled to at least neglect of the doctrine. This attitude helped pave the way for the more clearly defined Unitarian movement of the latter half of the century.

Not until 1774 was Unitarian effort formally organized, and then the direct impetus came from within the Establishment. In 1772 a petition drawn up by the Reverend Theophilus Lindsey (1723-1808), his father-in-law the liberal

Archdeacon Francis Blackburne, and others, and signed by nearly two hundred clergymen, asked Parliament for relief from subscription to the articles of the Church. The Bible was to be the only essential "article." The House of Commons, after a debate lasting eight hours, in which Burke was the chief speaker for the opposition, rejected the petition by a vote of 217 to 71. The size of the minority was larger than might have been expected. The following year, after a similar attempt had again failed, Lindsey obeyed his conscience and left the Church. From his studies he had arrived at the Unitarian position without first having been an Arian. In 1774 Lindsey began conducting Unitarian services in a room in Essex Street, London, where later a chapel was built, the first to be openly consecrated to Unitarian worship. Some of the Presbyterian ministers now avowed themselves as Unitarians, but Lindsey failed to attract many followers from the Church. From this time forward, however, there was organized Unitarianism.

While it was Lindsey who resolved the crisis, the great name in the movement of this period is Joseph Priestley (1733-1804). He cannot be called the founder of English Unitarianism, but it was the weight of his influence that gave it most impetus. His theological views gained credence and influence in good part because of his reputation as a man of learning and as a scientist. In our own day he is honored chiefly for his scientific achievements, especially his discovery of oxygen, and his theological writing is largely neglected, though he himself and many of his followers regarded his theological work as of more importance. A disciple of Locke and Hartley, he was a leader in the cause of civil and religious liberty. Although, unlike Dr. Price, he did not engage actively in politics, he supported the American-cause, and what in the end proved more dangerous to his safety, the cause of the Revolution in

France. Essentially a controversialist, he imparted an even stronger militant tendency to the Unitarian movement than it had originally possessed. The charge long leveled at his followers that their religion was cold, unfeeling, more of the head than of the heart, was in part at least, due to his example.

Brought up among the Independents and educated at Daventry Academy, Priestley discarded early the Calvinistic theology of his youthful training. At Daventry he became for a time an Arian. Soon after taking up his first pastorate at Needham Market, Suffolk, in 1755, he came to reject the doctrine of the atonement and the plenary inspiration of the Scriptures. In 1758, while a teacher and minister at Nantwich, he attacked the Pauline theology in his essay *On the Character and Reasoning of St. Paul.* His removal to Warrington in 1761 as tutor in languages and belles-lettres opened up to him opportunities for wider contacts with prominent Nonconformists. Each year he spent a month in London, where he soon became the intimate friend of Richard Price and Benjamin Franklin. His *Essay on First Principles of Government* (1768), written during his Warrington years, furnished Jeremy Bentham with the idea for his greatest-happiness principle, the foundation stone of the Utilitarian philosophy. During the five years of his ministry at Leeds (1767-1772), Priestley became an avowed Unitarian, expressing his belief in the simple humanity of Jesus. By the publication of his *Appeal to the Serious and Candid Professors of Christianity* (1770), which sold some 30,000 copies, his theological and philosophical teaching became dominant in Unitarianism. In 1769 he began the publication of the first Unitarian periodical, the *Theological Repository,* of which more will be said later.

The seven years which he spent as secretary and companion to Lord Shelburne (1773-1780) gave Priestley freedom to pursue his varied studies. From 1780 to 1791 he was a minister in Birmingham; his residence there was terminated by the riots of the latter year. After a short ministry at the Gravel Pit Chapel in Hackney, he emigrated to America in 1794.

In addition to Lindsey and Priestley, a third important leader in the Unitarian movement was Thomas Belsham (1750-1829), one of the most able writers of the denomination. For a number of years a tutor and, later, head of the Dissenting academy at Daventry, Belsham resigned in 1789 after adopting Unitarian views. With Priestley he superintended during its brief existence a college at Hackney. In 1791 Lindsey, Priestley, and Belsham were leaders in the founding of the "Unitarian Society for Promoting Christian Knowledge and the Practice of Virtue by the Distribution of Books." From 1805 to 1829 Belsham presided in the leading church of the Unitarians, Essex Street Chapel.

Priestley and Belsham in great part shaped the trend of Unitarianism down to about 1835. They placed chief emphasis in doctrine upon the human nature of Jesus, who was "a man constituted in all respects like other men, subject to the same infirmities, the same ignorances, prejudices, and frailties."[15] The Bible was regarded as the sole source of authority in religion, although there were proved inconsistencies and mistakes in the received version. They rejected the doctrine of the atonement; said Belsham: "The rejection of that doctrine follows, of course, from the doctrine of Christ's proper humanity. For the Trinitarians will naturally say, What is that atonement worth, which a human being can offer to offended justice?"[16] In later years the doctrine of universal restoration was in some churches added to the other Unitarian doctrines.

[15] Thomas Belsham, *A Calm Inquiry into the Scripture Doctrine concerning the Person of Christ*, p. 447.
[16] *Monthly Repository*, XX (1825), 416.

Organized Unitarianism aroused extremely bitter orthodox opposition. Fairly typical of the orthodox attitude towards Priestley and his followers at this period is the poem *David against Goliath,* published in 1789 by an anonymous layman "to refute the tenets of Dr. Priestley as the redoubted hero of the Unitarian, Arian, and Socinian principles." A few lines of the doggerel tell much of the contemporary attitude. After attacking the Unitarians for, like the Devil, quoting Scripture for their own purposes of leading men astray, the author continues:

> But oh! how dreadful is the state of those
> Who use their wit God's wisdom to oppose!
> If they his myst'ries cannot comprehend,
> To carnal sense they try to make them bend;
> Whereas the nat'ral things they plainly see,
> They know not whence they came, nor whither flee.
> They move the human mind to deeds of vice
> When they the Scriptures into pieces slice.[17]

The hatred of Unitarianism was even carried over into orthodox religious services; many a sermon attacked the Rational Dissenters, and at least one Methodist hymn invoked the Almighty's especial wrath:

> Stretch out thy arm, thou *Triune God!*
> *The Unitarian fiend* expel,
> And chase his doctrines back to Hell.[18]

Priestley's modern reputation as a consistent philosopher and theologian—as scientist also—might have suffered less had he been more careful about rushing into print. His collected works, edited by J. T. Rutt in twenty-six volumes (1817-1832), contain much that was hastily thought out and hurriedly written to meet the need of the moment. His

[17] *David against Goliath* (London, 1789), p. 8.
[18] Hymn 431 of (Methodist) Large Hymn Book, quoted from J. Nightingale's *Portraiture of Methodism,* in the *Monthly Repository,* III (1808), 103.

scholarship, though wide, was neither profound nor always accurate. James Martineau, who was to lead the Unitarians in new directions in the nineteenth century, away from the Priestley-Belsham domination, said in an article in the *Monthly Repository* in 1833:

> To refer to a Catalogue of Dr. Priestley's works is like consulting the Prospectus of a Cyclopedia; and it is impossible to remember that they are all the productions of one individual, without the impression that his mind was more adventurous than profound, more alert than gigantic, and its vision more telescopic than microscopic.[19]

Leslie Stephen in his *History of English Thought in the Eighteenth Century* lashes Priestley's inconsistencies, his hasty and sometimes superficial thought:

> Priestley caricatures the ordinary English tendencies to make a compromise between things incompatible. A Christian and a materialist; sympathizing keenly with the French Revolution, and yet holding to the remnant of the doctrines to which it is vitally opposed; a political ally and a religious opponent of the spirit which spoke through Tom Paine; abandoning the mysterious and yet retaining the supernatural elements of Christianity; rapidly glancing at the surface of opinion, and incapable of appreciating its deeper tendencies—he flashes out at times some quick and instructive estimate of one side of a disputed argument, only to relapse at the next moment into crude dogmas and obsolete superstitions.[20]

Stephen's criticism is harsh, but it has a measure of validity. Almost as much might be said of Unitarianism itself as manifested in Priestley's day and later. The Unitarians placed extraordinary emphasis upon the Bible as the essential in the Christian armory, rejecting creeds as man-made

[19] *Monthly Repository*, N. S., VII (1833), 85.
[20] Leslie Stephen, *History of English Thought in the Eighteenth Century*, I, 431.

and misleading, but they proceeded to choose among texts those that would support their own unusual beliefs. They insisted upon the simple humanity of Jesus, but accepted the miracles as authentic. Their insistence upon the need of using reason in interpreting revelation sometimes led them into strange resorts when revelation proved unreasonable. They resented the charge of Deism so often hurled at them, but their methods were similar to those of the Deists. They were at a "halfway house" which provided no very comfortable lodgment.

Harriet Martineau, reared in a staunchly Unitarian family, and herself an apologist for the sect in the early years of her career, before she eventually became a follower of Comte, attacks this weakness of Unitarianism in her *Autobiography*. One must of course make some allowance here for a measure of animus behind her remarks.

Unitarians took any liberty they pleased with the revelation they professed to receive. . . . They were issuing an Improved Version, in which considerable portions were set aside (printed in a different type) as spurious. . . . Having begun to cut away and alter, there was no reason for stopping; and every Unitarian was at liberty to make the Scriptures mean what suited his own views. Mr. Belsham's *Exposition of the Epistles* is a remarkable phenomenon in this way. To get rid of some difficulties about heaven and hell, the end of the world, salvation and perdition, etc., he devised a set of figurative meanings which he applied with immense perseverance, and a poetical ingenuity remarkable in so thoroughly prosaic a man; and all the while it never seems to have occurred to him that it could hardly be a revelation designed for the rescue of the human race from perdition, the explanation of which required all this at the hand of a Belsham, after eighteen centuries. . . .

Unitarianism is a mere clinging, from association and habit, to the old privilege of faith in a divine revelation, under an actual forfeiture of all its essential conditions.[21]

[21] Harriet Martineau, *Autobiography*, I, 29, 31.

Both Harriet Martineau and Leslie Stephen refused to stop at the halfway house; but for many along the way Unitarianism provided a refuge in the face of storms that science and agnosticism were to raise. The Unitarians of the Priestley-Belsham stamp made no pretense of having reached ultimate truth; they made no effort to force upon anyone the truth that they had found; and their emphasis upon the function of reason in searching for that truth cannot be regarded with scorn. And not the least of their virtues, they were in the thick of the fight to free religion from political control when to fight in that cause brought disrepute and even persecution.

So closely concerned were the Unitarians in the political reform battles from 1790 to 1832 that the charge made in the *Christian Remembrancer* as late as 1825 echoed an oft-voiced complaint: "The Unitarians are a political rather than a religious sect—radicals to a man."[22] But the Dissenters as a whole—except the Methodists— were also involved in politics; their situation as Dissenters postulated that. Walter Wilson, the biographer of Defoe, in a speech printed in the *Monthly Repository* in 1823, asserted: "A dissenter, whatever may be his theological opinions, . . . is eminently a political character, being made so by the state. It is his duty therefore, never to lose sight of his situation, nor to forego any fair opportunity for urging its amelioration."[23] None of the Nonconformist sects, however, was so consistent as the Unitarians in the support of political and religious freedom. Some Dissenting sects fought bitterly every proposal for Catholic Emancipation and exulted in the harsh prosecutions for blasphemy of freethinkers and atheists, whereas the Rational Dissenters, as they liked to call themselves, may be said to have supported every movement in the di-

[22] *Christian Remembrancer*, VII (1825), 372.
[23] *Monthly Repository*, XVIII (1823), 394.

rection of greater political and religious freedom in the period culminating in the Reform Bill of 1832.

Early in the course of the French Revolution the Unitarians became identified in the public mind with revolutionaries and Jacobins. At first, orthodox Dissenters, as well as heterodox, looked upon the Revolution as destined to promote the cause of long-overdue reform in England; they looked with envy upon the sudden victory gained over clerical absolutism and for tolerance in France, while they themselves were still subject to the humiliations of the Test Act. But when the Jacobins went to extremes, the orthodox Dissenters became frightened almost as soon as Churchmen and Tories.

Dr. Price's discourse in 1789 before the Society for Commemorating the Revolution of 1688 did much to identify Unitarianism with Jacobinism.[24] His declamation on liberty was probably no more inflammatory than other discourses that had been delivered before Dissenting societies; it was the occasion and the expressed sympathy with the French revolutionists that raised the storm of protest. Both Price and Priestley held really moderate views with regard to political reform, yet they became the chief targets of the conservatives' hatred. R. V. Holt has pointed out that Priestley was attacked from every wing: by the rationalist Gibbon, the orthodox Bishop Horsley, the conservative Burke, and the radical Cobbett.

In the wave of reaction that swept England in the last decade of the century, Unitarians were the frequent victims of mob attack and legal persecution. Unitarian churches were burned in the Birmingham riots of 1791, and the homes of several of Priestley's congregation as well as his own. Priestley himself was popularly labeled "Gunpowder

[24] Price was an Arian rather than a Unitarian, though, as has been seen, the difference was relatively slight and one not easily grasped by the public. Besides, Unitarianism by this time was fast absorbing Arianism.

Joe." He and Gilbert Wakefield shared honors with Godwin and Paine as bogie men; conservative orators attacked them in Parliament, scribblers damned them in doggerel, and the mobs howled for the destruction of Presbyterians and Jacobins. Gilbert Wakefield was imprisoned for two years for asserting that the laboring classes were so badly off that they could lose nothing by French conquest. William Frend, a fellow of Cambridge, was excluded from the University for his Unitarian beliefs. A Unitarian minister at Dundee, the Reverend T. F. Palmer, was transported to Australia for having corrected the proof of a handbill which urged the reform of Parliament. In at least one town the effigy of the Unitarian minister was burned in company with that of Paine. Benjamin Flower, editor of the *Cambridge Intelligencer,* which the *Anti-Jacobin* called "the most infamous paper that ever disgraced the press," was jailed. It is small wonder that Unitarians felt that they were "a sect every where spoken against."

By degrees, however, legal restrictions upon religious belief in England were abolished. Although the Toleration Act had been amended in 1779 to permit subscription to a belief in the Bible in place of subscription to the Thirty-Nine Articles, not until 1813 was the anti-Trinitarian law repealed; the law had actually, of course, been null for many years. In 1837 Unitarians gained the long-sought privilege of performing marriages in their own chapels. Unitarians fought zealously for the emancipation of Catholics, not achieved until 1829, one year after the repeal of the Test and Corporation Acts. The prosecution of atheists and Deists for blasphemy they opposed as a violation of civil rights. They were ever on the side of freedom, in government as well as in religion.

That the movement never gained wide popularity was not due to its political radicalism alone. Its intellectualism could appeal only to a limited class, the antithesis of that which Methodism usually attracted. Unitarian congregations, almost never large, consisted chiefly of the educated middle class. Coleridge, an apostate from Unitarianism, noted in his "Lay Sermon" (1817) "that the number of its secret adherents, outwardly of other denominations, is tenfold greater than that of its avowed and incorporated followers"—especially "in our cities and great manufacturing and commercial towns, among lawyers and such of the tradesfolk as are the ruling members in book clubs." Coleridge remarked that Unitarianism had "a particular charm for what are called shrewd knowing men."[25] Like the other Dissenting sects, the denomination lost many who, by way of the social ladder, climbed into the Anglican fold. "A wealthy dissenting family is but rarely known to continue steadfast in the principles of Nonconformity for more than two generations," said Walter Wilson.[26] Such losses were hard to replace, for Unitarians were little given to proselytizing; their ministers were seldom popular preachers, though they were ordinarily well educated, thoughtful men. For years the movement tried to avoid sectarianism. A few Independent churches, one branch of the Baptists, and even a few rural Methodist societies became Unitarian, but the movement had most success in the declining Presbyterian churches; by 1800 virtually all the traditional English Presbyterian churches had gone over to Unitarianism. Never very great in numbers, never very militant as a sect, it achieved its greatest results in breaking down dogmatism and denominationalism, and establishing in their place freedom and the rule of reason.

Rufus M. Jones, distinguished Quaker thinker and writer of our day, has summed up well the claims of Unitarianism:

[25] S. T. Coleridge, *On the Constitution of Church and State*, pp. 372-73.
[26] *Monthly Repository*, XVIII (1823), 394.

It began in revolt and vigorous protest. It aroused an almost unbelievable tide of theological hate. It invaded many communions. It produced divisions in homes and churches. The old debates are dull, sad reading. There was narrowness on both sides and failure to apprehend the deeper truths which underlay both wings. But there can now be no doubt that the Unitarian protest has helped in the end to bring a truer conception of God and man, a broader Christian spirit, a more liberal theology, a larger humanitarianism, and a sounder Biblical scholarship.[27]

[27] R. M. Jones, *The Church's Debt to Heretics*, p. 250.

2: "News from Heaven": English Religious Periodicals to 1825

> News from Spaine *so engrosses Men's whole time, that few en-quire what* News from Heaven, *(how it stands 'tween God and their own Souls,) or reflect on that Eternity they are posting to; . . . whilst all, or most, thus mistake their happiness, I shall endeavour to find it by enquiring,* What News from Heaven, *(what we must do to be saved?) and in order to this, I shall settle the best correspondence I can with some* Post-Angel, *and live so as I may secure his ministry to, and care for me.*

THUS DID John Dunton, that indefatigable projector of periodicals, declare the purpose of his monthly *Post-Angel* (1701-1702), perhaps the earliest forerunner of the numer-ous influential religious miscellanies of the eighteenth and nineteenth centuries. "News from Spaine," in the periodi-cals of political and social history, of literature and criticism, has hitherto received adequate attention in the histories of English journalism. "News from Heaven," however, as heard and interpreted by mortals in the periodicals devoted to religion, has been in the main neglected. Painstaking studies have been made of the great magazines like the *Gentleman's* and *Fraser's,* of the great reviews like the *Edinburgh,* the *Quarterly,* the *Westminster,* and the *Fort-nightly,* but little attention has been paid to such influential and even more widely circulated religious periodicals as the *Evangelical* and *Methodist* magazines, the *Christian Ob-server,* the *British Critic,* and the *Eclectic Review.* That neglect, from the point of view of anyone interested in the development of English thought and mores during the past two centuries, cannot be justified. While religious periodicals usually have little importance as literature, they are of genuine significance not only as a record of the clerical and the lay mind but also in many instances as a kind of common denominator of the general reading public.

In these periodicals one should naturally expect to be able to trace the course of theological controversy, the great revival led by John Wesley and George Whitefield, the subsequent development of the powerful Evangelical movement within the Established Church, the rise of the Tractarian movement, and the irreconciled conflict between science and religion in the Victorian era. Less expected but no less welcome is the considerable light thrown by these publications upon English common life, the literary tastes of lower-and middle-class readers, the survivals of Puritanism, and the development of what has popularly been called Victorianism. Since there has hitherto been no comprehensive study of English religious periodicals, I have attempted in the present chapter to furnish a brief survey of the development of religious journalism in the eighteenth century and to describe in somewhat more detail the various denominational periodicals from the time of the French Revolution to 1825. Within the confines of a single chapter it has not been possible to discuss all such publications, but an attempt has been made to include all the major periodicals and a good number of the minor ones.

It is, of course, no safer to generalize about religious magazines that about other periodicals. Their range is somewhat narrower, it is true, but there is variety enough to provide for every class of reader: from the penny *Tract Magazine* and sixpenny *Baptist Magazine* to the half-crown *Eclectic Review;* from the ultra-Calvinist *Gospel Magazine* to the Arminian *Methodist* to the Unitarian *Monthly Repository;* from the polemical *Scourge* to the Quaker *Herald of Peace;* from the High Church *British Critic* to the Low Church *Christian Observer;* from the blind orthodoxy of

Mrs. Trimmer's *Family Magazine* to the open-eyed heterodoxy of Joseph Priestley's *Theological Repository* and the leering blasphemy of Peter Annet's deistic *Free Enquirer*. Nor does any rigid system of classification seem practicable. In the main, however, six leading types may be discerned:

1. The journal of religious news or "intelligence," devoted to reporting the religious activities of a denomination or party, like the *Baptist Annual Register;* or to missionary work, like the *Missionary Register;* or to the activities of specific religious societies, like the *Biblical Register* of the British and Foreign Bible Society and the *Jewish Expositor* of the London Society for Promoting Christianity among the Jews.

2. The eighteenth-century single-essay sheet, following the vogue set by the *Tatler* and the *Spectator,* like the *Weekly Miscellany* and the *Independent Whig.*

3. The learned journal, devoted to theology, sacred criticism, and ecclesiastical history, like the *Theological Repository.*

4. The controversial or polemical periodical, devoted to defending the dogma and practice of a particular sect or party, and to attacking the opposition, like the *Scourge* and the *Protestant Advocate.*

5. The review, for the endorsement or reprobation of current publications, depending upon the agreement of their views with those of the sect in whose interest the review is published, like the *Censura Temporum* and the *British Critic.*

6. The magazine or miscellany, by far the dominant type, including all the afore-mentioned materials, with the addition of religious poetry, moral essays, general information, obituaries, biography, sermons, news summary and editorial comment, like the *Evangelical, Christian's* and *Gospel* magazines.

Most of the miscellanies were designed to attract the widest possible audience of lower- and middle-class readers, though some were directed to a more limited range; for example, the large number of juvenile papers (which we shall not consider), such as the *Youth's Magazine,* and those for specific classes or trades, such as the *Sailor's Magazine.* Of these six types the most interesting and the most profitable for study are the review and the magazine or miscellany.

FROM 1700 TO 1790

The origins of English religious journalism are buried in obscurity, and any attempt to unearth them must be considered beyond the scope of our purpose here. In the turbulent seventeenth century and later, religion and politics, religion and everyday life, were so inextricably interwoven that even what purported to be secular periodicals often treated, necessarily, of religious matters. The various *Mercuries* of the Civil War period were devoted quite as much to ecclesiastical as to political controversy. Then and later, militant Protestantism seized upon the periodical as a weapon in its armory for the fight against Roman Catholicism. Late in the reign of Charles II, fear of possible Roman domination led to the publication of such sheets as Henry Care's *A Pacquet of Advice from Rome; or the History of Popery* (1678, 1679), continued under somewhat varying titles at intervals in the succeeding decade.[1] Only

[1] It was also known as *The Weekly Pacquet . . . , The Anti-Roman Pacquet . . . ,* and *The New Anti-Roman Pacquet. . . .*

The remainder of the title page of Volume I will sufficiently indicate the nature of the work: "A Deduction of the Usurpations of the Bishops of Rome, and the errors and superstitions by them from time to time brought into the Church. In the process of which the Papists Arguments are answered, their Fallacies detected, their Cruelties Registred, their Treasons and seditious Principles Observed and the Whole Body of Papistry Anatomized. Perform'd by a Single Sheet, coming out every Friday, but with a continual Connexion. To each being added, The Popish Courant: or some Joco-serious Reflections on Roman Fopperies."

in a limited sense can this be classified as a religious periodical; it was solely devoted to fighting Roman Catholicism. Like many a later religious periodical it was directed to the lower classes: "to furnish meaner Capacities with such familiar Arguments, as every Judicious Christian ought to have at hand; and which may be enough to Guard their Reason, and baffle the attempts of Jesuitical Assailants."[2]

The early progenitors of the modern literary periodical also devoted much space to religious matters. One of the earliest, the ponderous *Works of the Learned* (1691-1692) by Jean de La Crose, was devoted to translations and abstracts of moral and religious books rather than criticism. "Plays, satyrs, romances and the like" were purposely neglected as being "fitter to corrupt men's morals, and to shake the grounds of natural religion, than to promote learning and piety."[3] The *Compleat Library: or News for the Ingenious* (1692-1694), conducted by John Dunton,[4] was virtually a continuation of La Crose's work, though it carried in addition occasional original articles and "Notes on the Memorable Passages" of each month. Its few original articles treated only of scriptural interpretation and controversy. Something in the nature of a forerunner of the later religious reviews like the *British Critic* may be seen in the Reverend Samuel Parker's *Censura Temporum* (1708-1710), a monthly of thirty-two pages in which discussion of the "good or ill tendencies of books, sermons, pamphlets, etc." was cast in dialogue form. Only those works which "promote or oppose the Interests of Religion

---

In 1682-1683 the paper was conducted by William Salmon. See *D.N.B.* According to a note in the Columbia University copy it was conducted by George Larkin in 1689.

[2] *A Pacquet of Advice from Rome,* I (1678), 2.

[3] Quoted in Walter Graham, *English Literary Periodicals,* p. 40.

[4] Richard Wooley was named as the author. Dunton had become the printer and licenser of the *Works of the Learned* by January, 1692. See T. M. Hatfield, "John Dunton's Periodicals," *Journalism Quarterly,* X (1933), 209-25.

and Vertue" were considered. In theology it was Anglican and as a consequence opposed Socinians, Deists, and Latitudinarians of various shades, including such writers as Le Clerc, Locke, Whiston, and Toland.

As has been pointed out at the opening of this chapter, the nearest approach among these early periodicals to the later religious miscellanies was John Dunton's *Post-Angel*. Some doubt, however, may be expressed as to the complete sincerity of Dunton's purpose: he was a bookseller and not a cleric. This enterprising Whig was one of the earliest publishers to recognize the practical wisdom of sugar-coating moral and religious instruction with entertainment.[5] In the *Post-Angel* the sugar coating was more evident than the pill. Moral and religious instruction was provided by a "spiritual observator" in marginal comments, "the Design being Divine Emprovement of every Remarkable Occurrence under the Sun."

The monthly was at first divided into five parts (later eight). The first section, occupying roughly half of the eighty-page numbers, regaled the credulous with remarkable "providences": an Amazon who had been in the French armies for eighteen years, the dying words of a Lithuanian burned for blasphemy, the miraculous cure of a nun at Venice by swallowing the thread of a deceased Cardinal's girdle, strange voices, the appearances of good and bad angels, the Christian experiences of private men, atheists, drunkards, swearers, and Sabbath-breakers, the wonders of

---

[5] One may also suspect him of realizing—like the modern publishers of "confession" magazines—the commercial possibilities of pornography when decked out with moral platitudes. Dunton's *Night-Walker, or Evening Rambles after Lewd Women, with the Various Conferences held with them* . . . (1696-1697) professedly was concerned only with the exposure of vice and the reformation of prostitutes, but his nocturnal rambles among the street-walkers were related with an eye to the pruriency of his readers. T. M. Hatfield *(op. cit.)* conjectures, with some degree of certainty, that the companion of Dunton's rambles was the Reverend Samuel Wesley, one of his coadjutors in the conduct of the *Athenian Mercury*.

nature, children marked in the womb, hermaphrodites, etc., etc. Part II related, with "improvements," the lives and deaths of eminent persons, with especial emphasis upon their dying words. Part III revived Dunton's earlier successful question and answer paper, the *Athenian Mercury,* "resolving the most nice and curious Questions proposed by the Ingenious of either Sex." Part IV summarized, again to the accompaniment of a Spiritual Observator, the news at home and from abroad. Part V briefly catalogued books published and at press. Departments added later included a "Poetical Project," consisting of poems on the most remarkable passages in the Bible and on what passed for philosophy —panegyrics on virtue, and satires on vice. Another department, the "Gentleman's Library," containing "Essays on all manner of diverting subjects," may have been the germ of the Addison-Steele papers. This section helped to make good the boast of the subtitle: "A Universal Entertainment." The last four numbers (March-June, 1702) added dialectic: "An Honourable Challenge between the Author . . . and a Cambridge Scholar." After eighteen months Dunton (for reasons of health, he says) turned the project over to a Society of Clergymen; in their hands it quickly died.[6]

The leading type of religious periodical in the first half of the century was that which printed a single essay in each number. The vogue of the religious essay sheet probably may be accounted for by the success of the *Tatler* and *Spectator* papers, which led to many imitations. Several of the religious essay periodicals, however, preceded Steele's *Tatler.* For example, there was the openly didactic *Mercurius Theologicus; or the Monthly Instructor* (1700-1701), published by a "Divine of the Church of England" to ex-

---

[6] *Life and Errors of John Dunton,* I, 200. In 1709 and again in 1713 Dunton published a short-lived *Christian's Gazette,* more political and personal than religious.

plain and apply "all the doctrines and duties of the Christian religion . . . necessary to be believ'd and practis'd in order to Salvation." Designed for "the meaner sort of Readers, who must be taught their Duty, both as to what they shou'd *Believe* and *Do,* in the most familiar manner," the object of the publication was to go through a body of divinity, "by short and plain and cheap essays." Here no attempt was made to entertain. Typical discourses included "Of the Happiness of Man in this Life," "Of Natural Law," and "Of the Immensity of God." The publication offers at least one curiosity: page lists of all manner of subjects were printed and the reader was invited to draw up his own index!

Representative examples will indicate the scope of the essay periodical as adapted to religious purposes. *Serious Thoughts; or A Golden Chain of Contemplations* (1710) and the *Silent Monitor* (1711) were dominated by didactic purpose, while the others were chiefly devoted to religio-political controversy. The *Scourge, in Vindication of the Church of England* (1717), a small eight-page Jacobite, High-Church paper by Thomas Lewis, specialized in polemics against the Dissenters and particularly against the Presbyterians as "the most formidable Enemy of the Church of England . . . , an Enemy, subtil, secret and implacable, full of Stratagem, Refinement, and Revenge. . . ." The *Independent Whig* (1720-1721) by John Trenchard and Thomas Gordon, sought to "illustrate the beauty of Christianity, by exposing the Deformity of Priestcraft," that is, in the Established Church.[7] Essays appeared on such topics as "The Unfitness of the Clergy to Teach Others," "The

---

[7] *Independent Whig,* 3d edition (1726), p. 49. Collected in book form, this periodical gained wide circulation; by mid-century it had gone through at least seven editions in England, two in America, and one in France. Cf. C. B. Realey, "The London Journal and its Authors, 1720-1723," *Bulletin of the University of Kansas, Humanistic Studies,* V (1935), 3.

Enmity of the High Clergy to the Reformation," and "The Enmity of the High Clergy to the Bible." The *Occasional Paper* (1716-1719), an organ of liberal Whig Dissent, was dedicated to the cause of religious liberty and free inquiry.[8] Each paper presented a moderate, unusually well written essay of about twenty pages on some such subject as bigotry, orthodoxy, Protestant principles of civil government, or the doctrine of the Trinity. According to Alexander Gordon, largely to the influence of this serial may be attributed the action of the non-subscribing majority at Salter's Hall in 1719. To it and the *Old Whig, or the Consistent Protestant* (1735-1738), edited under similar auspices but more devoted to the political causes of the Dissenters,[9] may legitimately be traced the periodical activity of the liberal Presbyterian-Unitarians which culminated in the *Monthly Repository*.

Considerably different in tone and point of view was the *Weekly Miscellany, Giving an Account of the Religion, Morality, and Learning of the Present Times* (1732-1741), the leading religious periodical of its decade. Though published as by Richard Hooker of the Temple, its real author was the Reverend William Webster. Appearing each Saturday for 444 numbers, at five shillings a year, it was designed "to promote the real Interest of Religion . . . , to guard the Faith and Morals of the Body of the Nation from the Infection of Infidelity and Immorality, so industriously spread and propagated; to defend our Established Church, as the best support of the Christian Religion, in its Purity and Perfection." With the growth of the Methodist move-

---

[8] This is sometimes referred to as the "Bagweel" Papers, a name formed from the surnames of the editors and contributors: Reverend Simon Browne, Dr. Benjamin Avery, Reverend Benjamin Grosvenor, Reverend Samuel Wright, Reverend John Evans, Jabez Earle, Reverend Moses Lowman, and Reverend Nathaniel Lardner, biographies of all of whom may be found in the *D.N.B.*

[9] It was edited by Dr. Benjamin Avery, with the assistance of G. Benson, S. Chandler, B. Grosvenor, C. Fleming, M. Towgood, and J. Foster.

ment in this decade, the *Miscellany* led the bitter Anglican attack upon Wesley and Whitefield.

George Whitefield, leader and evangelist of the Calvinistic Methodists in England and America, seems to have been responsible for the establishment of perhaps the earliest weekly religious intelligence: the *Christian History* (more often, the *Weekly History); or, an account of the most remarkable particulars relating to the present progress of the Gospel* (1741-1748). Though printed and sold by J. Lewis, it was really under the control of Whitefield.[10] Its chief purpose was to recount the successes of Whitefield and his followers. Printed originally as a small folio of four pages, price one penny, it was changed after number 84 to a pocket size. Like the later *Arminian* or *Methodist Magazine* it was hawked at the chapels.[11]

From 1760 on, the number of religious periodicals increased so rapidly that we shall be able in this chapter to touch only briefly upon the more important ones. In the sixties appeared three miscellanies with titles thereafter frequently used: the *Christian's,* the *Spiritual,* and the *Gospel* magazines. The *Christian's Magazine; A Treasury of Divine Knowledge* (1760-1767) had as its chief writer or editor the Reverend Dr. William Dodd, chaplain to the King, hanged in 1777 for forgery. The careful departmentalization of this periodical may well have made it the model

---

[10] L. Tyerman, *Life of George Whitefield,* II, 107, note 1.

[11] Whitefield's weekly was probably the immediate inspiration for at least three other periodicals of similar title: the *Christian History* (Boston, Mass., 1743-1745), a small eight-page weekly conducted by Thomas Prince, Jr., and devoted to reports of the progress of the "Great Awakening" in New England; the *Christian Monthly History* (Edinburgh, 1743-1745), conducted by the Reverend James Robe; and the *Glasgow Weekly History* (1743). These were composed of letters and journals narrating the progress of the great religious revival in England and America. The Edinburgh *History* was perhaps the first British periodical to relate almost exclusively to American affairs. Of especial interest in it are letters from Jonathan Edwards and Thomas Prince, an extended account of Scott's mission to the Indians, and the Journal of Azariah Horton, missionary to the Indians of Long Island.

for many other religious miscellanies.¹² In theology it was
Anglican and conservative. It was generally well printed
and its engravings were somewhat above the standard of
most religious magazines.

The *Spiritual Magazine; or Christian's Grand Treasure*
(1760-1784?) carried a variety of secular as well as sacred
materials.¹³ It included foreign and domestic news, lists
of civil and military promotions and ecclesiastical prefer-
ments, prices of stocks, and even a lottery advertisement on
occasion. On the religious side it printed a good deal of
"poetical divinity," and much practical divinity and moral
preaching. Like its numerous successors in the title during
the following century, it was almost violently Calvinistic.

Little difference is to be seen in the first series of the
Gospel Magazine, or Spiritual Library (1766-1773), which
with varying subtitles and in many series, has continued
down to the present century. Of the ultra-Calvinist school,
the *Gospel* led the attack on the Arminian Methodists;
John Wesley called it a "twin-sister" of that "miscreated
phantom," the *Spiritual Magazine,* and accused it of supporting predestination "with arguments worthy of Bedlam
and with language worthy of Billingsgate."¹⁴ The *Gospel*

¹² The eight departments of the *Christian's* included: (1) Systematical Divinity, exposition of the principles of Christian faith and doctrine, drawn from
English and Continental divines; (2) Historical Divinity, lives of the most
celebrated Church Fathers, Reformers, and Divines, such as Cranmer, Donne,
Sherlock, and Bishop Hall; (3) Physico-theology, the wonders of nature (often
illustrated) to reveal "the Wisdom and Wonders of God in Creation"; (4)
Antiquities of the Jewish and the Christian Church; (5) "Occasional or Miscellaneous Divinity," critical, controversial, and practical pieces; (6) Poetical
Divinity, original and reprinted; (7) Literary Divinity, listing moral and theological works of the month, occasionally with extracts; (8) A "brief Diary" of
the most material occurrences at home and abroad, plus a record of births,
deaths, and marriages.
¹³ According to W. T. Whitley's *History of British Baptists* and the *D.N.B.,*
an earlier *Spiritual Magazine* was begun in 1752 by the none too reputable
Baptist preacher, John Allen of Salisbury. I have been unable to locate any
record of extant copies of this.
¹⁴ *Arminian Magazine,* I (1778), Preface.

in retaliation anathematized Wesley, calling him a "prowling wolf," an "unfeeling and unprincipled flatterer," and a "lyar of the most gigantic magnitude." Among the contributors to the first series were John Newton, Isaac Harmon, and John Stafford. It regarded itself as non-sectarian and invited all denominations to join in the fight against "the self-sufficient proud Arminian and the blaspheming Arian."[15] Typical contributions included "Predestination Calmly Considered," "The Office and Work of the Holy Ghost," "Deists Proved to be Defective in Integrity and Common Sense," Newton's "On the Advantages of a State of Poverty," and such religious verse as "The Anatomy of the Christian's Heart" and "Thoughts on the Death of the late pious Captain Hill."

A second series of the *Gospel* (1774-1783), with the subtitle *Treasury of Divine Knowledge,* for a time (1775-1776) achieved considerable popularity under the editorship of the Reverend Augustus M. Toplady, known today chiefly as the author of the hymn "Rock of Ages," which first appeared in the *Gospel.*[16] Toplady seems to have made no change in the character or tone of this bitterly controversial sheet. Typical of its orthodox, literal acceptance of the Scriptures is this sentence from the preface to Volume III (1776): "*Time* is now 5779 years old: and hastens on to that grand period, when, like a drop that has been severed from the ocean, it shall again be absorbed in that eternity out of which it was taken. . . ." On the literary side, an interesting survival of the popularity of the "character" may be seen in such pieces as "Mercator; or the Tradesman,"[17] "Famula;

---

[15] *Gospel,* VII (1772), Preface.

[16] According to Thomas Wright's *Life of Augustus M. Toplady* (p. 98), the editor of the first series of the *Gospel* was a Mr. Gurney. William Mason preceded Toplady as editor of the second series, and Erasmus Middleton succeeded him. Wright identifies many of Toplady's contributions and some by John Berridge, Joel A. Knight, John Newton, John Ryland, and William Tucker.

[17] *Gospel,* 2d series, I (1774), 424-28.

or the Maid Servant,"[18] and Toplady's "Sketch of the Modern Female."[19] A "Monthly Chronology" briefly recorded such events as the Boston Tea Party, robberies, murders, sudden deaths, etc., usually with "improvements" for the guidance of the reader. In typography, printing, paper, and general make-up the magazine was inferior. A third series, begun in 1784, soon merged with the *Spiritual Magazine*. Other series, from 1796 to 1839, will be noticed later in this chapter.

The decade of the founding of the last three mentioned periodical champions of orthodoxy also saw the establishment of the first Unitarian periodical, Joseph Priestley's *Theological Repository; Consisting of Original Essays, Hints, Queries, etc., Calculated to Promote Religious Knowledge*, which made its first appearance on January 2, 1769, in Leeds. Since this is of importance in the history of Unitarian thought and as a forerunner of the *Monthly Repository*, it is advisable to treat of it in more detail than has here been given to other eighteenth-century periodicals.

The idea for the *Repository* occurred to Priestley upon seeing some short discussions of passages in the Bible by his friend, the Reverend William Turner, of Wakefield; he decided to provide a periodical for preserving valuable notes which might otherwise be lost. Such a publication would make it unnecessary to publish small notes and criticisms in book form. Ambitiously Priestley designed it as "a common channel of communication which shall be open for the reception of all new observations that relate to theology; such as illustrations of the scriptures, the evidences of revealed religion, with objections of all kinds, etc., etc."[20] Its pages were to be open to the writers of any denomination and also to non-believers. The editor promised complete impartiality and the preservation of anonymity for contribu-

---

[18] *Ibid.*, I (1774), 471-73.   [19] *Ibid.*, III (1776), 104-6
[20] *Theological Repository*, I (1769), Introduction.

tors. Except for translations, only original contributions were to be admitted. The new venture began with the approval of leading liberal Nonconformist ministers such as Richard Price and John Aikin. Sponsors included Newcome Cappe of York, Andrew Kippis of Westminster, Samuel Clark of Birmingham, William Turner, Thomas Scott of Ipswich, and Samuel Merivale of Exeter.

Three volumes were published in the first series, from 1769 to 1771. The numbers appeared at irregular intervals, usually four times a year, and the price varied with the number of pages, from one to two shillings a number. Little attempt was made to attract a wide public; it was a periodical for the clergy and the learned, sometimes printing texts from Scripture in Greek, Latin, Hebrew, and Syriac. The invitation to Deists to contribute did not help to win favor for the *Repository* among the orthodox, even though no Deist or atheist accepted. Only a few of the Arians contributed; the rest were Unitarians. The periodical lost money from the first; it was subsidized, but publication ceased at the end of 1771. Thirteen years later, after Priestley had failed in an attempt to persuade the Society for Promoting the Knowledge of Scripture to publish something similar, he revived the *Repository*. Three volumes were also published in the second series, in 1784, 1786, and 1788, at Birmingham. This series fared in popularity and sales no better than the first.

Throughout its six volumes the periodical stressed Biblical science rather than doctrinal controversy, but there were numerous articles on the doctrine of the atonement, the preexistence of Christ, and the inspiration of the Scriptures. One of the editor's chief contributions was an attack on the doctrine of the virgin birth. The Reverend William Hazlitt, father of a more famous son, contributed notes in illustration of passages of Scripture. Gilbert Wakefield sub-

mitted specimens of his translation of the Bible. Samuel
Badcock discussed the Socinian hypothesis. Edward Evanson attacked Sabbatarianism. Joshua Toulmin challenged
the historical evidence of Old Testament miracles. Priestley
was by far the most voluminous contributor, using a variety of pseudonyms.[21] At least a third of the six volumes
was his work. So closely was anonymity guarded at the
time of publication that the editor himself often did not
know the names of contributors. At least once a father
unknowingly attacked a paper by one of his sons; Priestley
published one article in answer to another of his own. Herbert McLachlan in *A Nonconformist Library* has appended
an identification of seventy-four of the ninety-three signatures used in the six volumes; he points out that twenty of
the forty-one identified contributors are the subject of articles in the *Dictionary of National Biography*.

Perhaps of most interest to the modern reader, unless
he is a theologian, is Priestley's sturdy advocacy of freedom
of inquiry and his belief in the advantages of controversial
discussion. Even lip service to the principles enunciated in
the following quotations would be hard to find in the
periodicals of his orthodox contemporaries.

Nothing but the free discussion of any question of importance,
by persons who have different views of it, has ever produced
all the evidence for or against it; and till a serious enquirer has
a persuasion that he has before him all the evidence that he
can reasonably expect, he naturally hesitates, and does not form
a decided judgment. . . .[22]

On no account. . . should any persons be discouraged from
enquiring, with the greatest freedom, into everything relating
to Christianity, or revelation in general, or from publishing the
results of their enquiries, wherever they may have led them. . . .[23]

[21] Cf. *Monthly Repository*, XII (1817), 526 ff.
[22] *Theological Repository*, IV (1784), viii.
[23] *Ibid.*, p. 26.

Unitarians for years afterwards subscribed to these principles, maintaining that it was better for Christians to discover the weaknesses of their religion for themselves rather than to permit Deists and atheists to ferret them out.

Principal McLachlan has summed up well the significance of the periodical:

As a pioneer in Biblical research, the *Theological Repository* is entitled to respect for its scholarly articles on textual, historical, and exegetical subjects, and it stands to its credit that various writers anticipated modern critical verdicts in the fields of translation and hermeneutics. As an open journal of liberal theological opinion, it also enabled divines and laymen of different schools to exchange their views and place them before the rather limited public interested therein at a time when religious periodicals generally were under the domination of dogmatic prejudice and ecclesiastical bias.[24]

Some evidence of the growing realization of the importance of the religious periodical at this time, not so much as an organ for converting the unregenerate as for defending and maintaining the morale of the faithful, may be seen in the fact that at seventy-five years of age the venerable founder of Methodism established a miscellany for his followers, the *Arminian Magazine*. Since 1778 this periodical has continued uninterrupted to the present day, though with various changes of title: 1798-1821 as the *Methodist Magazine,* 1822-1913 as the *Wesleyan Methodist*

[24] *The Unitarian Movement in the Religious Life of England*, p. 171.

Deistic or atheistic periodicals in the eighteenth century received short shrift, if they did not collapse quickly of their own accord. For example, Peter Annet in 1761 began a weekly essay periodical, the *Free Enquirer*. Only nine numbers were published (Oct. 17-Dec. 12) when Annet was arrested for blasphemy, imprisoned in Newgate, pilloried, and sentenced to hard labor for a year. The avowed purpose of the *Free Enquirer* was to unmask "wolves in sheep's clothing," and to explode the absurdities of miracles and mysteries. Nos. 3-9 were devoted to a debunking history of Moses, the tone of which must be admitted to be offensive. Richard Carlile, Deist bookseller and publisher, reprinted Annet's periodical in 1826.

Magazine, and since the year 1927 with the 1798 title. Opposing magazine to magazine, John Wesley projected the *Arminian* to combat the "deadly poison"—Calvinism— which had been "spread through England, chiefly by means of those pestilent declamations, *The Gospel* and *The Spiritual* Magazine";[25] and also to provide his largely unlettered followers with an entertaining and useful miscellany. It further provided him with a medium for wider circulation for some of his books which had not sold well because of their price. Until his death in 1791 Wesley gave the magazine his close personal supervision;[26] his hand and his personality are everywhere evident in the earliest volumes. Without those frequent glimpses of Wesley these volumes would be far drearier reading than they are.

As projected, each monthly number of about eighty pages, price one shilling, was to contain "no news, no politics, no personal invective, nothing offensive either to religion, decency, good nature, or good manners," but an abundance of extracts and original articles to advance the Arminian doctrine that "God willeth all men to be saved." In addition to defenses of Methodist doctrine, the magazine from the first contained Christian biography, accounts and letters of pious persons, and a good deal of verse. Each number usually carried the engraved likeness of some Methodist worthy. Among the early biographies were those of Arminius, Luther, Archbishop Ussher, and John Donne, the last lifted from Walton with no acknowledgment and with few alterations. More interesting are the many autobiographies of the early Methodist preachers which appeared from month to month at Wesley's request. These are invaluable for the history of the movement and in their sim-

[25] Letter to Thomas Taylor, Jan. 15, 1778, quoted in L. Tyerman, *Life and Times of John Wesley,* III, 284. T. W. Herbert in his *John Wesley as Editor and Author* devotes a chapter to the *Arminian.*

[26] Thomas Olivers for a time served as editor but was relieved of his position for not following instructions and for poor proofreading.

ple, often moving prose, not without literary significance.[27] Of letters there were sometimes as many as fifty or sixty to a volume, most of them recounting spiritual experiences. In the verse columns the editor promised "not to insert any Doggerel; nothing which shall shock either the understanding or the taste of the serious reader." Not all the poetry was religious, and not all the poets were Methodists. Selections appeared from the works of Dryden, Pope, Watts, Goldsmith, Cowper, John Newton, Mrs. Barbauld, and Prior.[28] Many of the Wesley family's poems also appeared, of course, including some by the unfortunate Mehetabel.

Wesley contributed heavily of his own writings and boasted that there was little likelihood of his running out of materials. For some years he printed his own sermons, each divided into two installments. His other contributions included many letters, some biographies, extracts from his book on natural science, *The Wisdom of God in the Creation,* "Predestination Calmly Considered," "On Persecuting Papists," etc. In the volumes for 1782 and 1783 he printed extracts from Locke's *Essay concerning the Human Understanding* and Bryant's *Analysis of Ancient Mythology;* in answer to protests that these were hardly for common readers, Wesley countered tartly:

[27] T. B. Shepherd in his *Methodism and the Literature of the Eighteenth Century* (pp. 143-44) sums them up well: "The accounts are full of stories of mobs and the sufferings of simple men for the cause in which they believed, vivid tales from soldiers at Dettingen and Fontenoy, moving descriptions of prison and execution scenes, and detailed reports of conditions at sea and of the slave trade that make Smollett's accounts pale in comparison with their realism. Nevertheless, the writers are chiefly concerned with the story of their spiritual development, and often give psychological details of their own early fears, their conversions, and their backslidings. In this they offer comparison with a book to which many of them refer, Bunyan's *Grace Abounding."*

[28] Protests against the printing of the fourteen-page love story in verse by Prior, "Henry and Emma, a Dialogue," as unsuitable to the magazine, Wesley answered by saying that it was "one of the finest poems in the English tongue and that anyone who could "read it without tears must have a stupid and unfeeling heart."—Tyerman, *op. cit.,* III, 317.

But did I ever say this was intended for common Readers only? By no means. I publish it for the sake of the learned as well as the unlearned Readers. But as the latter are the greater number, nine parts in ten of the work are generally suited to their capacity. What they do not understand, let them leave to others, and endeavour to profit by what they do understand.[29]

Not the least of attractions for the nine-tenths, no doubt, were the numerous pious deathbeds, the confessions of thieves and murders, the accounts of voyages, shipwrecks, and marvelous lands, and the narrations of witchcraft and strange apparitions. Wesley frequently seems as credulous as his common readers, though it must be admitted in fairness to him that there was much more of this sort of thing in the magazine after his death. In serving its purpose as a useful as well as improving miscellany there often appeared articles of the nature of these titles selected at random: "A Method of Saving Frozen Limbs," "Of Planting Potatoes," "A Remedy for the Palsy," and "A Cure for Cancer." All in all, the *Arminian* served well the needs of the nine-tenths. Subsequent series of the magazine will be considered later in this chapter.

During the 1780's appeared at least eight or nine religious miscellanies, all short-lived. With the exception of the *Philadelphian* (1788-1789), the most important of these were attached to the Established Church; the *Philadelphian* was the organ of the newly founded sect of Universalists, led by the American Elhanan Winchester. The Reverend Charles de Coetlogon, an Anglican clergyman, published the *Theological Miscellany* (1784-1789), and Mrs. Sarah Trimmer the *Family Magazine* (1788-1789); both belonged to the High-Church wing. The *New Christian's Magazine* (1782-1784?), and the *New Spiritual Magazine* (1783-1785)

[29] *Arminian,* VII (1784), Preface. Wesley's contributions to the *Arminian* are identified in the bibliography compiled by Richard Green, *The Works of John and Charles Wesley.*

were two of a kind, both ardently Calvinist, both designed for lower- and middle-class readers, and both published by one Alexander Hogg. They seem to have been a publisher's venture for profit, though Hogg claimed that the whole was undertaken by a "Society of Clergymen of the Diocese of London." Both were carefully departmentalized in the usual fashion. Their tone is distinctly inferior to that of the *Arminian* under Wesley's editorship.

More interesting was Mrs. Trimmer's *Family Magazine; or Repository of Religious Instruction and Rational Amusement,* which was patently written down to the needs of serving girls and laborers.[30] It appeared monthly from January, 1788, to June, 1789. The title page of Volume I announced that it was designed to counteract "the pernicious Tendency of immoral Books, etc. which have circulated of late years among the inferior Classes of People, to the Obstruction of their Improvement in Religion and Morality." The usual number of seventy-two pages, small octavo, was divided in two parts: I, "Sunday Employment," consisting of sermon extracts, religious verse, and prayers; II, "Amusement and Instruction for Leisure Hours in the Week Days," moral tales and discourses, essays on household management, gardening, and child rearing, fables in verse and prose, and a comparative view of foreign countries, always designed to show the "superior advantages of the British laborer." One of the purposes of the magazine clearly was to combat revolutionary tendencies among the working classes:

There is no evil which Englishmen can endure under the present form of government, that can be compared to those which attend upon civil commotions in a nation; and those men are the greatest enemies of the people who strive to make them discontented with the English government. Those who are the

---

[30] For details of Mrs. Trimmer's work and influence, see M. J. Quinlan, *Victorian Prelude.*

head of it have a great deal of care and anxiety upon their minds, and are by no means objects of envy to those below them.[31]

The evident bias of Mrs. Trimmer against "combinations" of laborers to raise their wages may be seen in the account of the trial of some journeyman smiths who had attempted to organize.[32] The leading fiction feature was a series of twenty-six "Moral Tales," loosely connected, about a benevolent squire and his wife and how they converted their villagers from evil ways. The department of "Home News" recounted and "improved" shipwrecks, executions, and the like. The obvious desire of the *Family Magazine* to mollify and win over the laboring classes is evidence of the growing concern among the upper classes over the spread of revolutionary sentiments. In the next decade religion was increasingly called upon to man the ramparts against revolution, and religious periodicals played their part.

FROM 1790 TO 1825

John James Tayler, Unitarian minister and teacher, in 1839 called attention to the great development towards the close of the eighteenth century of controversial periodical literature on fundamental questions of human rights:

The American first, and then the French Revolution aroused men's minds to an intensity of thinking on these momentous topics, before which every lighter interest at once gave way. The organs of popular literature, which had entertained the public mind with elegant trifling, with an amplification of universally-admitted axioms, with the playful artillery of good-natured satire, with criticisms on the drama, or with the discussions of questions of taste, seasoned now and then with a passing *innuendo* at political measures or political men, abandoned now the easy and pleasant style of the friends and impartial instructors of every class of society, took part in the thickening fray, and assumed forthwith a more emphatic and impassioned tone.

[31] *Family Magazine*, I (1788), 57.   [32] *Ibid.*, II (1788), 501.

From this time may be dated the rise and rapid increase of the moral influence of the newspaper press, with the endless division and subdivision of periodical literature. . . .[33]

In England the reaction to the French Revolution not only stirred up a swarm of pamphlets;[34] it also gave an impetus to the production of periodicals designed for the furtherance of all manner of political and religious causes. From 1790 to 1825, as compared with the preceding thirty-five years, in the religious field alone new periodicals increased fourfold; over a hundred were begun during these years. There is also reason to believe that circulation increased tremendously, though there seems to be no accurate way of estimating it. Within a short time virtually every party or sect had its journal or journals. Party spirit was bitter and vituperative. Conservatives feared the downfall of the British Constitution and the Church, the breakdown of public morale, the coming of anarchy; and such periodicals as the *Anti-Jacobin* and the *Quarterly Review* were created to serve the conservative cause. Liberals were less fearful about the dangers of reform—so long as it was kept in proper hands, those of the well-to-do middle classes—and tried to effect their reforms through the medium of such reviews as the *Edinburgh* or the *Westminster*. Radicals hailed the British Constitution but thought that human rights were more important than property rights; welcomed, in some quarters the coming disestablishment of the Church, and in others deep-searching reform; worked in general for the democratizing of the government. These attitudes are apparent in such periodicals, opposed to each other as they often were, as Cobbett's *Political Register*, Leigh Hunt's

[33] "On the Influences and Responsibilities of Periodical Literature," *Christian Teacher*, N.S., I (1839), 8-9.

[34] Burke's *Reflections on the Revolution in France* provoked some thirty-eight pamphlets in attack and an unknown number in defense within the space of several years. Cf. P. A. Brown, *The French Revolution in English History*, p. 41.

Examiner, Benjamin Flower's *Political Review,* and the *Monthly Repository.* In general the religious magazines—especially those of the Evangelical and Methodist persuasion, which had the largest circulation—exerted a strong conservative influence both socially and politically.

Recent studies of the leading secular reviews of the period have revealed the extent to which political beliefs and affiliations affected their criticism not only of political and social institutions but also of poetry and belles-lettres. In the article by J. J. Tayler already quoted, there is contemporary recognition of this fact:

> Discussion of first principles seems to be at an end. Each party takes its stand on its own view of the controverted question, and, through its constituted organ, summons literature, opinions, institutions, to its tribunal, and tries them by the canons which it has established. The verdict to be pronounced upon a work can be confidently anticipated from the principles which it espouses, and the court before which it is arraigned.[35]

The religious reviews followed closely in the footsteps of their more politically minded brethren in thus enthroning party spirit, except that for *party* one must often substitute *sectarian* or *denominational.* They were often as severe in their judgment of a work because it offended their own special interests or beliefs, as ever the *Edinburgh* and the *Quarterly* were. Rather too frequently, one might think, did periodicals whose title pages bore texts of brotherly love and affection, utter tirades against their opponents.

The chief fare of the religious miscellanies continued to consist of (1) theological discussions on points of doctrine or dogma; (2) moral essays to strengthen the heart of the believer and improve his conduct or his opinions; (3) defenses of the peculiar doctrines of the sectarian or denominational sponsor; (4) devout poetry, usually inferior; and

[35] Tayler, *op. cit.,* p. 9.

(5) religious intelligence of the activities of the clergy, the church societies, and philanthropic organizations. This intelligence bulked increasingly greater with the tremendous growth of committees and societies for the reformation of this or the abolition of that. With foreign missionary effort assuming added importance in carrying the "banner of civilization" into Africa and the Antipodes, mission news became a staple of the miscellanies, and exclusively missionary periodicals were also established. On the home front, evangelical effort to convert the unregenerate poor led to the publication of many tract magazines full of pious models for emulation and horrible examples for reprehension. Sensationalism of the sort now more commonly expected of yellow journalism was not limited to these penny papers, however; in the well-established denominational miscellanies may be found stories of fallen women, drunkards, highwaymen, and murderers, of wife-burning in India, the cruel customs of the Hottentots, and the strange goings-on of apparitions—all standing side by side with weighty discussions of Arminianism, the Last Judgment, and the Unforgivable Sin. Somewhat fewer sermons were printed than in the earlier period, and usually only in part. Some took no notice of things secular; others printed columns on politics and added scraps of news from foreign countries culled from the daily or weekly papers. Some, like the *Eclectic,* printed only reviews or what purported to be reviews (often simply independent articles headed by the title of a book or two); others printed no reviews. In short, during the period under consideration there was some type of religious periodical for virtually every class of English society. The principles of Milton's *Areopagitica* were being carried into practice.

For the purposes of this survey, since the number of these periodicals is so considerable, some kind of grouping seems necessary. Consequently they have been arranged, so far as practicable, according to the denominations, sects, and parties, orthodox and unorthodox, whose causes they espoused.

1. The Established Church

By the end of the eighteenth century there were in the Established Church two great camps, the High Church party and the Evangelical; in addition there was a band of irregulars, or Latitudinarians, who sometimes occupied a middle ground (with all the disadvantages of being a target for both sides) and sometimes wandered completely away from the battlefield. The Evangelicals were by far the most zealous of the three in all manner of religious concerns, including the publication of religious periodicals.

At the time of the founding of the *British Critic* (1793), the High Church party, though it received generous support in such secular periodicals as the *Gentleman's Magazine* and the *Anti-Jacobin Review,* had no critical publication of its own. To remedy this deficiency, the *British Critic,* a monthly, was projected, largely as the result of the deliberations of a short-lived "Society for the Reformation of Principles," made up of a small group of High Churchmen led by the Reverend William Jones of Nayland.[36] In the beginning the *Critic* was distinctively High Church; later, under the editorship of Archdeacon Robert Nares, it became more moderate. In politics it was uncompromisingly Tory: "To protect property is, indeed, the chief end of society. . . . Whoever does not see that a reform of representation, made on the principles of equal right to dictate laws, must totally subvert all branches of the constitution, has surely very little

---

[36] Jones has sometimes been called the originator of the *British Critic,* but he was never its editor and never contributed to its columns. Cf. J. H. Overton, *The English Church in the Nineteenth Century,* p. 200. The Reverend William Beloe was the first editor.

claim to praise of political sagacity."[37] Needless to say, the review strove hard to combat revolutionary ideas of the rights of man.

Not confining itself to religious works, the *British Critic* ranged through, among others, the fields of science, history, and literature. The novel, it is true, did not at this time command sufficient respect as a serious literary form to warrant much space being given to it, but no number passed without at least brief critical notice of perhaps half a dozen examples of current fiction. The *Critic* was less prejudiced against the reading of novels than were the Evangelical periodicals. It praised highly Mrs. Radcliffe's *Mysteries of Udolpho* and printed copious extracts.[38] The reviewer of Godwin's *Caleb Williams* and Thomas Holcroft's *Adventures of Hugh Trevor,* though deploring their moral and political philosophy, nevertheless admitted "that the opposition to revealed religion and to civil society can boast of two very amusing novelists among its advocates."[39] Jane Austen's *Sense and Sensibility* was also favorably presented.[40] Published plays were frequently noticed. The poetry of Rogers and Scott was praised, as was the first publication of Byron's *Childe Harold.*[41] Of scientific works those most frequently reviewed related to medicine. Here is evident little of the prudishness so characteristic of Evangelical publications; the treatment of venereal disease was a subject openly discussed. One of the features of the review throughout the first series was a half-yearly preface which gave summary criticism and recommendations of the best works in various fields for the preceding six months.

In general, reviews in the *British Critic* were reviews and not independent articles, as so often in the *Edinburgh* and the *Quarterly.* Its criticism was ordinarily moderate

---

[37] *British Critic,* I (1793), 64-65.
[38] *Ibid.,* IV (1794), 110-21.
[39] *Ibid.,* p. 71.
[40] *Ibid.,* XXXIX (1812), 527.
[41] *Ibid.,* pp. 478-82.

in tone, except when it encountered radical or unorthodox political and religious works. Its writers included some of the most able of the conservative Churchmen; their writing was sound but not always spirited.[42]

Most influential of the Church periodicals undoubtedly was the *Christian Observer* (1802-1877), organ of the Evangelical party. Anyone who wishes to study the origins of what is commonly labeled "Victorianism" cannot afford to neglect this magazine. Its founders and sponsors included the brightest lights among the Evangelicals: William Wilberforce, Josiah Pratt (the first editor), William Hey, Henry Thornton, John Venn, Thomas Babington, Charles Grant, Hannah More, and Zachary Macaulay, who, after the first three months, edited the magazine for sixteen years.

A primary object of the *Christian Observer* was "to explain and enforce the pious tendency of her [the Established Church's] Rites, Ceremonies, and Liturgy"—at least as the Evangelicals interpreted these. The reforming purpose of the monthly miscellany was revealed in its prospectus:

At a period like this, when Dramatick Compositions, Novels, Tales, Newspapers, Magazines, and Reviews are disseminating doctrines subversive of all morality, and propagating tenets the most hostile to piety, order, and general happiness, some friends of civil government and revealed religion, have felt it incumbent on them openly to oppose the progress of lawless opinions, to strip scepticism and imposture of their artful disguise, and, by displaying the true features of libertinism and impiety, to expose them to deserved contempt and abhorrence.

[42] Towards the end of 1811, dissatisfied with Nares' editorship, Joshua Watson and Henry Handley Norris purchased the review. For a very short time William Van Mildert (later Bishop) served as editor. Cf. Edward Churton, *Memoir of Joshua Watson*, I, 96. Other editors of the new series included Thomas Fanshawe Middleton, Thomas Rennell, and W. R. Lyall. In 1824 the *British Critic* became a quarterly. At the conclusion of three volumes of this third series, it merged with the *Quarterly Theological Review* in 1827, though retaining the title *British Critic*.

Regular departments included (1) religious communications, comprising religious biography, Biblical criticism and interpretation, Christian evidences, theological essays, and disquisitions on the virtues of the Establishment; (2) miscellaneous articles, anecdotes, and poetry, usually of an improving order; (3) a review of new publications on religion and morals; (4) intelligence, literary, philosophical, religious, and political; and (5) obituary. For a time a regular feature was a Review of Reviews: it attacked the *Anti-Jacobin* as opposed to "spiritual religion" and as having "popish" tendencies; castigated the *Critical Review* for its great tenderness to authors of a sectarian, democratic, or sceptical cast; labeled the *Monthly Review* as dangerous and Socinian; and praised early numbers of the *Edinburgh,* except for their lukewarm religious views and the Reviewers' evident "pride of talents."

Though Calvinistic in doctrine, as became an organ of the Evangelicals, the *Observer* tried to gloss over the differences between Arminians and Calvinists as being of minor importance or at any rate as involving questions impossible for man to resolve. It followed the Evangelical party-line in its advocacy of "vital" religion, its Sabbatarianism, its hostility to the theatre and the novel, its opposition to Catholic Emancipation, and its hatred of latitudinarianism and Socinianism. Approving the prosecution of blasphemous and heretical publications, it upbraided the *Eclectic,* the *Monthly Magazine,* and the *Monthly Repository* for their advocacy of complete freedom of the press. In its political-economic theories it adhered to the laissez-faire doctrines so popular among the prosperous middle classes. During the agitation among the Manchester cotton .spinners in 1818, the *Observer* contended that wages depend upon demand for labor and that manufacturers cannot, and have no desire to, keep wages below their natural standard:

Nothing can be more unjust or more senseless than the outcry which is occasionally raised either against the government
or the great capitalists of the country, as if those distresses originated with them; except, indeed, inasmuch as they may be parties to the continuance of evils arising from the poor-laws and
the game-laws, from the multiplication of gin-shops, from the
institution of lotteries, or from a deficiency of sound instruction.
With this exception, it is impossible for any set of men to regulate the complicated relations of the manufacturer and his em-
ployer, so well as they will regulate themselves.[43]

While an ardent advocate of the abolition of slavery, the
Observer felt no qualms in supporting British imperialism.
An interesting justification of imperialism may be seen in
a series of articles which appeared in 1808-1809, "On the
Probable Design of Providence in Subjecting India to Great
Britain." The argument runs that since Britain is pre-eminent in those manufacturing arts whereby less mechanically
skilled countries, including her enemies, are obliged to buy
back their own raw products, at a hundredfold increase in
price, therefore the benighted Hindoo "may be moved to
do homage to the genius of that nation and adopt its religion"! Then this advocate of sanctified imperialism waxes
hortatory:

Let our people, as far as national security permits, beat their
swords into ploughshares; let them go forth with the Bible in
one hand, and the loom in the other; let the Hindoos see, that,
far from perishing as they do in the shade of their superstition,
art and science flourish under the wing of Christianity; and,
forced to recognize our skill, . . . conclude that the wisest people
must have the best religion. . . .[44]

On the subject of the drama, the *Observer* revealed the
strong Puritan strain in Evangelicalism. Throughout these
years it declared itself an enemy of the theatre as a cor-

[43] *Christian Observer*, XVII (1818), 621-22.
[44] *Ibid.*, VIII (1809), 83-84.

rupter of the imagination and of morals. It did not even believe that reform was possible; in 1806, agreeing with a correspondent that *The School for Scandal* was a "disgrace to a Christian community," it refused to agree, however, with those "who allow themselves to believe that a theatre is likely, under any regulations, to be converted from what it now is, a school for *vice,* into a school for *virtue,* or be rendered a fit entertainment for Christian men and women."[45] Declared the editor in 1824: "A truly virtuous theatre is a solecism."[46]

Prejudice against the early nineteenth-century theatre because of the corruption in which it flourished is pardonable, but the *Observer* went further. It labeled as dangerous even the reading of drama, including Shakespeare, in the privacy of one's home, away from the corrupt influences of the theatre. A review in 1808 of Thomas Bowdler's expurgated *Family Shakespeare* furnishes ample evidence of the Evangelical attitude.[47] The reviewer remarks that a true Christian would hesitate to disseminate a taste for the drama among young people, even though he admits that the study of the drama is "one of the highest kinds of gratification"—that is, intellectually, not morally. It is not the rude and uncultivated who need to be warned of the "danger connected with the study of Shakespeare, Otway, and Congreve," but rather "those whose imagination and passions are not curbed and made tractable by principle." A taste for the drama is likely to be particularly injurious to the young by enervating and deranging the mind when it ought to be preparing for the realities of this life and of the eternal state. "It is scarcely possible for a young person of fervid genius to read Shakespeare [and all other dramatic poets, too, says a footnote] without a dangerous ele-

---

[45] *Ibid.,* V (1806), 524.   [46] *Ibid.,* XXIV (1824), 200.
[47] *Ibid.,* VII (1808), 326-34. The reviewer was John Bowdler, Jr. Cf. *Letters of Hannah More to Zachary Macaulay,* pp. 23-24.

vation of the fancy." The drama is too much concerned with the passions and is consequently unfavorable to the development of a sober and collected habit of mind. "It may be safer to entrust a pupil with Robinson Crusoe, than with Shakespeare." Even if his plays do have a "good moral," that is not the lasting impression. And in point of religion, though the great poet's creed is generally orthodox, the religious characters are not of much importance. Shakespeare's low-life scenes are too natural, and expurgation of crudities, as in Bowdler's edition, is therefore to be welcomed.[48]

The basic complaint of the *Christian Observer* against both the novel and the drama was that they continually overfed the imagination and served no useful purpose, since they did not strengthen moral sentiment or encourage the performance of duty. Even novels portraying common life so divested it of its sorrows and its mediocrity as to make the young dissatisfied with actual life. "By feeding continually this craving imagination, novels become a constant, solitary source of enjoyment,—a private dissipation. . . ." Britons should remember: "The last age in France was characterized by the number of profligate novels, and behold the consequences in the total corruption of the present. . . ."[49] Dangerous were even the Waverley Novels, which, glumly admitted the *Observer,* peeped forth, "Go where you will . . . from the breakfast table to the recesses of the American forest." No review of the Scott novels appeared until the publication of the thirty-ninth, *The Pirate.* "These specious works" were breaking down the barriers between Christianity and worldliness; "and an opening for injurious or

[48] Evangelical prudishness objected to realistic language in others than dramatists: the Reverend George Burder was upbraided for using in a sermon on public amusements "expressions so gross, and descriptions so particular" (*Christian Observer* IV, [1805], 241), and the editor reprobated the publication of "indelicate expressions" to be found in the works of early theologians.—*Ibid.,* VIII (1809), 64.　　　　　　　　　　　[49] *Ibid.,* XIV (1815), 512-17.

trifling reading being once admitted, it is not easy to anticipate where the evil may stop." Though Scott is admittedly
less blameworthy than most novelists, even he is wasting
his time and that of thousands of others.[50] Occasionally, it
is true, there was protest against the *Observer's* hostility to
novels; one such protest is to be attributed to the editor's
son, young Thomas Babington Macaulay.[51]

Scott's poetry fared better than his fiction. In *The Lay
of the Last Minstrel,* "Mr. Scott never kindles a blush on the
cheek of modesty, nor insults the awful dignity of religion."[52] In *The Lady of the Lake,* however, the soldier's
song was "too offensively immoral to be passed by."[53] Byron
was at first admonished to learn that "a great writer must
be a good man,"[54] and later castigated as "that man whose
writings display the resources of the finest genius in dark
and unnatural connexion with the worst qualities of a perverted heart." The British public was warned against suffering itself "to be held in the silken chains of a poetical
enchantment."[55] —Much safer were the bonds of Crabbe
and Southey.

The *Christian Observer* had as contributors almost all
the Evangelical leaders of its day: Wilberforce, Hannah
More, Henry Thornton, Thomas Scott, John Venn, Charles
Simeon, Lord Teignmouth, Legh Richmond, and others,
in addition to some from outside the strictly Evangelical
circle, such as Bishop Burgess, Bishop Heber, and John
Bowdler the younger. The magazine never attained, however, the intellectual level of the best years of the *British
Critic* or, on the other side, the *Monthly Repository.* Perhaps for that reason it appealed to a wider circle of readers.

Of less importance within the confines of the period we

[50] *Ibid.,* XXII (1822), 157-72, 237-48.
[51] "Observations on Novel Reading" (signed Candidus), *ibid.,* XV (1816),
784-87.
[52] *Ibid.,* IV (1805), 739.   [53] *Ibid.,* IX (1810), 389.
[54] *Ibid.,* XI (1812), 386.   [55] *Ibid.,* XVIII (1819), 667.

are considering, but more influential later, during the period of the Oxford Movement, was the *Christian Remembrancer; or the Churchman's Biblical, Ecclesiastical, and Literary Miscellany,* founded in 1819. It was begun largely as the result of the efforts of Henry Handley Norris and Joshua Watson, leaders in the High Church party, for the purpose of stimulating the clergy to a more lively interest in theological studies. "The country clergy," remarked Norris, "are constant readers of the *Gentleman's Magazine,* deep in the antiquities of the signs of inns, speculations as to what becomes of swallows in winter, and whether hedge-hogs, or other urchins, are most justly accused of sucking milch-cows dry at night. . . ."[56] To turn clerical scholarship in other directions, Norris persuaded a young clergyman, the Reverend Frederick Iremonger, to undertake the quarterly. William Van Mildert lent assistance and counsel; it was on his recommendation that the *Remembrancer* printed some abridgments of standard theological works. From the first it sought to combat the influence and power of the Evangelicals within the Church and of the Methodists by now without, and to promote and defend "all and everything contained in the Book of Common Prayer." Said the Introduction to Volume I:

. . . we seek not to conceal our alliance with those men [of the High Church party], and see little or no prospect of extending the influence of Christianity, except through the instrumentality of the Church. . . . An attempt to maintain the character and pretensions of the Establishment, upon popular arguments, will be the distinguishing feature of the work.[57]

The general plan of the *Remembrancer* included scriptural criticism, ecclesiastical history, religious miscellany, reviews of new books, sacred poetry, a monthly register of religious intelligence, and a "political retrospect." While

---

[56] Quoted in Edward Churton, *Memoir of Joshua Watson,* p. 278.
[57] *Christian Remembrancer,* I (1819), 1-2.

usually an opponent of the *Christian Observer,* it took, for instance, much the same stand on the bowdlerizing of Shakespeare,[58] and likewise endorsed the prosecutions of Richard Carlile.[59] It defended, however, the famous Eighty-seven Questions of the Bishop of Peterborough, who sought to eliminate from the clergy the adherents of the opposed party. Of Wesley it remarked that, on the whole, he "did more harm than good."[60] The *Remembrancer* in its early years was ably enough conducted, but one wonders whether it was sprightly enough to draw many of the country clergyman even from their antiquarian researches in Mr. Sylvanus Urban's repository.

Of the other Church of England periodicals, the *Christian Guardian and Church of England Magazine* circulated more extensively among the lower classes. Its origins date from the establishment in Bristol in 1798 of a monthly miscellany, *Zion's Trumpet,* to furnish religious knowledge to the poor. This was superseded in 1802 by the first series of the *Christian Guardian,* subtitled *A Theological Miscellany.* The new and enlarged series, begun in London in 1809, survived until 1849. It characterized itself as "a cheap and popular magazine devoted to the cause of vital religion, as professed and established in the Church of England." Selling at sixpence a number, it claimed in 1820 upwards of twenty-five thousand readers in the middle and lower ranks, probably meaning a circulation of four or five thousand. The *Guardian* was markedly Calvinistic and Evangelical; it carried out on a lower level the same purposes as the *Christian Observer.* It printed miscellaneous religious and moral essays, a "Youth's Remembrancer" (often recounting the deaths of incredibly pious children), brief book reviews, poetry, and a department of missionary and general religious intelligence. It specialized in the gospel tract; in its col-

[58] *Ibid.,* I (1819), 370-71.
[59] *Ibid.,* pp. 681-86. [60] *Ibid.,* II (1820), 486.

umns, for instance, first appeared the Reverend Legh Richmond's famous tract, *The Dairyman's Daughter,* which
within twelve years was translated into eighteen languages
and circulated three million copies.[61] The *Guardian* was
violently anti-Catholic: "Popery is the religion of the vicious,
in all ages and places."[62] It promoted the work of the
Bible Society (which the *British Critic* opposed) and other
Evangelical organizations. In its reviews it usually neglected
works of a political cast or on ecclesiastical polity, and devoted its attention to doctrine and practical divinity. An
excellent sketch of Church history in the late eighteenth
century, as seen by Evangelicals, appeared in 1820-1821.[63]

The *British Critic, Christian Observer, Christian Remembrancer,* and *Christian Guardian* may be ranked as the most
important Anglican periodicals during the period under
consideration, but there were numerous others, most of them
short-lived. Some of these were published to advance specific causes sponsored by the almost innumerable Evangelical societies.

Longest-lived was the *Gospel Magazine: and Theological
Review,* a revival of forerunners in the title which have been
discussed earlier. Edited by W. Row from 1796 to 1839, it
has been published in various series down to the present
time. A miscellany like its predecessors in the title, it
continued to advocate extreme Calvinism. Such "high-fly-
ing" Evangelical divines as Toplady, Romaine, and Cadogan
were extravagantly praised; Arians, Arminian Methodists,
Swedenborgians, and Deists were almost viciously scourged.
A review of an attack on Swedenborg reveals in passing the
Gospel's attitude towards Wesley: "When we hear of John
Wesley detecting the errors of Swedenborg, it puts us in

[61] *Christian Guardian,* II (1810), 63-67, 99-104, 176-82, 300-4. See also
ibid., XIV (1822), 293.

[62] *Ibid.,* II (1810), 141.

[63] "Ecclesiastical Memoir of the Four First Decades of the Reign of George
III," *ibid.,* XII (1820), 121-27, 161-67, etc.; XIII (1821), 1-6, 41-47, etc.

mind of a common adage, which says—'Set a thief to catch a thief.' "[64] It described the *Evangelical Magazine,* which was professedly Calvinistic, as being "daubed over with the honeyed varnish of Arminian ingredients, for the purpose of catching flies."[65] In a series of articles in 1799 it castigated the *Anti-Jacobin Review,* a supporter of the High Church party, for the Review's aspersions on the leading Evangelical divines and for its unfriendliness to missions, lectureships, and Sunday Schools, but not, of course, for its anti-Jacobinism. The *Gospel* was ever a last-ditch defender of the plenary inspiration of the Scriptures and warned its readers against both scholars and novelists who even by implication attacked the authenticity of Holy Writ.[66]

The *Orthodox Churchman's Magazine* (1801-1808), a monthly, supported High Church doctrines. Its first editor was W. Hamilton Reid, a journalist adventurer who later became a Unitarian. It professed tolerance and charity towards all moderate Dissenters but attacked Deists, Unitarians, Latitudinarians, and Methodists. Preferring to endorse the reviews in the *British Critic* and the *Anti-Jacobin,* it printed only a brief account of new publications.

The *British Review and London Critical Journal* (1811-1825), while not exclusively a religious periodical, reflected faithfully the Evangelical point of view. This was the ponderous quarterly edited by William Roberts which Byron

---

[64] *Gospel,* II (1797), 479.   [65] *Ibid.,* p. 41.

[66] Said T. J. Mathias in 1798 in a review of Dr. Alexander Geddes' translation of the Bible: ". . . the tendency of *all* the proceedings of our scholars and guides in literature, should be carefully watched. The open blasphemy and low scurrility of Thomas Paine has been set aside, and the law of the land has armed itself against its effect in society. Mr. Lewis, *Member of Parliament,* has attacked the *Bible,* in another, and in a shorter manner, [in *The Monk*] *blasphemous as far as it goes,* and tending to discredit and traduce its authority. And last, Dr. Geddes, a Translator of the Bible, versed in original languages and in Hebrew criticism, has now *begun* his attack also on the *historical* parts. . . . It is difficult to say where these attacks will end. . . ." Soon, if care were not exercised, "might the whole fabric vanish into air, into thin air."—*Ibid.,* III (1798), 85-86.

in *Don Juan* scornfully labeled "my Grandmother's Review." In its later years it reviewed a considerable number of religious books.

The short-lived *Quarterly Theological Review and Ecclesiastical Record* (1824-1826), of the High Church wing, attempted as a digest of divinity to notice every publication that might be called theological. A bulky periodical of over three hundred pages a quarter, it printed reports of Parliamentary debates and legal proceedings relating to the Church and proceedings of the Universities and Church Societies. At the end of 1826 it merged with the *British Critic*.

The large number of periodicals sponsored by Church societies testifies to the unceasing activity of these organizations. Two of them, the *Bible Magazine and Theological Review* (1815-1819) and the *Biblical Register* (1818) carried forward the work of the British and Foreign Bible Society. The first-mentioned had a somewhat wider scope, printing articles labeled as biblical research, religious communications, reviews (usually one or two fairly detailed criticisms), and departments of biography, obituary, and intelligence. The *Missionary Register* (1813-1855), an Evangelical organ, recounted the work of mission societies in general, but in particular of the Church Missionary Society. The *Jewish Repository* (1813-1815) and the *Jewish Expositor and Friend of Israel* (1816-1831) were the periodicals of the London Society for Promoting Christianity among the Jews. Product of the Church opposition to Catholic Emancipation was the *Protestant Advocate* (1812-1816), eventually discontinued to form a department of the *Anti-Jacobin Review*. The British and Foreign Seamen's Friend Society began in 1820 the *Sailor's Magazine and Naval Miscellany* to promote "the work of God in our marine world."

2. Dissent

Certain of the religious periodicals of this period may be classified as non-denominational, or perhaps tri-denominational, since most of them catered chiefly to the needs of the "Three Denominations," the Presbyterians, the Independents (or Congregationalists), and the Baptists. In a few instances these periodicals were inclined to coöperation with the Establishment, but most of them were zealous for the advancement of Nonconformity.

By far the most important of these that cut across sectarian lines was the *Evangelical Magazine*. Founded in 1793 by the Reverend John Eyre, with the assistance of the Reverend Matthew Wilks,[67] as the joint production of Dissenters and Evangelical Churchmen, it soon became the most widely circulated religious miscellany in England. As early as 1813 it claimed to have one hundred thousand readers.[68] Tributes to its power and influence may be gained from widely varying sources. Robert Southey in a letter of 1808 referred to its contents as "offal and hog's wash" and was horrified by the "presumptuous ignorance" and intolerant spirit of its Evangelical sponsors, but he conceded readily that the magazine was "a powerful engine,—the most powerful in this country."[69] In 1835 Southey wrote that he had subscribed to it for many years, "as the best means by which I could estimate the state of knowledge and the temper of that portion of the public among whom it is intended to circulate."[70] An article in Benjamin Flower's radical *Political Review* for 1807 labeled the *Evangelical*

[67] Cf. *Evangelical*, VIII (1801), Preface, and *ibid.*, N.S., VII (1829), 93.

[68] Eyre claimed for it a circulation of 12,000 in 1803, the *Monthly Repository* conceded it 18,000 in 1806, and the editor of the 1823 volume said that at one point it had reached 22,000. As at the present time, estimates of the number of readers were often formed by multiplying the circulation figures by four or five.

[69] Letter to J. Neville White, Nov. 28, 1808.—J. W. Warter, *Selections from the Letters of Robert Southey*, II, 112.

[70] Letter to Charles Craddock, Dec. 8, 1835.—*Ibid.*, IV, 428.

as "the Bible of a myriad of well-meaning but unenlightened Christians" and "a formidable engine of influence," which, "low as it ranks in point of literature and theological merit, ought on account of its power to be narrowly watched."[71]

The preface to Volume I of the *Evangelical* promised the by now familiar miscellany: biography and memoirs to excite emulation; essays to recommend Evangelical doctrines and practice; striking providences and the words of dying Christians, to display the goodness of God; reviews to recommend and reprobate; foreign and domestic intelligence, "improved" to stir readers to "prayer, praise, zeal, and good works"; ecclesiastical history and antiquities; sacred criticism; and pious verse to charm the ear while it instructed. Short contributions of not more than two or three pages were favored. Politics was excluded, since the editors strove to direct readers "to higher objects, and matters of superior consideration." The work was designed to be "level to everyone's capacity."

Profits of the enterprise were devoted to the support of missions and the widows of ministers. In 1823 it was stated that over £11,000 had been so contributed. Much of this income was derived from advertising, for the nature of which the editor on occasion felt compelled to apologize.[72] Trustees of the funds and stated contributors to the magazine included prominent ministers, among others: David Bogue, Samuel Bottomley, George Burder, Andrew Fuller, Samuel Greatheed, John Hey, Timothy Priestley, John Ryland, John Townsend, Rowland Hill, Alexander Waugh, and John Pye Smith. In later years the connection with Churchmen was more or less broken, though one was main-

[71] *Political Review*, II (1807), 45-46.

[72] Since the advertising has not been preserved in the bound volumes we must depend upon contemporary descriptions. The *Monthly Repository* in 1820 (XV, 540) described a current number of the *Evangelical* as having a blue wrapper of sixteen pages, containing 111 advertisements, plus fourteen pages of bills stitched into the wrapper.

tained with the Evangelical wing of the Scottish Church. Eyre remained editor until 1802, when he was succeeded by George Burder, Independent minister and secretary to the Missionary Society. From the first the *Evangelical* was vigilant in promoting missions; from 1813 on, the subtitle *and Missionary Chronicle* was added, and thereafter at least one-fifth of the space was given to missions.

Like most of the Calvinistic periodicals, the *Evangelical* subscribed to a strictly literal interpretation of the Scriptures. "We had better give entire credit to the word of God, then shew that we are slow at heart to believe. . . ."[73] It fought Catholic Emancipation, favored the abolitionist cause, and, though not hostile to the Establishment, upheld Dissent. In its literary prejudices it resembled the *Christian Observer*. "Novels, generally speaking, are instruments of abomination and ruin," and even untainted, instructive books "will, if they preclude punctual attention to the duties of our respective stations be read too much."[74] The title of one of Rowland Hill's "Village Dialogues" reveals sufficiently the *Evangelical's* attitude towards the drama: "On the Evil Nature and Effects of Stage Plays."[75]

Contemporary poets were criticized on the basis of conformity to Evangelical doctrine and practice. Bernard Barton was upbraided for his "Verses on the Death of Percy Bysshe Shelley": "We confess we were somewhat surprised to see the chaste and Christian muse of our 'Quaker poet' stooping to write verses on this dissolute and unhappy infidel." Fortunately for Barton's repute in Evangelical circles he had remarked that he wanted to guard young persons from "dangerous sentiments in the beguiling guise of poetry."[76] Readers were warned against Byron's *Cain* as a "foul and scandalous libel upon the character and operations of that Being whom angels admire and adore." Byron

[73] *Evangelical*, I (1793), 30.
[74] *Ibid.*, pp. 78-79.
[75] *Ibid.*, IX (1801), 227-32.
[76] *Ibid.*, XXX (1822), 522.

was described as "well read in the worst part of ecclesiastical history, the writings of the ancient heretics," and as having "borrowed much of his reasoning, and even imagery, from the Gnostics and Manicheans."[77] Like most of the religious magazines, the *Evangelical* printed extracts from a correspondence between John Sheppard and Lord Byron, the purpose of which was to show that the noble poet was not beyond redemption.[78] Religious folk in general, though abhorring the poet's life and principles, admired his talent and eagerly accepted any evidence to show him as at least religious below the mocking exterior.

Far superior in talent and execution, in fact probably the ablest orthodox Dissenting periodical, was the *Eclectic Review*. Founded in 1805 by the joint action of a group of Dissenters and Churchmen, it endeavored, "by entering into a compact of neutrality on disputed points of secondary importance," to engage the support of persons from every denomination. This hope was not realized, and at the end of the first year the Anglicans withdrew their assistance; Robert Hall's articles on "Zeal without Innovation" (1810) led to the Evangelicals' denunciation of the *Eclectic*. At the beginning of a new series in 1814 the "compact of neutrality" was formally renounced.

Modeled after such reviews as the *Monthly* and the *Critical,* the *Eclectic,* in keeping with its title, sought to select for discussion whatever books appeared "to be sanctioned by reason, experience, and revelation." It avowed its support of the British Constitution, "which happily combines the advantages of Monarchy, Aristocracy, and Democracy," and of the doctrines of the Church of England so far as they were congenial with those of the Scottish Church and of the principal Dissenting sects.[79] Profits were pledged to the British and Foreign Bible Society. In keeping with its

[77] *Ibid.,* pp. 192-93.
[78] *Ibid.,* N.S., III (1825), 49-50.   [79] *Eclectic,* I (1805), Preface, ii-iii.

intent "to induce the religious world to cultivate literature, and the literary world to venerate religion," the *Eclectic* reviewed a wide variety of publications, devoting not more than approximately a fourth of its space to religious and moral works. Desiring to escape provincialism, the editors included at least a short department of review of foreign literature.

Editor for the first year was the Reverend Samuel Greatheed, of Newport Pagnel. He was succeeded by Daniel Parken, a young lawyer,[80] at whose death Theophilus Williams took charge until 1814. When for lack of success the original proprietors were about to abandon the project, it was taken over on January 1, 1814, by Josiah Conder, who edited it successfully for the next twenty-three years. For some years under Conder the regular staff of the periodical included Reverend Robert Hall, Reverend John Foster, Dr. Olinthus Gregory, and Isaac Taylor (1787-1865).[81] Foster contributed 174 articles during 1806-1819 and perhaps a dozen more, 1819-1839.[82]

In later years most closely attached to the principles of the Congregationalists, it was a zealous advocate of the Bible Society, foreign missions, religious liberty, and the abolition of slavery. Advocacy of religious liberty, however,

[80] Cf. Memoir in *Evangelical*, XX (1812), 373-79.

[81] In a signed "Farewell Address, on Concluding the Third Series of The Electic Review" at the end of Vol. XVI (1837), Conder also listed the following as among the regular or more occasional contributors: Reverend J. P. Smith, Reverend Dr. Chalmers, James Montgomery, John Ryley, Reverend J. Robertson, Reverend Henry Steinhauer, Dr. Benjamin Robinson (Physican to the London Hospital), Dr. Uwins, Professor Park, Dr. Polidori, Reverend Cornelius Neale, James Mill, Charles Marsh (of the East India House), Reverend W. Orme, Reverend Dr. Redford, Reverend Joseph Gilbert, Reverend Dr. Payne, and Reverend T. Morell. Occasional papers had been contributed by: Reverend T. Binney, Reverend F. Watts, Reverend Dr. Styles, Reverend S. Thodey, Henry Rogers, Henry Dunn, and James Douglas, of Cavers. John Ryley contributed articles of criticism during nearly the whole period.

[82] For identification of his contributions, see J. E. Ryland, *Life and Correspondence of John Foster*, pp. 380-85.

did not mean tolerance of Deism, the "fiendlike Paine," Unitarianism, or atheism. Occasionally, liberal points of view were revealed even on such sacrosanct subjects as the text of Scripture; a review of new translations of the Bible in 1809 expressed willingness to label the controversial "Three-Witness" text (1 John v. 7, 8) as spurious and a gross interpolation. Though usually no friend to Methodism, the *Eclectic* upbraided the *Edinburgh* for printing Sydney Smith's critiques on the sect, because of "his conceited pertness, his affectation and bad taste, his insolence and buffoonery." It was a "triumph for infidelity" to have "a clergyman to officiate as the ape of criticism."[83] In politics the *Eclectic* was surprisingly liberal for a religious periodical. Towards America it was cordial: her literature was encouraged,[84] and Foster in his review of Charles Janson's *The Stranger in America* even envisioned the day when England, having become one of the inferior states of Europe, might "boast that it is in *America* that she appears in her glory."[85]

In its reviews of literature the *Eclectic* was slightly more liberal than most of its orthodox contemporaries. Though it shared the Evangelical distrust of novel reading as a habit that "in general, tends to dissipate, and commonly to mislead the mind,"[86] it nevertheless did occasionally offer reviews of the reprobated productions. In poetry, Byron was regularly reviewed, as were Crabbe, Scott, and Southey. A severe review of Wordsworth's 1807 volumes began with praise for the *Lyrical Ballads* "as one of the boldest and most fortunate adventures in the field of innovation." The reviewer objected, however, to Wordsworth's theories of poetic diction, citing lines from "Tintern Abbey" to show that the poet in his most successful pieces violated his pro-

[83] *Eclectic*, VI (1810), 749.
[85] *Ibid.*, III (1807), 463.
[84] *Ibid.*, I (1805), 54-55.
[86] *Ibid.*, I (1805), 60.

fessed principles: "This is no more the language, than these are the thoughts of men in general in a state of excitement: language more exquisitely elaborate, and thoughts more patiently worked out of the marble of the mind, we rarely meet with. . . ."[87] The new 1807 volumes were censured as presenting "every style and character from sublimity to silliness. . . . A more rash and injudicious speculation on the weakness or the depravity of the public taste has seldom been made." The sonnets were thought to maintain the best level of excellence in the volumes. "Resolution and Independence" was considered the best poem, and the "Ode on Intimations of Immortality" perhaps the worst:

. . . the reader is turned loose into a wilderness of sublimity, tenderness, bombast, and absurdity to find out the subject as well as he can. The Poet assumes the doctrine of pre-existence, *(a doctrine which religion knows not, and the philosophy of the mind abjures)* and intimates that the happiness of childhood is the reminiscence of blessedness in a former state.[88]

The reviewer concluded that, while in the poet's earlier volume each poem had a purpose, these "seem to have been written *for* no purpose at all, and certainly *to* no good one." The *Eclectic's* standard for poetry was still based on eighteenth-century preferences and upon Evangelical insistence on moral utility in poetry. But despite these shortcomings, the *Eclectic* is the best representative of orthodox Dissenting criticism.

Before concluding this section on non-denominational Dissenting periodicals, we should at least mention a few lesser magazines. The *Protestant Dissenter's Magazine* (1794-1799), published with the assistance of ministers of the Three Denominations (though it was careful to disclaim being the work of the Dissenters as a body), was a liberal miscellany of biography, ecclesiastical history, sacred criti-

[87] *Ibid.*, IV (1808), 38.   [88] *Ibid.*, p. 42.

cism, doctrinal and practical divinity, reviews of theological publications, devotional poetry, essays, and intelligence. In view of the troubled political situation, the editors chose not to arouse opinion further against the Dissenters, and promised to print nothing inflammatory. Despite this promise, the general tone of political comment was almost uniformly more liberal than in most religious periodicals of the day—a fact which may in good part be attributed to the writings of such liberal Unitarians as John Evans, John Marsom, Abraham Rees, Edmund Butcher (editor of the later volumes), John Towill Rutt, and Joshua Toulmin. Theological controversy was not excluded, though "practical" pieces were preferred. The magazine contains some valuable biographical and historical material relating to Dissent, much of it contributed by Toulmin. It sought to note all new works in divinity, giving extracts to allow the reader to form his own judgment; authors were invited to analyze their own works—if they signed the analyses.

The *Theological Magazine* (1801-1814?), a monthly publication by a committee of London and Bristol Baptist and Independent ministers, showed no departure from the usual religious miscellany; it regarded itself as more liberal than the *Evangelical* and *Methodist* magazines. The *Home Missionary Magazine* (1820-1846), a sixpenny monthly devoted to the work of the Home Missionary Society, provided a good deal of tract material, anecdotes, verse, and a few short reviews of practical religious works; on occasion it attacked the Established Church. The *Evangelical Pulpit* (1824), a twopenny sixteen-page weekly, featured extracts from sermons by contemporary Evangelical preachers; it also provided a miscellany of scriptural illustrations, anecdotes, religious verse, and portraits of ministers. After six months it combined with the *Pulpit,* a similar kind of periodical, which continued until 1871.

3. *Methodist*

After John Wesley's death in 1791, the *Arminian Magazine* was carried on without interruption by the Connexion, under the editorship of George Story until about 1803. In 1798 the title was changed to the *Methodist Magazine,* but otherwise there was almost no alteration in plan or content. The growth of the magazine's circulation must be attributed to the increase in the membership of the denomination and to the growth of the lower-class reading public rather than to any improvement in the character of the periodical. It continued to be vended in the chapels. By 1820 its circulation was probably larger than that of any other monthly or quarterly publication, religious or secular—in the neighborhood of 25,000, representing at least 100,000 readers. About this time a smaller number was published for the "pious poor," a selection selling at sixpence.

Under the editorship of Joseph Benson (*c.* 1804-1821) some slight changes were made. In 1804 was begun a department of religious and missionary intelligence, consisting largely of letters; in 1805, a department of obituary to supplement the longer accounts of exceptionally pious deaths. By 1807 the following departments were standard: (1) Biography; (2) Divinity, sermons and theological discourses; (3) "The Truth of God Defended," controversial articles and reviews; (4) "The Work of God Illustrated," chiefly through anecdotes; (5) "The Works of God Displayed," remarkable natural phenomena; (6) "The Providence of God Displayed," miraculous rescues from shipwreck and the like; (7) "The Grace of God Manifested," especially in pious deaths; (8) Miscellaneous Articles; (9) "The Kingdom of God Enlarged," religious intelligence; (10) Obituary; (11) Poetry. Though there were scattered reviews during these years, not until 1821 was a regular department of review established.[89]

[89] Wesley had refused to include such a section. "I would not, at any price,

The narrowness and illiberality of the *Methodist* with regard to politics, religion, and literature seemed to intensify with the passage of years. When Jabez Bunting, who ruled Methodism with an iron hand for many years, took over the editorship (1821-August, 1824), he boldly jettisoned any pretense of permitting "free discussion." Said the prospectus of the new series, entitled the *Wesleyan Methodist Magazine:*

Many might thus receive the poison of error, whom the antidote would never reach, or who "love darkness rather than light." It betrays great practical inattention to the doctrine of our natural depravity, when men boldly assert that truth has nothing to fear from *any kind* of discussion, and that therefore we may freely, and *ad libitum,* give audience to the subleties of error, and innocently lend ourselves to its diffusion, under the notion of its eventual impotence.[90]

Such a spirit was hardly calculated to draw readers from other denominations, but with the constantly growing numbers of the Methodists the proprietors did not need to worry about circulation.

Other Methodist periodicals, generally of less importance during the years under consideration here, included: the *Methodist Monitor* (1796-1797); *Missionary Notices* (1816-1904); the *Primitive Methodist Magazine* (1819-1898); and the *Evangelical Register, or Magazine for the Connexion of the late Countess of Huntingdon* (the Calvinistic Methodists), which ran from 1825 to 1842.

4. Baptist

Both wings of this denomination, the General and the Particular Baptists, were active in the field of religious

---

be bound to read over all the present religious productions of the press."— Letter to W. Churchey, Oct. 18, 1777, quoted in Tyerman, *Life of Wesley,* III, 282.

[90] *Methodist,* 3d series, I (1822), Prospectus.

journalism. John Rippon was responsible for what seems to have been the first official publication of the sect, the *Baptist Annual Register* (1790-1802?). The Baptist Missionary Society began its *Periodical Accounts* in 1794. Among the early miscellanies of the denomination were the following: the *General Baptist Magazine* (1798-1800), sponsored by the New Connexion and edited by Dan Taylor; the *New Theological Repository* (1800-1808), conducted at Liverpool by William Jones; the *Theological and Biblical Magazine* (1801-1807?), conducted by J. W. Morris of Clipstone; and the *General Baptist Repository,* begun by Adam Taylor in 1802 and continued with various changes in title throughout the century.[91]

More successful than any of the aforementioned, though inferior to the *Evangelical,* was the *Baptist Magazine,* founded in 1809 by Thomas Smith, of Tiverton. In one series after another, absorbing several rivals, owned by a syndicate or by an individual, it maintained a semi-official connection with the denomination for nearly a hundred years. Evangelical in tone and designed for "plain, serious readers," it made no pretense of serving other than Baptists. Theology and controversy were avoided in favor of practical and devotional pieces. It was staunchly Calvinistic; in a review of a work by Robert Owen on his project at New Lanark, the *Baptist* urged fair play for Owen but held out little hope for the success of his plans for the reason "that man in his native state is universally and totally corrupt; and that no actual, no imaginable circumstances will essentially change the rebellious creature independent of the forgiving and renewing grace of God."[92]

The *Baptist* supported Dissenting political views but usually paid little attention to politics. It gave much more space to severe attacks on card-playing, dancing, fox-hunt-

[91] For a brief survey of these early Baptist periodicals, see W. T. Whitley, *A History of British Baptists.*   [92] *Baptist,* XIII (1821), 353.

ing, Sunday-traveling, and even oratorios. It denounced German literature: "The extensive mischief done to morals and good taste by many translations from the German poets, as well as the sacrilegious boldness and unholy familiarity of their biblical criticisms, have led us to regard translations from the German press with a jealous eye."[93] The *Baptist's* reviews were only short critical notices, Evangelical in bias. A commendatory review of James Montgomery's *The World before the Flood* remarked: "Works of taste are too frequently the instruments of instilling erroneous principles into the mind, or the means of collecting the scattered embers of unhallowed passion and blowing them into flame."[94] Byron was referred to as "that highly-gifted infidel, whose evil genius breathes like a pestilence, and infects our youth of all classes throughout the land"; but it was hoped that the noble lord was "not yet beyond the reach of divine mercy."[95]

Appended to the *Baptist* from 1819 on were the *Missionary Herald,* containing news of the Baptist Missionary Society, and the *Irish Chronicle,* devoted to Baptist proselytizing in Ireland. Somewhat more liberal than the *Baptist,* though also orthodox in its Calvinism, was the *New Evangelical Magazine and Theological Review* (1815-1824?) supported by Sandemanian Baptists. A *New Baptist Magazine,* begun in 1825 by the Particular Baptists, was incorporated after December, 1832, with the *Baptist.*

5. Congregational

Less given to proselytizing than other sects, the Independents or Congregationalists for long had no separate periodical. In 1818 was begun the *London Christian Instructor, or Congregational Magazine,* after 1824 known by the subtitle. The first series sought in particular to educate

[93] *Ibid.,* I (1809), 418.
[94] *Ibid.,* VI (1814), 290.   [95] *Ibid.,* XIV (1822), 388.

the young people of the denomination in the orthodox principles of the sect. The miscellany included biography, short discourses for families, essays, reviews, and an epitome of missionary and religious intelligence. It zealously supported Dissenting political causes, but shared the Evangelical horror of latitudinarianism and Unitarianism. Evangelical pre-Victorian prudishness was also evident; a critic of the King James version of the Bible for its occasional indelicacy of expression, said: "Something must be wrong, when it is scarcely possible to read a number of passages in a mixed audience."[96] Altogether, it is safe to say that the *Eclectic,* which in its later years usually reflected the views of the Independents, gives more flattering testimony to the talents of the denomination than does the *Congregational Magazine.*

6. Roman Catholic

Prior to what is known as Catholic Emancipation (1829), Roman Catholic journalism played an almost negligible role in England. The number of Catholics was small, and the membership seems to have been chiefly divided between the two extremes of old, well-to-do families who had maintained their faith for generations despite repressive laws, and of lower-class groups, often of Irish extraction. The high rate of mortality among early Catholic periodicals in England may be taken as an indication of very limited circulation.[97] Not until 1813, with the establishment of the *Or-*

[96] *London Christian Instructor,* I (1818), 469.

[97] I am indebted to John R. Fletcher's "Early Catholic Periodicals in England," in the *Dublin Review,* CXCVIII (1936), 284-310. This largely bibliographical account has been supplemented by consulting Fletcher's sources, chiefly articles by F. C. H. [Husenbeth] in *Notes and Queries* for 1867, and Joseph Gillow's *Bibliographical Dictionary of the English Catholics.*

Husenbeth lists a *Catholic Magazine,* published from about 1790 for three or four volumes, as the earliest Catholic periodical but gives no information about its editors or contributors. A short-lived *Catholic Magazine and Reflector* appeared for seven months in 1801, edited by one Fr. William Hyacinth Houghton, *thodox Journal and Catholic Monthly Intelligencer,* edited, printed, and published by William Eusebius Andrews, was there an even moderately successful Catholic periodical.

Andrews is the most important person in the development of Catholic journalism down to 1830. A native of Norwich, son of convert parents, he began his career as a printer in the office of the *Norfolk Chronicle,* later becoming its editor. For the fourteen years before his removal to London in 1813 he was recognized as the great champion of Catholicism in Norfolk. The chief object of the *Orthodox Journal,* aside from the primary one of advancing the faith, was to combat the influence and activities of the Cisalpine group, represented by the Catholic Board, a prominent lay leader of which was the lawyer Charles Butler. Andrews' *Journal* almost at once gained the active support of Bishop John Milner, an aggressive Ultramontanist, who was engaged in internecine war with the Catholic Board and Bishop Poynter. In 1820 Milner was forbidden by the Papacy to contribute to the *Orthodox Journal* on pain of being relieved of his mitre. This, together with a quarrel with Andrews, led to the suspension of the *Journal* in December, 1820. It was revived in 1823 and 1824, with the numbers in consecutive sequence as if there had been no interruption, and again in 1829-1830. In all, twelve volumes were published.

Other periodicals by Andrews included: the *Catholic Advocate of Civil and Religious Liberty* (1820-1821), apparently the first Catholic newspaper in England; the *Truth-Teller* (1824); fourteen volumes of a weekly political pamphlet, also called the *Truth-Teller* (1825-1829); and a brief-lived *Catholic Friend* (1825). Andrews was also the real editor in 1822-1823 of the *Catholic Miscellany* (1822-

---

O.P., chaplain at Fairhurst Hall, Lancashire; and a *Catholic Magazine and Review* is said to have appeared briefly about 1810.

1830).[98] This differed in almost no respect from the pattern of Protestant religious magazines, comprising biography, moral and doctrinal essays, poetry, and religious intelligence.

The chief rival to Andrews' *Orthodox Journal* was the *Catholicon, or Christian Philosopher* (1815-1818, 1823-1826), edited by George Keating.[99] Fairly moderate in tone, it was in good part devoted to notices of Catholic publications and to strictures on anti-Catholic productions. Other Catholic periodicals of the time included: the *Catholic Gentleman's Magazine* (1818-1819), the real editor and chief supporter of which was Charles Butler; the weekly *Catholic Vindicator* (1818-1819), written by George Andrews in answer to a Glasgow sheet called the *Protestant*; and the *Monthly Catholic Advocate* (1825). The chief energies of all these were directed to combatting Protestant prejudices and advancing the cause of Emancipation. The tone of their criticism was somewhat less bitter than that of the Evangelical Protestant periodicals.

7. *Unitarian and Universalist*

Four years after the publication of the last volume of Priestley's *Theological Repository,* Benjamin Kingsbury and John Holland attempted to provide Unitarians and other liberals with a more popular type of periodical, the *Christian Miscellany; or Religious and Moral Magazine* (1792). In comparison with its orthodox contemporaries, it was ably conducted, liberal in sentiment and well written, but its evident Unitarian character, at a time when feeling was running especially high against the radical Dissenters, un-

[98] This was printed and published by Ambrose Cudden, who edited it from 1823 to 1828. The Reverend T. M. McDonnel conducted it during 1828-1830.
[99] It began as the *Publicist* (1815) and was revived in 1823, after a five-year lapse, as the *Catholic Spectator, Selector, and Monitor or Catholicon* (1823-1826).

doubtedly contributed to its failure at the end of only eight
months. The *Christian Miscellany* strongly supported religious liberty, the abolition of slavery, and other humanitarian causes. Favorable reviews appeared of writers who
seldom received a fair hearing in other periodicals: Priestley, Lindsey, William Turner, Joshua Toulmin, Timothy
Kenrick, and Mary Wollstonecraft. Its poetry maintained
a higher standard than was usual in the religious magazines.

In 1797 began the publication of William Vidler's *Universalist's Miscellany; or Philanthropist's Museum*, like the
earlier *Philadelphian Magazine* designed as "an Antidote
against the Antichristian Doctrine of Endless Misery." Vidler (1758-1816) ran the gamut of religious affiliations, and
his periodical followed the veerings of his later religious
beliefs. Reared as an Anglican, he began to preach as an
Independent Calvinist in 1777, three years later switched to
the Particular Baptist Church, and in 1792 professed Universalism. In 1794 he accepted a call to assist the American
Universalist, Elhanan Winchester, at the chapel in Parliament Court, Artillery Lane, London, and was later appointed Winchester's successor, a position which he held
until 1815. Universalism, however, was not destined to be
his final faith; in 1802 he became converted to Unitarianism
by Richard Wright, later known as a Unitarian missionary
to the outlying districts of England. Vidler's frequent
changes of faith seem to have been no more conducive to
his success as a minister than they were to his conduct of
a periodical, and in 1796 he set himself up as a bookseller
in an attempt to bolster his income. The *Universalist's Miscellany*, projected and published by Vidler with the aid of
Thomas A. Teulon, Unitarian bookseller, was ill calculated
for financial success. Reared to the trade of stone mason and
largely self-educated, Vidler "excelled in nothing so little as
in the office of editor of a magazine."[100]

[100] *Monthly Repository*, XII (1817), 134.

Selling at sixpence a month, five volumes were published under the original title. Chief emphasis, of course, was placed upon advancing Universalist doctrine. During these five years it was almost completely barren of literary interest, and it made few contributions to liberalism in politics or religion. Most noticeable in this direction were the editor's attempts to advance the liberal, unprejudiced study of the Bible. Vidler's *Miscellany* advocated the extension of scholarly methods to Biblical criticism, though at the risk of offense to orthodox Christians: "even should some of the passages which they have long looked upon as a principal bulwark of divine truth be overturned."[101] Demonstrations of these methods, however, were sometimes poorly executed, as may be seen in the attempts to prove that Jonah had been imprisoned in a cavern of rock rather than in the belly of a whale,[102] and that Samson had tied together, not foxes' tails, but sheaves of wheat.[103] Vidler himself at times sounds more like an Evangelical than one of the Enlightened. He censured Goethe's *Werther* as "one of those poisonous *novels,* of which the present age has produced so great a number, to injure the minds of unthinking youth."[104] In advance of its day, however, was a series of "Letters on Women" in Volumes III and IV, probably by Richard Wright, which urged the extension of women's rights and privileges. Other contributors included Nathaniel Scarlett, J. H. Prince, J. Cue, Samuel Thompson, and Joseph Thornhill. Not until Volume V was a regular department of review included.

When Vidler became a Unitarian, he changed the title of his periodical in 1802 to the *Universal Theological Magazine: Intended for the Free Discussion of Religious Subjects,* and again, two years later, to the *Universal Theological*

---

[101] *Universalist's Miscellany,* I (1797), 58.
[102] *Ibid.,* pp. 51-58.
[103] *Ibid.,* pp. 119-28.   [104] *Ibid.,* III (1799), 74-76.

Magazine and Impartial Review. The editor's conversion to Unitarianism lessened the circulation of the periodical, but by moving into the orbit of that denomination he acquired abler contributors. On this foundation, weak though it was, Robert Aspland built the *Monthly Repository.* At the close of 1805 Aspland bought Vidler's rights in the magazine and at once began his new Unitarian periodical. Many of the contributors to the *Universal Theological Magazine* continued to write for the *Repository:* Edward Taylor, Thomas Belsham, Edmund Butcher, John Evans, John Fullager, Richard Wright, William Turner, 2d, R. Allchin, David Eaton, Edward Evanson, William Richards, J. T. Rutt, Samuel Palmer, and John Kentish. Aspland himself had contributed some of the best articles in Vidler's periodical.[105] Like the *Repository,* Vidler's magazine comprised biography, communications on a variety of religious, moral, and historical subjects, biblical criticism, book reviews, obituary, religious intelligence, and a few scattered literary notices. It published the first complete life of Priestley,[106] and lives of Dr. John Taylor, William Turner, and other Unitarians. The magazine was not without talent to draw upon, but Vidler was ill equipped as editor to make the most of it. The Unitarians were fortunate when Aspland, as will be seen in the next chapter, bought out Vidler and began the *Monthly Repository.*

Aspland was also responsible for another Unitarian periodical, the *Christian Reformer; or New Evangelical Magazine,* which he edited from 1815 to 1844. Originally designed to diffuse religious knowledge and promote Unitarian views among a humbler class of readers than those for whom the *Repository* was intended, the *Reformer* was less controversial and of a more "practical" bent. The early volumes were largely written by Aspland himself, who at

---

[105] For a list of these see note 6, p. 108.
[106] *Universal Theological Magazine,* N.S., I (1804), 171-89.

the same time, in addition to editing his other periodical, was preaching, running an academy, and serving on numerous committees and as secretary of the Unitarian Fund. A number of the *Repository's* contributors came to his aid, especially Mary Hughes, Unitarian tract writer, John Marsom, Richard Wright, and J. T. Rutt. Occasionally writers left it to the discretion of the editor to publish their articles in whichever magazine he chose.

The political and religious views of the *Reformer* agreed with those of the first series of the *Repository,* which will be examined in the next chapter. Its columns were more devoted to moral and religious essays than to controversial articles, and it printed fewer reviews and less religious intelligence than the older magazine. While designed chiefly for the less well educated, it was seldom guilty of obviously being written down to its readers; unlike most early religious magazines for the poor, it maintained dignity and reserve and was usually written in good taste. In 1834, when the *Repository,* which had been taken over by W. J. Fox, had ceased to represent the Unitarians, Aspland began a new and larger series of the *Christian Reformer,* which continued until 1863 with the subtitle, *Unitarian Magazine and Review.*

Less successful was another Unitarian periodical for the lower classes, the *Christian Reflector and Theological Inquirer,* published at Liverpool, 1819-1829. It was chiefly devoted to furnishing those who had little access to books with short expositions of Scripture and essays on Evangelical truth. In paying attention to local controversies in Liverpool it tended to restrict the circle of its readers.

Still further to the left than any of the afore-mentioned, at least in religious matters, were the *Freethinking Christian's Magazine* (1811-1814) and the *Freethinking Christian's Quarterly Register* (1823-1825), the organs of an obscure sect which began in the closing years of the eighteenth century under the leadership of one Samuel Thompson. The Freethinking Christians opposed even the limited sacerdotalism of the liberal Protestant sects, and displayed especial animus towards the Unitarians for their refusal to go to extremes in their hostility to existing establishments. Largely composed of former Baptists, the sect renounced all established opinions and practices in religion, and sought by turning to the Bible alone to get back to what it regarded as the primitive purity of the Christian church. It "rejected public prayer and singing, all pulpit preaching, all observance of sabbaths, holydays, and outward ordinances, believing them to be inventions of priestcraft and popery."[107] On the doctrine of the Trinity the Freethinking Christians agreed with the Unitarians, but otherwise the Unitarians were targets of their bitterest scorn; Volume I of their magazine contained a vitriolic satiric description of a Unitarian anniversary dinner.[108] These two periodicals are of interest only as a manifesation of extreme Protestantism, so extreme in fact that if it were carried to its logical conclusion, each individual might well constitute a sect in himself.

The circulation of all these liberal or radical Protestant religious magazines was evidently small. Unitarian writers and principles, however, dominated a number of secular periodicals of wider circulation.[109] The *Analytical Review* (1788-1799), a quarterly founded by Joseph Johnson, "father of the book trade" and friend of Lindsey and Priestley, was conducted by Thomas Christie. It numbered among its Unitarian contributors Anthony Robinson, who controlled its department of politics and economics, William Enfield of Norwich, and William Turner, and regularly gave fa-

[107] *Freethinking Christian's Magazine*, II (1812), 52.
[108] "Christian Jollification; or a Peep at the Unitarians' Annual Dinner," *ibid.*, I (1811), 340-46, 390-400.
[109] For a survey of Unitarian contributions to periodical journalism in the nineteenth century, see McLachlan, *The Unitarian Movement*.

vorable attention to Unitarian publications. The *Monthly Magazine* (1796-1843), founded by Sir Richard Phillips, a friend of Priestley, was edited to 1806 by John Aikin, M.D., (1747-1822), son of Dr. John Aikin. It avoided discussion of theological controversy and Biblical criticism but clearly showed Unitarian sympathies and supported Dissenting political interests. Its Unitarian contributors included Sir James Edward Smith, George Dyer, William Taylor of Norwich, who contributed nearly eight hundred articles, and Charles Lamb, who may be classed as a Unitarian though he was scarcely a militant sectarian. Aikin, after relinquishing the editorship of the *Monthly,* began in 1807 and continued into 1809 the *Athenaeum: a Magazine of Literary and Miscellaneous Information.* Modeled on the *Monthly,* it included as contributors, in addition to the above, Eliezer Cogan, J. T. Rutt, Henry Crabb Robinson, Catherine Cappe, Lucy Aikin, John Jones, Thomas Rees, and John Bickerton Dewhurst. The *Annual Review* (1802-1808), edited by Arthur Aikin, was also markedly Unitarian. Charles Wellbeloved, principal of Manchester College, ran its theological department; the Reverend William Wood, of Leeds, its department of natural history; William Taylor, the departments of politics, history, and German literature; John Dewhurst, the classical department. Mrs. Barbauld and Dr. Lant Carpenter contributed, and the last volume (1808) was edited by the Reverend Dr. Thomas Rees of Stamford Street Chapel, London. With all this support, Unitarians gained a hearing out of proportion to their numbers, even though their religious periodicals circulated little beyond the rather limited confines of the denomination itself.

THE RELIGIOUS PRESS VS. JOHN MILTON, HERETIC

As a final illustration of the respective points of view and the critical methods of the periodicals that we have been examining, a consideration of the reception accorded to John Milton's posthumously published *De Doctrina Christiana* (1825), is revealing. Milton's long-hidden heretical treatise makes an excellent test case, for it was widely reviewed upon publication,[110] and Milton's long-established reputation as the great English religious poet made it necessary that his departures from orthodox theology, as first unmistakably revealed in the Treatise, be examined and refuted. The publication of the *Christian Doctrine* will be remembered also as the occasion of two famous articles on Milton: in Britain, Macaulay's famous *Edinburgh Review* essay; and in America, William Ellery Channing's "Remarks on the Character and Writings of John Milton."[111]

Milton's *De Doctrina Christiana,* the Latin manuscript of which was discovered in 1823 in the State-Papers Office, was published two years later by royal command, edited and translated by the King's chaplain, the Reverend (later Bishop) Charles Sumner. Appearing thus under unimpeachable auspices, the Treatise administered to English religious sensibilities a shock as unexpected as it was widespread. Only the long-established reputation of the poet and the acceptance of *Paradise Lost* as second in importance only to the Bible, plus a growing tendency evident among religious folk by 1825 to pay less attention to involved questions of theology, prevented the cloud of proved heresy from obscuring forever the brightness of the poet's renown in religious circles.

Prior to this time there had been little suspicion of grave heterodoxy in Milton's theology. Dr. Johnson, ever

---

[110] I have examined forty-nine articles in twenty-eight English and American periodicals directly dealing with the Treatise, and a number of others dealing with it in part. This probably does not exhaust the list of reviews, but it undoubtedly includes the most important and representative items. For a more complete examination of this evidence, see "The Critical Reception of Milton's *De Doctrina Christiana,*" by the present writer in the *University of Texas Studies in English,* 1943, pp. 115-47.

[111] Macaulay, *Edinburgh Review,* XLII (1825), 304-46; Channing, *Christian Examiner* (Boston), III (1826), 507-47.

suspicious of the poet for his political radicalism, nevertheless declared that he was "untainted with any heretical
peculiarity of opinion," and such biographers as Todd and
Symmons had likewise endorsed Milton's orthodoxy. Every
sect and denomination, established and dissenting, orthodox
and unorthodox, had paid homage to Milton as the great
religious poet of England. It is true that with regard to
his prose writings there had been less unanimity: Anglicans
found these tainted with republicanism, regicide, and revolt,
while the Dissenters cherished them for their defense of
toleration and religious liberty. In the main, however, the
prose writings were little read, except for one or two, like
the *Areopagitica*. And in *Paradise Lost* there was sufficient
vagueness in Milton's treatment of disputed points of theology to permit readers to place their own interpretations
on troublesome passages. Trinitarians had even quoted from
the epic to support their doctrines.[112] Now, with the publication of the poet's mature views on theology, unequiv-
ocally expressed and free from rancor or polemics, refuge
could no longer be taken in ambiguity. Milton, by his own
declaration, now stood forth an Arian, a Materialist, a Polyg-
amist, an anti-Sabbatarian—"and in fact," said the *Evangelical,* "an abettor of almost every error which has in-
fested the Church of God."

To ignore the evidence was impossible, for the discovery
of the manuscript had been widely heralded, and its publication had been demanded in the House of Commons.
The religious magazines hastened to make the best of the
situation. Readers must be warned against the most heretical portions of the Treatise. Each sect found cause for
some comfort: High Churchmen, in Milton's general agree-

---

[112] Only a year before the publication of the *Christian Doctrine,* a Unitarian
noted, to his annoyance, that Milton's theology was highly admired by Trinitarians and that *Paradise Lost,* "regarded as a powerful auxiliary to their cause,"
was often quoted to strengthen their position.—H. Clarke, "Theology of Milton's
Poem," *Christian Reflector,* V (1824), 33-37.

ment on many fundamental points with their beliefs; the Baptists, in his advocacy of immersion; the Independents, in his defense of congregationalism; the Unitarians, in his anti-Trinitarianism. All but the Unitarians deplored the poet's Arianism as his most fundamental error. All rejected his views on polygamy as preposterous, and only one, the secular *New Monthly Magazine,* endorsed his views on divorce. In general, every religious periodical followed its respective "party-line" in approving or reprobating various tenets of the poet's theology.[113]

The two leading Evangelical periodicals of the Church, the *Christian Observer* and the *Christian Guardian,* seem to have ignored the Treatise entirely, but the High Church *British Critic* and *Quarterly Theological Review* both gave it long reviews. It should be remembered that High Churchmen had long before this regarded with suspicion the Milton of the prose tracts, the supporter of revolution, regicide, and disestablishment, and that therefore they were not now placed in so embarrassing a position as the Dissenters in having to apologize for Milton's heresies. Release even the greatest religious poet from the protection of the formularies of the Church, and these were the errors one might legitimately expect to find.

[113] Though the secular reviews of the Treatise will not be examined here, as being beyond the scope of this chapter, it may be pointed out that they likewise criticized it as it accorded with the religious and political sympathies of their sponsors. Macaulay in the *Edinburgh* paid scant attention to the Treatise itself but glorified Milton as an apostle of liberty. The Tory, High Church *Quarterly Review, Blackwood's Magazine,* and *Gentleman's Magazine* had less occasion to apologize for Milton, since they had consistently opposed his views on church government and his political opinions. *Blackwood's* even attacked Milton for disingenuousness and lack of integrity. The *Monthly Review,* usually hostile to the Establishment, did not go out of its way to puff the Treatise. The *Monthly Magazine,* by now less under Unitarian influences, dismissed it with a semi-facetious paragraph, but its rival, the *New Monthly,* was in general favorable. *Knight's Quarterly Magazine* (Charles Knight, a friend of Sumner, was the publisher of the *Christian Doctrine*) hailed the publication enthusiastically. For fuller consideration of these and other secular reviews of the Treatise, see my article cited earlier.

The *British Critic*[114] rejoiced to find that Milton's theology "was very far from being a fanatic or puritanical cast," and that the poet's temper had been purged by age and religion of its "former ungovernable and savage vehemence." It predicted that members of the Established Church, except for the high Calvinistic Evangelicals, would find little fault with Milton's views on the divine decrees, especially in relation to the problem of man's freedom of will. But his Arianism, "probably higher than the highest Arianism known to antiquity," was deplored, though not feared, because of the salutary demolition of that heresy since Milton's day by the great defenders of the Trinity, Bull and Waterland. The reviewer confessed that, during some parts of his task, he felt very much as if he had been filling his belly "with the east wind." He did not question Milton's sincerity of purpose, but thought that his "love of independence" had "betrayed him into such extravagancies" that his theological work might as well or better have remained buried. Only as a literary curiosity and as a relic of his genius was publication of the Treatise to be justified, and translation of it was open to question.

The *Quarterly Theological Review*[115] paid tribute to Milton as "among the proudest names of English Literature," but warned that reverence for his genius must not be allowed to "palliate error, or to sanction heresy." The poet was praised for his moderation of expression, for his piety and his purity of motive, and the Treatise itself was admitted to be not altogether without merit. That Milton had not endorsed the Calvinistic doctrine of Reprobation was comforting. His notions on baptism were "degrading," but on the doctrines of Justification, Adoption, Assurance, and final Perseverance he was said to be generally correct, since here he seemed to agree with the Church. Milton had added

[114] *British Critic*, N.S., II (1825), 279-310.
[115] *Quarterly Theological Review*, III (1826), 42-65.

nothing new on Arianism or on divorce. His lax opinions on ministerial authority and ecclesiastical jurisdiction, as well as his "Erastian notions," were attributed "to his having imbibed a portion of the malignant spirit of the age which subverted the altar and the throne." On this score was contrasted Dr. Johnson, "who was as much superior to Milton in giant force of intellect, as he was below him in imaginative invention." Disdain of authority in religion had led the poet lamentably astray. Though the work would not add to his reputation as a writer, scholar, or theologian, his fame was already so great that even the defects of this Treatise could not tarnish it.

Of the orthodox Dissenting periodicals, the *Evangelical* devoted the longest continued attention, printing a total of seven monthly articles designed chiefly to confute "the most unscriptural parts" of the Treatise. A brief introductory article[116] regretfully conceded the authenticity of the production; it was only "too lamentably evident" that towards the close of his life, Milton was, on many points "wretchedly erroneous and unscriptural." Though Baptists might now be inclined to boast of Milton's endorsement of their distinguishing rite, their triumph should be moderated by the fact that his "extreme heterodoxy in other particulars must forever annihilate him as a theological authority." And then the *Evangelical* reviewer sounded the note most frequently to be heard in the orthodox Dissenting periodicals:

How little alas! can mere genius effect in protecting the human mind from the influence of pernicious error . . . ! How affecting it is to see the most stupendous intellects falling victims to the sorcery of an ingenious though deceitful theory, while the unlettered peasant holds on in the even tenour of his way, believing what God has said, and obeying what he has commanded!

[116] *Evangelical*, N.S., III (1825), 506-7.

But if Milton could be confuted, nothing need be feared from inferior quarters.

The confutation, comprising a series of six articles, began to appear in January of the following year, 1826.[117] The author can be identified as the Reverend John Pye Smith, prominent Dissenting scholar and controversialist, and author of *The Scripture Testimony to the Messiah,* quoted in some of the other reviews to refute Milton. Smith offered some apology for Milton: the poet's highly imaginative mind was probably incapable of "patient and laborious investigation"; the excesses of the Presbyterians (Smith himself was an Independent) had no doubt repelled him from their system; and his generous sympathy for the oppressed must have inclined him to favor the Socinians of Poland and the Remonstrants of Holland.

Smith in his first essay admitted, "with grief," that Milton was an Arian (though he was "high above the lower parts of the slippery steep"—that is, Unitarianism), and proceeded to demolish the heresy. The second essay attacked the poet's opinions on the properties of the Deity and rejected Milton's attaching literal meanings to terms used only figuratively in the Bible. The third criticized Milton's too ready acceptance of the abrogation of the Mosaic Law. The remaining three attacked the poet's views on marriage and divorce, on the observance of the Sabbath, and on the obligation of veracity. But with all Milton's errors of opinion, Smith confessed amazement that they had had so little influence on his practice or his character. The poet manifested no inclination to commit polygamy, he forgave his recreant wife, his chastity of life defied calumny, and in

---

[117] "On Milton's Treatise on Christian Doctrine," *ibid.,* N.S., IV (1826): Essay I, "The Doctrine Concerning Christ and the Holy Spirit," pp. 50-53; Essay II, "Anthropomorphism," pp. 92-95; Essay III, "The Abrogation of the Law," pp. 137-40; Essay IV, "The Sabbath and the Lord's Day," pp. 371-75; Essay V (misnumbered IV), "On Marriage, Polygamy, and Divorce," pp. 463-66; Essay VI, "On Veracity and Falsehood," pp. 555-58.

spite of his bad theories on veracity he "maintained the loftiest integrity in circumstances of peculiar trial and temptation." In concluding, Smith could not forbear a parting shot at the Baptists: though Milton had shared their views on baptism, he had not abjured his own infant sprinkling and submitted to immersion!

In contrast with the *Evangelical*, the *Methodist Magazine* paid little attention to Milton's Treatise; while it belatedly noted the discovery of the manuscript,[118] it offered no review. It did, however, notice and comment upon Bishop Burgess's attack the following year upon the authenticity of the manuscript and his defense of Milton's orthodoxy.[119] Distressed to find that the poet "was the secret advocate of principles subversive of the Christian faith," the *Methodist* approved the Bishop's attack, for if the Treatise really were Milton's it would seem "impossible to vindicate him from the charge of base and unprincipled dissimulation."[120]

The Baptists' rejoicing at Milton's support of their most characteristic doctrine was temperately expressed, at least in their periodicals. The *Baptist Magazine* first noticed the work by simply extracting the poet's views respecting Baptism and Communion.[121] The *New Baptist,* which made no attempt to analyze or review the Treatise, headed its page of extracts with the exclamation: "Milton a decided antipaedobaptist!"[122] The *Baptist* returned to the subject with three articles in ensuing months. The first[123] recounted the discovery of the manuscript and announced that since the size and price of the work (large quarto, £2 10s.) would prevent many from reading it, the editors would

---

[118] *Methodist*, XLVIII (1825), 558.

[119] John Milton, *Protestant Union. A Treatise of True Religion. . . . To which is prefixed a Preface on Milton's Religious Principles and Unimpeachable Sincerity.* By Thomas Burgess, Bishop of Salisbury. London, 1826.

[120] *Methodist*, XLIX (1826), 335-36.   [121] *Baptist*, XVII (1825), 387.

[122] *New Baptist*, I (1825), 335-36.   [123] *Baptist*, XVII (1825), 413-16.

furnish an analysis of the contents and print extracts on some of the more important points. Essay II[124] endorsed Milton's method in constructing his Body of Divinity from the Scriptures but criticized his introduction of metaphysics. His Arianism was passed over in "silent regret," as was also his materialism. Essay III[125] praised Milton's views on church government (for coinciding with those of the Baptists and Congregationalists) and his defense of religious liberty. The conclusion of the article reiterated the vanity-of-human-genius refrain noted earlier in the *Evangelical*.

Oddly enough, the most scornful review in any religious periodical appeared in the *Congregational Magazine*. A preliminary short notice in August, 1825,[126] evidently written by a different author or before thorough reading, was enthusiastic, though it facetiously dismissed Milton's plea for polygamy. The writer of the more extended review in November,[127] however, was not only disappointed but deeply indignant. After two years of waiting for the manuscript to be published, meanwhile allowing his imagination to dwell on the riches of theological wisdom to be unfolded, he now found the work to be "literally, a bundle of as dry bones as ever critic sat down to pick." The book was "an absolute and total baulk," which, even if it could be read, "would do nobody any good." It would delight Unitarians, Arians, and "other triflers with sacred Scripture" and confuse the wavering. The only possible importance of the Treatise was "as an exponent of certain ambiguities in Paradise Lost," which might better have remained ambiguities. The execution of many parts of the Treatise was conceded to be "able, and not unworthy of Milton's pen," but on the whole it was pronounced " a production of his dotage."[128]

---

[124] *Ibid.*, pp. 463-67. [125] *Ibid.*, pp. 510-13.
[126] *Congregational*, N.S., I (1825), 434. [127] *Ibid.*, 588-92.
[128] That the *Christian Doctrine* did not permanently affect the *Congregational's* admiration for Milton may be seen in the long review (N.S., III, 33-40) of Todd's revised *Life of Milton* early in 1827.

The *Eclectic Review,* published under much the same doctrinal auspices as the *Congregational,* was more temperate and reasoned in its detailed criticism.[129] This reviewer admitted sharing in the almost universal disappointment over the Treatise but did not believe that it in any way lowered the poet's character or endangered his reputation. Milton both as theologian and poet stood alone. "Too heterodox for the orthodox, he is by far too orthodox for the sceptical and misbelieving school." He dwelt apart, though within the pale of the true church, "an intellectual hermit, a sect consisting of an individual."

The *Eclectic's* criticism paid most attention to Milton's Arianism, the heresy thought most likely to mislead the unwary. Arian views had not previously been detected in *Paradise Lost* because of the "poetical necessities of almost anthropomorphous representation of the Eternal Father." Milton was clearly no sceptic or freethinker, as was demonstrated by his uniform deference to the Scriptures as the final law of faith. His other departures from orthodoxy were dismissed more briefly: his views on the creation of matter were described as "singularly puerile"; his materialism as "dangerous"; his anti-Sabbatarianism likened to Paley's; his reasonings on polygamy and divorce were "shallow and perverted" and tending to immorality, though "From the slightest relaxation of the moral discipline of the country, Milton would have shrunk with abhorrence." The critic expressed his belief that the Treatise contributed nothing to theological science or to history. The poet's opinions were, however, of genuine historical interest, and there was little real likelihood that they would make error more attractive. At least the Treatise would illustrate Milton's piety and integrity, if not his intellect. His failure must be excused by the failures of his times and of his judgment. "We still retain entire our admiration of his Muse, his

[129] *Eclectic,* N.S., XXV (1826), 1-18, 114-41.

greater self, and our conviction that he deserved, far more
than most of his contemporaries, the high name of patriot,
sage, and saint."

If an orthodox journal could still refer to Milton as "patriot, sage, and saint," in spite of his now proved heresy on
fundamental points, it should scarcely be a matter of surprise that the unorthodox sects should be even more ready
to pay tribute. The Unitarians found much to praise in
Milton's system of theology, though even they made certain reservations, notably on divorce and polygamy. Since
the Unitarians believed in the simple humanity of Christ,
they could derive no direct comfort from Milton's Arianism,
which held Christ to be divine, though inferior to the Father; the poet's attack upon orthodox Trinitarianism, however, was sufficient to make the Unitarians regard him as
a valuable ally. The *Monthly Repository* long before this
had paid frequent tribute to the poet as a defender of religious liberty. (See pp. 125-27.) Of the Treatise, after preparing its readers with several notices of the discovery,[130]
the *Repository* printed an extended account in three numbers, less a review than a summary: "Milton, of all men
that ever lived, is entitled to speak for himself." The three
installments were largely made up of quotations.[131]

The editor revealed his admiration for Milton in his refusal to attack those of his doctrines which were not held
by Unitarians. He conceded that Milton's doctrine was "entirely Arian," though "not the highest Arianism." The
poet's exposure of "the absurdity of the conceit of eternal
generation" and his refutation of "the commonly received
doctrine of the Son being one in essence with the Father"
were noted with approval, as was also the fact that he gave
"the Unitarian sense of most of the texts alleged by Trinitarians." Hope was expressed that the Unitarians might

[130] *Monthly Repository*, XIX (1824), 124, 253, 638.
[131] *Ibid.*, XX (1825), 609-13, 687-92, 748-50.

publish these portions in cheap form for general circulation. The account concluded with temperate criticism. In form the Treatise was declared to be too scholastic to be popular, the lengthy successions of texts tedious, and Milton was throughout "the grave and even severe divine." The Treatise was regarded as a curiosity to be valued by posterity as a lasting memorial to Milton's independence and integrity of mind; its influence would be seen "in taking off the edge of the *odium ecclesiasticum* from what is called heresy."

In addition to this three-installment account, the *Repository* printed two articles by the Reverend John Evans, General Baptist minister. Both articles took their departure from other periodical critiques of the Treatise. The first, "On Milton's New Work,"[132] attacked the reviews in the *Evangelical* and the *Congregational*. Evans took up the *Evangelical's* taunt to the Baptists; the triumph of the Particular Baptists might be moderated because of Milton's heterodoxy, but for the most part the General Baptists (many of them Arian or Unitarian) exulted "without reserve" in finding the poet among their ranks. Evans was not above a *tu quoque* in excusing Milton's more flagrant heresies of polygamy and materialism: an Evangelical clergyman had advocated polygamy as a remedy for the evil of prostitution; Bishop Law and Archdeacon Blackburne, "the brightest ornaments of the Church of England," and even Luther himself had maintained materialism. As an antidote to the bigotry of the *Evangelical* and the *Congregational,* Evans quoted the closing paragraphs of Milton's preface.

Evans' second article, "Estimate of Milton's Theological Work,"[133] was largely devoted to a discussion of eleven reviews of the *Christian Doctrine*. He claimed that only two

[132] *Ibid.*, pp. 710-13.   [133] *Ibid.*, XXI (1826), 724-31.

of the monthlies, the *Christian Moderator* and the *Monthly Repository,* and three of the quarterlies, the *Edinburgh,* the *Quarterly,* and the *British Critic,* had done the volume justice. Large excerpts were quoted from the *British Critic,* with commendation for its moderation, "considering that Milton blows up the whole fabric of episcopacy." The article closed with a comparison of Milton and Priestley.

The *Christian Reformer,* Aspland's miscellany for the poor, published a series of ten articles by J. T. Rutt, consisting largely of extracts.[134] According to Evans, the *Christian Moderator,* a short-lived (1826-1828) Unitarian-Universalist miscellany, endorsed the Treatise enthusiastically:

Notwithstanding the intermixture of some curious theories and novel opinions, Milton was a very diligent, and, on the whole, a very successful inquirer into the meaning of Sacred Scripture. The wonder is, not that he should have fallen into some mistakes, but how he was enabled to discover so much at the time when his countrymen were so blind to the light of unadulterated Christianity as he was to the sun! He looks, among his contemporaries, like one who had anticipated the progress of time by a century.[135]

In conclusion, it may be said that these varying attitudes towards Milton's heretical Treatise which we have examined reveal more than merely the respective denominational and theological prejudices of the religious periodicals of 1825; they reveal more even than the transcendent, enduring brightness of Milton's reputation, which clouds of political and religious prejudice could not eclipse. These criticisms reveal something of the genius, the nature, of a many-sided Protestantism which had developed to a point where it could withstand the shock of discovering that its greatest religious poet was infected with heresies, could combat them by

[134] *Christian Reformer,* XI (1825), 236-42, 281-85, 317-19, 353-59, 386-90, 421-27; XII (1826), 29-33, 74-79, 123-27, 205-11.
[135] Quoted, *Monthly Repository,* XXI (1826), 725.

reason and argument rather than by suppression and still pay high tribute to their author. If Milton had published his Treatise in his own life-time, he might have been liable to extreme punishment and the work itself would probably have been suppressed. If he had been alive in 1825 to witness the reception of his views, he could not have liked it in all respects, but he would have rejoiced to see the principles of his *Areopagitica* being carried into practice in the multiplicity and diversity of English religious and secular periodicals.

The Monthly Repository

3. The First Series: *From 1806 to 1826*

> *To do something to instruct, but more to undeceive, the timid and admiring student;—to excite him to place more confidence in his own strength, and less in the infallibility of great names;— to help him to emancipate his judgment from the shackles of authority;—to teach him to distinguish between shewy language and sound sense;—to shew him that what may tickle the ear or dazzle the imagination, will not always inform the judgment;— to dispose him rather to fast on ignorance than to feed himself with error.*

THROUGH MOST of the years of the first series of the *Monthly Repository*, this paragraph appeared as a motto on the title page of each successive volume. Its source, the conclusion of Jeremy Bentham's *Fragment on Government*, gives a clue to a connection of the great founder of Utilitarianism with the Unitarians; and its sentiments give a key to the character of the *Repository* throughout the editorship of Robert Aspland, 1806-1826. In the twenty-one volumes of the first series may be found many articles designed to instruct but more that were concerned with undeceiving the public with regard to religious and political questions of the day. The *Repository* always endeavored to rally Unitarians to an awareness of their own strength and to encourage them to accept authority, even when it was that of Dr. Priestley himself, only after questioning. Its readers were seldom confronted with showy language, though, unfortunately, they did occasionally meet with what could not be labeled as sound sense; certainly no effort was made to tickle the ear or dazzle the imagination—a deficiency which the modern reader is less inclined to praise. And as for the connection with Utilitarianism, the social and political philosophy of the periodical—as far as a miscellany to which anyone may contribute can be said to have a philosophy—was essentially that of Bentham and his followers, though modified by religious prepossessions that did not ordinarily affect the leading Benthamites.

The origins of the *Monthly Repository* can be directly traced to the periodicals published by William Vidler, which have already been described: the *Universalist's Miscellany* and the *Universal Theological Magazine*. Robert Aspland, in 1805 appointed successor to Thomas Belsham at the Gravel Pit Chapel, Hackney, where he served for the next forty years, had not been long in the Unitarian camp before he perceived the need of the denomination for union and organization. The lack of some form of central organization had been one of the important factors in the drift of the English Presbyterians to Arianism and Unitarianism and also in their decline in numbers and importance as a denomination. Nor had their propaganda agencies fared well. The Unitarian Bible Society, founded in 1783, had been virtually superseded by the short-lived second series of Priestley's *Theological Repository*. The Unitarian Book Society, established in 1791, had not prospered in the decade of the anti-Revolution reaction; by 1804 it had published thirteen volumes of tracts, works by Price, Priestley, Lindsey, Belsham, Frend, Hartley, and several others, and had expended somewhat over £2,500. In 1805 the subscription list carried less than 150 names, and the Society raised less than £200 a year. It published no periodical, and none existed to serve the wider needs of the denomination. To remedy this deficiency and to advance the Unitarian cause, young Aspland on his own responsibility embarked upon the conduct of the new periodical. For nearly forty years he was to serve as a Unitarian editor; after selling the *Repository* in 1826, he continued until his death in 1844 as editor of the *Christian Reformer*.

Aspland had been a contributor to Vidler's failing *Universal Theological Magazine,* and at the close of 1805 he contracted to take over the property with its liabilities. The diminished reputation of Vidler's miscellany urged the need of a new name. After some playing with the title, *The Inquirer* (ultimately the name of another Unitarian publication), Aspland settled upon *The Monthly Repository of Theology and General Literature,* probably because of the associations with the title of Priestley's periodical. The prospectus of the proposed magazine stated that it was the editor's purpose

to blend literature with theology, and to make theology rational and literature popular; to be the advocate of Scriptural Christianity; to guard the Protestant privilege of liberty of conscience; and, acting on the principle that a bold and manly habit of religious investigation is favourable to truth and virtue, to open the pages of the *Monthly Repository* to all writers of ability and candour, whatever their peculiar opinions.[1]

The original plan provided for two main sections: one to contain "biographical sketches, moral and theological disquisitions, political criticism, select poetry, and miscellaneous original contributions"; the other, reviews of selected works on morals and theology. Three other departments were added: obituary; a catalogue of new publications; and "intelligence" of religious activities, chiefly Unitarian, of politics, and occasionally of literature. The price was one shilling.

The new magazine appeared on the first of February, 1806. The inexperienced editor, we are told by his son, sat up the whole night but one before the publication, in the printer's office in Paternoster Row, correcting proof. To a modern reader the first number is not prepossessing. Its fifty-six pages in typography, format, and content, did not differ radically from its predecessor, Vidler's defunct *Theo-*

[1] R. B. Aspland, *Memoir of Robert Aspland,* chap. 12.

logical Magazine. The first article was an installment of a two-part biographical sketch of Edward Evanson, an Anglican clergyman who had gone over to Unitarianism, signed J. S. (Joseph Spurrell, a Hackney businessman). There followed a department of miscellaneous communications including the following: "Indiscretions of Preachers" by A Constant Reader (Mrs. Catherine Cappe, a Unitarian tract writer); "An Inquiry concerning the Author of the Whole Duty of Man," signed Episcopus; "Strictures upon the Twelfth-Day Ceremonies at Court" by Gogmagog; "Vindication of the Nonconformist's Memorial," by its author, the Reverend Samuel Palmer, Dissenting minister at Hackney; a "Dialogue on a Reflection of Dr. Jortin's," by the Reverend Rochemont Barbauld, husband of the most distinguished woman poet of the day; a "List of Dissenting Congregations in the Counties of Northumberland and Durham," unsigned but by the Reverend William Turner of Newcastle, son of the friend of Priestley; an article on Biblical criticism, "An Explanation of Christ's Being Made Sin," extracted by Mrs. Cappe from her husband's sermons. The department of review included an examination of *Cappe's Discourses,* by the Reverend John Holland; of Samuel Parker's *The Old Testament Illustrated,* by John Evans; of funeral and thanksgiving sermons (the latter for Nelson's victory), probably written by Aspland. Of obituary there were four items, one of them on William Pitt. With joy the Intelligence Department noted that the American Congress had voted to abolish the slave trade. New publications listed included chiefly works on theology. In the poetry columns appeared a reprint of Thomas Campbell's "Ode to Winter," and three translations from the German of Herder and Goethe, signed Viator but identifiable as by Henry Crabb Robinson, recently returned from a prolonged stay in Germany.

Other writers of the first year may be mentioned: John Towill Rutt, a drug merchant but an untiring antiquarian of Nonconformist history and biography, who had helped Aspland to establish the *Repository* and who was later the editor and biographer of Priestley; Benjamin Flower, editor of the *Cambridge Intelligencer* and of the *Political Review;* the Reverend John Kentish, one of the leading scholars of his denomination; the Reverend Lant Carpenter, of Bristol; the Reverend Jeremiah Joyce, who in 1794 with Horne Tooke and several others was arrested for high treason; the Reverend Thomas Belsham, after Priestley's death the leading minister of the Unitarians; William Hamilton Reid, first editor of the *Orthodox Churchman's Magazine,* who had been converted to Unitarianism; and the Reverend Charles Wellbeloved, of York. Rutt and Kentish contributed to each of the twenty-one volumes of the first series; the Reverend John Evans, General Baptist minister in London, and William Turner, to most of them; and Dr. Joshua Toulmin, Dissenting historian and biographer, up to his death in 1815. Contributions were usually anonymous or signed only with pseudonyms. Most of the writers were Unitarians; as with Priestley's *Repository,* few of the orthodox accepted the invitation to contribute.

ROBERT ASPLAND

Aspland was twenty-four years old at the time he began the new periodical; he had been a Unitarian for less than five years. His break from Calvinism, since it was typical of that of many of the rational Dissenters, may be of some interest to recount. He was born in 1782 in the village of Wicken, county of Cambridge. His parents were Baptists, and it was under the auspices of that denomination that he prepared for the ministry. The ferment of liberal doctrines infected Aspland, Senior, in politics if not in religion. We are told that he held the strongest dislike for Pitt and the repressive measures of the Tory party, and did not hesitate even in public to excoriate the government. Since paid informers were everywhere abroad, such criticism could not be uttered without danger. Several times during his father's absence young Robert sat up late with his mother in order to allay her fears that her husband had fallen into the hands of government spies. The elder Aspland's views accorded with those of Benjamin Flower, imprisoned for libel in 1799. The boy was undoubtedly influenced in favor of the liberal cause; at twelve, on a visit to the Tower of London, he was shown some of the state prisoners, members of the Society for Constitutional Information: Horne Tooke, Jeremiah Joyce, Thomas Hardy, and several others.

Young Aspland pursued his education at the local grammar school, at a school in Islington for the two years 1793-1794 with the Reverend Edward Porter, of Highgate, and at the Reverend John Eyre's establishment in 1795. At fourteen he purchased and read Paine's *Age of Reason* and also Bishop Watson's *Apology for the Bible.* Soon thereafter he wrote home to his parents: "Paine is utterly unable to cope with the Bishop. Like the feeble javelin of aged Priam, his attack on Christianity has scarcely reached the mark. It has fallen to the ground without a stroke."[2] His letters of the next year or two contain numerous references to his "many inward struggles" over Calvinism and to the shock of Deistical writings upon him. Sometimes he seems to be whistling to keep up his courage:

Though I received a material shock by reading the *Age of Reason,* yet I have reason to bless God that I have been led to see the fallacy of the author's arguments, and obliged to fly to Revelation in order to enjoy any true comfort. . . . At least it has stirred me up to greater watchfulness. I sometimes fear that I shall one day or other fall by that monster, Deism. . . .[3]

[2] *Ibid.,* p. 12.
[3] *Ibid.,* letter to Andrew Fuller, 1797, p. 26.

In the year of this letter (1797) he joined the Baptist Church and was admitted as a Ward's Foundation scholar at the Bristol Academy to prepare for the ministry. Still suffering doubts, he continued to insist upon reason as the arbiter of truth.

I conceive an increasing disgust to some enthusiastic, irrational proceedings of the age. . . . *Reason,* however spoken against, shall be my attendant in all my researches, the standard of my faith and practice. . . . When I use the term *Reason* I would be understood to mean Reason aided and assisted by the simple and sublime truths of Revelation.[4]

A visit in 1798 to see French prisoners confined near Bristol filled him "with poignant indignation against the promoters of war." He complained to the young lady whom he eventually married, Sara Middleton, that his fellow students were "cramped by party spirit" and "afraid to investigate." Occasionally there is in his letters at this time a slight tone of rodomontade that may have been unconsciously designed to arouse the tender fears of his beloved:

The apparent contradictions and mysteriousness of Scripture have sometimes almost driven me to despair. Frequently have I sighed for non-existence! Frequently have I lamented that my lot was not cast in some remote part of the globe, where I might have lived at ease and indulged the native sentiments of my heart. . . . And I assure you I have often been a prey to Deistical reflections; and though examination has tended to Christianize my mind, you will readily believe that scepticism is not wholly excluded. . . .[5]

In the course of the same year as this letter, he was stirred to anger by the brutal trials in Scotland of Joseph Gerrald and Thomas Muir for sedition. On one occasion at least he bought boots from Thomas Hardy and discussed politics with that hero of the London Corresponding Society.

[4] *Ibid.,* letter to his parents, 1797, p. 53.
[5] *Ibid.,* Oct. 15, 1798.

In the fall of 1799 Aspland proceeded to Scotland, in keeping with Dissenting practice, to complete his education for the ministry. At Marischal College, Aberdeen, within a year he finally revolted against "hard and dry" Calvinism and adopted heterodox views, not without many an inner struggle. As a result, he was formally dropped from membership in the Baptist Church; he resigned his scholarship and further study at the college. Returning to England, he spent the winter of 1800-1801 in business with his prospective father-in-law. In the spring came a call to the General Baptist church at Newport, Isle of Wight. Aspland accepted the call, married Sara Middleton, and began his first pastorate. His theological views at this time, like those of many of the General Baptists, were Arian, but he soon came to accept the simple humanity of Christ. His congregation followed him into Unitarianism.

The young minister took an active part in the formation of the Southern Unitarian Association. On the occasion of Thomas Belsham's sermon to the Association in 1803, Aspland first became acquainted with that recognized Unitarian leader. In the same year appeared Aspland's first printed sermon, "Divine Judgments on Guilty Nations," published by Benjamin Flower, who contributed to the pamphlet a prefatory attack on the orthodox leaders, Robert Hall and Andrew Fuller. About this time Aspland began to contribute to Dissenting periodicals, and especially to Vidler's *Universal Theological Magazine*.[6]

In July, 1805, he became the successor of Belsham, Priestley, and Price at the Gravel Pit Chapel, Hackney, no small recognition of his abilities. For the remainder of his life

[6] Some of his identified contributions include the following: a letter, signed "A Nazarene," reprobating the demand for a confession of faith at a minister's ordination; "Cant Religious Terms"; "Remarks on J. M[arsom]'s Observations on John xi:40, 41"; "A Reply to J. M."; "A Brief Sketch of the Life and Works of Archdeacon Blackburne"; a review of Blackburne's works; a life of Paley; and a review of Foster's essays. Cf. *Memoir*.

he was pastor of that church. The location was fortunate, for many of the most influential Unitarians lived nearby: Belsham, Dr. Samuel Pett, the Reverend John Pickbourne, and John Towill Rutt, in Hackney; others in London suburbs: the Barbaulds at Newington; the Reverend Jeremiah Joyce at Highgate; the Reverend John Evans at Islington; Dr. James Lindsay at Bow; the Reverend Eliezer Cogan, one of Disraeli's teachers, at Walthamstow; and in London, Dr. Abraham Rees, Theophilus Lindsey, and George Dyer. David Ricardo, the economist, while he lived in the vicinity, was a member of the Gravel Pit congregation.

With the establishment of the *Repository,* Aspland soon became recognized as a leader of the denomination. February, 1806, also saw the founding of the Unitarian Fund, with Aspland as secretary. In 1809 he established the Christian Tract Society, and served as its secretary. In 1810 he edited a hymnal for Unitarian use. Always active in the affairs of the Three Denominations, he served on numerous committees for the protection of civil and religious rights. The Non-Con Club, which he founded in 1817, numbered among its members leading Dissenters of London and vicinity. In addition to the *Christian Reformer,* he also edited the *Test-Act Reporter* from 1827 until the repeal in the following year of the Test and Corporation Acts. Throughout his life he was an indefatigable worker in the Unitarian cause, and to that cause his editorship of the *Repository* contributed incalculable services.

GENERAL CHARACTER OF THE SERIES

In format the *Repository* was scarcely designed to attract readers. It was printed two columns to the page (after Vol. II), in approximately nine point type, and with certain departments in seven point. Octavo in size, a single number usually contained from sixty-four to seventy-two closely packed pages. Little attention was paid to securing attractive make-up, the various contributions simply being strung together, one after the other, with no discernible purpose in the arrangement. The division into departments has already been described. Proof-reading was fairly accurate, but there seems to have been little attempt, if any, to standardize the usage and punctuation of contributors. There were no illustrations, except for an annual frontispiece for the bound volume; ordinarily this was an engraving of some Unitarian worthy or chapel. On one occasion some music was printed. The magazine carried a wrapper of advertisements, but since these have not been preserved in the bound volumes, it is difficult to estimate the amount. Contrary to modern practice, numbers were published at the end of the month rather than at the beginning.

Most of the articles appeared in the form of letters to the editor, who assigned titles and running heads. Leading articles, however, were frequently cast in essay form. Most of the contributions were relatively short, three or four pages being the usual limit; many were only a column or a page long. The few longer articles, even book reviews, were often divided and published over two or three months. The writers were not, of course, remunerated. Free to sign contributions or remain anonymous, many of the regulars eventually adopted the practice of affixing their signatures. Some used pseudonyms like A Churchman (Anthony Robinson), Ben David (John Jones), A Plain Christian (Benjamin Flower), and Discipulus (Harriet Martineau). More used initials, which within the relatively small Unitarian circle sometimes proved easily identifiable, especially when the letters bore the *locus* of the writer.

The *Repository* proved worthy of its name in serving as a storehouse of materials for the history of Dissent. It printed many articles about Dissenting worthies of the eighteenth century, and not alone of Presbyterians. Letters,

journals, scraps of church and educational history, which
have otherwise disappeared, may be found in abundance.
Records of Nonconformist academies and churches appeared
frequently, many of them contributed by J. T. Rutt, William Turner, and Joshua Toulmin. These three also furnished much biographical material; for instance, in the
years 1818-1819, Rutt supplied the correspondence of Locke
and Limborch. Obituaries in the *Repository* are notable for
their freedom from the fulsome eulogizing and the death-
bed testimonials of the evangelical periodicals; its necrology
is usually reliable biography, temperate and factual, though
of course not without praise for the worthy departed. One
of the chief functions of the periodical was to serve as a
public record of Unitarian and Nonconformist biography
and history. It regularly printed accounts of the meetings
of Unitarian organizations and of the Society for the Protection of Religious Liberty. Parliamentary debates on questions of religious and civil liberty it often reported in considerable detail.

LITERATURE AND CRITICISM

The weakest side of the *Repository* lay in its literary
character, a fault recognized when the new series was begun
in 1827. "General Literature" in the title of the first series
was given a narrow interpretation; little of what might be
called literature appeared in its pages, and seldom did any
of the great literary works of the period receive attention
in its department of review.

A page or two of poetry was included in most numbers,
and the twenty-one volumes presented altogether something
over five hundred poems. Of this amount, as might be expected, over half was religious or devotional, including many
hymns. These, in keeping with Unitarian doctrine, stressed
the unity of the Godhead, the love of the Father, and the
promises of Restoration; they tended to be more stately and

dignified in tone and diction than the popular Methodist songs. The most notable contributor of devotional songs to the *Repository* was John Bowring, several of whose hymns are still widely sung in Protestant churches, the best known being "In the Cross of Christ I Glory." In all, Bowring contributed some sixty poems to the first series, many of them translations which will be noted later. Included among the leading contributors of religious verse were Mrs. Barbauld, some of whose work Wordsworth admired greatly, Emily Taylor, writer of children's books, and three ministers, Richard Fry, of Kidderminster, John Johns, of Crediton, and Robert Wallace, of Chesterfield. In addition to hymns there were paraphrases and expansions of Biblical themes, like Joseph Nightingale's "The Lamentation of Jephthah's Daughter,"[7] and the Reverend Jacob Brettell's "The Encampment of the Israelites on the Plains of Moab";[8] there were also poems commemorative of religious anniversaries, on the duties and rewards of Christians, and memorial verses for departed friends and relatives.

Well over a tenth of the poems were elegiac; among the less obscure of those commemorated were such Unitarians as Theophilus Lindsey, Jeremiah Joyce, William Vidler, and such public figures as Thomas Jefferson, John Adams, Charles James Fox, Sir Samuel Romilly, the Princess Charlotte, and Queen Caroline of famous memory. Political sympathies intruded even in elegiacs; in "Lines on the Death of Queen Caroline" the writer (probably Bowring) invoked the "Royal Sufferer" to "go to courts above, *too good* for courts below." There, free from the "yells of spite and faction," she might enjoy the "sunshine of eternal rest."

> Stung with remorse, may thy repentant foes
> Abhor themselves, and mourn thy bitter woes;

[7] *Monthly Repository*, 1st series, III (1808), 441. Except where otherwise noted, all references in this chapter are to the first series of the *Monthly Repository*.   [8] XXI (1826), 360-67.

Confess the injustice of their foul misdeeds,
And hide with shame their self-condemning heads.[9]

One finds it hard to picture George IV's being "stung with remorse" in losing the queen whom he had for years been vainly trying to divorce.

The *Repository's* secular poetry consisted largely of descriptive and occasional verse. Occasions commemorated ranged from the presentation to "the Author's wife of an ornamented workbox," to a wedding anniversary, to the re-establishment of the Inquisition in Spain, and the fall of Napoleon. Favorite political themes were the woes of war and the blessings of peace, toleration, independence, and liberty. On the latter subject, Thomas Noon Talfourd, an enthusiastic admirer of Wordsworth, to whom he had been introduced by Charles Lamb, published four "Sonnets Supplementary to Wordsworth's Sonnets to Liberty." The young poet in a footnote modestly deprecated any comparison with the poems he imitated. Talfourd's poetry, then and later, was less marked by simplicity and naturalness than by high-flown rhetoric. Since his early poetry seems hitherto unnoticed elsewhere, quotation of one of his two sonnets "To the South American Patriots" may be of interest as illustrative of his manner:

> Think not, undaunted champions! that the sea
> With all its waves can part us from the cause
> In which you struggle;—that 'neath English laws
> We sit in cold and mute tranquillity,
> When mightiest nations combat to be free.
> No! we are form'd of one celestial blood,
> The children of one Sire;—and we have stood
> For freedom's cause in earth's Thermopylae!
> E'en nature mingles feelings from afar—
> The ocean, and the winds, and clouds are free,
> And the unbridled coursers of the sun,

[9] XVI (1821), 555.

> And the sweet moon and every silent star,
> All that both Continents can look upon
> Breathe, with one deathless voice, of LIBERTY![10]

Radical Dissenting sympathies with the revolutions in France and America were still evident years later. To illustrate the Dissenting attachment to liberty, a stanza from "Independence" by George Dyer, the kindly hackwriting friend of Charles Lamb, will perhaps suffice. The poem refers throughout to America.

> Whilst we view yon lamp of fire;
> While we feel its genial ray;
> May Freedom British hearts inspire,
> May Honour rule with sovereign sway!
> Hail, Independence, reign supreme;
> Ours be thy more than chartered plan;
> And never will we Briton deem,
> Who spurns the noblest rights of man.[11]

Not all the poems in the magazine represented original contributions; nearly one-fifth were acknowledged excerpts from books and periodicals, and a number of others were taken without acknowledgment. The favorite source of extracts seems to have been the *Morning Chronicle,* a Whig newspaper. Five poems were quoted from works by Tom Moore, and four each from Byron and the Irish poet William Drennan. Southey's "Battle of Blenheim" was reprinted, as well as Bryant's "Thanatopsis" and Mrs. Hemans' "The Lament of the Last Druid." William Roscoe, a Unitarian, was represented with three. Some attention was paid to the work of unlearned poets like John Jackson and Charlotte Richardson and occasionally to some juvenile effusions. Three or four University prize poems were printed in whole or in part.

Altogether, poetry in the *Repository* was not distin-

---

[10] XII (1817), 371.   [11] V (1810), 306.

guished, though it compared favorably enough with that in contemporary religious magazines. Much of it was uninspired, amateur work. For models, diction, and measures it tended to favor eighteenth-century standards rather than the new ones of its own generation, though there were occasional signs of revolt against the old rules. The sonnet was popular, at least a tenth of the poems aspiring to that form. If extenuation need be urged for the character and quality of the *Repository's* poetry, it may again be pointed out that the magazine's avowed interests were not in the field of belles-lettres.

In translations from foreign poetry the *Repository* completely eclipsed rival religious periodicals. In part this was due to the accident that the sect numbered among its adherents two devotees of foreign literature, Henry Crabb Robinson and John Bowring, though it must be remembered also that the Unitarians were more receptive to foreign influences, particularly German, than were the orthodox sects. The Unitarian-dominated *Monthly Review* and *Monthly Magazine,* and the indefatigable critic and translator William Taylor of Norwich, made important contributions to the cause of German literature in England, while Unitarian theologians followed with interest and profit the labors of German theological research and criticism.

Somewhat over ten per cent of the *Repository's* poems were translated from Continental languages. Nearly half of these translations were from the German. Herder was the favorite; fifteen of his poems appeared in translation between 1806 and 1816, all but one the work of Crabb Robinson.[12] These are of some importance in connection with Herder's reputation in England, since, as V. Stockley has pointed out, Herder was seldom noticed in England before

---

[12] For a listing of these and other contributions by Robinson, see Appendix, p. 397.

1800, and almost never between that date and 1820.[13] Only one Goethe lyric appeared in the *Repository*[14] and but two by Schiller.[15] John Bowring contributed a dozen translations from the Portuguese, three each from the German, Italian, and Spanish, two from the Russian, and single examples from the Persian and the Finnish. Occasionally translations of Latin poetry, ancient and modern, exercised the skill of contributors. In most of the translated verse, fidelity to the original was not an outstanding characteristic; in this respect perhaps the best of the translators was Robinson.

In the field of prose, the *Repository* paid almost as much attention to the literature of the Continent as of England, though this statement should not be taken to mean that there was emphasis upon foreign literature. Two translations from Schiller, "The Mosaic Mission" and "On the Migration of Nations," appeared in 1825.[16] To Volume I Crabb Robinson furnished a translation of a parable by Lessing and the first rendering into English of Lessing's *Education of the Human Race*,[17] which years later was the subject of several articles by Harriet Martineau in the second series of the magazine. Robinson also wrote "Remarks on the Genius and Writings of Herder" for Volume III,[18] and years later, for the second series, nine articles on Goethe. (See pp. 316-20.)

The forte of John Bowring (1792-1872) in literature lay in his wide knowledge of languages, acquired in the first instance for commercial rather than literary pursuits. In addition to his many hymns, religious verses, and translations of foreign poetry, he contributed to the *Repository* a

---

[13] *German Literature as Known in England, 1750-1830*, pp. 107-18.
[14] "The Spirit's Greeting," translated by Robinson, I (1806), 55.
[15] VIII (1813), 526; XI (1816), 174.
[16] XX (1825), 194-204, 577-81. The latter is signed Comar Yates.
[17] I (1806), 412-20; 467-73.
[18] III (1808), 173-79.

number of articles on such subjects as these: "A Sketch of the History and Literature of the Spanish Jews,"[19] "The State of Religion in Sweden,"[20] "Ultra-Catholicism in France,"[21] and "The Present State of the Vaudois Churches in Piedmont."[22]

Heartily disliked by a number of his contemporaries, particularly in the Utilitarian Radical camp,[23] Bowring was highly regarded among the Unitarians. A "self-help" sort of young man, he was possibly at times none too scrupulous in pushing his way up the ladder, but he did manage to get up. Born at Exeter in 1792 of a mercantile family, he left school at fourteen, worked as a clerk in Exeter for five years, meanwhile ardently studying French, Spanish, Portuguese, German, and Dutch, and then went into a London trading firm in 1811. His linguistic ability (in addition to the above, he later added Swedish, Danish, Russian, Serbian, Polish, Bohemian, and many more) earned him a position as a commercial agent on the Continent, first in Spain in 1813. For a time he engaged in the Mediterranean trade. Through the Norwich firm of Thomas Martineau and Sons he became acquainted with George Borrow, who also prided himself on his linguistic accomplishments. For years Borrow hung to Bowring's coattails, but eventually after a quarrel he scurfed Bowring sharply as "The Old Radical" in *Romany Rye*.

Bowring had been educated under two Unitarian ministers, Lant Carpenter and James Hews Bransby, and he made the most of his Unitarian as well as his political connections. In fairness to him, however, it must be noted that open avowal of Unitarianism was not the accepted road to success in politics. In 1822 he was arrested in France for bearing secret dispatches to the Portuguese ministers, and

---

[19] XIV (1819), 345-52.   [20] XIX (1824), 193-200.
[21] XV (1820), 325-32.   [22] *Ibid.*, pp. 629-31.
[23] See G. L. Nesbitt, *Benthamite Reviewing*, pp. 28-34.

sentenced to perpetual exile from the country, a sentence later rescinded by Louis Phillipe. The *Repository,* reporting his arrest, said: "Our own Government seem to have done everything in their power to vindicate the rights of an English subject, and to relieve the distress of Mr. Bowring's family and friends; and of friends no man living has a wider circle, or in the circle more that from qualities of both head and heart make their friendship valuable."[24] A captious critic might hazard the guess that Bowring sought out those whose friendship would be valuable. Of his imprisonment in France he made literary capital; the *Repository* reviewed his account of the experience[25] and extracted his "Lines Written in the Prison at Calais."[26]

Bowring became the toadying disciple of Jeremy Bentham, and as a result the first editor of the *Westminster Review* and also Bentham's biographer and editor. He published volume upon volume of poetry translated from the Russian, Spanish, Magyar, Batavian, Polish, Serbian, etc., often apparently with insufficiently acknowledged help from some starveling linguist. His political career achieved more success than his commercial; he represented the British government on many business missions all over the world, served as British plenipotentiary in China for ten years, was elected to Parliament, and eventually was knighted by Victoria. In addition to many volumes of verse he wrote numerous articles on social, economic, and political reform. As a Unitarian he stood always on the side of religious and civil liberty, and in the affairs of Unitarian associations he took an active part. While his contributions to the *Repository* have little interest as literature, they were valuable in giving somewhat more substance to the too slender literary character of the periodical.

Not much can be said for Aspland's discernment in

---

[24] XVII (1822), 656.
[25] XVIII (1823), 167-69.   [26] *Ibid.,* pp. 103-4.

choosing literary works for review, and many of the reviews were little more than short critical notes or summaries; the *Repository's* proper field of criticism lay rather among religious and didactic works. As a result, many a dull sermon received notice while the works of the great poets and novelists were neglected. Of John Keats, for instance, aside from reprinting his and Leigh Hunt's sonnets "On a Grasshopper,"[27] there was no word except for the curt notice of his death: "—Jan. 23, at Rome, of a decline, JOHN KEATS, the Poet, aged 25."[28] Shelley's name was mentioned only a few times, and then in connection with the Chancery suit of *Westbrook* vs. *Shelley*[29] and with the prosecution of the printer of his "atheistical libel," *Queen Mab;*[30] a very brief notice of his death was reprinted from the *Monthly Magazine.*[31]

The *Repository's* attitude towards Byron was revealed in 1824 in a short article, "The Testimony to Christianity from Lord Byron." The "testimony" was an ambiguous passage in *Don Juan* which the commentator thought showed some "glimmering of returning piety." Said the writer:

We seldom introduce the name of Lord Byron into the *Monthly Repository.* We dare not express admiration, and we are unwilling to join the ranks of those that, from such different motives, raise their voices against him. He is now employed in a good work, the assistance of the Greeks, and happy shall we be to see that in this philanthropic service he is making amends to mankind for any injury which he may have done to society by his writings.[32]

The Reverend John Evans contributed an article, "On Lord Byron's Infidelity," which compared the reasons for the infidelity of Gibbon and Byron.[33] Earlier, in 1819, the maga-

---

[27] XII (1817), 299.
[28] XVI (1821), 181.
[29] XII (1817), 60, 180-81.
[30] XVII (1822), 717.
[31] *Ibid.*, p. 577.
[32] XIX (1824), 200-1.
[33] XX (1825), 1-7.

zine had protested against the prosecution of poor parodists
when rich, noble ones escaped punishment: "The grossest
parody of modern times is one upon the Ten Command-
ments in Lord Byron's *Don Juan,* published and republished within a few months, by *Murray,* of Albemarle Street,
the publisher of the *Quarterly Review,* and of other 'orthodox' and 'loyal' works."[34] The writer of an article on devotional poetry thought that Byron's "Hebrew Melodies"
breathed "more the soul of Jewish patriotism than of Christian devotion."[35]

The "wandering bards," "Coleridge, Southey, and Co.," whom
in 1798 the *Anti-Jacobin* represented as moving "in sweet accord
of harmony and love" and tuning all their "mystic harps to
praise Lepaux," the French Theophilanthropist, are still con-
sentaneous in their movements but their harps are tuned to another theme, the demerits of the Unitarians,

began the reviewer of Coleridge's "Lay Sermon" in 1817.[36]
Only infrequently did the *Repository* notice the "lost liberals," and then usually in relation to their political and
religious views and their attacks on Unitarianism. The
known radicalism of Wordsworth, Coleridge, and Southey
in their youth was contrasted, to their disadvantage, with
the now evident desire of their maturity for a reputation
of orthodox respectability. Though lamenting their defection from the liberal cause, sometimes with mingled resent-
ment but more often with regret, the *Repository's* recognition
of their poetic merit tended to temper criticism of their
apostasy. In tone much of this criticism is surprisingly close
to that of Browning's "A Lost Leader"; Browning voiced
the feeling of many Dissenting Liberals, evident as early
as 1817.

Of the three, Southey, because of his official position as

[34] XIV (1819), 716.
[35] XXI (1826), 253-60.   [36] XII (1817), 299.

the poet laureate and his numerous attacks on the Dissenters in the *Quarterly*, was the target of the sharpest barbs. Unfortunately for Southey's peace of mind, the youthful radicalism of his past came stalking forth in public to confound him; in 1817 a piratical bookseller brought out, unauthorized, his till then unprinted and unknown, republican, revolutionary drama, *Wat Tyler*, written in 1794. To the delight of radicals and Dissenters, Southey failed in his attempts to suppress the publication. The *Repository* waxed satirical: "Mr. Southey is thus consigned to his own lash: his self-castigation will we hope subdue his angry spirit: if it should have this effect, we would recommend to him, as a work equally fitted to his literary researches and his experiences, a new History of the Flagellants."[37] William Smith, staunch Unitarian M.P. for Norwich, rose up in the House of Commons, with a *Quarterly Review* containing a Southey article in one hand and *Wat Tyler* in the other, to chastise their author. Southey countered with a published "Letter to William Smith, Esq., M.P.," which the *Repository* reviewed:[38] "Although he has written more epics than Milton and probably as much history as Hume, we are not fully convinced of the equity of his title to immortality. . . ." Singled out for attack were Southey's support of the suspension of the Habeas Corpus Act, his advocacy of Church control of education and of the suppression of a free press. The same volume continued the assault on the laureate with a review, signed "Renegade Northey," of *The Spaniard's Letters from England*,[39] an epigram on the letter to Smith,[40] and a reprint of his early radical poem, "To the Exiled Patriots, Muir and Palmer."[41] After this volume, except for an article on his *Life of Wesley*,[42] the *Repository* paid little attention to the laureate other than an occasional hostile allusion.

[37] *Ibid.*, p. 172.
[38] *Ibid.*, pp. 274-75, 301-2.
[39] *Ibid.*, pp. 281-84, 350-54, 406-9.
[40] *Ibid.*, p. 371.
[41] *Ibid.*, pp. 622, 739.
[42] XV (1820), 652-55.

Coleridge also received most attention in the 1817 volume, the result of his denunciation of Unitarianism in his "Lay Sermon . . . on the Existing Distresses and Discontents." In this Coleridge attacked the Unitarians' reliance on common sense as a guide to religious truth and their rejection of mystery in religion. Their creed, he said, was made up more of negations than positive articles of faith; his catalogue of the latter listed only six. Unitarians were declared to be a class of men who read the Scriptures "in order to pick and choose their faith . . . for the purpose of plucking away live-asunder, as it were from the divine organism of the Bible, textuary morsels and fragments for the support of doctrines which they had learned beforehand from the higher oracle of their own natural common-sense."[43] This, of course, could not go unanswered in the *Repository,* especially since Coleridge had once been a Unitarian, and, for a short time, even a preacher of the sect. The reviewer of the "Lay Sermon" did not forbear to remind the poet of "the time that he officiated as an Unitarian teacher at Shrewsbury and elsewhere," and hastened in sharp tones to rectify Coleridge's possibly purposeful lapses of memory.[44] The same volume had earlier printed two letters,[45] signed S.N.D. (possibly a pseudonym for Thomas Noon Talfourd), which answered in more detail Coleridge's charges. The second letter closed with an expression of regret that the poet had left his proper path for "the lower walks of controversy, political or religious." Coleridge was said to be "one whose proper sphere is above this world and not amidst its storms," and "who may live in the hearts and imaginations of brighter ages, when the very names of those whose cause he now condescends to gild over are utterly forgotten.[46] Other than for excerpting a *Monthly Review* attack on the renegade

---

[43] *On the Constitution of Church and State,* pp. 373-74.
[44] XII (1817), 299-301.
[45] *Ibid.,* pp. 213-16, 268-72.   [46]*Ibid.,* p. 272.

Unitarian,[47] the first series devoted no more attention to him.

Wordsworth received somewhat more attention and respect than either Coleridge or Southey, though he too had to be reproached for anti-Unitarianism. In a series of articles "On Poetical Scepticism" in 1816, the writer (again, probably Talfourd) reproved Wordsworth for his unfriendly remarks in the notes to his volume of the previous year. The poet had said that readers of religious poetry tended to be strongly, even violently, prejudiced for or against an author as his sentiments agreed with theirs, and that those sects "whose religion, being from the calculating understanding, is cold and formal" were most liable to such excesses. Of a religion founded upon the pride of reason,

what can be expected but contradictions? Accordingly, believers of this cast are at one time contemptuous; at another, being troubled as they are and must be with inward misgivings, they are jealous and suspicious;—and at all seasons, they are under temptation to supply, by the heat with which they defend their tenets, the animation which is wanting to the constitution of the religion itself.[48]

Though repelling these insinuations of the poet, S.N.D. paid high tribute to Wordsworth. "In acute sensibility, in the philosophy of nature, in the delineation of all that is gentle in man, and in the power of rendering earthly images ethereal, I believe him to be surpassed by none in ancient or modern times. . . ."[49]

The same writer in another article of this series[50] made use of Wordsworth's poetry to attack orthodox Calvinism, with its doctrines of original sin and natural depravity, as a blight upon poetry. After quoting "Heaven lies about us in our infancy," he remarked: "It seems scarcely possible to

[47] XVI (1821), 595.
[48] Wordsworth, *Poems* (1815), I, 346.
[49] XI (1816), 218.   [50] *Ibid.*, pp. 278-80.

link anything which is beautiful or exalted with the belief
that the heart of man is naturally corrupt, his faculties
morally depraved, and his earliest emotions sinful." Such
a creed, which teaches that the veriest infant is "under the
wrath and curse of God," can scarcely be expected to produce lofty poetry. Calvinism blights the joyousness and
purity of childhood, the source of true poetry. There is an
intimate connection between poetry and "the sacred feelings of childhood, . . . and these are the affections over
which Calvinism casts its shadow. They are 'the fountain
light of all its day.'" The true poet is one who believes
that "we have all of us ONE HUMAN HEART." Wordsworth's
support of this conclusion was cited from "The Old Cum-
berland Beggar," of which S.N.D. declared: "No one can
read the whole of this exquisite poem, and be *for the time*
a Calvinist. If Mr. Wilberforce should write for ages on the
total corruption of man—these lines would be more than an
answer to the most eloquent exaggerations he could produce."[51]

Not all the *Repository's* writers admired Wordsworth's
theories of poetry. The reviewer of a volume of Cowper's
poems took occasion to criticize the theories of poetic diction
exemplified in the *Lyrical Ballads,* and refuted the proposition that the conversational style of humble life is suited to
poetry. "For the poet, like the painter, must copy *general,*
not *individual,* nature. . . . He must elevate what is mean,
he must soften what is harsh; and these objectives he will
not reach if his style is familiar and provincial."[52] Cowper
was praised as one who held a middle rank between the
poets of Pope's school and "those who introduce the language of common life into compositions professing to be
poetical."[53]

Only once did the *Repository* review any of Words-

[51] *Ibid.*, p. 280.
[52] *Ibid.*, p. 161.   [53] *Ibid.*, p. 162.

worth's books. An article of five pages on his *Ecclesiastical Sketches* and his *Memorials of a Tour on the Continent* appeared in 1822.[54] The writer was probably John Bowring; his criticism was not in all respects discerning.

Wordsworth, who, touched by an habitual sense of beauty and melody, seldom fails to communicate their influence to the expression of his thoughts and feelings—too eager and enthusiastic to follow the gradual workings of the mind, usually breaks forth in the strength and impetuosity of his genius, and becomes exhausted in the first fervour of his song.

The character of Wordsworth's genius is such as to give a charm to whatever he touches;—to "the vast and the minute"— "the meanest flower that lives," as well as the mightiest orb that rolls. He is the true alchemist. . . .[55]

The chief emphasis of the article was upon Wordsworth's defection from the liberal cause. "In truth, since Wordsworth changed his politics, his writings have lost much of their charm." When the poet chooses a subject from the past, he can give expression to his love of freedom; "but when he approaches modern times, he dares not . . . give vent to the thoughts that must intrude upon him." He no longer loves liberty. "But *we* [the liberals] have no commissionerships of stamps and taxes to give." The liberals should be consoled, at any rate, that they have had the best of his services. But with all his political sins, "Wordsworth is indeed a great poet. If his admirers be few, they are chosen from among the best of our species. . . . Though noiseless as the voice of time, he has produced a deeper and more lasting influence on modern English poetry than any writer of his epoch."[56]

The one English poet whom the *Repository* was always eager to honor was John Milton, but it is clear that Milton's reputation as a Puritan and as a not altogether orthodox

[54] XVII (1822), 360-65.
[55] *Ibid.*, p. 360.   [56] *Ibid.*, p. 365.

thinker on theology, influenced this preference. The publication of Milton's *Christian Doctrine,* as has already been seen, was hailed as a triumph for the cause of rational Christianity. In 1809 Aspland reprinted from the *Times* a translation of some of the Italian sonnets.[57] Extracts from Milton's prose were reprinted in successive months of 1813, arranged under such headings as "Acts of Grace," "Catholic Faith," "Calvin," and "National Church."[58] Volume XX printed a poetical version of a passage from the prose.[59] In 1825-1826 the Reverend John Evans, who had once edited *Paradise Lost,* contributed four articles on Milton: one defended his domestic character,[60] another discussed his person and his blindness,[61] and two examined the varying reception accorded the *Christian Doctrine* by the periodicals.[62] Writers in the magazine were fond of quoting from the Puritan poet. For example, as if by way of anticipatory answer to Matthew Arnold's criticism years later in *Culture and Anarchy* of the dissenting contribution to culture, Christopher Richmond, in the peroration of his Non-Con Club address on "The Cause of Nonconformity as Connected with Literature,"[63] said:

Does anyone still hesitate to pronounce Nonconformity to the State religion compatible with the expansion and cultivation of genius, imagination, fancy, and taste, let him look upwards to the venerable form of *Milton.* . . . The country which gave him birth will not cease to derive a growing lustre from so rare and perhaps unparalleled a combination of all the majesty of genius with all the grace of science; but more especially may those who enlist under the banners of Protestant Nonconformity, that glorious cause which called forth the most powerful energies and moulded the loftiest conceptions of his mind, fearlessly

[57] IV (1809), 45-46.
[58] VIII (1813), 27-31, etc.　　　[59] XX (1825), 306.
[60] XXI (1826), 657-63.　　　[61] *Ibid.,* pp. 590-94.
[62] XX (1825), 710-13; XXI (1826), 724-31.
[63] XIV (1819), 24-30.

go forth, armed in the mental and moral strength of their immortal champion, so long as

"New foes arise
"Threat'ning to bind our *souls* with secular chains."[64]

The extent to which theological bias could sometimes influence literary judgment is illustrated by a letter from the Reverend Thomas Howe, of Bridport, in 1821. He attacked Bunyan's *Pilgrim's Progress* for being "as pernicious in its tendency as it is erroneous in principle." Howe believed that an allegory which represented Christians as having to pass through a Slough of Despond, presented "needless discouragement . . . not warranted by divine revelation." The contest between Christian and Apollyon was "more calculated to promote *superstition* than genuine piety." *Paradise Lost* was also declared to be guilty of spreading false ideas of God's goodness and mercy, though *Pilgrim's Progress* was more dangerous since it was read more widely by those of "common capacities." Howe recommended a new edition, *"revised* and *corrected"*—evidently according to Unitarian principles.[65]

In general, the *Repository's* contributors chose to deal with literature only as it bore upon religion and morality. This deficiency was made up in part for Unitarian readers by the *Monthly Review,* with its rather marked Unitarian bias. The fact that Aspland's periodical did not pay for contributions must have discouraged some writers and poets from submitting their wares. The editor's readiness to accept pieces that would lend a more literary character to his periodical, however, did give the encouragement of print to several young writers who eventually achieved distinction.

Of these, the best known is Harriet Martineau. Her first published work, entitled "Female Writers of Practical

[64] *Ibid.*, p. 30. [65] XVI (1821), 16-18, 72-74.

Divinity," and signed Discipulus, appeared in two installments in the *Repository* for 1822.[66] At the outset of her
career the youthful Norwich aspirant for literary fame revealed her unbending Protestant and Unitarian training.
As proof of the superiority of the Protestant faith to the
Catholic, she pointed to the fact "that England has produced in one age so many female writers on morals and
divinity." In reading the works of Catholic females, "soon
is our pleasure alloyed by discovering some defective morality, some hidden licentiousness, or at least some artificial
sentiment . . . ;" the reason is, of course, that these ladies
"have drawn their ideas from that source which is tainted
by the foul admixtures of superstition." It is the differences
in religion which have made Hannah More's works superior to those of Madame de Staël or of Madame Genlis.
Not that Harriet approved of all Hannah's doctrines—Hannah, after all, was an Evangelical—but she found in them
"nothing really offensive" to her feelings and much that
excited her admiration. Despite her extravagant praise of
Mrs. Barbauld, she criticized that lady's *Thoughts on Devotional Taste* as being too imaginative: "there is too much
of the language of poetry and romance, instead of that
calm, though warm, that sedate, though animated tone of
feeling, which the theme demands." Calmness and sedate-
ness—and more than a measure of priggishness—marked
Harriet's own excursion into the field of practical piety.
Another of her articles, "On Female Education," will be
noted later. To her are probably also to be attributed two
poems signed H.M.: "Lines Occasioned by the Controversy
on the Origin of Evil," and "On the Death of Lieutenant
Hood."[67] Of Miss Martineau's voluminous contributions to
the second series of the *Repository* we shall have much to
say in Chapter V.

[66] XVII (1822), 593-96, 746-50. For an account of the occasion of her first
contribution and of its reception by her family, see her *Autobiography*, I, 90-92.
[67] XIX (1824), 43-45.

Another young literary contributor was Thomas Noon Talfourd, later the highly though briefly acclaimed author of *Ion, a Tragedy* (1836); often known as Serjeant Talfourd, famous for his work in securing copyright laws for English authors, he is perhaps even better known as the literary executor and editor of Charles Lamb. Talfourd married J. T. Rutt's eldest daughter, and as a young man he was active in Unitarian and Nonconformist causes. He contributed a number of poems and articles to the *Repository* and several addresses given before the Non-Con Club, of which he was a charter member. Harriet Martineau in her *Autobiography* recalled the attention accorded one series of Talfourd's early papers, "On the System of Malthus," which "had nothing to do with the real Malthus and his system, but was a sentimental vindication of long engagements."[68] Harriet confessed long afterwards, she says, to Malthus himself that she had for years labored under misapprehensions about his real meaning, as a result of these papers. If she had taken the trouble to re-read Talfourd's articles, she would have found that she had misapprehended them also. (See p. 162.)

One of Talfourd's Non-Con Club addresses bore the imposing title, "On the Supposed Affinity of the Poetical Faculties with Arbitrary Power and Superstitious Faith."[69] It was an attack upon a thesis of Hazlitt in an essay on *Coriolanus* that "The language of poetry falls naturally in with the language of power. . . . The principle of poetry is a very anti-leveling principle. . . . Poetry is right royal." Talfourd remarked scornfully that this was the principle of Burke, who "made the cause of tyranny appear the cause of the imagination and the affections." Poetry is not right-royal; it is "right-human," and does not put might before right. Nor are the objects of power "the stateliest or the most enduring things for a poet to celebrate. The meanest

---

[68] *Autobiography*, I, 54. [69] XV (1820), 95-99.

objects of nature have an antiquity more venerable than the Pyramids. . . . The splendours of tyrants are dim compared with the gorgeous visions of childhood." No religious belief is "so fitted to the offices of a poet as the Christian faith, in the free goodness of God, and the universal brotherhood of man."[70]

That faith the *Repository* carried over into its criticism of literature as well as into its discussion of religion, politics, and society.

RELIGION

Since the primary object of the *Repository* was the advancement of the Unitarian cause, much space was devoted to the defense of the denomination's theological position. Attacks on the Anglicans and the orthodox Dissenters were of common occurrence, sometimes lending spirit to otherwise uninteresting religious discourses. The Unitarians were small in number, but they gained a deserved reputation for being strong in controversy. They attracted attention out of all proportion to their numbers, partly because of the able learning of their ministers and writers.

That learning was frequently turned to account, particularly in the illustration and interpretation of the Bible. These contributions, many of them slight, often only of several paragraphs, perhaps on the interpretation of a single verse, distinguished the periodical from many of its religious contemporaries. No other devoted so much attention to textual criticism, and at the close of each bound volume was printed a list of the texts explained during the course of the year. Chief among the writers of this kind of criticism were Thomas Belsham, Joseph Jevons, John Kentish, and John Jones.

It must be remembered that a century earlier in England the whole New Testament, from beginning to end, had been

[70] *Ibid.,* p. 99.

almost universally regarded, especially by Protestants, as the infallible revelation of the Divine Will. Christian doctrines, it was held, were simply inferences from the Sacred Text. But early textual study, particularly in England by John Mill (1707) and in Germany by J. J. Wetstein (1751), proved the existence of important variations in the text, even in the days of primitive Christianity. Unitarians were naturally committed to accepting these new principles of criticism, since to establish some of their doctrines certain verses had to be proved to be interpolations in the original text. Like most Dissenters they insisted that the Bible and nothing but the Bible was their religion, but, unlike most other sects, they also insisted upon using all the forces of reason to arrive at a true version. To them, reverence for the Bible as a whole did not mean yielding to every published verse in the King James translation.[71] To tolerate textual corruptions was to encourage infidelity.

William Frend in 1825, discussing the need of a new translation, said: "It is needless now to expatiate on the imperfections of the Bible now in general use. . . . If the authors of it were now alive, they would gladly avail themselves of the advantages which a greater insight into manuscripts, and a more improved criticism has produced." He attributed the defects to the corrupt state of the text and to "the imperfect knowledge of languages from which the translation was made." Frend, who had once undertaken a translation for Priestley, endorsed Griesbach's edition (1774-1775) as completely surpassing the received version in accuracy. Frend proposed a Bible to be issued without

[71] A reviewer of pamphlets on the Scottish Unitarian controversy (probably Dr. Southwood Smith) said: "Unitarians revere the Scriptures; but they do not hold the English translation sacred: Unitarians revere the Scriptures; but they know that every syllable of the received text is not an exact transcript of the original record; they are therefore anxious to distinguish what is genuine from what is spurious. . . . They wish to show their reverence by deducing their religious opinions entirely from a pure text, aided by liberal and enlightened criticism. . . ." XII (1817), 412. Cf. also Vol. I (1806), 88-89.

note or comment, with variant readings, with divisions and chapters indicated in the margin only, bound in small parts rather than in one volume, and to be available in cheap form.[72]

In 1819 a refutation, probably by Belsham, of objections to a published Unitarian "Improved Version" enunciated these principles of Biblical criticism forty years before similar statements in *Essays and Reviews* aroused mid-Victorian horror:

> The meaning of the sacred writings is to be made out precisely in the same way as that of any other writers of equal antiquity. First by a correct text; then by the grammatical construction of the words, and by philological criticism. If this be not sufficient, . . . recourse must be had to the context, to the object and design of the writer, to the habits of thinking, and the peculiar phraseology of his age and country. And finally, it is impossible to avoid taking into consideration the general principles of the writer and the doctrine he proposes to establish.[73]

The *Repository's* contributors paid frequent tribute to the pioneer work of German scholars in this field,[74] especially Wetstein, Griesbach, and Michaelis. In a "Memoir of Wetstein," Edgar Taylor, a lawyer but by avocation a Biblical scholar, praised highly the eighteenth-century scholar, particularly for having been the first "to affirm that, in adjusting the balance between two readings, the most orthodox ought to bear the character of suspicion."[75] Unitarian scholars were the first to recognize the superiority of and to publish Griesbach's text of the New Testament. Said a reviewer of Griesbach's labors in 1807: "By laying

---

[72] XX (1825), 193-94.   [73] XIV (1819), 403.

[74] Crabb Robinson, in Germany for five years at the beginning of the century, was surprised to find that Germans had no name for rationalists in religion, Socinians or Deists, because, as a schoolmaster told the young traveler, "All our men of learning are so."—Edith Morley, *Life and Times of Henry Crabb Robinson*, p. 14.

[75] XIV (1819), 248-56.

open the scientific principles on which an edition of the New Testament is founded, they have checked that licentiousness of conjecture and neglect of critical authority which have perpetuated many difficulties, but can never remove one."[76] A sketch of Griesbach's life and works appeared in the next volume, probably by John Kentish.[77] Belsham attacked the accounts of the miraculous conception in the opening chapters of Matthew and Luke as "no more entitled to credit, than the fables of the Koran, or the reveries of Swedenborg."[78]

The Old Testament also was subject to criticism. Belsham in his old age boldly rejected the account of the creation in Genesis as unbelievable in the light of modern science. In a reply to a fellow Unitarian's criticism of his views on "the philosophical ignorance of Moses" he defended his right "to call in question the truth and inspiration of the first chapter of Genesis," and pointed to an honored son of the Church, the Reverend John Hey, an eighteenth-century professor of divinity at Cambridge, who had said that that portion is "not a literal description of fact, but an allegorical story, like the Pilgrim's Progress."[79] A number of the *Repository's* correspondents enunciated critical principles which would have shocked the English religious public deeply if the periodical had been widely read. In 1818 a communication "On the Connexion of Science . . . with Religion and a Future State," defending the study of science, declared:

It may be laid down as an infallible canon for Scripture interpretation,—*that no interpretation of Scripture ought to be admitted which is inconsistent with any well-authenticated facts in the material world;* or, in other words, *where a passage is of doubtful meaning, or capable of different interpretations,* it ought

[76] II (1807), 151.   [77] III (1808), 1-9.
[78] I (1806), 587.   [79] XX (1825), 416.

to be explained in such *a manner as will best agree with the established discoveries of science.*[80]

"An Attempt to Distinguish between Genuine and Spurious Christianity" rejected divine inspiration for the whole Bible in forthright terms: "nothing can be more groundless." The writer did, however, get into deep water in maintaining that divine revelation is proved by prophecy, which must have come from God, and that the prophecies predicted the many textual corruptions.[81] One John Higman had earlier rejected in good part the necessity of revelation as the basis of morality: "There is nothing in the morality of the Bible but what reason can teach, and a near approximation to its precepts may be discovered in the writings of heathen philosophers."[82] Revelation was helpful, however, in speeding up the processes of moral perfection.

In addition to devoting much space to rational criticism of the Bible, the *Repository* printed many contributions on Unitarian doctrine and many reviews of sermons and books on the subject. Since the Unitarian position has already been outlined in the first chapter, perhaps a quotation or two here will suffice as indicative of the magazine's interpretation in general of the denomination's belief. (There were, of course, many somewhat variant interpretations, particularly on the nature of Christ.) Belsham rose up loudly in 1819 when the Western Unitarian Association proposed to modify its statement of faith so as to admit Arians; he referred to the Unitarian Society's original preamble which explicitly asserted:

the doctrine of ONE GOD, possessed of all possible perfections, the only proper object of religious worship: also that Jesus Christ is a *proper human being,* in all respects like unto his brethren, and distinguished from them only as being appointed by God

[80] XIII (1818), 483-84.
[81] XV (1820), 448-52.   [82] V (1810), 451.

to be the founder of a new and universal dispensation, and as being the greatest of all the prophets of God.[83]

Belsham was as optimistic as most Unitarians in believing that the acceptance of the doctrine of the human nature of Jesus would clear up all difficulties in religion. When that doctrine is accepted, "the huge fabric of error and superstition vanishes at once like an enchanted castle touched by the magician's wand, and nothing remains but the plain, simple, uncorrupted gospel, divested of all mystery, worthy of all acceptation, which will make men wise unto salvation."[84]

Turning from matters of doctrine to those of church organization, we find that the *Repository* lived up to the Unitarian reputation for stoutest Nonconformity. Its true principles, according to the Reverend William Hincks's address entitled "The Old Crab Stock of Nonconformity," were a "conviction of the right and duty of private judgment in matters of religion"; the disclaiming of "all immediate connexion with the powers of this world, deprecating as sincerely their baneful patronage, as their unjust and tyrannical persecution"; and "the perfect equality, as brethren and fellow-disciples, of all members of Christ's church. . . ."[85] Unitarians almost unanimously opposed the imposition of creeds, the requirement of subscription to any formularies, and civil establishment of religion.

Not all Dissenters were so consistent. The *Repository* often chided the orthodox for their "many gross derelictions" from the principles of Nonconformity. Said a writer in 1818: "Their jealousy of the Catholics loaded themselves and their posterity with the Test and Corporation Acts; . . . they it was who zealously concurred in excepting from the Toleration Act those who entertained different notions with regard to the Trinity. . . ."[86] The latter clause dragged forth

[83] XIV (1819), 658.
[84] XV (1820), 35.
[85] XVI (1821), 660-64.
[86] XIII (1818), 708-9.

one of the main bones of contention between the rational and the orthodox Dissenters: the orthodox were likely to be far more bitter in criticizing their heterodox brethren than in attacking their common rival, the Established Church. Talfourd in an address on the intolerance of orthodox Dissent deplored also their unwillingness to pursue "free inquiry."[87]

From 1818 to 1826 the *Repository* printed from time to time an interesting and valuable series of about thirty articles with the general title "The Nonconformist." The series consisted of addresses chiefly on Dissenting history and literature delivered before the Non-Con Club, founded in 1817 by Aspland for the discussion of subjects bearing upon civil and religious liberty. At the meetings each member presided in his turn and was required to give verbatim three standing toasts: "The Memory of the Two Thousand," "John Milton," and "Civil and Religious Liberty all the World Over." In the movement for the repeal of the Test and Corporation Acts, the Non-Con Club was a leader. Prominent among its members whose addresses appeared in the *Repository* were Bowring, W. J. Fox, Aspland, Samuel Parkes, Thomas Rees, Christopher Richmond, George Smallfield, Talfourd, Edgar Taylor, Richard Taylor, M. D. Hill, Walter Wilson, and Dr. Southwood Smith. Representative titles included these: "A Vindication of the Two Thousand Ejected Ministers"; "On the Opinions of the Puritans respecting Civil and Religious Liberty"; "On High-Church Infidels"; "On Religious Prosecutions." A complete list, with authors identified, will be found in the Appendix.

Unitarians opposed the beliefs and practices of the Roman Church as sincerely as did the orthodox Dissenters, but, unlike the latter, they spoke out boldly for the emancipation of Catholics from civil disabilities. A correspondent in 1812 enumerated five chief reasons for Catholic

[87] XIV (1819), 171-74.

emancipation: (1) "Justice demands it." (2) "It is a moral duty," for Protestants would want freedom if they lived in Catholic countries. (3) "It will render the liberty of Protestants more secure." (4) "The promotion of truth requires it," for only with the exercise of free inquiry can error and superstition be eradicated. (5) It will remove disaffection and bind Catholics to the British Constitution and government.[88] Other contributors attacked the Baptists and Methodists for opposing emancipation, especially since they themselves, as Dissenters, were still legally liable to disabilities.

With regard to the toleration of Deism or Atheism and to the advisability of prosecutions for blasphemy, the opinion of contributors was divided. Some maintained that punishment for publishing libels upon Christianity was just on the ground often held by the orthodox, that the Christian religion was "part of the common law of the land." Said one contributor:

This being the case, if the blasphemer, the scoffer, the daring violator of the national law, the reviler of the national faith, the misleader of the simple, the abuser of the ignorant, the corrupter of youth, the destroyer of all that is sacred and venerable—if this man be not a proper object of punishment, shew me the offender who deserves it![89]

The tone of this is more characteristic of the *Evangelical* or the *Methodist*. The majority of Unitarian leaders vigorously opposed the numerous prosecutions for blasphemy from 1815 to 1825. Aspland rendered active assistance to the bookseller William Hone during his trial in 1817 for publishing parodies of the litany, the Athanasian Creed, and the catechism of the Church.

The case of Richard Carlile attracted more attention. Indicted in October, 1819, for the republication of Paine's

[88] VII (1812), 230-31.   [89] XVI (1821), 13.

Age of Reason and Elihu Palmer's *Principles of Nature,* Carlile conducted his own defense in no very conciliatory style. He read into the court record the entirety of the *Age of Reason* and contended that the repeal in 1813 of the Anti-Trinitarian Law had given protection to Deists as well as Unitarians. The latter were only "Deists under a cloak." He also read certain professedly Christian writings on religious liberty, including an essay on blasphemy from Aspland's *Christian Reformer.* Carlile audaciously subpoenaed the Archbishop of Canterbury and other Church dignitaries, Thomas Belsham, and W. J. Fox, in order to show the diversity of opinion among Christians; needless to say, these witnesses were not allowed to appear. Carlile was found guilty, sentenced to three years' imprisonment, and fined £1,500. In reporting the case, the *Repository* avowed its conviction that "pains and penalties ought not to be attached to unbelief or misbelief" and that such treatment of unbelievers was contrary to the spirit of Christ.[90]

W. J. Fox, the most popular Unitarian preacher of the day, shocked many of even the anti-Trinitarians by his sermon on "The Duties of Christians to Deists" on October 24. Though proclaiming his faith in the Christian religion, he pointed out that, since its supporting evidence is neither mathematical nor demonstrable, "the Deists may be right and the Christian wrong." Prophecies might turn out to be only lucky guesses, and the Apostles might have been ignorant deceivers. Fox did not believe that Christianity might turn out to be a wicked sham, but he held that men must admit the possibility and be ever on the watch to detect it. Deists were entitled to free expression of their opinions.

The sermon was both attacked and defended in the *Repository.* The review of the published version agreed that Fox's main position, the inadvisability of such prosecutions, was unanswerable, but objected to a number of his con-

[90] XIV (1819), 645-46.

cessions to the Deists.[91] Another writer criticized the sermon on the ground that "there was no need of handing over weapons to the enemy." Fox ought to have avoided, and all Unitarians must avoid, even the appearance of evil. *"The duties of Christians towards Deists* are, most assuredly, not to seek out every possible excuse for their unbelief, but to expostulate with them on their unreasonableness. . . ."[92] In the same volume "Hylas" lamented that the sermon had been delivered because of the effect on the denomination's repute and its "tendency to confirm and justify the charge that a natural and close alliance subsists between Unitarians and Unbelievers."[93]

Belsham replied to Hylas in defense of Fox that nothing could promote the cause of atheism so much as persecution. "Let scepticism have fair play; let the infidel do his worst. . . . In the end, Truth, if left to her own energies, will be completely victorious." If prosecution for reviling Christianity is permitted, persecution of heterodoxy may also creep in. It will never be possible to purify the Christian religion "unless infidel writers are allowed their full scope."[94] J. T. Rutt also supported Fox by quotations from the "old" Unitarians.[95] Aspland, in letters reprinted from the *Times* explaining the basis of Unitarian doctrine, answered the charges of an anonymous clergyman who agreed with Carlile's definition of a Unitarian as a "Deist under a cloak."[96] Richard Taylor declared that the hackneyed excuse for such prosecutions—that Christianity was "part and parcel of the law of England"—placed its authority "on a level with a Turnpike Bill." If men were to be required to believe in the existence of a God in obedience to some enactment of Parliament, both the interests of civil liberty and of Christianity would be jeopardized. "The real value of

[91] *Ibid.*, pp. 701-2.

[93] *Ibid.*, p. 212.

[95] *Ibid.*, pp. 408-11.

[92] XV (1820), 31.

[94] *Ibid.*, pp. 346-48.

[96] XIV (1819), 707-12.

religion must depend on its being the subject of individual choice and belief."[97] The *Repository's* Intelligence department regularly reported prosecutions of this nature and uniformly reprobated the proceedings.

As Nonconformists, Unitarians naturally opposed the Church of England for the fact of its establishment. It was often slightingly referred to as "the sect established by law." Far less attention was paid in the *Repository* to attacking the doctrines of the Church than to the principle of establishment itself. A true religion, it maintained, would have no need of the support of the state. Belsham, almost alone of the Unitarians, believed in the principle of establishment; the Reverend Henry Turner expressed the more usual attitude:

A religion founded upon Divine Revelation, must contain within itself the best possible means of ascertaining and authenticating its real dictates; and the errors into which human weakness and fallibility might fall in regard to it, would be much more effectually corrected by the private exertions of learning and integrity, than by the ostentatious superintendence and controlling direction of the civil power.[98]

The alliance between Church and State was a "selfish contract . . . for mutual assistance in carrying on a conspiracy against the rights and liberties of mankind."[99] The imposition of tithes was "foreign to the generous spirit of the Gospel . . . , baneful to agriculture, and to the harmony of society."[100] Establishment, great wealth, and ecclesiastical power tended to corrupt both men and religion. Legal restrictions placed upon Nonconformists encouraged irreligion, fraud, and deceit, for such subscription meant nothing to the unscruplous. Establishment violated the spirit of the Protestant Reformation; spiritual usurpation had

[97] XVIII (1823), 371-72.   [98] XVII (1822), 193.
[99] *Ibid.*, p. 194.   [100] VI (1811), 662.

simply been transferred from the Pope to the King and
Parliament.[101] "The features of the 'mother of harlots'"
were "plainly drawn in the daughter."[102] Little was
changed but the name of Protestant for that of Papist.

The Anglican clergy were seldom spared. The Intelligence department regularly printed news of any act of
bigotry or persecution by a clergyman. The evils of nepo-
tism, simony, plurality, non-residence, and the impoverished
condition of the working clergy, the curates, all received
due attention. Occasionally a hot-headed contributor let
loose with a more than usually denunciatory blast; such
were two letters in Volume XV, signed A Nonconformist.
This writer declared that the clergy had always been more
anxious to curtail the liberties of the people than to preserve
them, and that they had "constantly endeavored to instil
into the minds of men the most slavish maxims, and taught
lessons of the most blind and abject submission."[103] So
scorching was the original text of the first of these letters
that the editor omitted some lines and said, "Prudence com-
pels us to make an hiatus here."[104] A reviewer in an early
volume described the Church as "truly 'a cage of unclean
birds,'" for among the clergy who had subscribed to its
articles were adherents of every heresy. The only compen-
sation for such bare-faced dishonesty was that it demonstrated the failure of national churches to answer "the only
end for which their institution can be justified, that is, the
securing of uniformity of faith."[105]

The bitterest scorn of the rationalists was directed against
the Evangelical wing of the Church, rapidly coming into
power. As early as 1808 a reviewer warned his readers of
the strength of the Evangelicals:

[101] XV (1820), 223-28.
[102] VI (1811), 662.
[103] XV (1820), 731.
[104] *Ibid.*, p. 279.
[105] II (1807), 262-63.

They have invaded the Navy, they thrive at the Bank, they bear sway at the India House, they count several votes in Parliament, and they have got a footing in the Royal Palace. Their activity is incredible. They are establishing new institutions for party purposes every day. . . . Scarcely a town or village of note in the kingdom but has a place or places set apart for Evangelical preaching, which is usually followed by crowds. . . .[106]

The writer feared that the Evangelicals would swallow up the Church and Dissent, only excepting the Unitarians, and that growing Evangelical political power would endanger liberty. The *Repository* attacked "enthusiastic" practices of the Evangelicals, their fondness for public confession,[107] their strict Sabbatarianism,[108] and their snooping societies for the suppression of vice.[109]

Outside the Church, in keeping with this hostility to the Evangelicals, the Methodists were the sect most singled out for criticism, though their rights to complete religious liberty were upheld, as was shown by the strong opposition to Lord Sidmouth's bill in 1811 to outlaw "tinker" preachers.[110] The Methodists were generally regarded by the Three Denominations as interlopers; their appeal to the lower classes and the extravagant nature of their religious emotion made them suspect in the eyes of even the orthodox. While it is undoubtedly true that Nonconformity was quickened into new life by the accession of the enormously successful Methodist movement, Methodism at this time was looked upon as a cause of decline in Nonconformity. This explanation was advanced by Walter Wilson in 1823: the Methodists, since they directed their efforts at the lower classes, "whose passions are more easily influenced than the judgment," soon supplanted the real Dissenters in the esteem of the multitude. They gave a "mystical turn to the

[106] III (1808), 505.
[107] *Ibid.*, p. 503.
[108] XI (1816), 228.
[109] VI (1811), 411-15.
[110] *Ibid.*, pp. 309, 495-501.

phraseology of Scripture," converted religion "into a fanciful intercourse with the Deity," and "deluded each other that they were the peculiar favorites of heaven, and, as such, the subjects of a miraculous inspiration." Their extravagancies served to illustrate "the danger of departing from the suggestions of good sense in matters of religion." The Methodists refused to have anything to do with politics and regarded discussions of ethics and philosophy with horror. Learning, to them, was "an impediment to spiritual improvement. . . . In fine, whatever may be thought of their pretensions to the next world, the tendency of their faith was decidedly to unfit them for the present."[111] The net result of Methodism, said Wilson, had been to change wholly if not to swallow up Nonconformity.

In 1824 in a series of translated articles drawn up for the *Repository* on "The Theological Controversies at Geneva" by J. J. Chenevière, occasion was taken to attack Methodist doctrine and practices. Amusing is the charge that Methodism has caused women to lose their natural modesty and reserve: "like the peacock spreading its admired plumage, they go about attracting attention, in what they call doing the work of the Lord, or revealing His counsel." Young girls lecture their pastors on piety.

Children gravely and shamelessly deny the Christianity of their parents, and pronounce sentence of damnation upon them; we often hear of them quoting the irreverent speech of *The Dairyman's Daughter,* who interrupted her father as he prayed and wept by the side of her death-bed, saying, "Father, weep not for me, but weep for your own sins."[112]

From all this it may be seen why Unitarians, even more than orthodox Dissenters, shuddered at the thought of Methodism. Zeal, enthusiasm, emotion, were scarcely the characteristics of the rational in religion. And rationality

[111] XVIII (1823), 388.   [112] XIX (1824), 131.

was ever the touchstone by which the *Repository* tested religion.

POLITICAL AND SOCIAL CRITICISM

Aspland's magazine paid considerably less attention to political and social questions than to religious but nevertheless contrasted favorably with contemporary religious periodicals in the amount of space devoted to temporal concerns. Some, like the *Methodist* and the *Evangelical*, in the main avoided discussion of politics as not in keeping with their higher mission. In general, however, Dissenting periodicals kept their readers informed on political matters that had bearing upon the status of Dissent; in this the *Repository* tended to follow, when it did not outdo, its more orthodox competitors. None was more vigorous or consistent in supporting liberal reform, particularly on issues involving religious freedom.

It should be remembered that when the magazine began its career in 1806, there was ample room for reform in English government and society, reform that in many instances had been delayed by the fearful reaction to the Revolution across the Channel in France. Before the Revolution there had been a growing consciousness of the need of parliamentary reform, and even Pitt had advocated moderate changes in the system of representation. But when both Whig and Tory conservatives began to fear the spread of revolutionary ideas at home, any suggestion of change came to be regarded as dangerous, Jacobinical. Not until 1832 could even a measure of change be effected in Parliament.

There were other matters too for the concern of reformers. In 1806 laws were still on the statutes to restrict religious freedom: the Corporation and Test Acts of the reign of Charles II, which excluded conscientious Dissenters from public office, were still in effect; the Unitarians until 1813 were legally though not actually liable to prosecution for blasphemy in denying the Trinity; the Catholics were to have to wait until 1829 for emancipation; all Dissenters were subject to the authority of the Church in the registration of births, deaths, and marriages, in the celebration of marriage, and in the performance of the rites of burial; Nonconformists were virtually barred from Oxford and Cambridge. In fields less immediately connected with religion, there was need of reform in education, in the criminal law, and in the care of the poor. On all these questions the *Repository's* contributors were usually to be found on the side of the liberals or the radicals. While it is impossible here to give a detailed picture of radical Dissenting politics over the twenty-one year period of the first series, a sampling of its views on the leading questions of the day may be helpful, particularly as background for an examination of the second series under W. J. Fox, when the magazine devoted much more attention to political considerations.

That there was a close connection in their political, social, and economic views between the Unitarians and the Utilitarian followers of Jeremy Bentham has been noted by R. V. Holt in *The Unitarian Contribution to Social Progress in England,* but the details of the connection seem never to have been completely examined. The *Repository* throws some light on the problem. Not all Unitarians were Utilitarians, but there was a considerable area in which their views coincided. Bentham attributed the discovery of his greatest-happiness-of-the-greatest-number principle to a passage in one of Priestley's works.[113] The extreme rationalism of Bentham's approach to the problems of society, of law, and of morals, differed only in degree from the Unitarians' approach to the problems of theology. Few of the Unitar-

---

[113] Modern scholarship, unable to locate the exact quotation in Priestley, has noted other possible sources. Cf. E. Halévy, *The Growth of Philosophic Radicalism,* pp. 22, 33. The idea was sufficiently current in the eighteenth century to make the problem of Bentham's sources difficult.

ians, however, were as ready as Bentham to pursue to extremes the logic of their position; Priestley, for instance, as has been noted in our opening chapter, for all his rationalistic study of theology, retained his belief in miracles. In the popular mind Unitarians and Utilitarians were identified to this extent, that their philosophy and their faith were thought to make them cold, analytical, and logical; to their critics and enemies, Unitarians were the Gradgrinds of religion. Unitarians and Utilitarians came largely from the same levels of society, the enterprising, successful middle class. Both groups were inclined to humanitarianism, but this, because of their faith in science, sometimes conflicted with their acceptance of the generalizations of the new political economy as statements of natural law. Neither group, however, was hampered, as the Evangelicals to some extent were, by any belief in original sin and the natural depravity of man. The followers both of Bentham and of Priestley believed in the perfectibility of man and society.

The *Repository's* use as early as 1811 of a quotation from Bentham for its title-page motto is significant, for Bentham was not widely known in England until in the 1820's. Many of his works were known chiefly on the Continent through the medium of redactions into French by Étienne Dumont. James Mill, who was to be so influential among the Philosophic Radicals, did not become acquainted with Bentham until 1808. Benthamite doctrine may be seen in the *Monthly Repository,* however, as early as 1807. Said the reviewer of a pamphlet on the education of the poor by Bentham's friend Patrick Colquhoun, a London police magistrate:

The whole business of life is a competition between individual and individual, to procure as great a portion of happiness as can be compassed by each single effort; and it is the superabundant quantity that is produced by the continued struggle, and found more than sufficient for individual use, that constitutes the public good. But the degree of happiness, either public or private, depends upon the struggle being conducted on equal terms; and if the competitive powers become engrossed on one side, both public and private happiness will diminish, and can only exist in proportion as this equality becomes restored.[114]

Aspland in his attack upon Brougham's Education Bill in 1821 questioned the advisability of compulsory education and betrayed sympathy with the negative, laissez-faire attitude of most Benthamites towards government: "The interference of governments with private concerns has been often mischievous, and as the world is managed their patronage is always suspicious." All the great moral and social changes "have been effected by private activity and benevolence, and commonly in opposition to political power."[115] In its views of reform in education and criminal law, the *Repository,* as will be seen later, approximated the Benthamite position.

There was some direct notice of Bentham in the magazine. Extracts from his published works were occasionally printed,[116] and in 1821 a poetical tribute to the aged philosopher, probably written by Bowring, was reprinted from the *Examiner.*

I have travell'd the world, and that old man's fame
   Wherever I went shone brightly;
To his country alone belongs the shame
   To think of his labours lightly.

The poet professed to see blended in Bentham "An infant child's simplicity By a sage's strength attended." Bentham, now a sun shrouded by clouds of folly and envy "soon shall emerge in light of love" and "shall the mists of night disperse."[117]

---

[114] II (1807), 383.   [115] XVI (1821), 25-26.

[116] For example, his views on penal law in matters of religion, XIII (1818), 360-62; his definition of felony, XVII (1822), 621; and his letter to the *Examiner* on the supposed independence of judges, XV (1820), 335.

[117] XVI (1821), 180.

Some close personal connections existed between Unitarians and Utilitarians. Bowring, a prominent Unitarian layman, was one of Bentham's closest friends and disciples; he edited the philosopher's works, wrote his biography, and was the first editor of the organ of the Philosophic Radicals, the *Westminster Review*. W. J. Fox wrote the leading article for the first number of the *Westminster* in 1824, and, as will be seen later, was closely associated with John Stuart Mill in the 1830's. Henry Southern, Southwood Smith, Edwin Chadwick, John Kenrick, and Crabb Robinson (though no Utilitarian) were among the *Westminster's* Unitarian contributors.

The chief contributor of political discussion to the first series of the *Repository* was, however, more a Whig than a Benthamite. This was William Frend (1757-1841), who for the eleven years, 1808 through 1818, conducted anonymously a department entitled "Monthly Retrospect of Public Affairs, or the Christian's Survey of the Political World." Aspland gave Frend a free hand, and he was solely responsible for the department. His views did not necessarily always represent those of the editor or of Unitarians at large, though there was essential agreement on fundamentals. Frend was an adherent of the reform wing of the Whigs, and, like Aspland, an admirer of Charles James Fox. Consequently, this department of the magazine reflected advanced Whig views, though with a leavening of more radical opinions.

Frend himself is of interest as one of those scholars who deserted the Established Church to become a Unitarian. Born at Canterbury, he was the son of a tradesman who had twice been mayor of the town. After a short business career, which involved for preparation study in France and a short stay in Quebec, he decided to enter the Church. Graduated from Christ's College, Cambridge, in 1780, the following year he became a fellow and tutor at Jesus College. Upon ordination as a priest in the Church of England in 1783 he was given the living at Madingley, near Cambridge. In 1788 after conversion to Unitarianism through his studies, he published an "Address to the Inhabitants of Cambridge," refuting the doctrine of the Trinity. He was also a vigorous supporter of a movement in that year to abolish the degree requirement of subscription to the Thirty-Nine Articles. For these derelictions from orthodoxy he was deprived of his tutorship in September, 1788.

After a long tour on the Continent, he returned to his studies, among them a Priestley-sponsored translation of the Old Testament. In 1793, at a time when Anglo-French relations were at the breaking point, Frend caused an academic uproar at Cambridge by publishing "Peace and Union Recommended to the Associated Bodies of Republicans and Anti-Republicans," a tract which advocated parliamentary reform, attacked existing social and political abuses, and condemned much of the Church's liturgy. He was promptly excluded from Jesus College by its Fellows and in May was prosecuted in the vice-chancellor's court for the publication. Refusing to retract his statements and confess his errors, he was banished from the University, though he was allowed to receive the income from his fellowship until his marriage in 1808.[118] The undergraduates of Cambridge, among them one Samuel Taylor Coleridge, held demonstrations in favor of the banished tutor, and college walls were chalked with the legend "Frend for Ever." Coleridge, who had evidently been influenced by the radical tutor, attracted attention at one point during his trial by applauding.

Going up to London, Frend supplemented the income

[118] Frend married a granddaughter of Archdeacon Francis Blackburne; their daughter, married to Professor Augustus DeMorgan, was the mother of the novelist, William Frend DeMorgan.

of his fellowship by writing and teaching. His radicalism did not prevent his prosecution of a successful career in business. In 1806 he helped form an insurance company, of which he served for years as actuary. An original, if at times eccentric, thinker in mathematics and astronomy, he has been called the "last of the learned anti-Newtonians." For some years he published a periodical, *Evening Amusements; or the Beauty of the Heavens Displayed* (1804-1822), to popularize the study of astronomy. He was active in Unitarian circles and a friend of many of the leading reformers of the time, including such men as Horne Tooke and Sir Francis Burdett.

In his "Monthly Retrospect" of the topics of current interest, Frend recognized the importance of parliamentary reform as the first requisite of other reform. As early as 1793 in his "Peace and Union" he had urged the shortening of the parliamentary term from seven to three years, reform of election methods, and some extension of the suffrage. Sixteen years later in the *Repository* he wrote: "The dreadful blows struck at the vitals of the constitution, by the establishment of septennial parliaments, and the admission of the dependents of the executive into the House of Commons, have produced all the evils the nation now so justly complains of. . . ."[119] The existence of rotten boroughs, he declared, stifled the voice of the people; and the obvious, gross traffic in seats, "sold as stalls in a market," degraded and nullified the principles of fair representation.[120] "If the representative part of our government is valuable, nothing can be more absurd than that stocks and stones in a park should be invested with a right of sending members, or that a peer by means of a dependent person, and three or four dependent tradesmen, should send two representatives to Parliament."[121] Without reform the boasted Constitu-

[119] IV (1809), 230.
[120] *Ibid.*, pp. 346-47.
[121] V (1810), 269.

tion would soon be discovered to be the veriest sham. "On the extension of the right of suffrage one would think that there could be only one opinion."[122]

R. V. Holt in his book previously referred to has delineated three periods in the history of the movement which led to the Reform Bill of 1832: a pioneer period, from about 1768 to the anti-revolutionary reaction about 1791; a period of persecution, lasting till the close of the Napoleonic wars in 1815; and a popular period, in which the movement was carried to success in 1832 under the leadership of professional politicians. Unitarians ardently supported radical reform throughout these three areas, but their efforts were most noticeable in the first two, when to advocate change was often dangerous. Testimony to the importance of Unitarian effort in the early days of the movement may be seen in G. S. Veitch's *Genesis of Parliamentary Reform,* which records again and again the labors of at least eight Unitarians prominent among the reformers: Price, Priestley, Lindsey, Jebb, Sir George Saville, Josiah Wedgewood, Sir William Jones, and "the father of Parliamentary Reform" himself, Major John Cartwright. To this heritage of allegiance to reform the *Repository* remained true.

It is fair to say, however, that not all Unitarians were numbered among the extremists who demanded the complete extension of the suffrage. Many, like most of the orthodox Dissenters, revered the memory of the Glorious Revolution of 1688 and the constitutional principles thereby established. To many of these people, reform was more a question of restoring the type of representation traditional before time had wrought changes in the distribution of population and the national wealth than a question of establishing universal manhood suffrage. Said an anonymous contributor in 1816: "I think the last twenty-five years . . . have very clearly shown how very impolitic it is to neglect

[122] XIII (1819), 406.

the people's voice until too late, when the whole fabric of
society may be destroyed in attempting to bring about a
reform, which if attended to as the times demanded, would
have had a gradual and very salutary operation." A constitutional representation is "the best method of collecting
together 'wise and virtuous people enough to keep the foolish and vicious in order.' "[123]   In the passage of the Reform
Bill of 1832 this was essentially the point of view that for
the time triumphed.   Less than half a million men were
enfranchised in 1832, but the adoption of the bill made
certain that further reform and further democratization
would eventually come.   That Unitarians had played an
important part in the agitation, even the Duke of Wellington conceded: "The Revolution is made . . . ; that is to
say, power is transferred from one class of society, gentlemen professing the faith of the Church of England, to
another class of society, the shopkeepers, being Dissenters
from the Church, many of them Socinians, atheists."[124]

But though parliamentary reform was consistently supported in the *Repository,* there was even greater unanimity
and considerably more zeal in advocating repeal of laws
restricting religious freedom.   Dissent, by the very fact of
its dissidence, was compelled to engage in political action,
if only in self-protection.   That orthodox Dissent, however,
was less concerned with maintaining the principle of complete religious freedom than with securing privileges for
itself, may be seen in the hostility of the orthodox to Catholic emancipation and to repeal of the law which made the
denial of the Trinity a penal offense.   That the Unitarians
paid more than lip service to the ideal of religious freedom and were not concerned solely with the protection
of their own interests, is evidenced, as has already been

[123] XI (1816), 335-36.
[124] Quoted in R. V. Holt, *The Unitarian Contribution to Social Progress in
England,* p. 132.

seen, by their unwavering support of Catholic emancipation and their general opposition to prosecutions of atheists and Deists. The *Repository* might well have carried on its title page as a motto Joseph Priestley's injunction in his *Essay on the First Principles of Government* (1768): "Let every member of the community enjoy every right of a citizen whether he choose to conform to the established religion or not."

Of fundamental importance were the repeal of the Corporation and Test Acts, not achieved until 1828. The Corporation Act, adopted in 1661, prohibited from employment in anything relating to the government of corporations any person who had not taken communion according to the rites of the Established Church within the preceding year. The Test Act (1672) considerably extended the restrictions; anyone convicted of taking public office without so qualifying was disabled from participating in any court action, serving as a guardian, or receiving any legacy or deed of gift, and was liable to a £500 fine. The two laws were originally designed as much to combat Roman Catholicism as Protestant Dissent, but in time ways of evading them were devised for Protestants without resorting to actual repeal. In the reigns of the first two Georges minor modifications were made, and for nearly a hundred years annual Indemnity Bills provided relief for the Dissenters. The practice of occasional conformity was winked at. Thus, while in practice admitting the unwisdom of the laws, adherents of the Establishment opposed their complete repeal as a measure that would weaken its foundations.

The *Repository* customarily reported the proceedings in Parliament relating to penal laws on religion, the meetings of Dissenting organizations seeking their repeal, and gave notice to books and pamphlets on the subject. In 1818 Aspland printed from Jeremy Bentham's *Traités de Legislation* a translation of a section entitled "On the Danger of Penal Laws in Matters of Religion," in which Bentham attacked the inutility of such laws:[125] "Every article of faith is necessarily hurtful, as soon as the legislator puts in activity penal and coercive motives to favour its adoption. . . . For the conformists, the coercive law is unnecessary; for the nonconformists, it is equally useless, because it cannot fulfill its object."

Perhaps the most complete statement of the Unitarian position on this subject may be found in a Non-Con Club paper by Aspland, published in 1819,[126] a brief summary of which should sufficiently indicate the usual tenor of the argument. Aspland claims that, despite the annual Indemnity Bills, the operation of these laws is not wholly set aside; they operate to the disadvantage of the conscientious and "by their indirect operation, they keep up a line of distinction between the Dissenters and others throughout the community generally." Even if they were entirely harmless, retention of them on the statute books operates as a "tax upon honour and conscience"; they divide the nation, engender discontent, and, above all, "pervert religion into an instrument of world policy." Taking the Sacramental Test proves nothing about a man's abilities. "It proves nothing but his desire of office, and his power of swallowing a morsel of bread and a drop of wine." The laws are really opposed to the best interests of the clergy, and discontinuance of the Test would not affect the Establishment. Repeal would not give the Dissenters more power, but only their just rights. "What we ask is not pardon, for we are not offenders, but justice. We feel the insult more than the injury of the bills of exclusion; and we demand their abolition. . . ."[127]

[125] XIII (1818), 360.
[126] XIV (1819), 426-30.   [127] *Ibid.*, p. 430.

In addition to seeking the repeal of the Anti-Trinitarian law, the Unitarians also sought to abolish clerical control of functions which they regarded as belonging to the State rather than the Church. Parish registers for the recording of births, deaths, and marriages were in the exclusive control of the Establishment and furnished revenue to its clergy. Dissenters who wished to marry had to accept the marriage ceremony of the Church; this was particularly galling to the Unitarians, for the ceremony made use of Trinitarian formulas and prayers. Many conscientious Unitarians adopted the practice of making a formal protest against having to undergo a Trinitarian ceremony; a number of these protests appeared in the *Repository*.[128] Even the *Edinburgh Review* in March, 1821, in what purported to be a review of Volume XIV of the *Repository*, admitted the justice of the Unitarian claims, but not until 1837 was relief obtained on this score. The Church burial service was required until 1880. Parish burying grounds were also in the control of the clergy, and Unitarian dead were sometimes excluded. Instances of any bigotry of this sort were brought to public attention in Aspland's magazine.

The remaining chief grievance of the Dissenters against Church control of what are now regarded as civil functions lay in the field of education. The *Repository*, however, paid less attention to clerical domination of the universities than it did to the problems of elementary education, and certainly from the point of view of the nation as a whole the latter was the more pressing problem. Only occasionally, and then usually in passing, was the question of higher education discussed. William Frend, once a tutor at Cambridge, revealed the typical Unitarian attitude in his delineation of the state of affairs at the two universities:

At Oxford prevails an absurdity, if we ought not to stigmatize it with the term of abominable wickedness, that of insisting upon

128 For example, see XIV (1819), 179-81.

every young man's subscribing, previous to his admission, to that farrago of nonsense, called the Thirty-Nine Articles. . . . At Cambridge such a subscription is not required, nor is any religious test laid down, unless the student takes a degree. . . . At Oxford, therefore, none but members of the established sect can be members of any college. Cambridge is open to all sects; and the sons of dissenters of wealth frequently go thither, to the no small advantage of the established sect; as very few frequent the meeting-house, after they have gone through the *discipline* of the university.[129]

At a later period, Unitarians were active in the establishment of the nonsectarian London University.

Like most middle-class Dissenters, Unitarians favored the provision of at least elementary education for all, though there was difference of opinion as to methods. Protestants, since they demanded a knowledge of the Bible, were bound to favor universal literacy, and the new middle class was fully aware of the practical advantages of education. The need was great: Patrick Colquhoun in 1806 estimated that two million children in England and Wales received no instruction. The Sunday School, which sought to enable poor children to learn to read their Bibles, in the course of forty years grew so that by 1820 nearly half a million children attended. But this was only a poor substitute for genuine popular education. Instruction throughout this period, and for years afterwards, was still almost exclusively in the hands of religious agencies: the endowed schools were private religious foundations, and most other schools were under clerical domination. Dissenting ministers, cramped by low salaries, ran schools to supplement their meager incomes. What little instruction the poor received was almost entirely provided by private philanthropy. Education was not yet generally recognized as a proper field for governmental control or support. As a result, educational effort

[129] VII (1812), 717.

was badly directed, too exclusively devoted to religious instruction at the expense of secular, and in any event too restricted in scope to provide for the rapidly increasing population, especially in the crowded manufacturing centers.

There were not wanting among the upper classes, of course, those who professed to see dangers to the established order in any system of genuine public education. For this attitude the *Repository* reserved its deepest scorn. In 1817 it attacked the Tory minister George Canning, "who is commonly supposed to speak the sense of the worldly-wise men of the country," for declaring that recent seditious plots and riots might "perhaps be traced to the education of the poor."[130] Ten years earlier the magazine had excoriated Colquhoun's proposal of "A New and Appropriate System of Education for the Labouring People" and had described as the object of his plan,

to prevent the children of the poor from being "educated in a manner to elevate their minds above the rank they are destined to fulfill in society," which he thinks would be the case if "extensive knowledge were diffused among them." . . . Is it not enough for the small minority which constitutes the great men of the earth, that they have reduced the majority of the human species to constant servitude, but they must degrade mankind to the state of mere machines?[131]

In the controversy over the respective merits of the educational schemes of the Quaker Lancaster and the Churchman Bell, the *Repository* naturally supported the Lancasterian plan, since it was neutral in its religious instruction, calling for the reading of the Bible but without catechism or commentary. Lancaster had opened his first school in 1798, borrowing and adapting Bell's monitor system. The chief virtue of both plans was economy; otherwise, there were serious disadvantages. The *Repository* once voiced a sus-

[130] XII (1817), 182.   [131] II (1807), 382-83.

picion that the High Church and Tory party had taken up Bell *because* he was opposed to Lancaster, supporting him not out of sympathy for the education of the poor, "but because they think that education cramped by the Church Catechism is a *less evil* than education made religious only by the lessons of the Bible."[132] Aspland was always ready to fight any plan for extending Church control of education. In 1820-1821 his magazine vigorously opposed Henry Brougham's education bill, which sought to set up a national but Church-dominated system with only minor concessions to the Dissenters. In his Non-Con Club address on the subject Aspland declared that though Dissenters were anxious for public education, the alternative was "not between this Bill and no national education at all."[133] Two writers in the same volume, one of them Mary Hughes, tract writer, criticized the bill because it did not provide for the education of girls.[134]

To the cause of female education, the *Repository,* in keeping with Unitarian tradition, was always friendly. Though Mrs. Barbauld had thought that the best way for a woman to acquire knowledge was through the intercourse of the family circle, and that "too great fondness for books is little favorable to the happiness of a woman,"[135] it was another Unitarian intellectual, Mary Wollstonecraft, who had begun the modern feminist movement with her *Vindication of the Rights of Women* (1792). The *Christian Miscellany's* support in 1792 of female education has been earlier noticed. In 1815 the *Repository* reviewed favorably John Morell's "Reasons for the Classical Education of both Sexes," interposing as its only objection, "the immorality and grossness of some of the popular Greek and Roman writers."[136]

[132] XII (1817), 182.
[133] XVI (1821), 33.   [134] *Ibid.,* pp. 113-15, 276-77.
[135] Lucy Aikin, "Memoir of Anna L. Barbauld," in *Works of Anna L. Barbauld,* pp. xvii-xix.   [136] X (1815), 243.

One of Harriet Martineau's earliest contributions to the *Repository*, "On Female Education,"[137] is perhaps the best and most complete treatment of the subject in the first series. Writing as "Discipulus," she refused to concede that women's intellectual powers were necessarily inferior to those of men, but only that in the past they had been "checked in their growth, chained down to mean objects." Properly to fulfill their duties as wives and companions, as mothers and teachers, women must be given a chance to improve their minds. Women must be educated to be "companions to men, instead of playthings or servants, one of which an ignorant woman must commonly be." What the course of instruction should be must depend on ability, fortune, and station in life;

but no Englishwoman, above the lower ranks of life, ought to be ignorant of the Evidences and Principles of her religious belief, of Sacred History, of the outline at least of General History, of the elements of the Philosophy of Nature, and of the Human Mind; and to these should be added the knowledge of such living languages, and the acquirement of such accomplishments, as situation and circumstances may direct.[138]

Once woman is allowed to "claim her privileges as an intellectual being," the follies, frivolities, and faults which men point to as arguments against her being educated, will gradually disappear. In the light of such defense of feminine rights, the emphatic advocacy of those rights in the second series becomes understandable.

To penal reform the *Repository* devoted little attention, but whenever it did treat the subject, it was unmistakably on the liberal side. The criminal law of England, as is well known, was then a "sanguinary chaos." A *Repository* writer in 1821 claimed that there were 223 capital offenses, and the list of these was almost completely haphazard, the

---

[137] XVIII (1823), 77-81.   [138] *Ibid.*, p. 80.

product of the accretions of many decades. It was a capital offense, for instance, to steal from a boat on a navigable river but not to steal from a boat on a canal. So unreasonable were the penalties that injured persons often refused to prosecute and juries to convict. Prisons were so badly managed that it was sometimes almost questionable whether death were not a more merciful punishment than imprisonment.

Repository writers, accepting the ideas of such reformers as Beccaria, Blackstone, Bentham, Howard, and Romilly, called for reform of the penal code. The author of an article on "Capital Punishments," citing some of these men in support of his position, declared that prevention, not revenge, should be the object of punishment. Differentiation should be made between greater and lesser crimes; revolting was the idea that the death penalty should be equally demanded for the murder of a man and the killing of a rabbit in a warren. The brutal penal code was accomplishing the moral degradation of the nation.[139] Another writer, in an "Essay on the Principles of Criminal Law," after formulating the proper purposes or ends of that law, advocated efforts to reform young offenders and quoted Beccaria and Montesquieu to the effect that certainty of punishment was more important than severity.[140] The capital punishment which the *Repository* most often singled out for reprehension was that for forgery. William Frend time and again in his "Survey" attacked the Bank of England for its insistence on retaining the death penalty for this crime: "The liberty of the subject must not be sacrificed to the interests, whatever they may be, of a commercial body.[141] A reviewer in the same volume declared that the punishment was unjust, since forgery was only theft, and life was "infinitely more than an equivalent for property."[142]

[139] XVI (1821), 8-11.
[141] XIII (1818), 407.
[140] XVIII (1823), 27-33.
[142] *Ibid.*, p. 645.

The untimely death in 1818 of Sir Samuel Romilly, the leading advocate in Parliament of legal reform, was mourned as a blow to the cause; a number of tributes to his work were published, and Talfourd wrote a eulogistic obituary notice.[143]

We have said earlier that the Unitarians tended to follow the Benthamites in accepting the generalizations of the new political economy. With one phase of that economy, however, contributors to the *Repository* in the main did not agree; like some other writers in contemporary religious periodicals,[144] they rejected the gloomy conclusions of the Reverend T. R. Malthus, first published in 1798, that the mass of mankind was doomed to misery and poverty because, while the means of subsistence increased in an arithmetic ratio, population increased in a geometric ratio. Religious and humanitarian considerations led contributors indignantly to reject the premises and conclusions of Malthus. In 1807 a review of a pamphlet by John Bone quoted with approval Bone's summary of Malthus: "that the world will be filled with misery a thousand years hence; and therefore we ought to begin to be miserable in good time."[145] Not until ten years later, however, was there further direct notice of Malthus. Anthony Robinson, under the pseudonym Homo, led the attack with a satiric article entitled "The New Morality."[146] He defined the system as a scheme "to prohibit the poor from contracting marriage, and their marriage according to his scheme is the greatest immorality." This, Robinson said, was unscriptural, for St. Paul had not considered it possible for all to live without marriage. Malthus' ethics lacked only a provision for permitting suicide; if the poor man's "circumstances are in-

---

[143] *Ibid.*, pp. 720-22.
[144] Cf. *Christian Observer*, IV (1805), 539-41; V (1806), 91-92; VI (1807), 450-66; VII (1808), 803-16.
[145] II (1807), 388.   [146] XII (1817), 152-53.

supportable except through vice and misery, he should be permitted to abandon a miserable existence to avoid vice and misery."

Robinson's article inspired the youthful Thomas Noon Talfourd to contribute three essays in an all-out attack on Malthus.[147] The articles were characterized by exuberant rhetoric and sentimentality. Malthus' system chilled "the heart of hearts," repressed charitable emotions, defended "the extravagant luxuries of the rich" while it represented as criminal "the most sacred affections of the poor." It was strange, declared Talfourd, that it had remained for this age to discover this melancholy secret; till now, population had never been regarded as the source of man's woes. No king had ever waged war to reduce surplus population. No, man's miseries came rather from his artificial desires, his extravagant hopes, his guilty passions, and these were largely independent of the means of subsistence. Malthus had founded his system on fallacious premises; he regarded man as a mere animal whose emotions and affections were to be matters of calculation. By debasing the character of man in supposing human love to be wholly sensual, he had thrown "a shade on the goodness of God." Talfourd denied that the means of subsistence increased only in an arithmetic ratio: both animal and plant life multipled faster than human; the world still had vast uncultivated areas; with the wonderful developments in applied science and the resulting division of labor, the improvement of the world might be made to increase in a geometric ratio.

Besides, said Talfourd, even if Malthus' conclusions should turn out to be true, they would constitute no reason for not moving forward; until a virtual millenium should arrive, with war abolished, knowledge made universal, and vice banished, no fatal overpopulation could occur, and by

[147] *Ibid.*, pp. 471-74, 532-35, 600-65.

that time man might himself have changed fundamentally for the better. Talfourd next turned the Malthusian conclusions against those of the upper classes who were using them to justify refusing charity and governmental relief to alleviate the sufferings of the poor. If, as Malthus contended, man has no right to subsistence "when his labour cannot fairly purchase it," then, said Talfourd: "All the higher orders, the possessors of wealth, . . . and the great proprietors of lands, as they do not earn their subsistence by their labours, have no right to enjoy it, and still less to revel in superfluous luxuries."[148] Though Malthus intended no such inference to be drawn, if his principle is true, must it not "include all those who do not labour with their own hands or intellects for the produce which they and their families consume? Does it not go thus far, that the constitution of that society is radically vicious which suffers any class to exist who live merely to enjoy? . . . If we cannot afford charity, still less can we afford pomp." All that makes life pleasant must be forsaken. "Government, nobility, property itself, must cease." But, fortunately for man, Malthus is wrong; nature's abundance is more than is merely requisite to preserve the human species. Talfourd closed with a grandiloquent peroration, pleading for the poor as fellow human beings. Talfourd's views may not, and probably did not, represent those of all Unitarians, but none arose to answer him in the *Repository*. Several correspondents praised the articles, and Harriet Martineau recalled in later years that they had created something of a sensation in Unitarian circles.

The ideas of Robert Owen, the wealthy founder of modern socialism who advocated coöperation as the solution for the evils of poverty, met with more favor in the *Repository*. William Frend, though sceptical of the practicability of

[148] *Ibid.*, p. 660.

Owen's plans, conceded many of his ideas to be good.[149]
Richard Taylor in a Non-Con Club paper, "Inquiry concerning Private Property . . . ,"[150] maintained that the spirit
and tendency of Christianity were directly opposed to the
acquirement of personal riches and the system of private
property. After learnedly tracing the history of the institution of a community of goods among the early Christians,
Taylor answered the usual objections to the practicability
of communism. To rid society of the evils of private property, he said, man "must look, not as some have done to a
return to a state of nature, but to a progress in refinement
and civilization." Only through a better knowledge of
human nature and of the arts of government could there
be hope for such a change. "The system of private property
belongs rather to the savage than the civilized state; or is,
at least, but the first step toward civilization." This system
may have been helpful in man's progress from a barbarous
to a civilized state; but when man has reached a higher
stage of civilization he may be able to adopt a better system.
In conclusion, Taylor referred his readers to Owen's publications and quoted long passages from Sir Thomas More's
Utopia, "which has been disgracefully neglected and mis-
understood by his countrymen."[151]

Two years later in the *Repository* appeared an anonymous but enthusiastic endorsement of Owen's ideas.[152]
This writer pointed out that Unitarians would find less
difficulty than other sects in accepting one of Owen's fundamental postulates: "that the character is formed *for* and
not *by* the individual" since this was one of the doctrines of
Philosophical Necessity, maintained by many Unitarians.
Admitting that Owen's ideas stood little chance of adoption
unless freedom and some continuance of the right of pri-

[149] XII (1817), 510.   [150] XVI (1821), 88-101.
[151] *Ibid.,* p. 99.   [152] XVII (1823), 450-57.

vate property could be guaranteed, the writer maintained that voluntary association, with some concession to private interest, could be made practicable. By the adoption of such coöperation, the national wealth could be increased for the benefit of all, men—and women—could be released from drudgery, national enmities would "gradually melt away, and eventually all mankind become one great family."[153]

Towards America, as might be expected from what has thus far been seen of the liberality of the *Repository's* views, Aspland's magazine always maintained a cordial, friendly attitude. Tory and old-line Whig party organs seldom praised things American for fear of encouraging democratic sentiments at home. One important factor in Dissenting friendliness to the United States was that she furnished an excellent example of religion freed from state domination. No church establishment adorned the American scene, yet Christianity flourished. This was always a telling thrust to make at supporters of the English Establishment.

Another reason for the *Repository's* interest in America was the connection between English and American Unitarianism. The progress of the movement in New England was recorded with joy and pride. Articles were frequently excerpted from American Unitarian journals. Some of the English Unitarians who emigrated kept up correspondence with the *Repository,* and numerous letters, particularly on the state of religion in the United States, were printed. For some years James Taylor, a Philadelphia minister who had come from Scotland, contributed a critical synopsis of previous numbers of the magazine. Francis Adrian Vanderkemp was another valued correspondent. The writings of such American Unitarians as Henry Ware and William

[153] *Ibid.,* p. 456.

Ellery Channing were praised; Channing commanded a considerable following in England, and later in the century strongly influenced English Unitarian thought. There is some reason to believe that the *Repository* enjoyed a respectable circulation in the United States; and it was often quoted in American Unitarian magazines. The *Repository* occasionally reprinted items from American newspapers—for instance, an account of the burial of the aged Indian chief, Skenandoa, at Hamilton College in 1816.[154]

In keeping with its policy of friendship to America and of opposition to war, it was natural that the War of 1812 should be condemned as "unnecessary and unnatural on both sides." America was reproved for not having "more sense and prudence than to follow the foolish fashions of the Old World."[155] The American's real triumph should lie in converting the wilderness into fruitful lands, not "in the wretched triumph which arises from the destruction of human life, laying waste the lands of the industrious, and destroying the mansions of civilized life."[156] The British conduct of the war was held up to scorn; announcing the capture and destruction of the city of Washington, Aspland remarked: "We call the Cossacks *barbarians;* yet they, coming from the smoking ruins of Moscow to the capture of Paris, religiously abstained from plunder and wanton destruction!" And upon the restoration of peace between the two countries, Aspland wrote lines as true in 1943 as in 1814:

The United States and Great Britain are in reality the only two free nations in the world: Providence has formed them for a close alliance; and it is our earnest prayer and our sincere hope that they will ever be a joint example and lesson to the

[154] XI (1816), 490-91.   [155] VII (1812), 476.
[156] X (1815), 62.

world of the necessary connection between liberty, civil and religious, and national prosperity and greatness.[157]

CLOSE OF THE FIRST SERIES

Throughout the twenty-one years of the first series, the *Repository* was solely Aspland's responsibility, financially and otherwise. For a long time the struggle to maintain it was hard; the Unitarians were not a numerous body and the magazine was not calculated to interest a wide audience in other circles. There were also external obstacles: in the early years some booksellers refused to stock the magazine because of its radical opinions, and as late as 1820 a Quarter Sessions Court in Lancashire banned twelve numbers from circulation in prisons under the Court's jurisdiction because of "gross and scandalous abuse" of the clergy.[158] Aspland in his diary recorded that in 1809, 1,250 copies had been printed of which about a thousand had been sold, including back numbers.[159] Twenty years later, the circulation of the second series was admitted to be no larger. In 1811 the price was raised from one shilling to one shilling, sixpence. In 1818 the sale, after twelve years of struggle, was said to be "not adequate to the expense, much less to the labour required to conduct it reputably."[160] Periodical literature, always quick to reflect hard times, suffered in the post-war depression in the years following Waterloo. An appeal to members of the denomination helped keep the *Repository* afloat. Eventually the magazine began to yield a slight profit, and Aspland probably would have continued to conduct it for many years, as he did the *Christian Reformer,* had it not been for developments within Unitarianism itself.

In 1825, on the same day that the American Unitarian Association was founded, came the formation of the British and Foreign Unitarian Association, resulting from the mer-

[157] IX (1814), 789.
[158] XVI (1821), 63-64.
[159] *Memoir of Robert Aspland*, p. 234.
[160] *Ibid.*, p. 408.

ger of several existing organizations. The new Association, of which Aspland was the secretary for the first five years, endeavored to pursue a more vigorous policy in the dissemination of Unitarian doctrines by books and tracts and by domestic and foreign missionary effort. In the hope that denominational management of the *Repository* could extend its usefulness and its circulation, at the close of 1826 the Association bought out Aspland and placed the conduct of the magazine in the hands of the committee of its Book Department, at the head of which was Dr. Thomas Rees. That the hopes of the Association were not realized will presently be seen. In August, 1828, W. J. Fox became the editor, and at the close of 1831 its owner and proprietor; in his hands the magazine broke away from its sectarian connections and became an important organ of the radical party.

Thus closed the twenty-one years of the *Repository's* first series. If from the point of view of literature its nearly 16,000 pages suffer in comparison with the more brilliant pages of the second series under Fox, the first series nevertheless has its claims upon the attention of the historian of early nineteenth-century England. To the student of Dissent, it is a storehouse of biographical and historical materials; to the student of the development of liberal political and religious thought in England it is of lasting value. In its devotion to the ideals of civil and religious liberty the *Repository* yields in comparison to no periodical of its time. That it pursued an independent and liberal course for more than twenty years, through days of war and a period of violent conservative reaction, is no small evidence of the idealism and the genuine liberalism of the Rational Dissenters.

4: W. J. Fox: *"The Bravest Of Us All"*

ON A FINE DAY in early September, 1806, seven months after the first appearance of the *Repository,* there embarked at Norwich upon the lumbering, double-bodied London coach a lumpish looking young man of twenty. He was William Johnson Fox, for seven years past a clerk in a Norwich bank, now bound for Homerton Academy to study for the Dissenting ministry. Few would have predicted for the shy, awkward, undersized youth, seated on top of that coach for his first trip of more than thirty miles, a successful career as preacher, teacher, writer, reformer, and finally as Member of Parliament. Few also would have predicted that Fox would make his mark as a Unitarian in religion and a radical in politics, for he had been reared in orthodoxy, nourished as he later said on "the sour milk of Calvinism," and Homerton Academy was staunchly Calvinist. None could have foreseen that he would become a leader too liberal for even the unorthodox Unitarians. To understand how that came about it will be necessary first, by way of digression, to offer some explanation of what had happened to Unitarianism by 1831, when Fox became the owner of the *Monthly Repository.*

In the preceding chapters much has been made of the liberalism of the Unitarians, their devotion to freedom of thought in religious matters and their championing of political and social reform. Evidence of that liberalism can, as we have seen, be substantiated by a study of the first series of the *Repository,* especially when it is contrasted with contemporary religious periodicals. What follows is therefore to be regarded as in no sense a retraction of what has been said. It is true that by contrast the second series during

Fox's ownership seems almost as far in advance of the first, as the original series in its day had been in advance of orthodoxy. So liberal were the *Repository's* views under Fox, in fact, that the magazine lost Unitarian support some time before its editor was virtually read out of the ranks of the denomination.

That there is no fixed, unwavering line of demarcation between liberal and conservative is a truism which every generation seems to have to learn for itself. Today's liberal is often tomorrow's conservative—and without any intervening commissionership of stamps, soul crisis, or profound change in ideas or opinions. Tomorrow's liberal is often simply carrying to a logical conclusion, even though perhaps beyond the bounds of respectability, the principles which today's liberal has been advocating. The present writer recalls that an older colleague of his—generally regarded as one of the staunchest of conservatives—once said, with a twinkle in his eye, in referring to his own early years on the faculty: "*We* were the young liberals then." What he had fought for then as liberal reform had been won— and now was being attacked as outmoded and reactionary. The example has point with reference to the Unitarians in the 1830's.

For long years the Unitarians had fought intolerance and bigotry. Almost perforce they had been reformers. But by 1832 much of what they had fought for had been won. True, they had not converted Christendom to a rejection of the Trinity. They had, however, secured legal recognition and toleration, disabilities had been largely removed, and principles of scientific criticism in Biblical studies seemed on the way to tolerance if not general acceptance. Also, the middle classes, from which most Unitarians came, by the Reform Act of 1832 had gained ascendancy in the Parliament. These reforms had been gained, and to many a Unitarian they seemed sufficient.

The Unitarianism of Priestley and Belsham, it must be admitted, had at its core a negativism akin to that of the French *philosophes*. It was often more concerned with the destruction of what it regarded as the false articles of the Christian faith than it was in defending and extending the positive articles of that faith. In its day that brand of Unitarianism had served well. Any revolution, whether in thought or society, must have its destructive, negative phase. The critical point in the revolution comes when, after the old has been torn down, the new must be built. It is at this stage that old comrades among the revolutionists fall out. The course of the Communist Revolution in Russia since 1920 is a modern case in point.

Unitarianism, as we have seen, while it achieved most success within the Presbyterian churches, had never been confined to a sect. It had permeated the thought of Latitudinarians among the Anglican clergy; it had swallowed up English Presbyterianism, dominated one wing of the Baptist Church, and even affected one small branch of Methodism. But the needs of Unitarians for defense against the highly organized and powerful orthodoxy opposing them led to the establishment of organizations for united effort. This movement, culminating in the simultaneous formation of the British and Foreign Unitarian Association and the American Unitarian Association in 1825, inevitably tended towards sectarianism. Sectarianism in turn tended to check freedom of thought and investigation. It tempted Unitarians to rest upon whatever laurels of respectability they had won rather than to press forward. Those who insisted upon pressing forward incurred suspicion, dislike, and virtually, to use the modern word, liquidation. This sectarianism was never so rigid as that of the orthodox denominations, but it became sufficiently marked to produce its rebels also: in America, such men as Theodore Parker and

Ralph Waldo Emerson; in England, James Martineau and William Johnson Fox. It is a tribute to Unitarianism that in the revolt against its early negativism and its temporary trend towards sectarianism it should have produced men of such calibre, men who were to carry the rational movement in religion into new directions and to exercise important influence on English and American life.

In this study we are concerned with only one of these rebels, and more immediately with the expression of that rebellion as manifested in the rebel's conduct of a periodical. When William Johnson Fox took over the editorship of the *Monthly Repository* in August, 1828, such a rebellion could hardly have been expected. For over ten years he had been the darling preacher of the Unitarians and a recognized leader in their councils. True, he had aroused the fears of some by his attack on the prosecution of Deists in 1819 and by his advocacy of vigorous missionary effort among the poor of London and other large cities. But his wide reputation within the denomination—and to some extent, without —coupled with his known literary talents and his evident faith in the principles of rational religion, made it probable that his conduct of the *Repository* would be creditable and advantageous to the cause of Unitarianism. Within four years, however, he had bought the periodical from the Association, divested it of its almost exclusively religious character, and made it the vehicle of enough social and political radicalism to frighten away many of the douce, respectable folk among its subscribers. Since the fortunes of the *Repository* in its later years were thus so closely linked to the career of its editor, it will be necessary to outline that career.

Fox was born on March 1, 1786, in a Suffolk village. His mother was daughter of the village barber, who also served as clerk in the Dissenting Meeting House. His father was a peasant farmer who after moving his family to Norwich in 1789 became successively shopkeeper, handloom weaver, and itinerant schoolmaster. In Norwich, at the school connected with the Independent Chapel, young Fox received his elementary education, the three R's and an extensive dosage of the Assembly's Catechism and Calvinistic doctrine. This schooling was interrupted before the boy was twelve by the poverty of the family. For a time he worked at home, helping his father at the loom, and this permitted mother and son to indulge in their favorite pastime of novel reading. While the boy filled bobbins, she read aloud to him over the hum of the wheel. When the weaving venture failed, he worked as an errand boy at two shillings a week, and then at thirteen moved up the social ladder a rung or two by obtaining a clerkship in a local bank, a position which he was to hold for seven years.

Though deprived of formal schooling during these years, Fox found ways to pursue his studies. Locke's *Essay on the Human Understanding* he digested bit by bit in time stolen from the noon hour allotted for dinner. Mathematics, however, was his best beloved subject. For several years he and his friend William Saint met often at five o'clock in the morning to study mathematics together until eight; during the dinner hour they read philosophy and history together, and three evenings a week learned Latin from an old tutor. Fox was also not without youthful literary ambitions and contributed numerous verse effusions to the Norwich *Iris* over the signature P. L., standing for *Philo Libertatis*. All in all, his life during these years was typical in its interests and aspirations of much of Nonconformist intellectual life in early nineteenth-century England.

Why at twenty Fox should have decided to enter the ministry is not altogether clear since his fragmentary autobiography omits discussion of the subject. No doubt after a conversion he experienced a "call," the product of his always religious temperament and of his intellectual and social aspirations. Something of the Puritan respect for the ministerial office still pervaded Nonconformity. To enter the ministry offered attractive possibilities of leisure for study and a not to be overlooked rise in social station. There is no reason, however, to doubt the sincerity of his motives or his whole-hearted acceptance at this time of the Calvinistic theology.[1]

Homerton Academy (later College), for which we have seen Fox embarking in September, 1806, was located in Hackney, a suburb of London. As an institution for the training of Dissenting ministers it was no worse and perhaps better than many of the Nonconformist colleges.[2] Founded in 1730 by orthodox Calvinists, for over a hundred years it drilled the Genevan's theology into its students. At six-month intervals students were called upon to subscribe to a Calvinistic creed of ten articles, a hurdle which years before had deterred Joseph Priestley from entering the institution. The usual course of six years at Homerton combined what would now be apportioned among the secondary school, the college, and the theological seminary. The first two years were principally devoted to the classics, and the last four constituted the "academical" course, with theological studies predominating. The main subjects of study were mathematics, natural philosophy (science), Classical and Hebrew literature, philosophy, Biblical criticism, and theology. Training in English composition and elocution was provided, with themes on moral and religious subjects chosen by the tutor. During Fox's residence, and for forty odd years afterwards, the important office of theological tutor was held by the Reverend John Pye Smith, one of the most distinguished Dissenting scholars.

---

[1] See his original confession of faith submitted to gain entrance to Homerton.—M. D. Conway, *Centenary History of the South Place Society,* pp. 24-25.

[2] For information of Homerton and other Nonconformist academies, see Herbert McLachlan, *English Education Under the Test Acts.*

Fox entered upon his studies at Homerton somewhat later than most of his fellow students, of whom there were about a dozen and a half. That he completed the course in three years instead of the usual six may be attributed to his ability and to his earlier independent studies.[3] No details are available respecting his years at Homerton aside from his own recollections of the misery of his early days there when shy, homesick, and mistrustful of his powers, he longed to escape. "Often did I go to my little box of a study, a place about five feet square, with a deal desk, a stool and one bookshelf, and throw my arms on my desk and my head on my arms and weep."[4] For a time he was acutely aware of his lack of the physical requisites for a preacher: he was little more than five feet tall, thick-set, plain-featured, scarcely the commanding presence so advantageous in achieving success in the ministry.[5] His voice in those days, he confesses, was unpleasant, monotonous, and often hardly audible at the other end of the room.

If Fox had completed his autobiography, we should probably have a none too favorable picture of Homerton, for in the outline he drew up may be found such items as "Humbug of college teaching" and "House meeting and rebellion." He might perhaps have castigated Dissenting colleges much as W. P. Scargill did in his *Autobiography of a Dissenting Minister,* a book which Fox praised upon its appearance in 1834.

Though rigid in its Evangelical discipline, Homerton did not always succeed in its proscription of such devices of the devil as cards and the theatre. Said Fox: "I learned to play whist within the walls of Homerton College, and

[3] McLachlan (*op. cit.,* p. 185) lists Fox as having been in attendance from 1803 to 1809. This is at variance with other available evidence, including Fox's own statement. Cf. Garnett, *Life of W. J. Fox,* p. 14.

[4] Quoted by Garnett, *op. cit.,* p. 18.

[5] Hazlitt in 1824 remarked his diminutive stature as a handicap, and W. J. Linton in retrospect thought that his physique had prevented his becoming the "royal leader of English democracy."

went thence on the first theatrical expedition from the time
of my conversion. Both became not infrequent practices.
. . . Our usual place was the two shilling gallery. We
thought it more secure from observation than the pit."[6] On
at least one occasion they encountered students there from
the rival orthodox college of Hoxton. There was, however,
some conscience in Fox's sinning: once, after walking the
six miles from Homerton to Covent Garden, only to find
that a modern comedy had been substituted for Shakespeare,
he turned around and walked back again. Such minor
aberrations as stolen visits to the theatre evidently did not
reach the ears of Dr. Smith, for when Fox finished his
course in 1809 he received the more or less usual compli-
mentary Latin testimonial. In his last year he was appointed
to deliver one of the English orations; it was entitled "The
Importance of an Accurate Study of the Philosophy of the
Human Mind in Promoting the Knowledge of Revealed
Religion."

The fledgling divine settled late in 1809 at the tiny village
of Fareham, in Hampshire. He had scarcely begun to
preach before he became obsessed by doubts and uncertain-
ties, at first over the doctrine of the Trinity and soon over
the whole Calvinistic scheme. As early as March, 1810, he
wrote of his trials to a friend: "My future lot becomes every
day more doubtful. I am hastening towards a time when
I can no longer be handed along by circumstances. . . . My
young friends say, Throw off the trammels of orthodoxy
now." Already he was moved to admire the intelligence of
the heretics in contrast with the blindness of the orthodox:
"But alas! the heretics understand one's discourse, and use
their powers; while the orthodox are such fools that one
may preach all the heresies in Christendom without their
knowing it, unless they are told so. . . ." Already he de-
spised the "ignorant and servile crowd" with whom he was

[6] Garnett, *op. cit.,* pp. 26-27.

compelled to associate and loathed their "spiritual conversation," which he described as "a nauseous chitchat, half scandal and half pure nonsense." Only an occasional event such as having tea with an intelligent currier, when the talk was a "pic-nic of Colonel Wardle, Ben Flower, Robinson, Independence, Liberty, etc., etc.," afforded a little relief.[7]

Meanwhile, his inner turmoil was intense. Years later he described the experience:

It was amid deprecations and agitations that I pursued my enquiries; external expressions of what was going on did but occasion coldness, suspicion, alienation. My path was through dark valleys shaken by an earthquake; it seemed as if there were a spell on me and I must go on, feeling that I was going wrong, toiling to arrive at the abandonment of heaven and diligently working out my own damnation. The investigation became more and more fascinating. It was as if I was under a spell; I thought, criticized, discussed (mentally) and read controversy with insatiableness. The work went on day and night: I used to take books on the Unitarian controversy to bed with me and read them for hours with the candle on my pillow.[8]

Though prejudiced by early training and background against Unitarianism, little by little he moved in that direction. First to go of the tenets of orthodox Calvinism were the doctrines of the Trinity and of original sin, a process completed within that first year at Fareham. In the next year, during which a schismatic church was set up in the village under his ministry, he gave up his belief in the pre-existence of Christ and in the atonement. Last to go was the dogma of everlasting punishment. By 1812 he was an avowed Unitarian, preaching his first sermon in that denomination at a meeting of the Southern Unitarian Association at Portsmouth.

[7] Conway, *op. cit.,* pp. 27-29.   [8] Garnett, *op. cit.,* pp. 22-23.

He now moved to Chichester, where he settled as the minister of a small Unitarian congregation. For nearly five years he remained there, reading widely not only in theology but also in fiction and poetry, perfecting his skill in oratory, ridding himself of his provincial accent, and unconsciously preparing for the wider ministry that lay ahead. There too he fell in love with Eliza Florance, the daughter of a local barrister. The affair encountered parental opposition, and the lover himself cooled at times. "She will never excite an enthusiastic passion, yet she may be very well loved," he wrote in his diary.[9] Propinquity, want of sympathy and an emotional outlet, and dissatisfaction with a "heartless" life narrowed by sectarian dissensions, led to a connection which eventually brought much unhappiness to both. In August, 1815, a semi-engagement was broken off. It would have been better if the matter had ended there.

In the meantime, Fox, was becoming known among the Unitarians for his oratorical powers. Unitarian like other Nonconformist preachers followed the practice of frequent interchange of pulpits, and numerous anniversary and association meetings offered opportunities for the display of homiletic skill. That Fox had early acquired extraordinary oratorical ability is evidenced in a diary entry for March, 1813, when he was in a mood of depression over the ill-success of his ministry as a Unitarian:

Shall I say, Oh that it were with me as in months past, when the candle of orthodoxy shone upon me? Shall I call up the times when listening crowds heard with visible emotion, when trickling tears proclaimed the vividness of the feelings, the pathos of my eloquence, the power of grace?[10]

Unitarians were perhaps harder to move to tears, since they prided themselves on their freedom from emotion in their religion. They could, however, appreciate oratorical power

[9] *Ibid.*, p. 33.   [10] *Ibid.*, p. 30.

as well as the orthodox, and Fox was not long denied recognition.

Late in 1816 he was invited to London to succeed the recently deceased William Vidler in the pastorate of Parliament Court Chapel, Artillery Lane, Bishopsgate Street. This church had been built in 1793 by the followers of the American Universalist and Baptist, Elhanan Winchester; its heterodoxy was limited at first to the doctrine of final restoration.[11] Winchestor's successor, William Vidler, who has been mentioned in another connection, by his conversion to Unitarianism split his congregation in 1802; for a while the Society was maintained only by help from the Unitarian Fund. By the time of his death, however, Vidler's congregation had flourished. Fox was given a salary of £200 the first year and £300 the second. For years Parliament Court maintained a technical connection with the Baptist church; not until several months after Fox's ministry had begun in April, 1817, was it legally registered as a Unitarian chapel.

The new position was worthy of Fox's abilities, and the removal from the provincial town to the metropolis offered stimulus and opportunity. From the first he made a favorable impression. At the services of April 2, 1817, to begin his pastorate, he refused ordination and declined to make any confession of faith, boldly avowing his unwavering belief in religious liberty and in the duty of free enquiry. Freedom he claimed for himself and would not deny to others.

In little more than a month he attracted favorable notice

[11] This religious society furnishes an interesting epitome of the development of radical Dissent from the late eighteenth century down to the present. The successive names of the organization, adopted or attributed, indicate the trends of its theology: Philadelphians, Universalists, Society of Religious Dissenters, South Place Unitarian Society, The South Place Society (after Fox had left the Unitarian body), The Free Religious Society, The South Place Ethical Society. Cf. M. D. Conway, *op. cit.*, p. x.

outside his church. An ardent advocate of the Lancasterian system of education, Fox in May at the festival of that Association's school in the City Road made so eloquent a speech that the Duke of Sussex (the one liberal in the Royal Family), the Lord Mayor of London, and several other notabilities complimented him warmly. For a time he even seemed threatened with lionization by the aristocracy. Recognizing his opportunities for the extension of his influence and his usefulness, Fox began the practice of delivering in his chapel evening lectures on great social, ethical, political, and religious questions. One set of these, delivered in November and December, 1818, was published the following year.[12] The book included discourses on "Antichrist," "Church of Englandism" (a term borrowed from Bentham), "Religious Liberty and Nonconformity," "Unitarianism," "On Creeds, Controversy, and the Influence of Religious Systems on Society," "War," and "Human Perfectibility." He defined Antichrist as all churches in which are "dominion over conscience, alliance with the temporal authority, mystery, idolatrous worship, blasphemy, hypocrisy, deceit and affected austerity, and persecution."[13] His scorn of illiberality was not to be confined to the Establishment: "Even Dissenters play their little game of tyranny, and make Christians pass to the Lord's table through the pool of Baptism, or under the forks of the Assembly's Catechism."[14] Most notable perhaps was his forthright attack upon war in every shape and form: *"War is one great crime . . . a repeal of the laws of morality and of God."*[15] Though years later Fox was to modify his extreme pacificism, his position three years after the close of the Napoleonic wars is interesting. A quotation will serve to demonstrate the style of his rhetoric.

[12] *A Course of Lectures on Subjects Connected with the Corruption, Revival, and Future Influence of Genuine Christianity*, London, 1819.
[13] *Ibid.*, "On Antichrist," p. 10.
[14] *Ibid.*   [15] *Ibid.*, p. 170.

It is the tendency of war to produce war, and thus to extend and multiply miseries. Treaties of peace seem little better than links to connect one war with another. They leave something ambiguous for future dissension, some germ of discord, which grows into a poison tree. Indeed, the professed object of hostility is seldom determined in favour of either party, by the peace. In the series of wars which have for ages desolated Europe, we may generally see one growing out of another. The various connexions and interests of nations serve to spread hostility when once commenced. This was particularly exemplified in the late contest, into which nation after nation was drawn or forced. The torrent of blood swelled, as it rolled on; still fresh sluices opened, till it spread and widened, and seemed without fathom or bound. Like the Glacier, from the mountain's top, it rushed on, accumulating as it fell, and finding in one work of ruin materials to render the next more wide and dreadful. It stretched from the old world to the new, wrapping both continents in its flames, and covering the earth as with a fiery deluge of desolation.[16]

More notoriety accompanied the delivery, during the trial of Richard Carlile in October, 1819, of Fox's sermon on "The Duties of Christians towards Deists." The controversy which it provoked has been discussed in the preceding chapter. Fox was aiming at bigotry among the Unitarians as well as among the orthodox; there were not wanting among the Rational Dissenters some respectable persons who feared lest the Deist label be attached to themselves. To such persons the little preacher's boldness, pushing to a logical conclusion the boasted Unitarian major premises of the rights of freedom of enquiry and of belief, was disquieting. Fox's congregation, however, rose quickly to the occasion, officially endorsed the address and requested its publication. His only concession to Mrs. Grundy in the printed version was a kind of prefatory confession of faith, which, as Garnett points out, "within a generation had become too narrow not

16 *Ibid.*, pp. 170-71.

only for him but for the leaders of Unitarian thought everywhere, and which probably would not now be accepted by a single Unitarian congregation in Great Britain."[17]

The sermon, while it alarmed some, did not seriously affect his growing popularity within the denomination. When the break eventually came, it was to arise more immediately from his personal conduct than from differences of opinion on religion and politics. An unfortunate and unhappy marriage, a cause of failure for many men, was for Fox the arduous path to a successful career in journalism and politics.

In 1819 the once broken off "semi-engagement" to Eliza Florance was renewed. There is ground for suspicion that this was not done without pressure from Miss Florance and her parents. Her father's fortunes had suffered some reverses, and Fox's success in London now made him a more eligible match. At any rate, she came to London in 1819, ostensibly to support herself as a teacher. Fox himself was at fault for allowing the affair to drift into marriage. Neither he nor Eliza seems to have been very much in love. A letter to his mother, justifying his engagement, may have attempted to placate her by a rationalizing of excuses for the step, but its tone is scarcely that of an ardent lover. He reports that he is tired of living in lodgings, and that his bride-to-be has "a very kind heart, and is no fool." In reply to the expected objection to her fortune, he counters: "She is, at any rate, as rich as I am, and we shall start in a house decently furnished, without debt, I want no more."[18]

With such modest expectations the marriage took place on April 20, 1820. Disillusionment did not take long. Years later, Fox wrote: "Very soon after my marriage I found I had made a blunder; and though a moderate share of comfort, a disposition to help me in my exertions, at least some sympathy with these, and economy in the management of

<hr />

[17] Garnett, *op. cit.*, p. 42.   [18] *Ibid.*, p. 44.

their fruits, would pretty well have contented me, I did not find even these."[19] Undoubtedly the unhappiness of the marriage was a major factor in the severe breakdown in health which Fox suffered in February, 1822. As a result, he was unable to preach for a whole year. In a sketch of Sandown Bay anonymously published in the *Repository* for 1832, Fox while describing how he found refuge from the demons of hypochondriasis in the beautiful scenery of the Isle of Wight, delineated his illness:

Anxiety, and exertion, and illness, had worked the animal machine so furiously, and so irregularly, and pulled it about in so many different ways, that the whole was in terrible disorder. Food had ceased to nourish me,—light had ceased to gladden me,—the reports of my senses were not to be trusted, my eyes saw sights, and my ears heard sounds, which were not sights and sounds, but only internal sensations, my muscles would often suddenly refuse to obey the will, and the limbs ceased to act, while the heart made up for their deficiency of emotion by the rapidity and violence of its pulsations. . . . Disease had generated a deep aversion to society, a shrinking from the presence of humanity.[20]

Solitude, rest, and the beauties of Wight's natural scene eventually restored him to his work.

By this time Fox had begun to engage in literary pursuits unconnected with his religious activities and by enlarging his circle of acquaintances had gained an entrée to several periodicals. His first ventures into the realms of secular literature[21] seem to have been contributions to the *Retrospective Review,* a periodical founded by Henry South-

---

[19] *Ibid.,* pp. 43-44.

[20] *Monthly Repository,* N.S., VI (1832), 272-73.

[21] Newman I. White in *The Unextinguished Hearth* (p. 63) makes a "pure guess" that Fox was the author of an anonymous *Reply* to Shelley's *Queen Mab* (1821). The guess seems unwarranted since the pamphlet is inconsistent with Fox's known views, and its style is unlike his. Also, contrary to Professor White's statement, Fox was not editor of the *Monthly Repository* at this time.

ern and largely devoted to a discussion of the great books of the past. Identifiable contributions by Fox include articles on "The Political Works of Andrew Fletcher," "Cudworth's Intellectual System," "On the Literature of the Occult Sciences," "The Dramas of Nathaniel Lee," and "Witchcraft." The last-mentioned is the most considerable piece of work. Fox in his early criticism, as well as later, displays always a tendency to find beauties rather than faults.

In the course of his Unitarian activities Fox formed a connection with the Benthamite Utilitarians, particularly through John Bowring and through Dr. Southwood Smith, a Unitarian preacher turned physician, who is remembered for his pioneer work as a sanitary reformer. Fox at this time served as secretary of the Unitarian Fund, with Bowring on the Fund's committee. Bowring once approached Fox with a request from Bentham that he edit the latter's heretical *Not Paul but Jesus,* intended to prove Paul an impostor. Fox declined the dubious honor though apparently without protest against the thesis of the work.[22] He must have had some repute among his friends for more than Unitarian heterodoxy, for a letter from Henry Southern of December, 1823, suggests the possibility that Fox review *Don Juan* for the first number of the *Westminster Review.*[23] Fox evidently refused, for no such review appeared.

He did, however, gain the distinction of supplying the leading article for the new Benthamite review, which began in 1824 with Bowring as editor of the political department and Southern of the literary. The nature of the subject probably determined the placing of the article. Ostensibly a review of *Men and Things in 1823,* a poem by a young

---

[22] The task was finally undertaken by Francis Place and published (1821, 1823), under the pseudonym of Gamaliel Smith. Bentham—or Place?—announced the publication in a letter to the *Repository* in 1821 (XVI, 108). It was reviewed by John Kentish ("N."), XVI, 231-35, and XIX (1824), 613-19.

[23] Garnett, *op. cit.,* pp. 52-53.

Oxonian, James Shergold Boone, it offered an opportunity for a survey of trends in contemporary English life.[24] Fox reveals his democratic sympathies and his anti-aristocratic bias in his singling out as the most significant tendency of the day the growing regard for and deference to the interests of the people at large. His allegiance to democratic ideals is boldly expressed: "The people no longer sit quietly by as spectators, while Whig and Tory, that is, a few great families with their connexions and dependants . . . play out the political game, in their own way, and for their own benefit." The people at long last are coming into their own; and everywhere, in politics, religion, and literature, tribute is rendered to their growing power. The Commons orator talks to the gallery rather than the benches. Dissenting religionists and their opposition both appeal to the public. "The multitude of theological publications, to say nothing of the pulpit, makes Britain appear like one great court of Areopagus, preparing for judgment on the 'setters forth of strange gods.'" Publishers are awake to the new and extensive market for books, and cheap editions pour from the presses. The public is now the great literary patron. The great poets write for the people. Fox names Scott as the one most notably affected by these tendencies; he says, however, that the desire to reach the many has affected them all, though Wordsworth "seems rather to chaunt a demonstration to the initiated few that the many should be sung to." The politician, the divine, the author, the reviewer, "All seem impressed with the rise of a new power, and, blessing or cursing, they pay to it a certain degree of homage." But with all this, full political emancipation has not yet come, as it must if the people are to be free. Parliamentary reform, says Fox, is not merely a question of diminishing public burdens; it is a question of public morale. "Mutual independence, and full liberty of speech and action, so far as

[24] *Westminster Review*, I (1824), 1-18.

they infringe not on others' rights, are what constitute a freeman; and he who desires not these loves not liberty, though he may hate taxation."

Fox's chief criticism of contemporary society concerns the vulgar utilitarianism of the age. "The one great thing on which we are intent is getting money; and our politics, religion, literature, are only branches of that pursuit. . . ." The spirit of *cui bono* has a bad effect on both learning and literature. The age may be eminently religious, but there is much cant and insincerity. Religious enthusiasm is the only fashionable enthusiasm. In literature and criticism there has been too much affectation of levity and heartlessness, probably because of Byron's influence. More encouraging is the enthusiasm of some of the popular reformers. Cobbett is praised for his share in rousing public intelligence, though condemned for his want of principle. Owen's doctrine of coöperation is favorably viewed as offering hope for the amelioration of the economic ills of the laboring classes. In general, this opening article by Fox reveals his agreement with the Utilitarian position, but it also reveals a deeper sympathy with the plight of the lower classes.

Fox wrote little more for the *Westminster,* despite the urgings of Bowring and, later, of John Stuart Mill. Though sympathetic to much of the program of the Philosophic Radicals and convinced of the validity of the greatest-happiness principle, he did not subscribe to all the Benthamite doctrines, particularly in their narrower applications. Continuance of his contributions to the *Westminster* might well have elevated the literary character of that periodical.

In February, 1824, was first opened in South Place the new Finsbury Unitarian Chapel which Fox's congregation had built for him. The years that followed were busy as he assumed an increasingly important role in the activities of the denomination. In 1825 came the amalgamation of the three chief Unitarian agencies into the British and Foreign

Unitarian Association; fifty years later at its anniversary celebration, James Martineau declared that Fox had been the real founder of the Association, with the consequent enlargement of the scope of Unitarian activity. Fox became the first Foreign Secretary of the new Association. When the organization decided to purchase the *Monthly Repository* from Aspland, Fox assisted in the conduct of the periodical. In August, 1828, he assumed the editorship, and continued it under the sponsorship of the Association until his purchase of the magazine in 1831. Meanwhile his reputation as a speaker grew with the years, and he was consequently in great demand at Unitarian gatherings throughout the country. Published versions of a number of his sermons, for example, the two volumes of *Christ and Christianity* (1831), extended his influence beyond his immediate hearers.

During these years Fox was also participating actively in reform politics. Like many Dissenting ministers in London he crusaded in behalf of the repeal of the Test Act in 1828, and, unlike many of the orthodox divines, in behalf of Catholic Emancipation. His efforts in behalf of the Reform Bill, however, went beyond those of most clergymen, even in his own denomination. In the stirring months preceding the adoption of the Reform Bill in June, 1832, Fox seems to have engaged in much subterranean activity in such radical organizations as the Political Unions. But his efforts were not confined to secret channels. John Saunders years later recalled in his sketch of Fox how,

When the Political Union stood forth to concentrate into one focus the energies of the people of London, notwithstanding the danger its members knowingly incurred of prosecution as an illegal body, . . . Mr. Fox stood forth among them, took up his position in the van, and addressed the people daily in Leicester-Square with a fearless and passionate eloquence that carried all before it. . . .[25]

[25] *People's Journal*, III (1847), 71.

Francis Place, veteran leader of the radical reformers, told
Saunders that Fox in those days was "the bravest of us all."
The best evidence available as to the extent of Fox's radicalism at this time is to be found in his many political
articles in the *Repository*, which will be examined in the
next chapter.

The extremes of Fox's radical political views alarmed
many of the moderate Reform Whigs among the Unitarians,
who thought that the Bill of 1832 accomplished all that was
needful, or indeed, all that was advisable if middle-class
dominance was not to be yielded up to the working classes.
But it was neither his political nor his religious radicalism
that brought about Fox's initial separation from the Unitarian denomination. In fact, so important a place did he
hold within its ranks that it is doubtful that anything short
of an offense against the social code of the day could have
dislodged him. It was his advocacy, in the *Repository* and
elsewhere, of the emancipation of women and the liberal-
izing of the divorce laws, and his solution of his own marital difficulties that led to his exclusion from the Unitarian
hierarchy. If Fox had been happily married, he would
probably have remained a Unitarian clergyman.

On September 7, 1834, the *London Sunday Times* carried in its columns a paragraph headed "The Fox and the
Flower." The paragraph was not an Aesopic fable to please
the children during a long Sabbath afternoon, but a scandal-
mongering squib to set the tongues of their elders a-wagging.

A *Fox*, not a little distinguished in his day, who has furnished
excellent sport on a variety of occasions, is reported to have been
very awkwardly chased on a late occasion. We shall be glad to
see him in his old fields as brisk and confident as heretofore;
but if *Sly Reynard* has demolished a fair *Flower*, under the circumstances some of his followers give out, the opinion will be,
the sooner he goes to earth the better.

Thus did one level of newspaper readers learn of the marital troubles of Fox and of his association with Eliza Flower.[26]

Eliza Flower was the elder of the two talented daughters of Benjamin Flower, the outspoken, radical editor and publisher of the *Cambridge Intelligencer* (1793-1800) and the *Political Review* (1807-1811). The earlier of these, a prototype of Leigh Hunt's *Examiner,* was one of the few liberal English weeklies of the decade of the French Revolution. The young Samuel Taylor Coleridge contributed at least six poems to the *Intelligencer,* and when his short-lived periodical the *Watchman* expired, he recommended Flower's paper as one to which his readers might with profit turn.[27] In 1799 Flower acquired distinction as one of the martyrs to liberalism at the hands of the Tory reactionaries. For what the House of Lords declared a libel and a breach of privilege in his criticism of the political activities of Bishop Watson, Flower was fined one hundred pounds and imprisoned in Newgate for six months.

Martyrdom proved to be not without its compensations. Among the visitors who came to offer their sympathy to the radical editor was Miss Eliza Gould, ex-schoolmistress of South Molton, Devon. Miss Gould had been one of Flower's most devoted subscribers, and in fact, had been obliged to give up her school because of her advanced political views and her refusal to cancel her subscription to the radical weekly. Miss Gould's visits to Newgate soon blossomed into more than the friendship of reformer and

[26] The matter had reached a crisis in Fox's congregation in July, and on August 15 he had issued a public letter to the Society, tendering his resignation. The letter was printed in the *Standard* of Sept. 2, 1834, the *Christian Advocate* of about the same date, the *Morning Chronicle* of Sept. 6, and the *British Magazine* for October (VI, 445-47). W. P. Scargill also reprinted it in his *Autobiography of a Dissenting Minister* (1834) as a document in his case against the Dissenting congregations' interference in the private lives of their pastors.

[27] For two letters revealing something of the connection between Flower and Coleridge, see *Monthly Repository,* N.S., VIII (1834), 653-55.

disciple; upon Flower's release the two were married early in 1800.

The veteran reformer had no more collisions with the law, but he never relaxed his vigilant devotion to the cause of political and religious liberty. Moving from Cambridge to Harlow in 1804, he conducted a printing business and published the monthly *Political Review*. For many years, though not ordained as a minister, he often served as a supply preacher. In his theological views an Arian of the school of Price, Flower nevertheless had among the Unitarians a wide connection of friends, one of the closest being Robert Aspland. He was a frequent contributor to the *Repository* during Aspland's long editorship.

Mrs. Flower at her death in 1810 left behind two daughters, Eliza, aged seven, and Sarah, aged five. The rearing of the two motherless girls has been described as "original and erratic." The epithets are justifiable if we are to believe the assumption of Mrs. E. Bridell Fox that Harriet Martineau's early novelette, *Five Years of Youth* (1831), was based on the life of Flower and his daughters. Because of their father's prejudices against the schools of the time, Eliza and Sarah were educated at home by "a few masters, the best that the little country village of Harlow afforded, a few lessons from the father and a good deal of traveling about the country in an old-fashioned, one-horse chaise, with the idea of cultivating their powers of observation."[28] Eliza at an early age displayed an unusual musical talent. Music was to become her life, and as a composer she achieved distinction beyond that of any other woman of her time.

In 1820, the year of Fox's marriage to Eliza Florance, Flower and his two daughters moved to Dalston, London. Nearby lived Fox, and an intimacy soon sprang up between the two families. This friendship was strengthened in 1823

[28] Quoted in H. W. Stephenson, *The Author of Nearer, My God, To Thee*, p. 19.

when an invitation to Fox to preach in Edinburgh gave him
an opportunity for a tour of Scotland. Included in the party,
which was organized by Dr. Southwood Smith, were Eliza
and Sarah Flower and their father, plus Mrs. Fox's sister.
The crowning event of the trip, an ascent of Ben Lomond,
was for years afterwards celebrated in an anniversary fête.
For some years the Flower sisters were frequent visitors in
the Fox household, apparently without objection on the part
of Mrs. Fox.

The little preacher became not only friend and religious
teacher to the two girls but also their mentor in literary and
cultural matters. When Eliza became acquainted in nearby
Hackney with a talented boy of twelve who wrote beautiful
verses, she made a copy of the poems which she submitted
to Fox for criticism—"Which verses," said the poet years
later, "he praised not a little, which praise comforted me not
a little."[29] The precocious poet was named Robert Browning. He became a friend of the sisters and an adoring admirer of Eliza, nine years his senior. It was probably she
who inspired Browning's first published poem, *Pauline*,[30]
and long years afterwards he still testified to his warm admiration for her and to his respect for her musical talents.
Sarah Flower and young Browning shared a devotion to
the stage and both had aspirations to become actors. Fox,
as we shall see later, was of great help to the poet in the
early years of his career, help which Browning generously
acknowledged long afterwards when he called Fox his "literary father."

That Fox was the confidant of Sarah as well as Eliza is
revealed in a letter of the autumn of 1827. Browning at
fifteen, as the result of a course of reading in Voltaire, had

[29] H. W. Griffin and H. C. Minchin, *Life of Robert Browning*, p. 42.

[30] M. Hovelaque in his *La Jeunesse de Robert Browning* makes out a case
that it was Sarah not Eliza that inspired *Pauline*. His evidence seems insufficient to establish the point.

turned sceptic and undermined Sarah's faith in Revelation. She wrote thus to Fox:

My mind has been wandering a long time, and now it seems to have lost sight of that only invulnerable hold against the assaults of this warring world, a firm belief in the genuineness of the Scriptures.

. . . The cloud has come over me gradually, and I did not discover the darkness in which my soul was shrouded until, in seeking to give light to others, my own gloomy state became too settled to admit of doubt. It was in answering Robert Browning that my mind refused to bring forward argument, turned recreant, and sided with the enemy. . . .

I have a firm belief in a resurrection—at least I think I have —but my mind is in a sad state; and before that goes, I must endeavour to build up my decaying faith. How is it to be done? . . .[31]

Just how far Fox was of help in restoring Sarah's shaken faith is not ascertainable; Moncure Conway, the most distinguished of Fox's successors in the South Place pulpit, in his *Autobiography* expressed his conviction that Sarah's doubts, thus initiated by the boy Browning, "or perhaps his [Fox's] efforts to move them, did away with his faith in a Biblical revelation."[32] Conway in his effort to trace the advanced rationalism of South Place Chapel as thus "primarily due to Robert Browning" has probably overstated the case, though we hesitate to challenge the opinion of one who had an intimate knowledge of the Fox and the Flower families. From available evidence, however, it does not seem clear that Fox lost his faith in a Biblical revelation at this time but rather at a considerably later date.

Eliza Flower early came to assist Fox in his work, copying articles and speeches for him and hunting up materials. The community of literary and cultural interests between

---

[31] Stephenson, *op. cit.*, pp. 22-23.
[32] M. D. Conway, *Autobiography*, II, 28.

them ripened by degrees into a romantic friendship. Denied the sympathy and affection which he needed at home, Fox seems to have turned more and more to the talented girl seventeen years his junior. The death of her father in 1829 served to strengthen the bond of affection, for Flower in his will appointed Fox an executor and trustee for his daughters.

By 1832 matters in the Fox household reached a crisis. In December Mrs. Fox resorted to the rather strange expedient of writing to her husband a formal letter of complaint. Divorce, in the then state of the law, was impossible; there was but one ground permitted for divorce, which could be secured only by act of Parliament. Since there was never any question of improper conduct between Fox and Eliza, the only alternative was some kind of arranged separation between husband and wife. The first arrangement lasted for nearly two years; by its terms, they were to consider themselves as separated, though they continued to live under the same roof in order that his means of providing for the family might not be impaired. Then, even more than today, public knowledge of marital difficulties was fatal to a ministerial career.

In the summer of 1834 Mrs. Fox, increasingly dissatisfied, confided her troubles to several members of the congregation. The result should not have been hard to foresee. The story spread, and disaffection in the congregation grew. One group wrote to Fox, demanding that he should set his house in order to Mrs. Fox's satisfaction or resign his charge. Fox at once chose to resign and on August 15 issued the letter to his congregation which has been noted.[33] In it Fox challenged their right to interfere in his domestic concerns.

Whatever may have been the trials of my domestic life, through many long years,—to whose, or to what fault (if fault there be)

---

[33] See above, note 26.

they are owing, are questions on which only continued and close intimacy can justify anyone in forming an opinion. Assuredly they are not fit subjects for argument before congregational authorities,—still less for decision by a self-constituted and secret tribunal, however respectable its individual members. . . .[34]

If Fox's account of the inquisitorial process is correct, the interference was intolerable. Selections were made from his private correspondence; his household accounts were analyzed; "the evils . . . of domestic inquisition grew around me"; and, most intolerable of all, under the circumstances, "of the proverbial delicacy of female reputation, advantage was taken the most unjust and base." Scorning to answer whispered charges of misconduct (as John Stuart Mill urged him to do),[35] Fox chose to regard his unpopular opinions as the true source of the trouble, and cited three of his *Repository* articles for 1833 ("The Dissenting Marriage Question," "A Victim," and "A Letter to a Unitarian Minister") as containing his considered judgment on the desirability of granting divorce for incompatibility.[36]

This was the ground upon which his critics based their

---

[34] *British Magazine*, VI (1834), 445.

[35] Mill, by now a close friend of Fox and himself in a somewhat equivocal situation with regard to Mrs. John Taylor, wrote Fox in July, urging him to deny the charges. "We all think it of great importance that every public mention of the charge should be accompanied by mention of your denying it. . . ." (Garnett, *op. cit.*, p. 164.) Mill clearly had the utmost confidence in Fox's integrity.

[36] Fox was not always guarded in his expressions. Crabb Robinson, a Unitarian but no very good friend of Fox—especially after what he regarded as Fox's ill-treatment of him in connection with his Goethe series in the *Repository* (cf. Chapter VII)—wrote in his Diary on December 5, 1834: "I have been reading the printed papers in Fox's affair with his wife in which he appears to have pushed frankness and sincerity to an extremity—He did not scruple to avow that though no illicit intercourse had in fact taken place between him and his friend (Miss Flower) it was merely accidental, there being nothing in their principles against their so acting—only prudence was against—and this being brought against him he very angrily retorts on his accusers as calumnious because they had represented him as being willing to sacrifice principle to prudence—In words he is right, but in spirit he is wrong in his elaborate defense of himself."—Typescript Diary.

case. When the congregation met in September, Fox was acquitted by a large majority and asked to withdraw his resignation. A minority of 46 members, with their families making a total of 120, withdrew from the church. At the earnest solicitation of the remaining three-fourths of the membership, Fox withdrew his resignation. He was to continue until 1852 as the preacher of South Place Chapel, though he dropped the title "Reverend."

When the commotion in his church subsided, he took an even more far-reaching step. A formal separation from his wife was arranged, whereby she received an allowance; Fox himself in January, 1835, moved to Bayswater, then a suburb, and established Eliza Flower at the head of his new household. Two of the children came with him, and one remained with the mother. Such a step, flouting the conventions of society, could not but bring notoriety, even though friends of Fox and Eliza never doubted the innocence of their relationship. From this time until her death in 1846 she presided over his household, tirelessly aiding him in every way she could. Some of the old friends— Harriet Martineau, for instance—dropped her, but there were new friends too, Macready and Forster, Richard Horne and Thomas Wade, Mary and Margaret Gillies, among others.

In the spring of 1835 the association of Presbyterian (really, Unitarian) ministers of London and vicinity met and formally expelled Fox from their ranks. Since he had not been given any opportunity to refute the charges against him, Fox protested vigorously, but to no avail.[37] Several of

---

[37] Robinson, still unsympathetic to Fox, wrote in his Diary on May 21, 1835: "A long chat today with Hardy about Fox's affair whose letter to the Dissenting Ministers I read at night—They have put themselves in the wrong having a good cause—not giving him notice of their meeting to expel him from their body as a presbyterian minister. Further he seems to have the advantage over them in this, that they allege as a ground of expulsion the secession of so many respectable persons of his congregation. He answers—a majority more

the younger, and later very influential Unitarian ministers, including John Relly Beard and James Martineau, while not agreeing with Fox's precepts or practice, wrote letters reprobating the action of the London ministers. To Beard Fox replied, assuring him that the confidence in his integrity was warranted: "Should I ever follow the example of Milton's intention, it will be with as little disposition to conceal or blink the transaction. I hold myself to be morally divorced—remarriage is quite another question."[38] The action of the association was arbitrary, but, in view of the disfavor which Unitarians still met in many quarters, understandable. For some time it had become increasingly evident that Fox was "among rather than of the Unitarian body," as Bowring years later put it. "His intellect entitled him to a very high, if not the highest place among the ministers who were his contemporaries; while the latitudinarianism, or perhaps better, the freedom of his opinions, tended to alienate their sympathies, and to make any very intimate or harmonious action difficult or impossible."[39]

Expulsion from the Unitarian inner circle was not without its advantage of freedom. For some years Fox had felt some disquiet over the performance of sacerdotal offices and had developed an increasing interest in journalism; in 1831 he had voiced his opinion that the pulpit was being "eclipsed by the greater power of a cheap and rapid Press."[40] It was therefore not without some sense of relief that Fox began

---

respectable in fortune and station have confirmed me in my office—and you in my absence without enquiry and having no original knowledge on the subject erect yourselves into a court of appeal and rescind the resolution of my congregation in my favour, in my absence and without notice. This often happens in litigation—the party essentially in the right loses by blundering the judgment which he should have in his favour."—Typescript Diary.

Other comments by Robinson may be found under dates of May 22 and July 4, 1835.

[38] Quoted in Herbert McLachlan, *Records of a Family,* pp. 17-18. For Martineau's letter to Fox, see Garnett, *op. cit.,* pp. 169-70.

[39] *Theological Review,* III (1866), 441.

[40] *Monthly Repository,* N.S., V (1831), 277.

his journalistic career, at first with the *Sunday Times,* then as leader writer and editor of the *True Sun,* and, after the demise of the latter, as literary and dramatic critic for the *Morning Chronicle.* Eliza Flower in a letter to Fox's sister in Norwich records that on the first day of his new work he said, on returning home, "There, I feel like an honest man who earns his bread by the sweat of his brow.[41]

Upon his removal to Bayswater, Fox gave up some of the pastoral duties of South Place, and divested himself as much as possible of the ministerial character, though he continued to serve as preacher for many years. The services at South Place became considerably secularized: texts were no longer appended to his sermons or lectures, prayers were shortened (under Conway, the Society later omitted prayers altogether), and the musical service was extended far beyond that common in Dissenting churches. Eliza Flower's great musical ability was put to good use at South Place. In 1841 *Hymns and Anthems* was published for the congregation with music by Eliza, and a number of hymns by Sarah, whose "Nearer, My God, to Thee" first appeared here. Fox's chapel continued to be sought out by distinguished visitors; Mill and Disraeli were sometimes to be found among the audience, and at least once Carlyle; Emerson and Theodore Parker, on the occasion of their visits to London; Longfellow, attending unannounced, was greeted by the singing of his own "Psalm of Life."

Freed from sectarian restrictions, Fox sought more and more to make Christianity a vital social force. Perhaps the best single sermon from which to gain an idea of his position in these later years at South Place is his address in 1842 on the occasion of the twenty-fifth anniversary of his connection with that church. The chief emphasis of the address is upon his reaffirmation of his belief in the duty and virtue of free enquiry, stated in his inaugural sermon of

[41] Garnett, *op. cit.,* p. 177.

1817. The address reveals how far freedom of enquiry had carried him and many of his congregation. He defines Deity, for instance, as "but the loftiest conception of each mind. As high as each soul can get in its notion of the true, the wise, the good, the powerful,—that to each is God. All else is verbiage."[42] Traditional religion which neglects the social and economic needs of men fares ill in Fox's hands:

Strange, indeed, is that system which lives so much in the past that it is almost dead to the present; . . . which dwells earnestly on the fact that when Cyrenius was governor of Syria, Judea was taxed by Augustus Caesar, but holds it almost profanity to allude to the fact of England being taxed by a Pitt or a Peel; which feels the liveliest concern about the massacre of the infants in Bethlehem, but thinks little of the massacre of men perpetrated at Manchester. It is in their application to ourselves and our own principles that the worth of moral principles consists. And in endeavouring to work out this, the Christianity of the present day, it has been my object to have a religion, which, while it shall not be less contemplative and imaginative than when it dwelt in its native towers, or looked upon those rich Eastern plains to the shining stars of that brilliant hemisphere; while it shall be rich in the recollections of earlier times, shall yet bring its treasures to our homes, dwell at our firesides, walk with us in the streets of this our actual London, share in the business of the shop and the mart, note well the proceedings of the Court of Justice and the Senate, find its way to the prison and the poor-house, make its influence felt throughout all the complications of social life, and establish itself, not as an antique conventionalism, but as a sustaining and inspiring principle, in which we live and move and have our being."[43]

More than to summarize Fox's career after 1836 is beyond the scope of our purpose here, which is to give some understanding of the man whose editorship was to transform the *Repository* into an able and advanced secular pe-

[42] Address, as printed in Conway, *Centenary History*, p. 127.
[43] *Ibid.*, pp. 130-31.

riodical of political and social reform. Nor shall we enter here into an exposition of his views on religious, political, and social questions during the years of his editorship of the *Repository,* since they are best to be considered in relation to the views of the able thinkers and writers whom he was to attract to the service of that periodical.

Fox continued in office as the minister of South Place Chapel till 1852, six years after the death of Eliza Flower, but during the last ten years of his ministry, his real work lay elsewhere. Perhaps the most effective period of his preaching fell between the years 1835 and 1840. He continued to deliver series of lectures on ethical and social subjects, some twenty-six of which were collected from reporters' notes and published from time to time as the "Finsbury Lectures." One set, "On Morality as Modified by the Various Classes into which Society is Divided" took up in succession the factors involving the conduct and interests of the poor, the aristocracy, the mercantile and middle classes, and of such professions as the legal, the military, the journalistic, and the clerical. In his definition of morality as the means, or the art, or science of happiness, "that which tends to the production of happiness, the greatest happiness of the greatest number," Fox revealed his Benthamite leanings; he listed Bentham with Socrates and Christ as the great teachers of the utilitarian theory of morality, though the recently dead philosopher was given a lesser place as "an appropriate teacher for the calculators—the continual calculators of modern times, and eminently of this commercial country."[44] These lectures are notable for a sympathetic understanding of the poor, a hearty dislike of an hereditary aristocracy, and a hopeful view of the virtues of the middle classes. "The *history of the Middle Classes* is the history of the advance of *Freedom and Civilization.*" The lectures are permeated with the spirit of moral idealism which was to

[44] *Finsbury Lectures,* Lecture I, p. 4.

affect so much Victorian thought, and, for both good and ill, to affect so many Victorian writers.

The principles of which Fox was the advocate in the *Repository* he continued to maintain as a journalist and politician. As editor of the *True Sun* he helped to increase its circulation by more than sevenfold. When, despite its increased circulation, the paper was killed in 1837, he joined the staff of the *Morning Chronicle*. Here expression of his radical views in politics was more constrained, and for a time he turned to writing dramatic criticism. A friend and warm admirer of the actor Macready, who was then engaged in an attempt to regenerate the moribund English theatre, Fox attacked the theatre monopoly, the low ideals and commercial nature of the popular drama, and praised the efforts of such men as Macready, Talfourd, Bulwer Lytton, Horne, and Sheridan Knowles to create a national drama lofty of aim and embodied in verse. The moralizing bent which years as a preacher could not have failed to give him, made Fox a perhaps over-enthusiastic admirer of the high-flown rhetoric and moralizing of this school of drama, but his genuine love of the stage makes understandable his enthusiasm for a movement which seemed to promise a rescue from the banalities and worse of the nineteenth-century theatre. One result of his friendship with Macready was not without its effect on the poetic drama: Fox's introduction of Robert Browning to Macready led to the poet's writing of *Strafford*.

But it was as an orator that Fox achieved his greatest fame in the decade after 1840. As early as 1840 Cobden entrusted the composition of an Anti-Corn Law League address to Fox as the person most capable of administering "a blister to the aristocracy and the House of Commons."[45] Convinced that the repeal of the Corn Laws was the most pressing of the needed reforms of the "Hungry Forties," he

[45] Garnett, *op. cit.*, pp. 258-59.

became a paid lecturer and writer of the League. As to the power of his wonderful eloquence in this cause there is contemporary testimony: Mongredien, for instance, thus describes his speaking at the first great public meeting of the League on September 28, 1843:

His large brown eyes flashed fire, and his impressive gestures added dignity to his stature. His voice displayed a combination of power and sweetness, not surpassed even by the mellow bass tones of Daniel O'Connell in his prime. His command of language seemed unlimited, for he was never at a loss, not only for a word, but for the right word. Not argumentative and persuasive like Cobden, or natural and forcible as Mr. Bright, his *forte* lay rather in appealing to the emotions of his audience; and in this branch of the oratorical art his power was irresistible.[46]

Though the names of Cobden and Bright are identified with the Free Trade movement, Guizot testifies that Fox's speeches contributed as greatly as theirs to the success of the cause in 1846. In his capacity as a journalist he also rendered valuable aid by a long series of popular and effective "Letters on the Corn Laws," signed "A Norwich Weaver-Boy," in the *League* newspaper.

From 1844 to 1846 Fox devoted his Sunday evenings to delivering popular lectures to large audiences of the working classes in the National Hall in Holburn. (Seventy-six of these were printed between 1845 and 1849.) The lectures included a series on "English Wars: Their Causes, Cost and Consequences," one on political and economic subjects such as the labor movement and the Chartist proposals, and one on ethical and literary topics; a series on "Living Poets," and discourses on "Suicide" and "The Chief End of Human Life." A sincere friend of the working classes, Fox never-

[46] *Ibid.,* p. 262, quoted from Mongredien's *History of the Free Trade Movement,* pp. 98-99. An excellent brief study of Fox's oratory is to be found in Graham Wallas' Conway Memorial Lecture, *William Johnson Fox.*

theless saw more for them to hope for in mass education than in trades unions and organization. Like many reformers of his day he thought popular education the one thing needful to all other reform. His open advocacy of woman suffrage was considerably in advance of his time.

Largely as a result of his public efforts for the repeal of the Corn Laws and of his popularity as a lecturer and orator, Fox came to be considered as an eligible candidate for public office. In 1847 he was elected Member of Parliament for Oldham, and except for two short intervals continued in that office for fifteen years. Entering Parliament at a relatively late age (sixty-one), he did not achieve great distinction there though he was a respected member of the Radical party. Perhaps his most noteworthy action was his introduction in 1850 of a bill for the establishment of compulsory secular education. Twenty years were to pass before anything approaching so far-reaching a change in English education could be adopted; the grip of organized religion upon education was not easily to be broken. For over thirty years Fox unceasingly fought to enlarge the educational opportunities of the working classes, and his wholehearted devotion to that cause is one of his chief distinctions.

In 1862 Fox retired from Parliament because of failing health, and two years later he died. To perpetuate his memory, his friends published an elaborate twelve-volume edition of his writings. The volumes have found few readers, as the uncut pages in library copies will testify. The fame of the journalist, the publicist, the orator, is more often than not short-lived, and Fox is no exception. Most of his writing and speaking was directed toward the accomplishment of reforms now become commonplace, but in their day they demanded vision and courage for their attainment. Not an original or systematic thinker, Fox was nevertheless an effective force as a writer, reformer, and public teacher. An epitaph might well have been devised for him out of his own description of Thomas Belsham, written in 1830: He "had no conception of dangerous truths and useful errors. He spoke as he thought and he wrote as he spoke. He had faith in truth, and left its tendency and influence to Providence."[47]

[47] *Monthly Repository*, N.S., IV (1830), 163.

5: The Second Series: *From 1827 to 1831*

The fear of not being sufficiently stimulant is the curse of English periodical literature,—the reason why, with few exceptions, it is the most vapid and frivolous of the sort in Europe. Those who want stimulants may read (if they can) the New Monthly Magazine, or the last new novel.—But those who wish to give a journal a durable and respectable character, to place it on a footing even with some of those of France, (which we are apt to suppose a land opposed to dulness,) must follow at a humbler distance the sterling value of some of the foreign works of a similar class. Let the Conductors choose their subjects for their real importance, not their accordance with the vanities of the day; and if they are not strong enough to lead in a good cause, at least let them not follow in a bad one by giving way to the frivolous tastes which disgrace both the public and those who cater for it.[1]

SUCH WAS THE gratuitous advice of an anonymous correspondent to the new editors and proprietors of the *Repository* in June, 1827. That it was advice uncalled for—unless, perhaps, as a left-handed endorsement of the policy of the new editors, the Book Committee of the Unitarian Association—even a cursory examination of the first volumes of the second series will reveal. One might almost suspect that some one of the new proprietors had written the anonymous communication to answer complaints of "heaviness." As has already been seen, the former series was never given over to "the vanities of the day" and was scarcely calculated to suit even mildly "frivolous tastes," but in comparison with the first years of the new dispensation it was considerably more interesting to the average reader. The magazine under

[1] *Monthly Repository*, 2d series, I (1827), 405. Unless otherwise indicated all references in this chapter are to the first five years of the second series of the *Monthly Repository* (1827-1831).

Aspland's editorship had been a genuine miscellany, fashioned after eighteenth-century models; the miscellany had by no means been of uniform quality or interest, but it had offered a sufficient variety of materials to gain the attention of lay as well as clerical readers. The new series was better designed for Unitarian ministers and scholars than for the rank and file of members. As a consequence, while it was ably conducted as a serious journal for the discussion of religious, moral, and philosophical topics, it lost (or did not gain) readers; in the five years, 1827-1831, the Unitarian Association sank in it £670. Since this represented over ten per cent of the Association's expenditures of about £5,000 during that period, it can be believed that Fox's offer to purchase the magazine in 1831 met with ready acceptance.

The most radical of the changes made in 1827, for the purpose of raising the *Repository's* literary character and reputation, lay in a shift from the eighteenth-century type of miscellaneous correspondence to something approaching the modern serious magazine, combining original articles with a department of review. This shift may be taken as a recognition of the fact that the day of the old-type miscellany had passed, even though the *Gentleman's Magazine* was to linger on for years as a kind of antiquarian oddity. Henceforth, letters to the editor were to occupy only a small part of the *Repository* instead of making up, as formerly, the major portion of most numbers. The dependence on miscellaneous correspondence had often led to the publication of mere scraps of information and hasty, ill-considered opinions. What was lost in the way of variety by this change was partly compensated for by the opportunity given for longer and fuller discussion of a more limited number of subjects. The periodical was even more narrowly restricted to religion than formerly; scarcely any attention was paid to literature not possessing religious or didactic value.

One alteration in the title gives a clue to a changed emphasis in the new series. The magazine became *The Monthly Repository* and Review *of Theology and General Literature*. The department of review was considerably enlarged, with a view to more adequate coverage of "works not in unison with popular opinions, especially on religious subjects." In their prospectus the new editors announced that they would select for criticism those works "which bear on the great controversies of the day, affecting Biblical knowledge and Religious Liberty, together with others which may appear to possess peculiar interest from the nature of their contents, or the acknowledged talents and celebrity of their authors." In addition to the longer reviews, a number of short critical notices were also included.

Other departments followed the pattern of the first series: obituary, and intelligence, religious, literary, and foreign. The new editors for a time strove to enlarge the amount of foreign news and commentary but soon relapsed into reporting events chiefly of interest to the denomination. The growing importance of the Unitarian movement in the United States found recognition in the attention paid to American religious activities and to Unitarian publications from across the Atlantic.

In format the new series showed improvement. More attention was paid to securing attractive make-up; poetry, for instance, instead of being relegated to a separate department, was now used to fill out incomplete pages. The same page size was kept, but a new and larger type (approximately ten-point) was introduced. A single column page for major articles replaced the double column used for many years. An average of about eight pages was added, the usual total running to seventy-two or eighty a month. The price of one shilling sixpence was continued, despite the increased cost of the improvements. The publication date was changed from the last to the first of the month.

While the *Repository* thus gained in appearance, the more fundamental need of securing new contributors and more interesting articles for lay readers was not met. Few new names appear as contributors to the early volumes of the new series. So far as they are named or can be identified, Unitarian ministers constitute the majority: such men as Robert Aspland, Lant Carpenter, Thomas Rees, John and George Kenrick, John Kentish, John Johns, Hugh Hutton, Jacob Brettell, Samuel Wood, Thomas Madge, W. H. Drummond, Eliezer Cogan, and William Turner, Jr., wrote more or less regularly for the magazine. At least two of the ablest young Unitarian ministers soon added themselves to the list: John Relly Beard and John James Tayler. Among lay contributors who had written for the first series were Emily Taylor, John Bowring, J. T. Rutt, T. F. Barham, George Dyer, James Luckock, and most important of all, Harriet Martineau, who became, as will be seen, the *Repository's* leading writer from 1829 to 1832.

The first number (January, 1827) furnished a reasonably typical example of issues that were to follow. The leading article of nine pages discussed critically the state of the principal religious parties in the Church of England. The Reverend Eliezer Cogan discoursed for three pages "On the Use and Abuse of Analogical Reasoning." An unidentified clerical scholar contributed the first installment of "Observations on the Controversy as to the Original Language of the New Testament." Practical Divinity was represented by "Thoughts on Christian Charity," in which readers were particularly admonished to exercise that virtue towards their ministers. The historical interests of Unitarians were served by the first of a series of brief memoirs of the Socini, probably written by Dr. Thomas Rees. An eight-page survey of the history and existing status of the Corporation and Test Acts completed the section of original contributions. Only two poems appeared in this first number: an "Evening

Hymn" and "The Dissenters' Plea." The latter sought to justify the Nonconformists' desire for

> Freedom of thought, the Christian's dearest claim;
> Freedom to judge, compare—to use the power
> Which Heav'n bestows, and humbly seek for more.[2]

The department of review disclosed a new emphasis upon German theology, for two of the three major reviews dealt with this subject. The third criticized the Reverend S. T. Bloomfield's *Recensio Synoptica Annotationis Sacrae*. Briefer critical notice was accorded to the following: a pamphlet on the inexpendiency of imprisonment for debt; a lexicon of New Testament Greek; pamphlets on the British and Foreign Bible Society; the Reverend John Mitford's *Sacred Specimens;* a Unitarian pamphlet; and a volume of *Rural Lays* by one Mary Ann Plomley. Obituary and Intelligence made up the rest of the eighty-page number.

Except for the addition in 1828 of a department of "Occasional Correspondence" and a column on "Public Affairs" which appeared only briefly, the pattern of the numbers for the succeeding five years differed little from that of this first month of the new series. When Fox became the single responsible editor in August, 1828, he made no appreciable changes so long as the periodical remained the official organ of the Unitarian Association. Not until the *Repository* became his own property did he divest it of its theological character and make it a liberal journal of political and social reform.

RELIGION

It is therefore as a religious periodical that the first five years of the second series must still be considered. But since the theological and religious views of the Unitarians in these years were substantially the same as those which

[2] *Ibid.*, p. 12.

have already been examined in the first series, the discussion here, to avoid repetition, will be confined to the few new trends revealed and to several of the more important young writers.

As has already been shown, Unitarians had been among the earliest in England to welcome scholarly, scientific study of the texts of the Christian faith, and as a consequence they had often availed themselves of the researches of German theologians. Unitarians had few of the prejudices against German rationalists so characteristic of most orthodox English believers. Connop Thirlwall, one of the few students of German theology among the Anglican clergy, wrote as late as 1841: "There is no English theological journal connected with the Church which does not *studiously* keep its readers in the dark as to everything that is said and done in German theology."[3] The orthodox Dissenting journals were even more fearful of the Antichrist with a Teutonic accent.

With these fears the new editors of the *Repository* had little sympathy. It would even seem that they began their work with the intention of championing German theology, since they singled out for review in the first number two significant German works which had been published two years previously. One was the then anonymous translation of Schleiermacher's *Critical Essay on the Gospel of St. Luke,* a bold example of the new higher criticism; and the other, the Reverend Hugh James Rose's *The State of the Protestant Religion in Germany,* a frontal orthodox assault on the rationalist ramparts. Schleiermacher's essay was characterized as "one of the most able and original which has appeared in this department of biblical criticism for a long time," and the anonymous editor and translator was highly complimented.[4]

[3] Quoted in J. C. Thirlwall, *Life of Connop Thirlwall,* p. 29.
[4] I (1827), 47. Such compliments were rare. J. C. Thirlwall (*op. cit.,* p. 33) says that only the *British Critic* gave the work a favorable notice.

The Reverend Mr. Rose, who will be remembered as one of the earliest movers among the Puseyites, fared less well. During the course of a vacation in Germany, Rose had found a cause. He returned to England convinced that practically the whole of German Protestantism had gone over to the Evil One, largely as the result of Theology's surrender to Carnal Reason. His findings and warnings he communicated to the English religious world in four lectures delivered at Cambridge and later published (1825). The *Repository's* review of the lectures was more than a defense of the Germans; it was also a defense of theology as a progressive science. Claiming for the Germans the merit of nearly all that had been done since 1750 for the improvement of Biblical criticism, it readily admitted that certain extremists had gone too far in depriving Christianity of "the essential characters of a Revelation." Though rejecting the anti-supernaturalism of the extremists, the reviewer took Rose severely to task for making no distinctions among those who made Reason the arbiter of Scripture: "We deny that the men who, either in England or in Germany, have led the way in the great change of theological opinion, followed any such principle as the exaltation of their own reason above the authority of Scripture." Such excesses as there have been "are no more than the natural consequence of the ardour with which the study has been pursued there." And better far the German ardor which has brought forth some weeds than the "absolute barrenness, such as the theological literature of the English Church has long exhibited."[5] Rose's book was evidently deemed important, for the *Repository* twice returned to it, printing the answers of two German theologians.[6]

"The singular want of practical, scholar-like theological and biblical learning in England, as compared with the

---

[5] I (1827), 49-51.
[6] By Bretschneider, *Ibid.*, pp. 831-36; and Sack, II (1828), 522-30.

continental school,"[7] was a theme to which the second series frequently reverted. The reviewer of an English edition of Schleusner's *Lexicon* of New Testament Greek raised a pertinent question: Why had there been such a host of valuable and learned works on the Continent, "perfectly impartial on, indeed carefully avoiding, all dogmatic questions, . . . zealously probing to the bottom every point of interest without stopping to inquire its bearing on the prepossessions or systems of anyone," while in England "almost *every* thing that appears owes its very origin to controversial feelings," and is unmistakably branded with sectarianism?[8]

One answer was to be found in the "extraordinary appetite" in England for proselytizing and doctrinal discussion. But the real answer, the reviewer charged, lay in the exclusive appropriation by the Established Church of almost the only agencies for imparting any profound theological or classical training. With the universities under Anglican control, the Dissenting scholar was without standing in both society and literature. "The exclusive circle of rank, preferment, or even of education which that circle labours to maintain to be the only one for a gentleman moving in any sphere, is for ever shut against him who moves out of the orbit which well-defined orthodoxy has traced out." As a result, despotism of opinion reigns within the Establishment, and party polemics among the Dissenters. Fearing ostracism, English scholars shun the cultivation of theological or biblical learning, and instead bestow their labors on the safe ground of Greek drama. "In short, where there is no catholic education, it is hardly to be wondered at that catholicism should form no feature of our theological literature."[9]

In Germany things were different, as several writers pointed out. "In Germany a university is a school for all, without distinction of creed, and all studies which are of

[7] I (1827), 62.
[8] *Ibid.*   [9] *Ibid.*

a general kind are carried on in common," wrote the translator of a discourse on the mythical interpretation of the
Bible by the German Catholic, Jahn.[10] Such an educational
system had had a beneficial effect even among the Catholic
theologians of Germany, whereas English Catholics, excluded from the nation's universities, had been restricted to
the narrowing discipline of their own seminaries. John Bowring in 1828 contrasted the "indefatigable ardour, the varied
learning, the critical sagacity" of German theologians to the
disgrace of "the slumbering dulness" of the English. A re-
nowned orthodox German professor had told Bowring:
"You boast of your *civil* liberty, but must come thither to
learn what *intellectual* liberty is. Your politicians may have
freedom of spirit, but your theologians have no freedom of
mind." Bowring gave the usual Unitarian reason for the
dearth of English theological learning: "How should the
worshippers of creeds and of authority have freedom? How
should the advocates of an establishment built up by tyranny
out of the wrecks of·ignorance, *dare* research?"[11]

Though occasionally the *Repository* offered a translation
of some piece of German research, as in the article by Jahn
cited above, more often the notice of German works took
the form of reviews and critical introductory articles: for
example, a review of a German theological journal,[12] Harriet Martineau's discussion of Lessing's *Education of the
Human Race*,[13] and J. J. Tayler's account of the "Life and
Writings of Herder."[14] In 1830 and 1831 Dr. John Morell
contributed from Heidelberg a series of interesting letters
on the state of theological opinion and religious liberty in
Germany.[15]

In contrast with its general tone of admiration for the

[10] *Ibid.*, p. 634.
[11] II (1828), 150.   [12] III (1829), 50.
[13] IV (1830), 300-6, 367-73, 453-58, 511-17.
[14] *Ibid.*, pp. 729-38, 829-43.
[15] *Ibid.*, pp. 545-48, 585-89, 808-14; V (1831), 30-34, etc.

state of religion in Germany, the *Repository's* attitude towards France was hopeful but slightly condescending. France was still too much under the dominion of the antipodal spheres of Catholicism and scepticism to produce much liberal theology, but every stirring of liberal Protestantism and every symptom favorable to religious freedom were noted with satisfaction. A writer in 1827 remarked: "At present there appears to be little medium between the abandonment of all religion or the adoption of some of its worst forms; the bitter fruits of a revolution founded on the renunciation of all religious principle, are and must long be felt and lamented by the best friends of constitutional liberty."[16] Orthodox French Protestantism seemed little likely to win over either the sceptics or the Catholics. Both Lant Carpenter and Robert Aspland, after surveying the situation at first hand, wrote articles suggesting that Unitarianism presented the only practicable solution.[17] In the establishment of a French Society of Christian Morality the *Repository* found with approval full recognition of "what Mankind ever have been and still are very slow to realize, that Christianity is a great moral system; . . . and that its doctrines are of little value separate from the moral ends which are made the test of their importance."[18] W. J. Fox, rejoicing in the triumph of religious as well as political freedom in the French Revolution of 1830, predicted: "The convulsions which have shaken down the props by which a superstitious and ceremonial system was supported . . . , must also cause the pillars of infidelity and scepticism to totter."[19]

Fox, like Thomas Carlyle and John Stuart Mill, was tremendously attracted to the "New Christianity" of the Saint Simonians, who sought to substitute in place of the medieval church's control of society a new religion of hu-

[16] I (1827), 306.   [17] III (1829), 666-68, 777-80.
[18] I (1827), 837.   [19] IV (1830), 624.

manity, the high priests of which should be the men of science. St. Simonianism projected a kind of religious technocracy in which the industrialist state was to be managed by scientists chosen for their ability to organize and administer production. The cause of the poor was to become a Holy Crusade for the new faith. Society must be organized in the best way possible to attain the amelioration of the moral, physical, and intellectual condition of the most numerous and poorest class—"in this, and this alone, consists the divinity of the Christian religion."[20] The humanitarian aims of this new faith were sure to attract many Unitarians and especially Fox, who was at the time urging the expansion of missionary work among the poor.

John Fisher, a member of Fox's congregation, supplied three articles in 1831 on the St. Simonians. The first recounted the life of the founder of the new sect and outlined the background of the movement.[21] Fisher gave qualified but generous approval. Though there were "some crude ideas and untenable positions," and though too few concessions had been made to the doctrines of historic Christianity, St. Simonianism was on the whole, Fisher declared, "a vast improvement on the mummeries of Catholicism, on the chilling, selfish spirit of nominal Deism and practical Atheism, and on the thirst for military glory. . . ."[22] His second article presented a translation of the *Revue Encyclopédique's* analysis of the new religion.[23] In the third, a review, Fisher maintained his belief that "nothing has occurred since the Reformation in which the interests of Christianity, that is, of humanity, have been so deeply involved as in the development of this new doctrine." Dissent as Unitarian Christians must from the St. Simonians' opinions of the Deity and of the scope of Christianity, that was not a sufficient reason to reject their whole system. "True Christians and

[20] V (1831), 85.   [21] *Ibid.*, pp. 83-88.
[22] *Ibid.*, p. 88.   [23] *Ibid.*, pp. 181-89.

true St. Simonites are own brothers, separated by the present conditions of their being, but destined to meet, with
an acknowledgment of kindred on their lips."[24]

Fox in his remarks revealed a similar sympathy. In his
series of dialogues entitled "The Conversations of Ebion
Adamson and his Friends," he (as Adamson) conceded that
the Simonians' theology was "a very crude affair"—an "extempore theology" unworthy of the French intellect, though
excusable in view of the need in France of some kind of
rational religion. But if the St. Simonians' theology was
deficient, not so their social gospel. "Their views of history,
the ways in which they trace the orderly progress of the
human race, are, however, a noble commentary on the
truth of a Providence; and their social objects seem to me
to be all one great application of the Christian principle of
man's fraternity."[25] Fox, ever concerned for the poor and
always critical of a privileged aristocracy, welcomed the
vision of a society in which every man should be placed
according to his capacity and rewarded according to his
works, in which none should be idle, none privileged by
birth, but all should be employed in increasing the common
good. If this social gospel was heresy, it was "the heresy of
Jesus of Nazareth."[26]

Fox's sympathies for the poor and his increasing interest
in political and social reform did not find their fullest expression in the *Repository* so long as it remained essentially
a religious magazine, but he was increasingly critical of the
Unitarians' failure to turn from doctrinal disputes to a practical application of their religion. There is noticeably less
emphasis upon scriptural criticism, for instance, in the later of the five volumes under consideration. Speaking in the
transparent guise of "Ebion Adamson" in 1831, he said:

[24] *Ibid.*, pp. 279-81.
[25] *Ibid.*, p. 194.   [26] *Ibid.*, p. 482.

Let criticism do its work, and a very needful and useful work it is; but there is much more to be done. We must advance from interpretation to application; from studying the letter of the word to imbibing its spirit; and that spirit must be made to bear upon the peculiar circumstances of the times and country in which we live.[27]

To those who objected that this would involve plunging religion into politics, Fox replied that politics, properly speaking, is a branch of morals and therefore must be a concern of religion. "Now-a-days, it is chiefly in politics that we must do, or violate, our duty to our neighbour. If Christianity does not apply to these circumstances, it is an obsolete religion, and we had better look out for a new one."[28]

In seeking to divert Unitarian energies from the barren mazes of doctrinal controversy into the paths of social usefulness, Fox was seeking not to make of Unitarianism a new religion but rather to have it fulfill what he regarded as its destiny. In his commemorative analysis of the work of Thomas Belsham, a few months after the death in November, 1829, of that redoubted champion, Fox named Priestley, Belsham, and the American, William Ellery Channing, as the embodiment of the three distinct stages of modern Unitarianism. Priestley, in this view, represented the first epoch of tentative speculation, of unbounded inquiry, of the "loosening of the foundations of ancient doctrine." There followed a period in which the dominant need was for selection, definition, and systematic controversy: "To Dr. Priestley, the universal inquirer, succeeds Mr. Belsham, the consistent controversialist."[29] Though this second, controversial stage had been a necessary and beneficial one, danger lay in considering it as anything more than a transitional period. To complete the work of religious reformation,

[27] *Ibid.*, p. 193.
[28] *Ibid.*, p. 194.   [29] IV (1830), 250.

there must be a third process, a development of the moral beauty, power, and tendencies, of the truth which had been sought so actively, and championed so ably. . . . This is the end which crowns the work. Doctrines now begin to be contemplated in their proper light, and to do their proper duty. They present themselves to the mind, not as hard propositions, but as living principles.[30]

It was this stage which Fox believed that Channing represented. Neither so original and versatile as Priestley, nor so intellectually sturdy as Belsham, Channing had a "stronger sense than either of the grand and beautiful," his powers were better fitted to the excitement of religious feeling and imagination, and to the extension of the "dominion of pure religion from the head to the heart."[31] Religion can not subsist upon reason alone or upon endless doctrinal controversy; it must kindle the imagination and quicken the heart; its principles must be applied to the elevation of human character and the improvement of human society.

In at least one young contributor to the *Repository* Fox found an able supporter of his views on the deficiencies and needs of Unitarianism. This was the Reverend John Relly Beard (1800-1876), then a recent graduate of Manchester College, York, and a Unitarian minister at Salford. He was to become influential in the denomination as the writer and translator of nearly forty volumes, as an editor of the *Christian Teacher,* the *Foreign Quarterly Review,* and the *Unitarian Herald,* and as the founder and first principal of the Unitarian Home Missionary College (now Unitarian College).[32] Beard in 1829 and 1830 contributed to the *Repository,* among other articles and reviews, a series of fifteen long papers in "illustration of the religious spirit of the age," under the general title of "The Watchman." Written in a vigorous style, replete with examples of the religious

---

[30] *Ibid.,* p. 251.   [31] *Ibid.*
[32] See McLachlan, *Records of a Family.*

extravagances of the day, and unsparing of criticism of his own denomination when occasion warranted, Beard's "Watchman" papers are today among the most interesting in these years of the magazine.

While the "Watchman" was ever on the lookout for instances of orthodox bigotry, he did not overlook Unitarian faults. His main complaint was that their faith was still too exclusively intellectual. "Our periodicals contain excellent nutriment for the mind, almost none for the heart." In the pulpit also, "intellect, instead of religious earnestness, too much predominates." Unitarian missionaries have worked "to demolish rather than to erect." Unitarian doctrine had been too negative. Intellectualism kept religious zeal at a low temperature, and the tendency to extreme individualism produced indifference to coöperative effort. The wealthy and better educated had neglected to exert themselves in spreading enlightened views of religion among the less fortunate classes.[33] In sum, "Unitarians, however far they are advanced beyond their fellow-Christians in the principles of their creed, are behind them, and the times in which they live, in activity and energy."[34]

The time was at hand, Beard believed, for Unitarians to exert themselves if their faith was not to perish. They had made some gains: there was a slight diminution in orthodox bitterness towards them; they were no longer subject to penal laws for the avowal of their beliefs; the repeal of the Test Act had raised them and all Dissenters to a "less unequal enjoyment" of rights and privileges; society seemed more disposed to inquiry and reform.[35] Impediments had been removed at the cost of long and bitter struggle; now the positive elements of Unitarianism must be made manifest to the world. Unitarians must show, said Fox, "what we can achieve through the Novum Organum which our

[33] III (1829), 699-704.
[34] Ibid., p. 846.   [35] Ibid., p. 856.

Priestleys and our Belshams had the honour of presenting to the world."[36]

Aside from their triumph, in company with all Dissenters, in the repeal of the Test Act, Unitarians at this time showed more rapid gains outside England than at home. In Ireland a bitter doctrinal dispute within the Presbyterian church led to the establishment of a Remonstrant Synod, largely of Arian rather than Humanitarian complexion. Many pages of the *Repository's* Intelligence were devoted to the progress of this schism in Ireland, and Harriet Martineau was moved to poetize the Irish ministers' stand for conscience in her "Address to the Avowed Arians of the Synod of Ulster."[37]

The other source of encouragement was the progress of the Unitarian movement in America. Reports of the meetings of the American Association appeared regularly in the *Repository*, and an increasing number of American sermons, tracts, and periodicals were reviewed. Channing, of course, was the American most frequently noticed, but Henry Ware, F. W. P. Greenwood, Orville Dewey, and others were not overlooked. The increasing popularity in England of published sermons by American Unitarians one reviewer attributed to their "eminently practical character" and to their direct appeal "to human feelings and the strength of human reasoning."[38] Channing's sermons were so popular that of one, preached in Boston on May 21, 1828, the *Repository* reported in October that three American editions had arrived in England and four reprints had been issued by English and Scottish publishers.[39] It was confessed that no English preacher could surpass him. Emily Taylor wrote: "He has kindled up more of true ardour, more of virtuous and independent feeling, among us, than all our critical scholars put together; and the reason is evident. *They* have

---

[36] V (1831), 664.
[38] *Ibid.*, p. 562.
[37] II (1828), 79-80.
[39] *Ibid.*, p. 657.

laboured successfully to pull down; *he* is endeavouring to build up from a better foundation."[40]

At home, the *Repository* continued to maintain "the dissidence of dissent" and to promote every movement for the enlargement of religious freedom. For Deists and unbelievers it continued to recommend complete toleration; it attacked a movement to void the competency of Deists as witnesses in legal proceedings,[41] and characterized as "disgraceful" the prosecution and imprisonment in 1827 of the Reverend Robert Taylor, an Anglican clergyman turned Deist.[42] It hailed the repeal of the Test Act with rejoicing, but, unlike many orthodox periodicals, it did not rest content until in 1829 the Catholics were also freed of legal disabilities. Granted that the sentiments of Catholics and Protestants might differ as widely as the poles, that still made no difference: "It is the broad principle of religious freedom that we, and all other classes of Dissenters, ought to contend for; the giving to every man the enjoyment of his opinions without let or hindrance."[43]

Anglican opposition to Catholic Emancipation was traced to fear of disestablishment of the Irish Church, that rich preserve maintained at the expense of a population overwhelmingly Catholic. This establishment the *Repository* described as "that most monstrous and scandalous anomaly in the history of political and ecclesiastical misgovernment."[44] The real dread of Emancipation was due to "an apprehension that, sooner or later, if things once begin to mend, the standing monument of iniquity and injustice which the Church of Ireland presents, must have its abase-

[40] IV (1830), 119. Only one of Channing's discourses, his bitter attack on Napoleon, aroused protest in the *Repository;* this was somewhat critically reviewed (II [1828], 340-41), and one correspondent strenuously attacked the American (III [1829], 200-5, 435-36). Another correspondent defended Channing (*ibid.,* 339-42, 503-4).

[41] I (1827), 77-79.

[42] *Ibid.,* p. 930; II (1828), 214.

[43] III (1829), 223.

[44] I (1827), 219.

ment."[45] One correspondent outlined a sweeping program
of reform for Ireland, including the abolition of all religious
distinctions in civil affairs, a reorganization of the administration of justice, the placing of Irish representation on the
same footing as the English, the commutation of tithes, and,
if the principle of public support of *any* religious worship
was to be maintained, provision for the decent support of
Catholic worship.[46] Adoption of such a program of reform
would have done much to meet the Irish problem, religious
and political, but the emancipation of Negro slaves in far-off
colonies and the conversion of the heathen in the Antipodes
long continued to be a matter of more concern to the majority of both Anglicans and Dissenters.

The evils of the Irish Establishment constituted but one
item in the Unitarians' bill of particulars against the English
Church. The fight continued against the principle of establishment itself.[47] Simoniacal practices were held up to scorn,
sometimes with evidence secured from the daily papers.
Such an advertisement as the following made a telling point
for the *Repository's* case:

To be sold, the next presentation to a vicarage, in one of the
midland counties, and in the immediate neighbourhood of one
or two of the first packs of fox-hounds in the kingdom. The
present annual income about 580 £, subject to curate's salary. The
incumbent is in his 6oth year.[48]

In a review of a pamphlet on "The State of the Curates of
the Church of England," J. R. Beard declared: "The history
of Church Property is a history of fraud. Its acquisition, in
almost nine cases out of every ten, has been effected in opposition both to the laws of man and the laws of God."[49]
Tithes, once free-will offerings, had been converted from

[45] III (1829), 106.   [46] *Ibid.*, pp. 4-6.
[47] See "On the Spirit and Tendency of Religious Establishments," II (1828),
12-20.
[48] Quoted, V (1831), 523.   [49] III (1829), 232.

custom into right. The wealth of the Church, with a gross annual income variously estimated at from four to nine and a half million pounds, was expended upon the perpetuation of an aristocratic hierarchy, while the working clergy, the curates, received barely enough to live.[50] But the day of reformation must come. "Public nuisances will be, if not removed, yet ere long abated, and among the greatest is the Church Establishment."[51] It was the creature of the legislature; it was a "Parliamentary Church" and by Parliament it could and must be reformed. Among the Dissenters the conviction grew in these years that reform in Church and reform in Parliament were inextricably linked.[52]

But while the *Repository* centered its biggest guns on the Establishment, it did not neglect to fire on intemperance, irrationality, and intolerance wherever they appeared on the religious front. Beard, as "The Watchman," assumed special charge of this sector of the Unitarian defense for the years 1829-1830. Chief among the enemies to rational religion that he singled out for attack were orthodox bigotry as revealed in sermons and periodicals, extravagantly enthusiastic practices among the more evangelical sects, revivals, special providences, millenarianism, and the extremes of Methodism. Though he criticized his fellow Unitarians for lack of zeal and for too great intellectualism, he warned the more zealous sects that they must not forget that religion "must affect the head as well as the heart."[53] In the waves of revivalism in the United States there had been "shameful extravagances" against which England must be warned. Among the revivalists "religion, instead of being regarded as the general habit of the mind, is a paroxysm."[54]

Though Evangelical religionists in England had not gone so far as some of the Americans, they were still to be

[50] V (1831), 303.   [51] IV (1830), 697.
[52] See Fox's review of *The Church Establishment Founded in Error*, V (1831), 517-26.
[53] III (1829), 185.   [54] *Ibid.*, p. 563.

criticized for intolerance and their overweening assurance
that the hand of God was upon all that they did. The orthodox periodicals still regaled and terrified their readers with
horrible examples of the sad effects of Unitarianism. Said
Beard:

Therein are tales innumerable, rivalling in number and merit
even the treasury of the Minerva press; tales for the old and
tales for the young; tales for the wise and tales for the foolish;
but above all, a plentiful collection entitled, "Tales of Horror,
or Death-bed Scenes, illustrative of the Effects of Socinianism;
humbly dedicated to the old Ladies of the Three United Kingdoms."[55]

Even more serious than some of this rather preposterous
bigotry was the widespread orthodox belief in supernatural
and extraordinary influence:

The age of miracles has appeared again. . . . Every puny institution, every little sect lays claim to the special aid and blessing of God. If the funds of a missionary society are increased,
the Lord has opened the hearts of the pious. If a minister at-
tracts an unusually large audience, God unseals his lips and
carries home his words to the heart.[56]

Methodists and Irving millenarians were not alone guilty
of such presumption; it was "woven into the very texture
of the religious community."[57] It was the "capital error"
of the religious world, for it encouraged the pretensions of
priestcraft, deluded the simple and ignorant, and debased
reason itself. No wonder that one of the Calvinistic spokes-
men for this kind of religion, the *Spiritual Magazine*
(which, as Beard noted, still carried as its motto the by now
admittedly spurious text, I John v:7) could declare: " 'The
march of intellect is the march of infidelity; and religious
liberalism the compromising of truth.' "[58]

[55] *Ibid.*, p. 272.
[57] *Ibid.*, p. 38.
[56] IV (1830), 37.
[58] Quoted, *ibid.*, p. 42.

Beard in his plea for a balance between the intellectual and emotional sides of religion may not have represented the views of all Unitarians of his day, but he approximated the position of many modern religious liberals:

Religion may be contemplated under two aspects, the moral and the intellectual. In the one it consists of something to be felt and done; in the other, something to be understood and believed. The one respects the head, the other the heart of man; the one is valuable in itself, the other chiefly as it leads to the first. The perfect Christian is he in whom both parts of religion are maintained in due proportion, and in vigorous activity. He thinks before he believes, he believes before he feels, he feels before he acts. But thinking, believing, feeling, and acting, are, with him, parts of one whole—links in one chain, connected, blended, and harmonized together, so as to make "the man of God."[59]

SOCIAL AND POLITICAL CRITICISM

It remains to speak briefly of some of the more temporal concerns of the *Repository* during the five-year period under consideration—briefly, because the periodical seldom ventured into fields not in some way connected with religion. The magazine in these years does not give so good a picture of liberal thought in more secular fields as does the first series. The abandonment of miscellaneous correspondence had produced more effective literary expression, but it had narrowed the range of subjects. Specialization had won out. The *Repository* was now a religious periodical; it was to become a magazine of advanced political and social criticism, almost to the exclusion of religion.

In its limited discussion of education during these years, the magazine devoted more attention to methods than to England's need of mass secular instruction. One reviewer endorsed a system of national education for Ireland,[60] and

[59] III (1829), 696-97.   [60] *Ibid.*, pp. 240-44.

Beard attacked the *Quarterly Review* for gravely maintaining that "education and reading have been pushed too far among the lower classes,"[61] but no thorough treatment of the subject was presented. Reforms of Church and of State were then matters of greater public concern. There was discussion, however, of the content of education, particularly in its higher branches. The writer of an essay entitled "Thoughts on Education"[62] revealed middle-class sympathies for a more practical curriculum than the traditional classical program. Conceding the value of Latin and Greek, the writer nevertheless called for a wider range of study. Most young men outside the higher ranks had not the time to acquire mastery of the classics along with other needful subjects. Teach the youth whose time is limited, therefore, "not Greek and Latin, but mathematics, chemistry, mechanics, and history; the philosophy of mind, the evidences of religion, the principles of the British constitution, and the objects, the nature, and the duties of civil government." Parents should resign for their children "the visionary idea of a *classical* for the invaluable attainment of a *general* education."[63] The same writer recommended lighter teaching loads, discussed the need of sound elementary treatises on the German model, and attacked the lecture system as a method of instruction.

The *Repository* was not asleep to the progress being made on the Continent in education. Occasionally there was discussion of the work of such reformers as Pestalozzi and Jacotot.[64] We have already noted its admiration for the German universities in contrast with the Church-ridden Oxford and Cambridge. The new London University was heartily endorsed, particularly for the advantages it offered to the large body of middle-class Dissenters. The writer of

[61] *Ibid.*, p. 388.
[62] *Ibid.*, pp. 44-48.   [63] *Ibid.*, p. 45.
[64] II (1828), 43-48; V (1831), 256-67.

an article on "Scientific Education and the University of London"[65] contrasted to England's shame her neglect of higher education as compared with its cultivation in practically every other civilized country. The writer especially blamed the Dissenters for their failure to establish adequate educational facilities; the Church at least professed to teach the higher branches. Most of the article was devoted to a discussion of the utility of higher education for those destined for middle-class occupations. A later article defended the new university's emphasis upon the sciences at the expense of the formal study of religion.[66] In sum, it may be said that the Unitarians advocated the secularizing and broadening of public education, with emphasis upon utilitarian rather than cultural subjects.

On political and social questions, except as they bore upon religion, the second series in its first five years had little to say. In January, 1828, appeared a brief column on "Public Affairs," somewhat on the order of Frend's "Christian's Survey" in the earlier series, but the column continued for only four months. In 1830-1831, under Fox, there was a slight increase in political discussion, but not nearly so much as one might expect, especially in view of the editor's pronounced political interests.

An unsigned article "On the Reign of George the Fourth,"[67] written by Fox soon after the death of the King in June, 1830, is interesting for its recountal of what a firm disciple of progress regarded as the improvements of the preceding decade. Fox confessed no admiration for the character of George IV but thought that, altogether, his reign had been propitious. Abroad, there had been triumphs for freedom, particularly in South America and Greece. There had been years of peace and a pacific policy, despite the errors, "we had almost said baseness," of British foreign policy.

[65] I (1827), 161-71.
[66] II (1828), 771-77.   [67] IV (1830), 505-11.

There had been welcome intellectual improvement among the people. The London University was a pledge of progress; even Oxford had done "homage to the spirit of the age and the principle of utility" by the establishment of a professorship of political economy. Popular education had been forwarded by "the lightness, the rapidity, the constant succession, the multiplicity, the cheapness of modern literature." Never before had there been such tremendous exertions for philanthropic objects. The science of government had advanced: witness the amelioration of the criminal code, the abolition of various restraints upon commerce, the progress towards a better system of taxation, the repeal of the Test Act, and the emancipation of Catholics. After such a retrospect, a disciple of progress might well be privileged to look forward with hope. On another occasion Fox remarked: "The reign of George the Third will always darken our annals; and they will always be brightened by that of George the Fourth."[68]

The *Repository's* avoidance of political controversy during these years may be gauged by the fact that so little discussion of the Reform Bill appeared in its columns. This was not because of lukewarmness. In April, 1831, Fox in a brief editorial maintained that the bill had united the nation; he urged the ministers to stand firm against those who would perpetuate corruption.[69] In June, after the elections had returned a majority for Reform, he prematurely anticipated success for the cause: ". . . the hopes of the nation can only be disappointed by the foulest treachery, can only be deferred by the most reckless infatuation. We apprehend neither the one or the other. The Bill is carried."[70] Unfortunately, the event proved that there could be both treachery and infatuation; a whole year was to elapse before the measure could be forced down the throats of the Lords

[68] V (1831), 728.
[69] *Ibid.*, p. 284.   [70] *Ibid.*, p. 431.

and Bishops. In November appeared the only article of any length of the subject.[71] By now less optimistic of the immediate adoption of the bill, Fox was bitter against the peers. If they could continue to thwart the will of the nation, a popularly elected House would be valueless. What hope could there be of reforming the temporalities of the Church, promoting the diffusion of political knowledge among the masses, or breaking up the Corn monopoly? The creation of new peers seemed the only answer, though it was "too late to dream of saving the order from degradation,"—and as for the phalanx of bishops against the bill, they had "sinned past political redemption."[72]

Thus it can be seen that there was no question where lay the political sympathies of the *Repository* and its editor. It was still primarily a religious magazine, however, and politics was but occasionally a topic for its columns.

LITERATURE AND CRITICISM

For its deficiencies on the score of literary criticism the *Repository* in November, 1829, made its own apology, at the same time promising a degree of reformation. Announcing the establishment of a new department of criticism, a "Monthly Report of General Literature," the reviewer remarked: "It has long been felt as a defect in the *Monthly Repository* that its notice of the current literature of the day is irregular, imperfect, and disproportionate." The amount of space devoted to reviews had varied unreasonably; at times inferior works had been noticed at length and important ones ignored; there had been little consistency either in selecting or reviewing, largely because of dependence upon voluntary contributions. Henceforth, through a new arrangement, it was hoped to remedy this situation. No promise could be made of elaborate criticism: "The

[71] "On the Present State of the Reform Question," V (1831), 775-79.
[72] *Ibid.*, p. 778.

promotion of a pure Theology and an enlightened Philanthropy must ever be paramount, with us, to the claims of mere Literature on our attention." But within its limits the magazine would henceforth supply brief critical notices of current general works. "The prevailing character, tone, and tendency of the Literature of the day, cannot but deeply interest us as friends of religion and morality. To observe, examine, and report upon it, with this peculiar reference, does, indeed, seem to be imperatively required of us."[73]

Prior to this time the reviews had been almost exclusively of works with at least a bearing upon religion: sermons, tracts, doctrinal and exegetical works, some history, a very few travel books, and a fair amount of religious and didactic verse. The closest approach to the novel was made in a review of Moore's *Epicurean,* which was criticized from the point of view of religion.[74] Only one class of popular books received attention—the omnipresent annuals, crammed with ornate engravings and the effusions of poets, near-poets, and poetasters. The innumerable *Gems, Keepsakes,* and *Forget-me-nots* were then and for years afterwards tremendously popular. The *Repository* in 1828 quoted an estimate of 100,000 copies for the current season, to be sold at a price above £70,000.[75] It hailed them as "at once a gratification and an encouragement to the taste of the British public,"[76] thus revealing no great critical profundity. Undoubtedly, however, the annuals, despite their sentimentality and ornate prettiness, did represent an improvement, as the *Repository* thought, over previous literary Christmas presents— "miserable stories for masters and misses with coarse wood-

---

[73] III (1829), 790. It has not been possible to identify with certainty the writer of this new department, but there is a tone throughout not unlike that of a Miss Harriet Martineau. As will be seen later, Fox, learning of the failure of the Martineau family fortunes, had sent Miss Harriet £15 and a parcel of books for review. This probably was the "new arrangement."

[74] I (1827), 901-09.

[75] II (1828), 728.   [76] I (1827), 918.

cuts" for the lower classes, and the extremes of Joe Miller or Methodistic piety for the upper classes: " 'A Grey Cap for Young Heads,' with a print of the laughing philosopher, or 'The Young Man's Monitor,' with a death's head for a frontispiece."[77]

Of contemporary poets, Mrs. Felicia Hemans was declared to be "the first in the roll of the annuals,"[78] and her other work was usually praised. On the more elevated ground of devotional poetry, however, she yielded the palm to Mrs. Barbauld.[79] Fox wrote in 1830: "Mrs. Hemans is the laureate of hearths and homes. . . . Songs of the Affections are what she should indite; songs of the senses would not beseem a lady, and we have enough of them from Moore, though he is a little better now; and she may leave the passions to Byron, the intellect to Wordsworth, and the soul to Coleridge." Fox nevertheless confessed that he had "sometimes thought that her writings were sickly, oftener that they were feeble, and almost continually . . . had been annoyed by their verbiage."[80]

Of the old poets none received more than occasional mention except Milton; he was frequently quoted in connections involving religious freedom. The Reverend Jacob Brettell, a minor Unitarian poet, in 1830 contributed a kind of autobiography of Milton, compiled from selections of the prose works.[81] Brettell was also the contributor of two short critical articles, one on Moore's poetry and one on Byron's. Neither is of much significance, but they represent the whole of the *Repository's* criticism of poetry in these years, except for brief notices. Both Moore and Byron might be thought a strange choice for a religious magazine. But Moore, once too much enslaved by his senses, had become "gradually emancipated from their debasing thraldom," and the "elegance and sweetness of his later songs"

---

[77] *Ibid.*   [78] *Ibid.*

[79] II (1828), 332.   [80] IV (1830), 631.

[81] "Anecdotes of Milton, Descriptive of his Feelings and Conduct, Related by Himself," IV (1830), 673-90.

had in part atoned for the days when his muse had been less chaste.[82] And Byron, to Brettell, was the greatest poet of his time, even though "moral gloom" was the most striking characteristic of his poetry. "Enthroned amidst the dark clouds of scepticism, this mighty, but evil, genius throws forth the illumination of his talent, like lightning in the storm, only upon mournful and distressing objects." His talent must be admired, though not the tendencies and influences of his work; one salutary moral antidote might be deduced from it, however—"the wretchedness of guilt and the miseries of scepticism."[83]

J. R. Beard in a review of Kennedy's *Conversations on Religion with Lord Byron*[84] came to the conclusion that the poet's temperament "was one fitted by nature to be eminently devout; and had it not been so perverted by Calvinism in his childhood, and by scepticism in his youth; had he possessed the advantage of a judicious and enlightened Christian for a guide . . . he would, we are assured, have been as eminent for his piety as he is for his poesy."[85] One wonders. Beard, to judge from his dwelling upon Byron's inability to comprehend the Trinity and the doctrine of eternal punishment, evidently thought that a good Unitarian could have been made of the poet. After all, Byron had read and liked Dr. Southwood Smith's *Illustrations of the Divine Government*.

As a partial extenuation of the *Repository's* failure to select much enduring poetry for notice, it may be recalled that these were years of a kind of poetic interregnum. The younger Romantics, Byron, Shelley, and Keats, were dead; the older, Wordsworth, Coleridge, and Southey, had survived their genius; and the new generation of Tennyson and Browning was yet to be recognized. In the meanwhile, Mrs. Hemans, Letitia Landon, and the two Montgomerys, James and Robert, held the stage. Since the work of the latter

---

[82] I (1827), 648-49.
[83] *Ibid.*, pp. 868-69.
[84] IV (1830), 605-13.
[85] *Ibid.*, p. 609.

two bore a religious character, they were briefly reviewed in the *Repository*. James Montgomery's *Pelican Island* was favorably presented,[86] but Robert Montgomery's *Satan* fared only a little better than at the hands of Macaulay.[87] The magazine did not carry its animus against the Church over into its criticism of Anglican religious poets. Bishop Heber's hymns were given only qualified approval because of their ornateness of style, occasionally jingling meters, and inaccurate prosody;[88] but Keble's *Christian Year,* despite its churchmanship, was praised for its "tone of sincerity and deep devotion."[89] Aside from these that have been mentioned, however, and the work of a few Unitarian poets, little attention was otherwise paid even to religious verse. One finds it hard to account for the mediocre quality of the *Repository's* criticism in these years, especially since, as will be seen, Fox was so soon to reveal himself as a critic of discernment and taste.

The magazine's original poetry during this period was neither good nor bad enough to warrant much comment— competent, respectable, are perhaps the best adjectives for it. Predominately religious verse, it reached an average of performance somewhat better than that of the first series. In keeping with Unitarian sentiments, it never rose to the mystical heights of the greatest religious verse, but neither did it sink to the level of many Evangelical effusions. The prevailing note is one of calm, reasoned faith, scarcely productive of emotional ecstasies. Translations were less frequent than in the earlier series: of German poetry Bowring supplied a piece by Novalis, and Harriet Martineau, one from Schiller; the French were represented by three translations from Lamartine; the Italian by two sonnets; and the Dutch and Hungarian by several from the pen of Bowring. Occasional and commemorative verse was also less frequently represented.

[86] II (1828), 394-97.
[88] I (1827), 681-83.
[87] IV (1830), 193-94.
[89] III (1830), 822-26.

Bowring continued to supply hymns. The Reverend John Johns, later a missionary in the slums of Liverpool, had a genuine poetic talent, but his work was uneven and marred at times by over-evident striving for effect. More versatile than most of the clerical poets, he essayed both religious and nature poetry, and versified historical and religious tales. His lines "On the Character of Napoleon Bonaparte" betray the English liberals' admiration and half-liking for the great conqueror but also their detestation of his tyranny.

> The rights of man—what were they but as dust,
> Strown in the path the aspiring soldier trod?
> The laws of Heaven—how faint in *them* thy trust!
> Power was thy Paradise, and Fate thy God.

And the concluding stanza:

> Hail and farewell! Thy glory was a curse—
> But who can curse the glorious—Chains, blood, tears,
> All were aton'd for in thy deep reverse,
> And the grave's bay no breath of lightning sears.[90]

The Reverend Hugh Hutton of Birmingham supplied hymns and paraphrases of Scripture. Emily Taylor, a writer of historical tales and sketches for children, contributed, in addition to verse, reviews and short prose pieces on religious subjects such as "Conscientious Deism" and "On Love to God." The sister of a leading Unitarian layman, Edgar Taylor, she eventually forsook Unitarianism for the Church under the guidance of Frederick Denison Maurice, who had himself been reared as a Unitarian. Her "Midnight Lines" are a good example of her less markedly religious verse:

> 'Twas a transient glance I caught of thee
> And thy starry train, O Moon!
> And anon a sable curtain fell
> O'er the lovely scene too soon.

[90] II (1828), 766-68.

But an image fair on my mind I bear
And it haunts me as I lie,
To think of the bright and beauteous things
That are travelling o'er the sky.

.   .   .   .

In such a time would I rest my head
Where thy beams should freely play,
And learn a lesson in wakeful hours,
Too rarely learnt by day.
Oh! blessed is he who readeth thee
With a meek and lowly mind;
He springeth on to the highest Heav'n,
And the Earth is left behind.[91]

Jane Roscoe contributed chiefly sonnets, generally graceful but marked by no very deep talent. Harriet Martineau's nature was not, as readers of her later work might surmise, eminently poetical, but the dozen poems she contributed to these volumes of the *Repository* reveal her as more than a mere journeyman at verse. Of several of her poems there will be occasion to speak presently in connection with her other work.

In sum, then, while the *Repository's* verse from 1827 to 1831, like the rest of the magazine, shows in general a higher standard of literary competence than that of the first series, it falls short of the excellence to be attained from 1832 to 1838. Before turning to these latter years, however, it remains to speak in more detail of the *Repository's* most voluminous contributor in the 1827-1831 period.

HARRIET MARTINEAU

"She is one of the strangest phenomena to me," said Thomas Carlyle, referring to Miss Martineau in a letter to Ralph Waldo Emerson on June 1, 1837.

[91] V (1831), 584.

A genuine little Poetess, buckramed, swathed like a mummy into Socinian and Political-Economy formulas; and yet verily alive in the inside of that! "God has given a Prophet to every People in its own speech," say the Arabs. Even the English Unitarians were one day to have their Poet, and the best that could be said for them too was to be said.[92]

Carlyle was ever as scornful of Unitarianism as he was of what he called the dismal science—political economy. He had once told Emerson, a Unitarian, that he was the only man of that persuasion whom he could unobstructedly like. Unitarians, he thought, using the familiar image, were "half-way house characters," who if they had had courage enough would have ended in unbelief. He preferred atheism to "'faint possible Theism'" and thought Unitarians deserved their fate—"the bat fate: to be killed among the rats as a bird, among the birds as a rat. . . ."[93]

The unfairness of Carlyle's attitude towards Unitarians does not, however, invalidate his judgment of Harriet Martineau. She *was* a strange phenomenon long before Carlyle became acquainted with her and before the tremendous vogue of her thinly fictionized tracts on political economy brought to her door staid and haughty members of Parliament to beg her to "illustrate" their pet principles or causes for the illumination of mankind. She was swathed in Socinian old clothes, even before she donned those of political economy. And, she was "verily alive in the inside of that!" —very much alive, as her opponents always soon found out. In a very real sense she was for a few years the Unitarian

[92] C. E. Norton, *Correspondence of Carlyle and Emerson,* I, 126. Carlyle was evidently impressed with his own description of Harriet. In another letter to Emerson over a year later (Nov. 15, 1838) he wrote: "The good Harriet! But 'God,' as the Arabs say, 'has given every people a Prophet (or Poet) in its own speech': and behold now Unitarian mechanical Formalism was to have its poetess too; and stragglings of genius were to spring up through that like grass through a Macadam highway!"—*Ibid.*, p. 200.
[93] *Ibid.*, Feb. 3, 1835, p. 38.

prophetess, though she was in later life to abandon the role and with it not only her belief in Unitarianism but in Christianity as well. In those later years she could outdo even Carlyle in scorn of the Unitarians.

But the Harriet with whom we have to deal is not the Miss Martineau for whose tales of the immutable laws of economics the Princess Victoria was said to wait eagerly each month, and for whose advice cabinet ministers held up decisions on matters of state; nor the Miss Martineau who professed agnosticism and Comtist positivism, and bedeviled the medical profession with her advocacy of mesmerism as a panacea for the ills of the flesh. The Harriet Martineau of this story is an unknown young lady of Norwich who wrote anonymously for the *Monthly Repository*. Like Carlyle, she had to undergo a long apprenticeship to the periodicals before achieving success with her books. Her apprenticeship was the harder because the *Repository* paid little— even that little was exceptional, for she was probably its only paid correspondent—but her success came the swifter. The *Repository* was her training school, and Fox was her master.

Miss Martineau's earliest contributions, in 1822, have been noticed in a previous chapter. For the following six years her contributions seem to have been only occasional: a defense of Hartley's doctrines of philosophical necessity, three or four poems, and several moral essays, such as "On the Dangers of Adversity" and "On Dignity of Character." Meanwhile she published anonymously, in addition to a number of tracts, two devotional works proper for a pious young lady who may have had ambitions to succeed Hannah More and Mrs. Barbauld as a popular female divine.[94] More significant as a forerunner of the type of writing which was later to make her fame and fortune, was the

[94] *Devotional Exercises, Consisting of Reflections and Prayers for the Use of Young Persons* (Norwich, 1823); and *Addresses, with Prayers and Original Hymns for the Use of Families* (Norwich, 1826).

publication of two little stories to educate the working classes: *The Rioters,* to discourage the operatives from breaking the machines that threw them out of work; and *The Turn-Out,* on the subject of wages. Not until some time later, after reading Mrs. Marcet's *Conversations on Political Economy,* did she realize (like the *gentilhomme* who unwittingly had spoken prose all his life) that she had been writing political economy without knowing it. All this represented a fairly considerable amount of writing for a provincial young lady who had to conceal her literary labors for fear of offending social conventions. But it was not writing that brought much financial remuneration, and of that there was presently to be need.

In the fall of 1828, while in Newcastle for medical treatment, Harriet read an advertisement by Fox, as the new editor of the *Repository,* appealing for literary aid as well as an increased circulation.[95] Her answer to the advertisement brought forth so cordial a reply from Fox that she was moved to offer him extensive assistance, even though he could at that time pay her no money. That he paid her in something more valuable than money, Harriet generously owned in her *Autobiography* years later: "in a course of frank and generous criticism which was of the utmost benefit to me. His editorial correspondence with me was unquestionably the occasion, and in great measure the cause, of the greatest intellectual progress I ever made before the age of thirty."[96]

[95] The "spirited advertisement" to which Miss Martineau refers in her *Autobiography* (I, 106) is probably the appeal, under the heading "Correspondence" (II [Sept., 1828], 656) for "voluntary assistance to render the work a worthy organ" of the Unitarians. "It is his wish that the Monthly Repository should, by the importance, the interest, the power, and the variety of its contents, and the faithfulness, freedom, and liberality of its spirit, verify its title to the honourable character of the *Unitarian* Review and Magazine; and unless it can be made to do so, he, for one, will feel little regret at its extinction."

[96] *Autobiography,* I, 106-7.

The first of Harriet's promised communications seems to have been her most ambitious poem, her "Ode to Religious Liberty," which appeared in January, 1829. The poem, an invocation to "Sacred Liberty," is the sole instance, as Garnett has pointed out,[97] of the influence of Shelley on the Unitarian poetess; she was generally more under the spell of Wordsworth. Milton's sonnet on the massacre of the Vaudois furnished the central motive for the ode, and the Puritan poet is celebrated as the "great High-Priest, the Prophet" of the universal reign of Religious Liberty. The penultimate stanza, relating to England, is among the best of Miss Martineau's verse (the second-person pronoun refers to the Spirit of Liberty):

> There is an island, rising from the main,
>   Where fields are green, and rivers flow,
>   And lakes reflect the sunset glow,
> And mountains tower above the plain,
> Whose people call on thee: O! must they call in vain?
>   They dwell not in the gloom of night,
>   Nor in the woes of slavery wail;
>   Thou blessest them with partial light,
> But dost from them thy full effulgence veil.
>   Withdraw the envious cloud
>   That doth thy features shroud,
> Receive their homage when they bid thee hail.
>   For fiery hearts are glowing there,
>   And earnest tongues are heard in prayer,
>   And hands are ready to prepare
>   A temple for thy dwelling place.
>   Speak but the word—its walls shall rise,
>   Its altars flame, its spreading dome
>   Shall echo with thy harmonies.
>   O! there unveil thy face,
> And choose that verdant island for thy home.[98]

[97] *Life of W. J. Fox*, p. 79.   [98] III (1829), 43.

Harriet's next identifiable contribution, "The Last Tree of the Forest," reveals a slightly romantic melancholy, to be noted also in some of her later prose sketches. The poem ends on the theme of the transitoriness of all earthly life:

> Thou hast outlived the brave, the wise, the gay:
> And, in thy turn, like all that's great, and all
> That's beautiful on earth, must pass away.[99]

Much more characteristic of the kind of fare she was to supply the *Repository* during the next few years was the essay published in March "On the Agency of Feelings in the Formation of Habits . . . ," and its companion piece, in April, "On the Agency of Habits in the Regeneration of Feelings."[100] These probably represent installments of a paper which Harriet confessed to Fox had once been rejected by the former editors because of its length. The two articles are chiefly notable as expositions of the Hartleyan associational psychology; allusions to and quotations from Wordsworth demonstrate that modern critics were not the first to recognize the links between Hartley and Wordsworth. Part of the first essay is virtually a commentary on the "Ode on Intimations of Immortality."

In June appeared an installment of Miss Martineau's first full-length review. The book examined, a *Natural History of Enthusiasm,* gave her an opportunity for expressing the views of Rational Christians on the subject and for warning against the "snares of enthusiasm."[101] In July came the first of a series of six "Essays on the Art of Thinking," for the benefit of those who had never studied Bacon, Newton, and Locke. Harriet avows herself the humble handmaiden of Reason: "An orderly mind is a temple where truth condescends to appear, and delights to be worshipped."[102] Subjects treated include the need of the dom-

---

[99] *Ibid.,* p. 81.
[101] *Ibid.,* pp. 417-25, 473-83.
[100] *Ibid.,* pp. 102-6, 159-62.
[102] *Ibid.,* p. 606.

inance of reason in human life, the importance of right subjects of thought, the supremacy of Baconian induction, the problem of cause and effect, cautions on the accurate use of words, mental discipline, and the importance of developing powers of observation. The Essays, a clear, orderly presentation of their subject, were twice accorded the distinction of being placed as the leading article of the month. Only two other contributions of 1829 can be identified with certainty: a two-part review of *Essays on the Pursuit of Truth* and a poem, "The Survivor." It is probable, however, that she was also the writer of the short critical articles in the new "Monthly Report of General Literature," which was begun in November. In all, the identified contributions for 1829 total fourteen; that number was to be nearly quadrupled in the following year.

The reasons for the flood of contributions in 1830 were at bottom financial. In June, 1829, the Martineau family fortunes, never very secure since the death of the father several years before, were wiped out in a disastrous bank failure. Left with "precisely one shilling" in her purse, Harriet could no longer afford the genteel luxury of writing for nothing. Family and friends tried to convince her that needlework was likely to be a more certain source of income. Not at once wholly rejecting the needlework, Harriet refused to give up her ambition, which was already in her mind taking on something of the character of a mission. She informed Fox, however, that she could no longer contribute to the *Repository* without remuneration. He apologetically placed at her disposal as much as he could command at that time—fifteen pounds a year, for which she was to do as much reviewing as she thought proper. Accompanying his offer was a package of nine books for review. Said Harriet years later: "Overwhelming as this was, few letters that I had ever received had given me more pleasure than this. Here was, in the first place, work; in the next, continued literary discipline under Mr. Fox; and lastly, this money would buy me clothes. So to work I went, with needle and pen."[103] One must picture her in the succeeding months at work early and late, alternating fancy needlework by day with reviewing and writing at night until one or two in the morning, and in spare moments studying German for recreation and inspiration. "It was truly *life* that I lived during those days of strong intellectual and moral effort."[104]

Fox, by his timely help and encouragement, had secured for his magazine a valuable writer. In addition to the now unidentifiable critical notices which she contributed in the fall of 1829, eighty-nine articles, reviews, tales, poems, and sketches can be attributed to her during the next two years, fifty-two of them in 1830. For lack of literary acquaintances and connections, practically everything she wrote went into the *Repository*.

The majority of her contributions were reviews, thirty-five in 1830 and thirty-three in 1831. Most of these were short critical notices often padded with generous excerpts, after the reviewing fashion of the day, but the labor represented was nevertheless considerable. Her chosen field for review lay in theology, morals, mental philosophy, and biography. What were regarded as the more important books received more detailed treatment; such reviews as those of Crombie's *Natural Theology*[105] and of *Physical Considerations Connected with Man's Ultimate Destination*[106] were in part original articles as well, though Miss Martineau was usually more conscientious in actually reviewing a given book than were many contemporary reviewers. Some of the reviews offered her an opportunity for the expression of her dearest convictions; a pamphlet on Negro slavery, for

[103] *Autobiography*, I, 110.   [104] *Ibid.*
[105] IV (1830), 145-54, 223-30.   [106] V (1831), 217-29.

instance, became the occasion for venting her abolitionist sympathies.[107] And the many sermons and controversial pamphlets given her for criticism enabled her frequently to champion her Unitarian views. Her judgment of books was, of course, in the main accommodated to the tenets of reason, the Unitarian faith, philosophical necessity, and, a little later, laissez-faire political economy.[108] Her reviews reveal a clear mind, sober, earnest, and forthright; her writing is calm, ordered, and generally concise. She was not an inspired reviewer but a thoroughly competent one.

One of Miss Martineau's most important contributions in 1830 was her series of four articles on Lessing's *Education of the Human Race,* of which the *Repository* twenty-four years earlier had had the distinction of presenting the first English translation, made by Crabb Robinson. Lessing's work was to have wide influence on religious thought, particularly for its contention that religions can and must be adapted to the progressive stages of civilization. By 1830 the work had been little noticed in England except by a few leading liberal theologians (including Bishop Marsh), and Miss Martineau's free paraphrase and running commentary on it seems to have been the first attempt to make its conclusions known to a lay audience. Strangely enough, students of Lessing's reputation and influence in England seem to have overlooked her contribution.[109]

Reviewing and theological discourse were not, however, enough to satisfy Harriet's ambitions. She continued to supply an occasional poem, a few translations from the German, but, of more importance to her eventual career, she

[107] IV (1830), 4-9.

[108] Not until 1832, however, did she approach politics and economics in the *Repository;* even then, it will be noticed, she paid little attention to such questions as parliamentary reform, for to her the education of the people in the principles of political economy was more important.

[109] See Sidney H. Kenwood, "Lessing in England," in *Modern Language Review,* IX (1914), 197-212, 344-58.

began to write didactic little tales. Inspiration for the latter came from Fox, who asked her to "send him two or three tales, such as his 'best readers' could not pass by."[110] First product of the request to appear in the *Repository* was "The Hope of the Hebrew,"[111] an attempt to represent in fiction the reception of the mission and teachings of Jesus in ancient Palestine. The story was well received, and before the year was out the author published a volume of such tales, under the title *Traditions of Palestine*. Fox gave the volume an appreciative puff.[112] The *Repository* was also supplied with several other tales of a different sort. "True Worshippers,"[113] in a simple combination of narrative and dialogue, taught that however sacred the communion between the individual and his God, he has need of the inspiration of spiritual brotherhood which comes from participation in organized religious services. "The Early Sowing"[114] preached the value of home missionary effort. "Solitude and Society"[115] is the story of a man who acquired a philosophy of society and coöperation during, oddly enough, a nine years' political imprisonment.

The problem of the recluse, the solitary, seems to have been much on Harriet's mind in these years—perhaps because of her own sense of aloneness in the years following her fiancé's death in 1827, or more likely because her own innate impulses to solitude had to be fought against. "The Solitary,"[116] one of a series of parables, again enforced the need of social worship; and one of her "Sabbath Musings" attacked ascetic withdrawal from the world.[117] Her poem "The Flower of the Desert"[118] may allude to her own experiences in the winter of 1829-1830, when she went to

---

[110] *Autobiography*, I, 110.
[111] IV (1830), 101-8.
[112] *Ibid.*, pp. 521-29.
[113] *Ibid.*, pp. 307-15.
[114] V (1831), 733-40.
[115] IV (1830), 442-49.
[116] *Ibid.*, pp. 361-62.
[117] V (1831), 763-70.
[118] IV (1830), 253.

London to consult with Fox about her literary labors. The final stanza reveals no longing for solitude, but the reverse:

A soul there is, as pure as thou and rare;
'Midst heartless crowds in solitude she dwells;
Conscious that kindred spirits breathe afar,
And cheer'd by that prophetic hope which tells
That flowers shall spring where now no promise shows,
And e'en this desert "blossom like the rose."

But if this much may be inferred from her evident preoccupation with the theme of solitude, there is little else in her *Repository* contributions to give a clue to her personality. With the possible exception of her "Sabbath Musings" and a few of her poems, almost everything she wrote at this time aimed at severe objectivity. Even from under the cloak of anonymity, little of the writer's personality was allowed to reveal itself.

On at least one occasion in these years Harriet was to go to extreme lengths to secure anonymity for the furthering of her literary ambitions. The story furnishes good evidence of her resourcefulness, her industry, and her will to succeed. In 1830 the Unitarian Association, awakening a little belatedly to the needs of evangelizing effort, with characteristic Unitarian faith in reason and the written word, held a prize essay contest. Three prizes were offered for three essays designed to present the case for Unitarianism to the Catholics, the Jews, and the Mohammedans. The prizes were evidently scaled according to the supposed difficulties involved: ten guineas for the Catholic essay, fifteen for the Jewish, and twenty for the Mohammedan. Careful rules were set up to ensure impartiality in the judging of the manuscripts. The Catholic essay award was to be made at the end of September, 1830, and the other two in March, 1831.

Harriet, returning to Norwich after a disheartening stay

in London, resolved to try, not for one prize, but all three. Confiding only in her mother and her aunt, she set to work and within a month had completed the first, *The Essential Faith of the Universal Church.* Extraordinary precautions were taken to assure anonymity; she paid a schoolboy a sovereign to copy the manuscript and dispatched it by a circuitous route to London. The period of suspense was not devoted to day-dreaming; she proceeded to write *Five Years of Youth,* which has been noted earlier in connection with the Flower sisters. The October *Repository* brought the news that she had won the first contest. The next day she began the Mohammedan essay, *The Faith as Unfolded by Many Prophets.* The Jewish essay, *Providence as Manifested Through Israel,* based in good part on Lessing, followed. Again the copying was done by different persons, and the manuscripts, "sent round by different hands (the hands of strangers to the whole scheme), done up in different shapes, and in different kinds of paper, and sealed with different wax and seals, were deposited in the office on the last day of February."[119]

There is no suspense in this story; such industry could not but achieve its reward. Harriet, attending in May the grand annual London get-together of the Unitarian Association—at which the most honored guest that year was the great Indian convert to Unitarianism, the Rajah Rammohun Roy, and, not the least honored, ex-President Kirkland of Harvard—was embarrassed by the applause of the gathering when it was announced that she had won all the prizes. Her essays were to be printed and broadcast by the Association. Unitarianism had its prophetess. The *Repository* in August, reviewing her *Five Years of Youth,* queried in passing, "how it happened that our ministers would not or could not prevent the honour of championing the cause

---

[119] *Autobiography,* I, 116.

of pure Christianity against the whole theological world from devolving on a young lady."[120]

Within a year England was querying how it happened that the role of recognized champion of the new political economy had devolved upon that same young lady. The publication of the first tale of her *Illustrations of Political Economy* in February, 1832, brought instant success, and thenceforth the Unitarian prophetess was the schoolmistress and oracle of the nation. The story of the publication of the Political Economy tales lies beyond our scope here; it can best be read in Miss Martineau's *Autobiography,* though that account should be corrected by reference to Garnett's *Life of W. J. Fox.* Her tremendous success in wider realms inevitably meant the end of her connection with the *Repository.* As will be seen later, Harriet continued to contribute throughout the first year of Fox's ownership of the magazine, but after that, save for one song, no more. One might infer from her *Autobiography* that the reason was that she soon lost faith in Unitarian Christianity; more probable reasons are the opening up to her of new media of publication, her estrangement from Fox because of his domestic troubles and because of her quarrels with his brother Charles, her publisher, and her departure for America in 1834. That she retained for some time yet her Unitarian connection may be seen in her writings for J. R. Beard's Unitarian magazine, the *Christian Teacher,* in 1839.

The first five years of the second series had secured the services of one outstanding writer; in the next five years it was to lose her services, but the loss would be more than counterbalanced by the contributions of John Stuart Mill, Robert Browning, Richard Henry Horne, Ebenezer Elliott, James Martineau, and others.

[120] V (1831), 538.

6: Fox's Repository: A Wider Audience

WHY FOX CHOSE to purchase the *Repository* and assume its full proprietorship is not altogether clear. On the financial score, the prospects of the magazine were scarcely encouraging: Aspland had often had to call for financial assistance, and the Unitarian Association since 1827 had spent well over a hundred pounds a year to keep it afloat. Its circulation, which had long been almost stationary, was largely confined to Unitarians. Nor were the prospects encouraging for the increase of its influence: the *Repository* had for too long been too exclusively identified with "a sect every where spoken against" to warrant expectations that the Unitarian label could be detached.

The real reason for Fox's decision to purchase the magazine is probably to be found in his dissatisfaction with the narrowness of sectarian religious effort and in his desire for a pulpit from which he and his friends could address a wider audience. Fox, like Carlyle, was fully aware of the growing significance and power of the press. Carlyle had declared in 1829, though not altogether with approval, "The true Church of England, at this moment, lies in the Editors of its Newspapers."[1] Unlike Carlyle, Fox welcomed the new medium: "The pulpit was a new power happily adapted to an age which had no other means of communication than conversation and manuscripts. Christianity has used that power well. It is now eclipsed by the greater power of a cheap and rapid press. Why should not Christianity use that too?"[2] Fox's definition of the scope of re-

---

[1] "Signs of the Times," *Edinburgh Review*, XLIX (1829), 439-59.
[2] *Monthly Repository*, 2d series, V (1831), 277. Unless otherwise indicated all references are to Volumes VI-X (1832-1836) of the second series of the *Monthly Repository*.

ligion, as has been shown, was broad enough to include most of the concerns of human life; control of the *Repository* offered a pulpit from which could be preached a liberal social and political gospel.

Transfer of the ownership of the magazine to Fox took place in the fall of 1831, probably in October, to judge from the announcement made of the removal of the editorial offices to the establishment in Paternoster Row of Fox's brother Charles, who had recently set himself up as a publisher.[3] Details of the terms of sale are not obtainable. Fox says that he paid the "fair and full worth" of the periodical, which, in view of the record of annual deficits, cannot have been judged to be great. He may have received some financial assistance to make the purchase, but there is no evidence that anyone else had a voice in the management of the magazine until he surrendered the editorship to R. H. Horne in June, 1836. Fox avowed his proprietorship more openly than was usual in that period of ordinarily anonymous journalism; the announced reason for this step was to free the Unitarian Association from responsibility, but the real reason may have been rather to free the magazine from the incubus of sectarianism. If the *Repository* was to succeed, it must circulate beyond the Unitarian limits.

The first step taken to detach the Unitarian label from the *Repository* was the elimination of denominational intelligence. After January, 1832, the magazine no longer published obituaries, news of Unitarian activities, or correspondence solely of interest to the denomination. But since, in a pecuniary view, this kind of thing had been the surest guarantee of a steady if limited circulation, Fox did not at once wholly abandon the publication of Unitarian intelligence. Instead, he began a complementary publication: the *Unitarian Chronicle, and Companion to the Monthly Repository*. Uniform in size, type, and paper with the *Reposi-*

---

[3] *Ibid.*, p. 796.

tory, the *Chronicle* consisted of a single sheet of sixteen pages, and sold at threepence a monthly number. By this expedient, Unitarians were provided, at a small cost, with more complete news of their denominational activities, and the *Repository's* pages were freed for larger purposes.[4]

The 1832 volume, the first completed under Fox's ownership, represents a transition from a religious to a secular magazine. Nearly half of its original articles and reviews relate directly to religion, and the Unitarian stamp is unmistakable. The roster of contributors shows few new names, and the only important new non-Unitarian contributor, John Stuart Mill, undoubtedly formed the connection through one of Fox's parishioners—Harriet Taylor. In addition to Fox, Beard, and Harriet Martineau, regular contributors continued to include John Johns, J. J. Tayler, Emily Taylor, Jane Roscoe, William Turner, John Bowring, and John Moggridge. Crabb Robinson was not new to the *Repository,* but his previous contributions had been scanty and sporadic. Sarah Flower may have been represented earlier, but none of her writing before 1832 can be identified. Harriet Taylor had written several book notices for the 1831 volume. Some of the older writers for the *Repository,* such as Hutton, Kentish, and Rutt, transferred their allegiance at once to the *Christian Reformer;* and after 1832 Beard, Bowring, Johns, Harriet Martineau, Emily Taylor, and William Turner, with a few unimportant exceptions, no longer wrote for Fox.

New contributors in the succeeding volumes more than made up for the loss of the Unitarian connection. In 1833

[4] The *Unitarian Chronicle* survived for two years, much of that time under the editorship of the Reverend Edwin Chapman. In 1834 the need for it vanished when Aspland, as the result of Unitarian alarm over the radicalism of Fox and his friends, began a new and enlarged series of the *Christian Reformer,* which for the next thirty years was to be the real continuation of the old *Repository.* In 1835 the Reverend John Relly Beard began the *Christian Teacher,* which lasted until 1845, then merging with the *Prospective Review.*

the new writers, in addition to Mill and Sarah Flower, included William Bridges Adams, Ebenezer Elliott, Mrs. Mary Leman Grimstone, W. T. Hayley, James Martineau, Charles Reece Pemberton, and Thomas Wade. In the following year were added to the list Robert Browning, R. H. Horne, Caroline Southwood Smith, William and Mary Howitt.

Once the predominance of clerical contributors had been broken, the *Repository* progressively substituted literary, aesthetic, social, and political subjects for religious. The proportion of original articles on religion fell from about fifty per cent in 1832 to twenty in 1833, twelve in 1834, and less than four per cent in 1835. Reviews of religious books declined in almost exactly the same proportions. Since religion was thus virtually to disappear from the *Repository's* columns, it may be well here to examine briefly its final treatment of religious matters.

RELIGION

Though the transitional 1832 volume still wore a Unitarian label, the defense of Unitarian doctrine received relatively small space. Beard contributed a discussion in four installments on "The Rise and Progress of the Doctrine of the Trinity,"[5] designed to show how "the doctrine of Christ's deity grew up by degrees, and crept almost insensibly into the Church." Emily Taylor attacked a movement to exclude Unitarians from the British and Foreign Bible Society.[6] Edward Higginson in a long review endeavored to convict orthodoxy of "the guilt of half the unbelief of an intelligent age."[7] Fox reviewed briefly several pamphlets growing out of a local Unitarian-Orthodox set-to[8] and at more length praised the publication of Harriet Martineau's prize essays.[9] The latter review offered an oppor-

[5] VI (1832), 15-23, 109-15, 259-66, 315-23.
[6] *Ibid.,* pp. 334-37.   [7] *Ibid.,* pp. 768-88, 829-40.
[8] *Ibid.,* pp. 345-49.   [9] *Ibid.,* pp. 475-84.

tunity again to reiterate his faith that Unitarianism was not
merely a *negative* system, nor "a corrected and amended
edition of Calvinism," but "a different view of the divine
plan." The 1832 volume gave brief critical notice to about
twenty Unitarian sermons and controversial works but seldom noticed them thereafter. Lingering traces of the *Repository's* Unitarian lineage may be seen the following year
in James Martineau's long review of the life and work of
Joseph Priestley[10] and in a brief review of Channing's collected sermons,[11] but by 1834 little can be found to be
labeled as peculiarly Unitarian.

The publication of religious miscellany also ceased with
the 1832 volume. To that volume John Johns, Emily Taylor, and Jane Roscoe each contributed a single devotional
essay, and Fox a portion of one of his sermons.[12] Religious
fiction was represented only by two of Harriet Martineau's
little parables and by perhaps the most attractive of her
didactic religious tales: "Liese; or, the Progress of Worship."[13] This story, the locale of which is the Germany of
Luther's time, recounts the progress of a nun, Liese, from
Catholicism to Protestantism and from asceticism to a full
life of religious and social service. The character of Liese
(Lizzie) takes on added interest from its evident patterning,
in part at least, after Eliza Flower. Liese, for instance,
serves as secretary to Martin Luther much as Eliza served
Fox, and she likewise composes beautiful hymns.

Under Fox the *Repository* also turned away from theology and scriptural criticism. William Turner and John
Beard contributed only a few items of the latter to the 1832
volume. German theology disappeared except for J. J. Tayler's four articles on "Herder's Thoughts on the Philosophy
of the History of Mankind"[14] and two on the work of the

[10] VII (1833), 19-30, 84-88, 231-41.   [11] *Ibid.,* pp. 132-36.
[12] "On Subornation of Insincerity," VI (1832), 699-705.
[13] VI (1832), 153-61, 239-48, 324-33.
[14] *Ibid.,* pp. 34-42, 86-97, 165-78, 217-33.

German preacher F. V. Reinhard.[15] The state of French
Protestantism was discussed in several communications from
a French minister, the Reverend Athanase Coquerel. The
tendency of some of the leading younger Unitarian ministers to turn to philosophy and ethics may be seen in J. J.
Tayler's "On the Influence of the Spirit of Gnosticism"[16]
and in James Martineau's critical examination of Bentham's
Deontology.[17]

The one religious subject to which the new *Repository*
devoted much space was the reform of the Church of England—and the reasons for this were as much political and
social as religious. The progress of political reform gave
the radicals hope that the glaring abuses of the Establishment might be eliminated. Next to Tories and unreformed
Whigs, the Church was the *Repository's* favorite target.
Chief grievances down to and after 1835 continued to be
Church control of parish registers and of marriage and
burial services, the exclusion of Dissenters from the Universities, and the compelling of Dissenters to pay tithes.
Since the main lines of attack followed those of the earlier
volumes, which have been previously examined, it will not
be necessary to consider the question further here except to
note one or two differences.

One difference lay in the more extensive use of satire
and irony in attacking the connection between Church and
State. When in the winter of 1832, for instance, the government decreed the observance of a fast day to invoke Almighty aid in averting a threatened outbreak of cholera,
Fox turned loose his scorn upon the politicians and the
ultra-Evangelicals. The emptiness and hypocrisy of the ges-
ture annoyed Fox most:

The fast day will come, and people will leave off working, but
nobody will abstain from eating, save those whom poverty com-

[15] *Ibid.*, pp. 734-41, 797-804.
[16] VII (1833), 564-75, 602-12.   [17] VIII (1834), 612-24.

pels to keep perennial fast. . . . The theatres will be closed, the churches will be open, and the shops will manage their shutters so as to hit the happy medium. Amongst the higher classes, a handsome dish of salt fish, at the head of the well-spread table, by way of addition not of substitution, will suffice to mark the day decorously. Our statesmen and senators will be in conclave, using their brief breathing time to arrange the tactics of the next week's debate, and plan how the next party blow is to be struck or parried.[18]

The appointment of a fast day was a political move to win ultra-Evangelical party support. Only cant or superstition would profess to believe that cholera, which obeys "the fixed laws of physical existence" could be averted by such mummery. "The efficacy of prayer is not in changing the course of nature." Furthermore, why select cholera for the bad eminence? Consumption annually destroyed as many thousands, and the high rate of infant mortality in London was far more serious. If fasting were possessed of any miraculous efficacy, the country should fast to eliminate greater evils—the delay of the Reform Bill, the sanguinary penal code, the ignorance, wretchedness, and crime perpetuated by inefficient social institutions.

Fox and his supporters in their desire to reform the Church went at least one significant step further than earlier reformers, perhaps because of the influence of Coleridge's *Idea of Church and State* (1828). They were not interested simply in abolishing the hated burden of tithes, nor had they any wish to destroy the Church as such. Separation of Church and State need not mean abolition. Instead, the funds of the national church should be used for the benefit of the whole nation. "What is called Church Property is a public trust for the spiritual culture of the entire population."[19] No advantage would be gained by seiz-

[18] VI (1832), 145.
[19] "Church Reform Considered as a National and Not a Sectarian Question," VII (1833), 809. The article was probably by Fox.

ing that property and dumping it into the quagmire of the national debt, or by making a present of the tithes to the landlords. Rather, the money should be used for the education, the moral and spiritual culture, of the nation.

To that end the *Repository* proposed a seven-point program[20] to be financed by these national funds: all church buildings "to be freely used for public worship by all according to the dictates of their consciences"; infant schools; grammar schools for all children up to fourteen years of age, with attendance made compulsory, as in Prussia; universities in all large towns, open to both sexes, and accommodated to the needs of indigent students; institutions for the cultivation of the higher branches of learning and for the training of teachers; "assistance in the formation of museums, libraries, exhibitions, scientific institutions, theatres, and similar means for promoting adult instruction, and the popular cultivation of sound knowledge and refined taste"; public provision, where necessary, for the support of men of learning, genius, or science. Such a program was advanced enough for its day to be ridiculed as Utopian; Fox regarded it as sound sense. Decades were to pass, however, before anything approaching its scope could be adopted.

Though the Church was the religious organization most attacked, Fox on occasion also lashed out at Dissent. His criticism in January, 1832, of the failure of orthodox Dissent to support Catholic Emancipation evoked a reply from the London ministers of the Three Denominations.[21] His review of William Howitt's *History of Priestcraft* criticized the author for overlooking priestcraft among the Dissenting ministers.[22] Fox's personal difficulties in 1834-1835 with his brother ministers no doubt influenced his increasingly critical attitude towards the whole clerical profession. In a re-

[20] *Ibid.*, pp. 811-12.
[21] VI (1832), 359-60.   [22] VII (1833), 505-6.

view of W. P. Scargill's blast against the voluntary system
in his *Autobiography of a Dissenting Minister,* Fox attacked
both the Church and Dissent.

The evils of both systems are enormous, and, it is to be feared,
irremediable, without much greater change than either party
is likely to be persuaded to adopt. Those of the Church press
heaviest, politically; but those of Dissent are very formidable,
in a moral and intellectual point of view. Both parties egregiously
overrate the advantages to be conferred on society by priests
and preaching.[23]

As long as ministers were so deeply entrenched, on the one
side in vested selfish interests, on the other in popular prejudices, Fox saw little to hope from organized religion "for
the practical adoption of schemes tending simply and solely
towards the spiritual well-being of humanity." As a consequence, he more and more turned to government and education as offering the best hope of ameliorating the ills of
society. The *Repository,* naturally enough, followed suit.

The repercussion among the ranks of the older Unitarians was sharp. The *Repository* had for too long been the
representative of their denomination to permit its transformation into a radical secular magazine without arousing
protest. In April, 1833, the Reverend Lant Carpenter of
Bristol, one of the leading ministers of the denomination,
wrote Fox with reference to the changes in the magazine:

As the year 1832 advanced, it was impossible not to perceive that
it was losing those peculiar characteristics by which it was the
bond of union and the medium of communication among Unitarians; and I found that some of my friends here proposed to
satisfy themselves with the Unitarian Chronicle alone, when the
year was out.

The real burden of Carpenter's complaint, however, concerned not what was being eliminated from the *Repository*

[23] VIII (1834), 876.

but the nature of the social criticism which was being sub-stituted. One of the strongest taboos of the English religious and social code was being openly attacked: the *Repository* was advocating divorce. "About two numbers back . . . ap-peared indications of views, on the dissolubility of the Mar-riage Contract, which have been more developed since, and which, in my judgment, are so inconsistent with the decla-ration of Christ on the subject, (Matt. XIX: 3-9.) that I can-not reconcile them with the reception of his Divine au-thority."[24] That such views should go forth to a hostile public under the name of a prominent Unitarian minister, and in a periodical long officially Unitarian, boded ill for the denomination's repute.

Still worse, said Carpenter, the number just published (April, 1833) contained statements and views more flagrant than ever before. Excerpts from the leading article, "On the Condition of Women in England," signed "Junius Redivi-vus," had been read at the monthly meeting of the local Reading Society; and as a result of "the coarseness and even grossness of some expressions," as well as of its unqualified advocacy of divorce, the Society had unanimously voted to suppress that number and to consider at the next meeting discontinuing its subscription altogether. Carpenter declared that the article presented "a very exaggerated as well as degrading picture, calculated to give an unjust and baneful view of the state of society." And even what did accord with reality was written "in a style adapted to awaken the con-ceptions of the sensualist, and to disgust the pure, refined, and reflective spirit." The *Repository* had always been a periodical that might be "fearlessly left on the side-board or work table"; this latest number Carpenter sorrowed that he could not read to "a circle of female friends" or give to a mixed company. He would not even read it to a group

[24] The letter was printed four years later in Aspland's *Christian Reformer,* N.S., IV (1837), 236.

of young men except to warn them against its views. To add further insult to his sense of injury, the same number carried an article of enthusiastic praise for the writings of Junius Redivivus, written (though Carpenter did not know the author) by John Stuart Mill.

Fox did not choose to let Carpenter's complaints go unanswered, especially since other influential Unitarian ministers (evidently including Beard and William Turner) were also protesting. In the May number he printed "A Letter to the Rev. ―――― ――――, Unitarian Minister of ――――, from the Editor of the Monthly Repository,"[25] which attempted to answer all his Unitarian critics. The letter is an invaluable clue to Fox's conduct of the *Repository*.

Fox at once acknowledged that there had been some falling off of Unitarian support but countered that this had been amply compensated for by the growth of the circulation in other quarters. He was still as willing as ever to be classed a Unitarian—if his interpretation of the name was to be accepted;

but if the appellation be construed to imply approval of qualities and conduct which cripple, for most useful purposes, the power of a body of intelligent, wealthy, and influential persons; and tend to degrade into a dwindling sect those who might, in conjunction with like-minded men of other classes, take the lead of public opinion; then I disclaim the term.

The hostility to the *Repository* he declared to be of the same species as that which had opposed his attacks on Deist prosecutions, and his efforts to establish city missions and to extend the scope of Unitarian effort. Too many Unitarians were lagging behind the times.

No religionists are so feeble as Unitarians for any little, narrow, mean, sectarian purposes; none so strong as they, did they but feel their strength, for general good. Their faith, taken con-

[25] VII (1833), 347-54.

troversially, is chiefly a string of negations; taken positively, it consists of the great and universally allowed principles of religion and morality. Of these principles, therefore, they are the natural advocates; of these principles in all their boundless and beneficent application to the concerns of public and private life, of national and individual conduct, of politics, literature, art, philosophy, and the condition of society. This advocacy is their mission, and I verily believe that they will flourish or fall, as they ought, in proportion as it is discharged or neglected.[26]

To this work and in this spirit, Fox declared that he had devoted the *Repository*. He had given his name as editor, accepting the inconveniences of such publicity, so as to absolve the Unitarians at large from responsibility for his opinions. He had rid the magazine "of technical theology, and petty details, and uninteresting, critical discussions, that its general usefulness might not be impeded." He had considered as within its scope every question which affects human affairs and had spared no effort "to render it an useful auxiliary in the great struggle for improvement, moral, mental, and physical." The result was that he had offended some by making the work *"less Unitarian."*

Fox claimed that an opposition magazine had been proposed within three months after his purchase of the *Repository*. Some did not approve his deleting "Theology and General Literature" from the title; others did not like the relegation of Intelligence to the *Unitarian Chronicle;* still others objected to the elimination of Miscellaneous Correspondence. All these steps Fox justified on grounds which we have previously indicated. To the charge that the magazine was no longer "a bond of union" among Unitarians, Fox retorted caustically:

Will nothing unite us but the dry, ceaseless, and reiterated assertion of two or three points of controverted doctrine, with the

[26] *Ibid.*, p. 348.

arguments and criticisms thereunto appertaining? Is theology never to be clothed with flesh and blood, and breathe the breath of life, and walk forth amongst men, and speak of all things pertaining to humanity, that by its sympathies, conjoined with its superiority, it may raise humanity toward heaven? If not, why then it seems to me that the "union" must be of little worth and brief duration.[27]

RADICAL POLITICS

The second major objection to the new policy of the *Repository* concerned its politics; that is, said Fox, "they object to *my* politics; as I should object to theirs, were they editors." But since the magazine was his sole property, whose politics but his should be advanced in its pages? There had been no more reserve on this point than on others. Frankly, earnestly, he had avowed his political beliefs; he could do no other if the magazine was to treat at all the stirring political questions of the time—and it must treat such questions to attain general interest and influence.

The gravamen of the *Repository's* political offense appeared to be that it was not supporting the new Whig ministry. Traditionally, as we have seen, it had supported the Reform Whigs, and Fox in general had continued this policy down to the passage of the 1832 Bill. Soon afterwards it had become obvious that the Whigs were interested almost solely in a narrow range of reforms that would benefit chiefly their own interests. Their refusal to repeal what the reformers labeled "taxes on knowledge" was alone enough to convict them of apostasy from any genuine concern for the welfare of the whole nation. Whigs were better than Tories, but not enough better. The *Repository* consequently became identified with the Radical, the "movement" party, which stopped only short of republicanism in its demands for reform.

[27] *Ibid.*, p. 350.

Much of the magazine's political discussion from 1832 to 1836 is occupied with details of political strife which are no longer of interest except as historical minutiae. Of more fundamental interest, however, are the broader lines of the Radical program, especially as seen in the writings of Fox, William Bridges Adams, and John Stuart Mill. To that program, therefore, we shall turn before considering the third and, in its day, the source of the most damning criticism of the *Repository*—its advanced social views, particularly as relating to the condition of women and the problem of marriage and divorce laws.

England in 1832 was undergoing a troubled period of transition, a fact which Fox emphasized in his leading article for January of that year.[28] The struggle for parliamentary reform was "the type and index of a wider, deeper, and mightier conflict." To reform the legislature was but a means to an end, the first step in achieving a multitude of other changes in the Church, the law, education, and the condition of the working classes. "The real battle has commenced," said Fox a year later, "the strife between the many and the few, to decide for whose benefit society is constituted."[29]

After months of bitter political skirmishing, of stubborn resistance by the King and the Tory Lords, of thronged public meetings led by Whigs and Radicals, of threatened commercial panic and revolution, the final passage of the Reform Bill in June, 1832, was to Fox less a cause for rejoicing than for a redoubling of effort to carry out the implications of the whole movement. That the Whig ministry and their supporters in the Commons were willfully blind to such implications soon appeared painfully evident to the Radicals, with whom Fox became identified. In the struggle for the Bill the Whigs had temporarily joined

[28] "On the State and Prospects of the Country at the Close of the Year 1831," VI (1832), 1-11.   [29] VII (1833), 498.

forces with the Radicals and had welcomed lower-class support, but once the Bill had passed and middle-class interests were assured of power, the Whigs proceeded to temporize with the Tories, shy away from the Radicals, and oppose any extension of power and privileges to the lower classes. Many of the Whigs were clearly of the attitude that "in getting the Reform Bill the people have got enough."[30]

How little that "enough" seemed to the Radicals may be seen in the extent of the reforms which they demanded. Briefly, their program called for (1) a further extension of the suffrage, with the abolition of property qualifications, the adoption of the secret ballot, and the substitution of triennial parliaments for septennial; (2) the establishment of a national system of education free from pecuniary barriers and Church control, plus the repeal of all taxes upon the press; (3) reform of the civil and criminal law, including the virtual abolition of the death penalty; (4) reform of abuses in the Church and abolition of compulsory tithes; (5) reform of the condition of the poor through the revision of the Poor Laws and the abolition of all monopolies, especially the agricultural monopoly maintained through the Corn Laws; (6) the abolition of all slavery; (7) proscription of the military and naval practices of impressment and flogging, and a reduction in the size of the armed forces; (8) abolition of sinecures and unmerited pensions.[31] How closely the *Repository* adhered to this program may readily be seen in a brief examination of its political articles.

Failure of the Whigs to carry electoral and legislative reform far enough was a basic source of complaint. The Bill of 1832, wrote John Stuart Mill, only created a *shopocracy* "in the place of, or rather by the side of, the aristocracy," and the people were "still to be sacrificed for the

[30] VI (1832), 848.

[31] For a full statement of the Radical position, see S. Maccoby, *English Radicalism, 1832-52*, especially Chapter 3.

joint benefit of both."³² Though the franchise had been extended, less than one sixth of the adult males held the privilege of voting. The *Repository* did not come out flatly for immediate, universal manhood suffrage, though it did advocate an eventual adoption of that principle; the lower classes must first be educated to use such a privilege wisely.

Fox went beyond the usual Radical position, however, in his advocacy of enfranchising women on the same terms as men. The point could not be pressed, for in that day to advocate woman suffrage was likely to bring down upon one's head the ridicule of many even among the Radicals. But Fox as early as 1832 was not afraid to call attention to the egregious anomaly by which a woman could be elevated to the throne of England while highly endowed and educated women were denied the lowest and simplest political function, that of voting. Woman "is vested with the entire power of the State, or not entrusted with its meanest fraction. She is a divinity or a slave."³³ Fox confessed that he did not attach "any particular importance to the continuance or the cessation of this apparent absurdity," for the whole condition of woman was "full of incongruities" which must first be rectified.

The present generation is so accustomed to the idea of the secret ballot in elections that it is difficult to comprehend the objections raised against it in the 1830's. Yet in 1833 a reasonably liberal periodical like the *Edinburgh Review* could find all manner of excuses to oppose its adoption as a part of the electoral machinery,³⁴ and even John Stuart Mill was not sure of its value, because of its supposed inculcation of cowardice. To the *Edinburgh's* list of imagined ills that the ballot would entail, the *Repository* gave short shrift:

---

³² VIII (1834), 170.   ³³ VI (1832), 638.
³⁴ *Edinburgh Review*, LVI (Jan., 1833), 543-64.

Is the life of every clubbist in St. James's a living lie, from the impending vengeance of pugnacious candidates who have been blackballed? Are the French particularly reserved as to their political opinions? Are they for ever haunted and struck dumb by the spirit of the electoral urn? And the Americans, are they all sunk in the profound, gloomy, and suspicious stillness which so appalls the reviewer?[35]

W. B. Adams noted two years later that "at the word ballot rise a host of Whigs and Tories, denouncing all secrecy as unmanly, un-English, and cowardly." What of it? asked Adams. Not all Englishmen were as bold as Hampden. If the coward could be strengthened by the ballot, so much the better.

In a country where the pressure of population, corn laws, and custom-houses reduces men to such a state of destitution, that large numbers of them consent to wear, for the sake of food, the badges, and liveries, and patchwork garments of their richer fellows—in such a country free and sturdy independence cannot be a national characteristic, and the rich will contrive to oppress the poor, unless insurmountable difficulties be thrown in their way.

In a "huge den of aristocracy" like England the ballot would guarantee the independence of the poor man.

More than independence, however, was necessary for the people if they were to have a voice in the affairs of the nation. The popular agitation which had culminated in the passage of the Reform Bill had uncovered a new-found power of public opinion, especially over the monetary system of the country. (Refusal to pay taxes and a threatened run on the Bank—*To stop the Duke, go for gold*—had been effective legal and non-violent measures to force reform.) The lesson which Fox and the Philosophic Radicals drew from the whole movement was the imperative need of uni-

[35] VII (1833), 81. [36] IX (1835), 476-77.

versal public instruction, including political instruction. To withhold or impede that knowledge would be dangerous in the extreme. The people had discovered their tremendous power, but if it was not to be abused or misdirected, "knowledge for its guidance cannot be too rapidly or extensively generated."[37]

First, therefore, on the list of pledges which Fox asked his readers to demand of candidates for the newly reformed Parliament was the repeal of all "taxes on knowledge,"[38] that is, the heavy stamp duties on newspapers and the various taxes on paper, advertisements, and imported books. Such taxes had served a dual purpose in the hands of reactionary ministries: they had provided revenue, but more important they had provided some check on the distribution of radical newspapers among the poor. Time and again Fox and his correspondents struck at the folly of such taxes. "Taxation should find other food to feed upon than public intelligence." Newspapers, periodicals, pamphlets, books, should be kept at as low a price as possible so that they might reach the great mass of the people. A free and popular press constituted "the best of all securities against the return of a reign either of terror or corruption, and for the full discussion and progressive adoption of all real ameliorations in the working of the government and the condition of the people."[39]

Repeal of the taxes on knowledge was not the only plank in the *Repository's* program for educational reform. As we have already seen, Fox proposed that the nation appropriate some of the fat revenues of the Church for the purposes of education. Harriet Martineau in one of her last contributions to the magazine characterized English education as "shamefully limited in extent, . . . vague in its objects, and

---

[37] VI (1832), 401.　　　[38] *Ibid.*, pp. 439-41.
[39] *Ibid.*, p. 440. Other articles on the subject may be found as follows: VI, 267-71; VIII (1834), 103-9; IX (1835), 347-48; X (1836), 69, 258-64.

absurd in its routine"; and called upon the Parliament to provide a system of national education.[40] John Stuart Mill, though in general opposed to any more interference of government in the affairs of society than was necessary, favored State provision for education,[41] and urged the establishment of normal schools for the training of teachers.[42] In his review of Sarah Austin's translation of Cousin's report on the Prussian educational system, Mill endorsed that system as worthy of imitation in England, since it provided "schools for *all,* without distinction of sect."[43] W. B. Adams advocated educational reform but thought that there was little chance for it so long as either Whigs or Tories were in power and so long as thousands were doomed to direst poverty.[44] The improvement of women's education, as we shall see later, was a perennial topic in the *Repository.*

Legal reform, a favorite topic of the Benthamites, received less attention but was by no means neglected. Fox in 1832 placed the amelioration of the civil and criminal code as second on his list of reforms to which Parliamentary aspirants should be pledged.[45] In the civil code he called for reform of bankruptcy laws and reduction of the costs, complexities, and delays of legal procedure. The interminable and ruinous proceedings of the Court of Chancery, later to be so effectively satirized by Dickens in the case of *Jarndyce* vs. *Jarndyce,* received special attention in another article.[46] The criminal code needed even more sweeping changes: clearer definition of crimes and punishments, more emphasis upon reformation of criminals, reduction of judicial discretion to a minimum in fixing sentences, and the restriction of capital punishment to the most atrocious crimes.[47] Harriet Martineau contributed two articles on the

[40] VI (1832), 693-94.
[41] VIII (1834), 441.
[42] *Ibid.*, pp. 356-59.
[43] *Ibid.*, p. 503.
[44] *Ibid.*, pp. 718-24.
[45] VI (1832), 440-41.
[46] "Lord Brougham's Chancery Reforms," VIII (1834), 122-29.
[47] VI (1832), 440-41.

subject in 1832,[48] attacking the barbarity of current practices in the custody and punishment of criminals. Her articles, as usual, stressed the need of formulating fixed principles for the administration of punishment, which should be keyed to the twin purposes of protecting society and reforming the offender. Universal education she believed to be the fundamental answer to the problem of crime, but classification and segregation of prisoners would aid the reformatory process. Transportation she attacked as ineffectual and outmoded. Harriet, like most of the reformers, urged limiting capital punishment to a very few crimes; a later correspondent, one G. E. Eachus, urged the total abolition of the death penalty.[49]

The humanitarian impulses which prompted measures for the amelioration of a harsh criminal code also moved the *Repository's* writers to call for the abolition of impressment and of flogging in the army and the navy. When a bill was presented to Parliament in 1834 to suspend the Navy's power to kidnap seamen into its service, Mill indignantly attacked the Whig Lords' plea of necessity for the practice. That the Whigs could abolish Negro slavery and yet justify the press-gang Mill attributed to obtuseness rather than knavery. For thirty years the crime and enormity of slavery had been dinned into their ears. "In thirty years more, by an equally intense expression of national abhorrence, their consciences might, we dare say, be awakened on the subject of impressment too."[50] W. B. Adams as Junius Redivivus in an article entitled "Civilized Barbarism" turned loose his bitterest rhetoric against the practice. His remedy was: "Increase the pecuniary and other advantages in the king's service, and abundant seamen will flock to it. Give good sailors the hope of becoming officers. Abolish caste, and

---

[48] "Prison Discipline," VI (1832), 577-86; "Secondary Punishments," *ibid.*, pp. 667-69.
[49] VIII (1834), 332-36.   [50] *Ibid.*, p. 241.

let fair play exist to all alike, and there will be no need of force to get men to enter."[51] Charles Reece Pemberton, who as a youngster had served in the Navy, made his *Autobiography of Pel. Verjuice,* which we shall examine later, an effective piece of propaganda against the brutalities of English naval discipline. Mill in an attack on the practice of flogging in the army declared: "It is a vice inherent in an army or a navy exclusively officered by gentlemen, that the soldiers and sailors must be treated like brutes."[52] Not until the aristocratic monopoly was broken and the common soldier was given a chance to rise in the ranks could there be much expectation of rational discipline.

On the problem of poverty the *Repository* perhaps most clearly revealed the influence of Benthamite radicalism. Fox and his contributors were genuinely friends of the poor and the enemies of a privileged aristocracy, but their faith in the doctrines of the orthodox political economists sometimes led them to advocate coldly scientific measures for the care of the poor. With all the literalness of the true radical, they sought to get at the roots of the evils of poverty. Indiscriminate doles and mistaken, shortsighted charity had only increased the demoralization and pauperizing of the lower classes. Misdirection of perfectly laudable benevolence, said William Turner, "has fostered the very evils intended to be removed: it has depressed and degraded, instead of elevating the objects of its bounty; and converted *poverty* . . . into *pauperism,* the permanent characteristic of an immense and increasing class, sunk in the lowest immorality and wretchedness."[53] The old poor laws, an accretion of centuries, supplemented by charity, had often placed a premium upon pauperism at the expense of the independent, hardworking poor.

The Radicals did not dispute the frightful amount of suf-

[51] *Ibid.,* p. 287.
[52] *Ibid.,* p. 599.   [53] VII (1833), 727.

fering among the English poor or the dire need of relieving it. "But why," asked Fox in a review of Harriet Martineau's Poor Law Tales, "persist in plans which only aggravate the evil, and while they extend the physical suffering, generate from it a noxious mass of moral degradation?"[54] Fox recommended that private charity be transferred from measures which tended to keep the poor dependent and improvident, such as passing out free food and blankets, to measures which encouraged education and thrift, such as free schools and savings banks. Idleness must not be encouraged at the expense of industry. No relief should be granted except in return for services rendered, and improvident marriages should be discouraged. All of these measures, however, would only palliate the evil. Vigorous effort must be made to get at more fundamental correctives, such as these specified by Fox: abolition of the Corn Laws, to give the laborer food at the lowest possible rates; elimination of all taxes on the necessities of life and substitution of levies on property; removal of all restrictions upon the freedom of labor; establishment of an efficient plan of education, for both children and adults; the extension of political rights, to allay discontent and to permit the lower classes to share in the processes of their own improvement; and an organized and permanent plan for systematic emigration.[55]

John Stuart Mill, Fox's most distinguished contributor on political subjects, undoubtedly would have concurred in these recommendations, but he limited his *Repository* writings on the subject to advocacy of the new Poor Laws of 1834. These laws Mill claimed to be founded on

the principle upon which all good government, and all justly-constituted society rest; that no person who is able to work, is entitled to be maintained in idleness; or to be put into a better condition, at the expense of the public, than those who contrive

[54] *Ibid.*, p. 371.   [55] *Ibid.*, pp. 372-74.

to support themselves by their unaided exertions. Any infringe-
ment of this principle, whether by rich or poor, is not only
immoral, but nine-tenths of the immorality of the world are
founded on it. The desire to live upon the labour of others, is
at the root of almost all misgovernment, and of most private
dishonesty.[56]

The 1834 regulations provided for abolition of "outdoor"
(or home) relief and of supplementing low wages by parish
grants; relief would be granted only in workhouses, where
the sexes were to be segregated. No one would be allowed
to starve, but the terms of relief would be such as to make
the laborer apply only when absolutely necessary. "To this
end, relief must be given only in exchange for labour, and
labour at least as irksome and severe as that of the least
fortunate among the independent labourers: relief, moreover, must be confined to necessaries."[57] To the cry of
critics who said that all this constituted treating poverty
as a crime, Mill replied that it was "but making pauperism
no longer a piece of good fortune."[58]

Unfortunately for the logic of Mill and the Reformers,
the severity of the new Poor Laws aroused a storm of sentimental and humanitarian protest on which the Tories late
in 1834 were able to capitalize at least briefly. And when
the Whigs did return to power they had lost any stomach
for further Radical reforms.

On labor questions, the *Repository's* policy was largely
determined by acceptance of the orthodox political economy,
though humanitarianism usually checked the too rigid interpretation of those supposedly immutable "laws." On the
shocking conditions of child labor the *Repository* strangely
had little to say. The writer of the one full-length article
on the subject[59] professed horror at the revelations made by

[56] VIII (1834), 360.
[57] *Ibid.,* p. 361.   [58] *Ibid.*
[59] "On the Factory System," VII (1833), 145-53.

the Tory Sadler's investigation in 1832 and reprinted mortality tables showing that in districts where the factory system operated, the death rate under twenty was appallingly high; the difficulty was to "find a cure without producing a greater evil." Any check upon the manufacturing system might have distressing results upon the economy of the whole country. The writer did, however, concede that a thirteen-hour working day might be too long for a child. If only the Corn Laws could be abolished, the resultant lower price of food would enable concessions to be made by manufacturers without endangering their foreign markets. By proper regulation the Factory System might be capable of producing great good.

This blind spot in the Philosophic Radicals' vision extended also to the subject of trades-unions. Acceptance of the wage-fund theory postulated that strikes could never succeed in raising wages. The inexorable laws of supply and demand decreed that so long as there was an overabundance of labor, wages could not advance; reduction of the supply of labor by emigration and by the lowering of the birth rate was the only way by which wages could be made to increase. Mill in his *Repository* articles revealed his belief in the wage-fund theory at this time—in later life he honestly confessed his error—but vigorously defended labor's right to organize. Aside from preventing violence, "any attempt to confine the liberty of combination among workmen . . . is systematic tyranny." True indeed, said Mill, combinations could not raise wages. Even so. "The working people are entitled to try: unless they try, how are they ever to learn? You, their employers, have not been wont to show either so infallible a wisdom, or so pure and disinterested a zeal for *their* interests, that you should expect them to take the proposition on your word."[60] Both Mill and Fox, like many of the orthodox political economists,

[60] VIII (1834), 247.

were benevolent in their attitude towards the working classes but thought that the workers must learn to employ the laws of economics to their own advantage. Labor could get nowhere by beating its head against a stone wall.

In sum, then, it is fair to say that the *Repository's* politics followed the main lines of the program of the Philosophic Radicals. Important exceptions must, however, be made. Fox, as we have already seen, markedly qualified his acceptance of the Benthamite philosophy. Nor was Mill at this period (or later) a thorough-going Benthamite, though, by virtue of the intensive indoctrination he had undergone at the hands of his father, he had once been an enthusiastic disciple—until about 1826.

JOHN STUART MILL

The story of Mill's spiritual crisis, of his awakening to the deficiencies and narrowness of an exclusively Benthamite philosophy, is beyond the scope of our purpose here; it can best be read in his *Autobiography* or as interpreted against the philosophic and economic background of the times in Professor Emery Neff's *Carlyle and Mill*. Suffice it to say that after a period of despair Mill had found new hope in the poems of Wordsworth, in a new philosophy of history which was being applied to the problems of society by the disciples of Coleridge, and in the positive philosophy of August Comte. But if he was no longer exclusively a Benthamite, neither was he a Wordsworthian, a Coleridgean, or a positivist. Carlyle, reading a series of articles by Mill in the *Examiner* for 1831, hailed him (mistakenly) as "a new mystic," and when the two shortly thereafter became friends, Carlyle for a time thought he had made a convert. Events were to disclose the gulf between them. Mill no longer could be satisfied with the negativism of Benthamite philosophy or with its attempt to establish a quantitative view of the elements of human happiness; there were whole sides of life, music, poetry, art, emotion, which the calculating philosopher had neglected but which Mill had come to value. On the other hand, Mill's long apprenticeship to Reason, to Science, disqualified him from accepting the mystical, intuitional gospel of Carlyle.[61]

The development of Mill's philosophy in the years from 1828 to 1838 was by no means in a straight line. At one time or in some one sphere, Benthamism seemed still dominant; at another time the influence of Wordsworth, Coleridge, Comte, or Carlyle seemed stronger. A detailed study of these yet formative years, based upon a complete examination of his letters, and his contributions to the *Examiner,* the *Monthly Repository,* the *London and Westminster Review,* *Tait's Magazine,* and various newspapers, is still a desideratum. Here we shall be able to consider only the partial light thrown on the problem by Mill's connection with the *Repository.*

Though Mill was undoubtedly acquainted with Fox in the early years of the *Westminster Review,* to which both contributed, it was not until the 1830's that the connection became at all close. Fox was twenty years the older of the two, and if it had not been for his radical political views, his position as a minister might well have repelled Mill, who had been prejudiced by his education against formal religion. Undoubtedly it was through Harriet Taylor that the tie between the two men became strengthened and that Mill became a contributor to the *Repository.*

Harriet Taylor was the young wife of John Taylor, a drysalter or wholesale druggist, who belonged to Fox's congregation. He was a man of some education and culture, kindly and affectionate, and to the outer world at least, a good husband. But the marriage, on the wife's side at any

[61] Cf. his remarks on Carlyle, *Autobiography,* p. 124.

rate, was not happy. Harriet Hardy had married at eighteen to escape from an unhappy home. Her husband was more than twenty years her senior; she appreciated his good qualities but did not love him. She was a woman of refinement and taste, interested in literature and questions of ethics and politics, but endowed with a strong emotional nature which kept her out of the bluestocking category. Carlyle in his *Reminiscences* superciliously called her "veevid," a "very will o' the wispish iridescence of a creature, . . . pale and passionate and sad-looking, a living-romance heroine of the royallest volition and questionable destiny."

Legend has it that Mrs. Taylor, emotionally depressed for want of intellectual companionship, turned to her pastor as a kind of father confessor, and that Fox recommended that she make the acquaintance of his young friend, John Stuart Mill, as a kindred spirit. The acquaintanceship began at a dinner party in the Taylor home at which Fox, Roebuck, and Harriet Martineau were also present. The meeting was fateful. Before long friendship between Mill and Mrs. Taylor had become a deep and abiding love, strengthened by intellectual interests and sympathies. For Mill, emotionally starved in the intellectual forcing process to which he had been subjected as child and youth, love for Harriet Taylor became the turning point of his life. Since both conscientiously obeyed the moral sanctions of the times, divorce or any irregular relationship was out of the question. Neither, however, could give up the solace of an intellectual companionship that gave meaning to their lives, though they could not thoughtlessly disregard the obligations due to John Taylor. Harriet confessed the truth to her husband, and eventually a *modus vivendi* was established whereby she remained in his home, in name his wife. On evenings when Mill came to dine with his Egeria, the husband considerately dined out. Since her health was delicate, she was obliged to spend much time in the country and abroad; Mill at times accompanied her and her daughter. The relationship, of course, caused a good deal of gossip, but there was never any attempt at concealment.[62] They knew their own integrity and it was never sullied. How much suffering the two underwent in the twenty years of this relationship, Platonic in the true not vulgar sense of the word, cannot be estimated.

Two years after her husband's death in 1849 they were married. The happiness of the following years, which ended with her death in 1858, was the high point of Mill's life. When she was gone, life was meaningless to him except as he could carry on the causes to which they had together been devoted. His love for her memory led him to utter such extravagant tribute to her intellect and talent as to evoke condescending and almost contemptuous remarks from his associates. However over-colored by emotion his estimate of her powers may have been, there can be no doubt that she was the saving grace of his inner life. Without her, John Mill might well have been a different person,

[62] The probable autobiographical significance of at least one passage of Mill's *Repository* articles gives it an interest which it cannot have had under the conditions of anonymous publication. Mill must almost certainly have had in mind the criticism of his own conduct when in 1834 he discussed a bill proposed by O'Connell which provided that in cases of private libel, truth should be a justification. Mill saw "insuperable objections" to permitting the details of private conduct to be subjected to judicial investigation whenever any accuser wished.

"Every one knows how easy it is, without falsifying a single fact, to give the falsest possible impression of any occurrence; and, in the concerns of private life, the whole morality of a transaction commonly depends upon circumstances which neither a tribunal nor the public can possibly be enabled to judge of. . . . The moral character of the transaction cannot possibly be understood . . . without a minute acquaintance with a thousand particulars of the character, habits, and previous history of the parties, such as must be derived from personal knowledge, and cannot possibly be communicated."—VIII (1834), 176.

The only proper tribunal qualified to judge of private conduct is the opinion of one's friends. "And even their knowledge, how insufficient it generally is!" That insufficiency of knowledge Mill himself was destined to suffer at the hands of his own friends.

but one can doubt that he would have been as fine, as understanding, or as great a man.

Harriet Taylor was a close friend of Eliza Flower. The similarity between Eliza's relationship to Fox and Harriet's to Mill probably served to bring the two men closer together. Mill developed a high respect for Fox's abilities, and when plans were drawn up for the establishing of the *London Review* as a radical journal in 1835, Carlyle was given to understand that Fox was Mill's choice for the editorship. The fact that Mrs. Taylor was interested in Fox's efforts to improve the *Repository* and that she had become, in a small way, a contributor to its columns, probably encouraged Fox to invite Mill's contributions. Mill replied on April 3, 1832, to the effect that, since he did not regard himself as a writer but simply as one who wrote when he could thereby aid the causes in which he was interested, he could make no promise; if occasion offered, he would be glad to appear under Fox's auspices.[63]

Before the year was out, such an occasion arose, and Mill's first article, an essay entitled "On Genius," was published in the September, 1832, *Repository* over the signature "Antiquus," later shortened to "A." This, together with several other essays and reviews, we shall postpone for later consideration, meanwhile here limiting ourselves to a brief survey of Mill's political articles. Altogether, in the three years, 1832 to 1835, Mill contributed somewhat over 350 pages to the *Repository*.

"The staple of all popular writings in the present crumbling condition of the social fabric, must be politics," said Mill in his third *Repository* article, a review of the writings of Junius Redivivus (W. B. Adams) in April, 1833. But politics, though important, were not all-important. Junius Redivivus was praised for realizing "the limits of what

[63] Garnett, *Life of W. J. Fox*, pp. 100-1.

laws and institutions can do"; no form of government can make people happy in spite of themselves, and if a people are as individuals ignorant and selfish, no "legerdemain of checks and balances" can

conjure up a government better than the men by whom it is carried on. . . . The individual man must after all work out his own destiny, not have it worked out for him by a king, or a House of Commons; but he can hardly be in a suitable frame of mind for seeing and feeling this, while he is smarting under the sense of hardship and wrong from other men. Nor is this the worst; for the laws of a country, to a great degree, make its morals. . . .[64]

Mill did not go so far as Plato, who "expected no great improvement in the lot of humanity, until philosophers were kings, or kings philosophers," but he did believe that until the world could be governed "at the least by honest men, and men who with adequate practical talents combine the highest appreciation of speculative wisdom," there could be little hope either for culture or for material well being.

Mill labeled Adams as a radical because of the latter's conviction that "power, without accountability to those over whom, and for whose benefit it is to be exercised, is for the most part a source of oppression to them, and of moral corruption to those in whom the power resides." On the same principle Mill classed himself also as a radical. In justifying his writing in periodicals, he declared "the great intellectual business" of his time, and its peculiar mission, to be the popularizing "among the many, the more immediately practical results of the thought and experience of the few." Periodicals were the only means of adequate access to the general public; through them one could not hope to reach posterity, but at the moment one's contemporaries were the audience that needed instruction.

[64] VII (1833), 266-67.

Mill's next political contribution to the *Repository,* written at Fox's request, was an attack on "a Whig homily on a Tory text" in the *Edinburgh,* on the house and window tax.[65] The subject itself is of little interest now, but at several points light is thrown on Mill's personal opinions. His strenuous advocacy of a property tax, as opposed to taxes upon consumption and industry, was orthodox Benthamite economics, but his scorn of the *Edinburgh's* "association of 'a fortune' with 'sagacity, ingenuity, and economy'" would scarcely have pleased wealthy Benthamite manufacturers.

One would suppose . . . that we lived in a country where wealth was meted out proportionally to the worthiest; society constituted according to the principles inculcated in our little story books and nursery tales; and the whole island one beautiful picture of "Virtue Rewarded." Of the great fortunes which are made, how many are made thus fairly?[66]

And the following sentence, important evidence of his turn to distribution, which did not appear under his name until 1848, would have shocked laissez-faire economists: "We hope the time is coming for more rational modes of distributing the productions of nature and of art, than this expensive and demoralizing plan of individual competition, the evils of which have risen to such an enormous height."[67]

If it had been signed, Mill's brief review in the following year of Harriet Martineau's compendium of political economy would have seriously alarmed loyal Benthamites. In a letter Mill had confessed to Carlyle that Harriet's Political Economy Tales had carried the application of the science to the point of absurdity. Although in his review he was somewhat more lenient, he took occasion to warn not only Harriet but the whole race of political economists. To the

[65] *Ibid.,* pp. 575-82.
[66] *Ibid.,* p. 576.   [67] *Ibid.,* p. 580.

elaborate treatises of all of them, perhaps it might be objected, said Mill,

that they attempt to construct a permanent fabric out of transitory materials; that they take for granted the immutability of arrangements of society, many of which are in their nature fluctuating or progressive; and enunciate with as little qualification as if they were universal and absolute truths, propositions which are perhaps applicable to no state of society except the particular one in which the writer happened to live.[68]

English political economists had adapted their conclusions so exclusively to the conditions of English society that their conclusions were often erroneous when applied to other countries where conditions differed. Mill believed that, though the science's method of investigation was still applicable universally, "it is, when not duly guarded against, an almost irresistible tendency of the human mind to become the slave of its own hypotheses; and when it has once habituated itself to reason, feel, and conceive, under certain arbitrary conditions, at length to mistake these convictions for laws of nature."

Just as lawyers, by their habit of referring everything to the existing system, generally become foes to reform because they cannot imagine any other system, so Mill believed English political economists were likewise in danger of becoming enemies of reform.

They revolve in their eternal circle of landlords, capitalists, and labourers, until they seem to think of the distinction of society into those three classes, as if it were one of God's ordinances, not man's, and as little under human control as the division of day and night. Scarcely any one of them seems to have proposed to himself as a subject of inquiry, what changes the relations of those classes to one another are likely to undergo in the progress of society; to what extent the distinction itself admits of being

[68] VIII (1834), 319.

beneficially modified, and if it does not even, in a certain sense, tend gradually to disappear.[69]

Mill admitted that the time for such enquiries was probably not yet. Certain reforms needed first to be made: the abolition of monopolies and trade barriers favoring particular classes; the paying off of the national debt by an impost on all kinds of property; the new-modelling of the whole fiscal system; the lessening of pressure on the labor market by systematic colonization, and "by ceasing to give, through the maladministration of the poor laws, artificial inducements to the increase of population, and on the contrary, giving all the force we can to the natural checks." The necessity of all these reforms the political economists had taught, and the reforms were already on the way to accomplishment. But, said Mill,

We only ask of those to whom we are indebted for so much, that they will not require of us to believe that this is all, nor, by fixing bounds to the possible reach of improvement in human affairs, set limits also to that ardour in its pursuit, which may be excited for an object at an indefinite distance, but only if it be also of indefinite magnitude.[70]

All this is perhaps evidence enough that Mill by this time seriously qualified his acceptance of Benthamism. At the same time, in the realm of practical politics, his sense of the importance of immediate reforms led him in the main to side with the Philosophic Radicals in and out of Parliament. In July, 1833, he wrote to his Coleridgean friend John Sterling: "I think I am becoming *more* a Movement-man than I was, instead of less—I do not mean merely in politics but in all things—and that you are becoming more and more inclined to look backward for good."[71]

[69] *Ibid.,* p. 320.   [70] *Ibid.,* p. 321.
[71] *Letters of John Stuart Mill* (ed. by H. S. R. Elliot), I, 56-57.

On March 2, 1834, Mill wrote Carlyle somewhat apologetically: "I have written in the last *Repository,* and mean to continue during the session [of Parliament] 'notes on the newspapers,' so as to present for once at least a picture of our 'statesmen' and of their doings, taken from the point of view of a Radical to whom Radicalism in itself is but a small thing."[72] In form resembling modern newspaper editorials, these eighty-odd pages of "Notes on the Newspapers," continued for the eight months from March through October, 1834, constitute a kind of political diary, and are perhaps the best extant record of Mill's day-to-day application of his political philosophy. A glance at the list of the titles of the "Notes," in the appendixed identifications in the present volume (pp. 418-19), will reveal the wide variety of subjects.

Mill is throughout contemptuous of the Whigs and generally disappointed with the new Radical members. Nowhere, he thought, did there seem to be a leader, whether for good or ill. Society was cursed with too many of "the half-honest, the men of feeble purposes."[73] Everywhere there were, quoting Wordsworth, "the weak, the vacillating inconsistent Good" whose hands were chained by a "thousand paltry respectabilities and responsibilities."[74] Said Mill: "We want rulers who do not wait to be told by us how we wish to be governed; men who can teach us what we should demand, who can at least anticipate our demands, not slowly and grudgingly obey them."[75] Carlyle, reading this in far-off Scotland, must have rejoiced to hear his echo.

The "Notes on the Newspapers" are replete with scornful attacks on the landlords, who like spoiled children were always dissatisfied.[76] The agricultural interests' demands for the retention of the Corn Laws Mill boiled down to:

[72] *Ibid.,* p. 95.
[73] VIII (1834), 162.
[74] *Ibid.,* p. 236.
[75] *Ibid.,* p. 162.
[76] *Ibid.,* p. 234.

"They cannot afford to be landholders unless we pay them for it. We must tax ourselves to give them salaries for being a landed Aristocracy. We thank them for nothing."[77] Though the principle of Aristocracy, whereby the drones governed the bees, was the chief obstacle to reform, middle-class selfishness was also at fault. Already the middle classes were taking advantage of their new power to shake off their own burdens at the expense of the poor. Mill saw no grounds to share middle-class fears that the laboring multitude were assuming too much importance in government.

On the contrary, they have notoriously but just emerged from a state in which they had no power of claiming attention from any one; in which laws were made, avowedly to prevent them from taking the commonest means of improving their condition; in which their education was reputed dangerous to church and state; in which they were actually kept at home, like cattle belonging to a master, for their very emigration was illegal; in which no legislative measure ever passed merely for the good of the working classes, when no powerful section of their superiors had an interest in it; in which their opinions were never appealed to but when some party of the aristocracy wanted a popular cry.[78]

The working classes were only beginning to emerge from the shadow of this sort of thing. Only by a progressive increase in their power could they force the propertied classes to give them a share in their own government.

Mill resented supposedly well-intentioned efforts by the upper classes to impose morality upon the working masses quite as much as he resented aristocratic indifference to their welfare. When in the spring of 1834 a bill was presented to permit arbitrary closing of beer houses and to prohibit the workingman from enjoying his beer in his favorite pub, Mill protested vigorously against attempts to legislate morality. Neither the government nor the higher classes had a

[77] *Ibid.*, p. 244.   [78] *Ibid.*, p. 436.

title so to legislate; they did not "know enough of the people," and they did not "feel enough" with them. "Their attempts to exercise a guardianship over public morals by acts of parliament, always end in some curtailment of the people's liberty, never in any improvement of their morality."[79] One hears as if by anticipation, twenty-five years early, the authentic voice of the author of the essay *On Liberty*. The hypocrisy of "beer-house purism" roused Mill to more than usual vehemence:

When we have surrounded a whole people with circumstances which, unless they were angels, *must* render them immoral; when, by the administration of the Poor Laws, we have placed them in a position in which none of the ordinary motives to good conduct can act upon them; when we have deprived them of almost every innocent amusement; when, by stopping up foot-paths and inclosing commons, we are every year excluding them more and more even from the beauties of nature; when, by our savage punishments for killing the game we tempt them with for our amusement, we have made our gaols little better than what the bitter patrician sarcasm of Appius Claudius termed the Roman prisons, the *domicilium plebis;* when, by whatever we have attempted, for them or against them, well meant or ill meant, we have been constantly labouring to alienate them from us, it is with a good grace, is it not, that, after letting loose the torrent, we attempt to dam it up with a straw? Make the people dishonest, make them disaffected, and then fancy that dishonesty and disaffection will be at fault for want of a place to meet in! With one hand turn virtue out of doors, and with the other try to refuse an entry to vice![80]

Altogether, the "Notes on the Newspapers" furnish a valuable index to the development of Mill's political philosophy. That his views were in essential accord at this time with those of Fox may be seen in a review (probably erroneously attributed to Mill) of E. L. Bulwer's *England and*

[79] *Ibid.*, p. 370.   [80] *Ibid.*

the English.[81] Whether or not the review was by Mill, the program it advocates is sufficiently identical with that of the *Repository* to serve as a final summary of the magazine's position. The root of the evils of English society and government the reviewer thought to be the spirit of aristocracy and privilege which pervaded English life. To eradicate the evils, constitutional reform must first be completed by extending the suffrage, adopting the secret ballot, and ensuring the responsibility of parliaments by shortening their term. Next in importance was the establishment of universal education by removing taxes on the press, developing a system of schools for all, and appropriating some of the Church revenues for this purpose. "Reading rooms, libraries, lectures, should be multiplied throughout the country; and we must also, by discussion and rational experiment, endeavour to mitigate that individual competition which so largely wastes the energy and vitiates the feelings of society."[82] The reviewer foresaw no early alteration of the monarchial form of government, but agreed with Bulwer that ultimately the tendencies of things pointed to a period when Englishmen should "perceive, slowly sweeping over the troubled mirror of the time, the giant shadow of the coming republic."

[81] "Characteristics of English Aristocracy," VII (1833), 585-601. Garnett in his *Life of W. J. Fox* (p. 104) attributes the review to Mill, as does the British Museum key to the *Repository* (though with a prefixed question mark). The present writer doubts that the review was written by Mill. Internal evidence would seem to point to Fox instead. Both Mill's correspondence with Carlyle (Cf. *Letters of John Stuart Mill,* ed. by H. S. R. Elliot, pp. 61, 70) and his own review of this number of the *Repository* (*Examiner,* Sept. 8, 1833, p. 567), in which he praises the article highly, would seem to argue against Mill's authorship. Also, the item does not appear in Mill's own bibliography of his writings. It is possible that the review of Bulwer's book has been attributed to Mill because of his defense of Bulwer in his "Letter from an Englishman to a Frenchman, on a Recent Apology in 'The Journal des Débats,' for the Faults of the English National Character," which appeared in the *Repository* for June, 1834 (VIII, 385-95).

[82] VII (1833), 601.

THE EMANCIPATION OF WOMEN

The *Repository's* politics, its urging of extreme radical
reforms, its stinging attacks on the Whigs, certainly helped
to alienate some of its Unitarian subscribers, but its advanced social views offended even more. In their politics
Unitarians had been traditionally radical enough that they
might have come to tolerate Fox's more extreme views. In
their social code, however, Unitarians were as conservative
as most middle-class Englishmen. Their social conservatism
may even have been strengthened by their radicalism in religion and politics: for their views in these fields they had
been for long so subject to attack that they were bound to
seek moral respectability if only to disprove their critics'
contention that adoption of their religious principles led to
moral degeneration. Also, they could hardly escape being
influenced by the ascendency of the strict Evangelical code
of morality among the English middle classes of the 1830's.[83]

We have seen that Unitarians were among the early advocates in England of the cause of women, though for the
most part their efforts were confined to the question of education. They believed that if women were better educated,
improvement in their social condition was bound to follow.
In this view Unitarians had no monopoly: Sydney Smith in
the *Edinburgh Review* for 1810 argued for the improvement
of women's education; Jane Austen, at least by implication,
attacked the vapid and frivolous nature of women's training; and the *Westminster Review* almost from the first
championed their cause.[84]

Unitarians as well as others seem to have paid less attention to the deplorable legal status of women. In 1832
and for years afterwards English law gave very limited

[83] Fox himself on occasion betrayed traces of Evangelical narrowness; in
1832, for instance, he refused to print Crabb Robinson's translation of one of
Goethe's poems because of its supposedly immoral tendency.

[84] See G. L. Nesbitt, *Benthamite Reviewing*, pp. 88-91.

protection to women. Marriage involved the surrender to the husband of almost every vestige of legal right.[85] A single woman at her majority could inherit and administer property; a wife held no right even to dispose of her personal belongings. After betrothal, before marriage, a woman had to gain the consent of her fiancé to dispose of her property. The husband secured title to all his wife's possessions, and if by her talents she was able to earn money, her earnings were also legally his. He held a vested right in her person: if she was unruly, he could lock her up; if she ran away, he could compel the return of the fugitive. Practically his only obligation was financial; he was liable for her support and for any debts she contracted, but for little more. No matter how brutal or profligate the husband, the wife had little legal redress. For her to obtain a divorce was virtually impossible; the only ground permitted was aggravated adultery, and the wife could not appear to testify as plaintiff, defendant, or witness. Divorce had to be obtained by act of Parliament and the cost was usually prohibitive. Legal separations could be obtained on the grounds of cruelty, adultery, and unnatural practices. In legal fact the wife was a veritable chattel or slave, though of course not all husbands took advantage of the letter of the law. There were kind slave owners, too.

It was perhaps inevitable that Fox, endowed as he was with warm humanitarian sympathies, should eventually have become concerned over the condition of women. His high moral and social idealism rebelled against injustice; his faith in progress postulated that one half of humanity could not develop its highest potentialities without the help of the other half, especially since to that other half the rearing of the next generation was largely entrusted. His close acquaintance with at least four talented women—

[85] For a summary of the status of women at this time, see Wanda F. Neff, *Victorian Working Women*, Chapter VI.

Eliza and Sarah Flower, Harriet Martineau, and Harriet Taylor—strengthened his confidence in the capabilities of the sex. In his discussion of the problems of marriage and divorce he was no advocate of laxer moral standards, as some of his critics charged; on the contrary, he argued his case on the highest moral grounds. Reform of the marriage and divorce laws he believed was essential to the elevation of English morality. As in the parallel case of Milton, Fox's argument for divorce is highly idealistic. But also, as in the case of Milton, he may be suspected of perhaps unconscious rationalizing. One finds it possible to doubt that either would have been so ardent an advocate for greater freedom of divorce if his own marriage bonds had not been irksome.

We have already noticed in another connection Fox's preliminary sparring for women's rights in September, 1832, when he tentatively advocated woman suffrage.[86] In the same article he outlined briefly a few particulars in which he believed there was great room for improvement in the condition of women: the restraints of custom and training which thwarted their physical development in the interests of achieving the admired feminine delicacy; and the limiting of female education to comparatively trifling objects and superficial attainments. He saw no reason to believe that women were not capable of solid intellectual achievement. And to the argument that genuine education would "raise them above their station," Fox replied, "All the better." They might thus shame men into "something like intellectual progress." The great trouble was that women were educated only to get married.

We understand not why one-half of the community should have no other destiny than irremediable dependence upon the other half; as long as women have nothing in the world to look to

[86] "A Political and Social Anomaly," VI (1832), 637-42.

but marriage, they cannot become qualified, in the best manner, for a married life; so long as the modes in which property is inherited, acquired, and distributed, leave them in utter dependence, they can never, in that institution, treat or be treated as independent parties, making a fair and equal contract for mutual benefit. Under the present order of things, a large proportion of them must remain as they are, fools to be cajoled, toys to be sported with, slaves to be commanded, and in ignorant pride that they are so. . . .[87]

Meanwhile, their real task in the world—purifying taste, reforming manners and morals, educating children, and helping to forward social changes and improvements—was not being fulfilled. Man had placed women in degraded circumstances, crippled their intellect, and thereby weakened his own. "In training a dependent, he has lost a companion."

In all this there was not much to which many Unitarians would have objected. Fox's next article to touch upon the condition of women, "The Dissenting Marriage Question,"[88] must, however, have made Unitarian ministers look askance. The occasion of the article was the Dissenters' effort to abolish the Church's monopoly in the performance and registration of the marriage ceremony. This long-standing grievance of orthodox as well as unorthodox Dissent was at last on the way to the settlement achieved in 1836. Fox, like many Dissenters, believed that the marriage contract should be regarded by the law as merely a civil transaction. He objected strenuously, moreover, to any measure by which the celebration of marriage should be merely transferred from the Episcopalian minister to the Dissenting. Any religious service attached to the ceremony should be purely voluntary; the contract should be "distinct from it, and complete without it." Otherwise, superstition could not be eradicated, and the Protestant ministry would take

[87] *Ibid.*, p. 641.   [88] VII (1833), 136-42.

on priestly functions. Said Fox, "The dissenting ministry already tends quite enough towards a priesthood." The magistrate should be the "only person known to the law in the formation of the marriage contract."

Fox's insistence on the abolition of the sacramental nature of marriage and the substitution of a civil contract, had a purpose. Once the principle that marriage was a civil contract was established, there could be hope for a rational divorce law. The existing system he thought pernicious for both the individual and society.

In many cases parties are inexorably bound together for life by the law, and by those anomalous relics of popery the ecclesiastical courts, who are neither one flesh nor one spirit, but, morally speaking, divorced, and without affection, if they live together, living together viciously. . . . Moreover, the streets of all large cities swarm with unhappy women, miserable agents of the temptation of which they were at first the victims, alike suffering and corrupting, and visiting on the other sex an involuntary but fearful retaliation for their own ruin.[89]

If marriage could be made a civil contract, then that contract could be dissolved, as it should be, like any other contract when the interests of the parties involved and of the community could be best so served. Fox in his attitude toward the problem reveals the influence of the German historical view of the Bible. "There never would have been any doubt on this matter, but for priests alike ignorant and meddling, who have strangely misapplied to legal and judicial divorce . . . that which our Lord said [Matt. xix:8] of the private and irresponsible right of divorce which the Jew possessed under the law of Moses."[90] Establishment of marriage as a simple contract, independent of priest or religious ceremony, would also have an effect in ameliorating the evil of prostitution. The great cause of that evil Fox believed to be

[89] *Ibid.*, p. 141.   [90] *Ibid.*

seduction, which in a moral view he regarded as marriage.
Even temporarily to tolerate polygamy would be infinitely
better than "this eternal flood of prostitution."

In the cause of women's emancipation Fox's most effective writing, both as literature and as propaganda, was an
article entitled "A Victim," which appeared in March,
1833.[91] In a "family gallery of stiff and starched portraits,"
A Biographical History of the Wesley Family by one John
Dove, Fox had found a lovely and affecting portrait to
adorn his case for the rights of women. This was a portrait
of Mehetabel Wesley, a younger sister of the founder of
Methodism, and a kind of modern Jephtha's daughter. The
story of Mehetabel, or Hetty, as her brothers called her, is
perhaps now so little known as to warrant brief summary
here, somewhat as Fox recounts it. She was, says Fox,

a beautifully-organized creature, and endowed with that peculiarity of the nervous system which is the physical temperament
of poetry; which quickens alike the organs of sense and the
apparatus of thought; which makes perception clear, imagination vivid, and emotion intense; and to which earth is either
heaven or hell, as external circumstance harmonizes or jars with
the internal constitution.

Her misfortune was to be born into what was once known
as "a well-regulated family"; her father, the Reverend
Samuel Wesley, a cold, austere, dogmatical Tory priest; her
mother, a feminine counterpart of the rector of Epworth,
who before she was thirteen years old had "examined the
whole controversy between the Established Church and the
Dissenters," and who lived her whole life severely according
to rule.

The gentle, lovely, sensitive Mehetabel's first calamity,
said Fox, was her education. Mrs. Wesley's rule in forming
the minds of her children was first to master their will; her

[91] *Ibid.*, pp. 164-77.

own statement is a sufficient indication of her success: *"When turned a year old (and some before) they were taught to fear the rod, and to cry softly. . . ."* Since, in her view, doing the will of God, and not one's own, constituted religion, the parent who did not break the will of his child was doing the devil's work and thereby damning his child eternally. Such a view of religion and education Fox thought to be the essence and perfection of tyranny. To him the object of religion—and of children's education—was to "make the human will *coincide* with the divine will, by enlightening the mind till it perceives the latter only consults the happiness of man."

Mehetabel's second calamity was an unhappy love affair, arbitrarily terminated by her father. In her despair she made a vow to accept the first man who offered to marry her. And when, as Fox phrased it, "a Caliban civilized into vulgarity by the pothouse had the audacity to offer the violence of marriage to his Miranda, her father compelled her to submit to the brutality." For twenty-five years she had to endure the burden of a loveless marriage to a rude clod. "It was only in the six and twentieth year of her suffering, that she was dismissed to tell Milton in heaven that his doctrine was still immoral upon earth." Fox's application of the story was trenchantly expressed.

Mehetabel Wesley was the victim, as woman is yet continually the victim, of bad education, perverted religion, and unequal institution. . . . The restraint which crippled her faculties, the awful rod which made her an infant slave, was an immorality. This was the source of her own errors. The twig was twisted, and so grew the tree, though graceful even in its distortion. Her marriage was an immorality. So was her continuing through life in a sexual companionship where mutual affection was impossible; not that she was conscious of viciousness, but the contrary; she no doubt thought her misery was her duty. Ill fare the machinery that wrought the perversion and the suffering.

For woman so situated there ought to be redress, open and honourable redress, in every country that calls itself civilized. . . . Savage man kicks and beats woman, and makes her toil in the fields; semi-civilized man locks her up in a harem; and man three-quarters civilized, which is as far as we are got, educates her for pleasure and dependency, keeps her in a state of pupilage, closes against her most of the avenues of self-support, and cheats her by the false forms of an irrevocable contract into a life of subservience to his will. The reason for all which is "that he is the stronger." And the result of which is that he often lacks an intelligent and sympathizing companion when most he needs one. . . . Truly he makes as bad a bargain as he deserves.[92]

To label as an immorality the long and faithful wedded life of a devout and virtuous woman may well have shocked a number of Fox's readers, but his publication as the leading article of the following month the intransigent Junius Redivivus' "On the Condition of Women in England" was the clinching blow. Adams' wholesale indictment of English social and moral standards, expressed in uncompromising and vigorous language, no doubt offended many readers, especially at a time when Evangelical prudery exercised a strong influence. Lant Carpenter did not speak for himself alone when, as we have already seen in his letter of complaint to Fox, he protested against Adams' "exaggerated as well as degrading picture" of the state of society, written "in a style adapted to awaken the conceptions of the sensualist." Without agreeing with Carpenter's condemnation, the modern reader may admit that Adams exaggerated certain aspects of the situation. Certainly Adams was somewhat too much of a fire-eater to win many converts to his views.

William Bridges Adams (1797-1872) was the son of a well-to-do manufacturer of coaches. After receiving his elementary education, he served an apprenticeship in mechanical engineering, but was forced to give up the profes-

[92] *Ibid.*, 176-77.

sion because of poor health. As a result he embarked upon a long course of travel, which took him through extensive areas of North and South America. Upon his return to England he interested himself in Radical Reform and published many controversial articles and pamphlets and a pseudo-Byronic poem, *A Tale of Tucuman*. His first wife was Elizabeth Place, daughter of the well known radical leader, Francis Place. His second wife we have already met —Sarah Flower, whose acquaintance he formed by reason of their mutual interest in the *Repository*. When by 1837 he had spent his patrimony, he entered business and became a manufacturer of railroad equipment. A competent and resourceful engineer, he was in later life a prolific contributor to scientific periodicals and the inventor of several devices still used by railroads.

As a person he was warm-hearted, generous, a foe to any kind of social injustice, but in some things eccentric—for instance, he abjured the use of buttons and held his clothes together with strings, tapes, and hooks and eyes. As a writer, he was possessed of an original, terse style, forceful and blunt rather than graceful, and at times ambiguous from the rapidity with which he wrote. The best estimate of his early writing is to be found in John Stuart Mill's article on the "Writings of Junius Redivivus" in the *Repository* for April, 1833.[93] Mill found particularly attractive Adams' "lively admiration and keen enjoyment of the beautiful in all its kinds, both spiritual and physical." This quality Mill thought had saved Adams from the error so commonly found among the social reformers:

the error of expecting that the regeneration of mankind, if practicable at all, is to be brought about exclusively by the cultivation of . . . the *reasoning* faculty; . . . forgetting too that, even supposing perfect knowledge to be attained, no good will come of

---

[93] *Ibid.*, pp. 262-70. Mill also wrote another article on Junius Redivivus for *Tait's Magazine*, June, 1833.

it, unless the *ends,* to which the means have been pointed out, are first *desired.*

Junius Redivivus' sensitiveness to beauty had quickened his intellect, expanded his views, and opened his eyes to "the importance of poetry and art, as instruments of human improvement on the largest scale." The criticism reveals the critic; Mill himself was no longer a reasoning machine.

Adams had been induced to write for the *Repository* because of his approval of its policies. In November, 1832, he had written to Fox, complimenting him upon the magazine: "The difference between your periodical and those of your more aristocratic contemporaries, appears to me to be, that your contributors are mostly *thinkers,* and those of your neighbors, *writers*—the former, striving to engage the judgment, the latter the imagination."[94] Fox, who earlier in the year had printed commendatory notices of two of Adams' pamphlets,[95] made this letter the text of some remarks on the conduct of the *Repository.*[96] In January, 1833, appeared Adams' first contribution, an article "On the State of the Fine Arts in England,"[97] and thereafter he was a fairly regular contributor on a variety of subjects. His articles were always signed Junius Redivivus. Altogether he contributed somewhat over three hundred pages: politics, poetry, social and dramatic criticism. He was not a great writer, and his work, confined as it was to current topics, has not survived, though it may still be read with some interest, if only for its rather heroic boldness of tone.

Adams' chief contribution to the *Repository's* condition-of-women crusade lay in his exposition of the degrees of women's servitude at different levels of society.[98] In all ranks they were slaves, he declared, just as much as the denizens of a Turkish harem, though in a different fashion:

[94] VI (1832), 793.
[95] *Ibid.,* pp. 139-41, 503-4.
[96] *Ibid.,* pp. 794-97.
[97] VII (1833), 1-13.
[98] *Ibid.,* pp. 217-31.

"the poor man seeks an efficient working slave, the rich man, an agreeable and well-taught harem slave. The man in middling circumstances endeavours, if possible, to combine both."

In the higher classes women's education was largely confined, said Adams, to the polite accomplishments, that is, "singing, music, and dancing, and dressing, and a peculiar carriage and capacity for gesticulation, whereby to excite the senses, and attract the notice of those of the male sex who are deemed sufficiently wealthy, or sufficiently noble, to be worth looking after as husbands." And when their training is finished they are "put up for sale at the fashionable shambles" to the highest bidder. Marriage is made a matter not of love but of bargain and sale—a legally sanctioned species of prostitution, or "at best but prostitution clothed in the robes of sanctity."

In the lower middle classes the difference in training was only in degree. "Such females are made to play a double part; they are to be housewives on ordinary occasions, and fine ladies when required. They must suckle the fools, and chronicle the small beer behind the scenes, and sing and play on the piano—whether with taste or without—whenever 'company' is collected." They must learn how to be useful as household drudges but be sufficiently skilled in meretricious arts "to get their legs beneath another man's table."

Among the poor, conditions were even worse, for poverty destroyed even the vestiges of refinement. "Visit the frightful dens at Manchester and elsewhere, where human beings, male and female, young and old, are huddled one amongst the other in unseemly contiguity, like cattle in the shambles, and amongst whom the very idea of delicacy has long been destroyed." Love and marriage in such surroundings could scarcely attain the ideal, but little improvement in these respects could be hoped for among the poor until their physical circumstances were improved.

As for the other classes, the entire system must be changed, said Adams. *"Women must be regarded and treated as the equals of men, in order to work the improvement of man himself."* They must be given the same education as men, for their part in society is fundamentally more important than that of men; men provide food and shelter, but women must, in bringing up children, "provide food for the mind." Also, educational equality was not all. *"Woman must be made morally the equal of man."* Like the Turks, Englishmen have required only one virtue of women—chastity; as a result, almost any other vice has been permitted. Meanwhile the male is permitted with impunity to break his marriage vows—because, having the power, he has so decreed it. Women, then, agreed Adams with Fox, must be freed from slavery by making marriage a civil contract, capable of being dissolved like any other contract. From irresponsible slaves they might be transformed by education into "glorious creatures."

Adams' article was the last important full-length treatment of its subject to appear in the *Repository,* but there were in the succeeding years frequent allusions to various aspects of the problem. Fox in his letter to Carpenter defended his own and Adams' position on marriage and divorce and restated their case.[99] In his review of Campbell's *Life of Mrs. Siddons* Fox defended, in passing, the virtue of actresses and went somewhat out of his way to deprecate the English ideal of chastity as the sole necessary virtue in woman. According to the English code, "she may be full of 'envy, hatred, malice, and all uncharitableness'; as ignorant as an ass, as obstinate as a mule, as blind as a beetle, as poisonous as an asp, and as savage as a hyæna, and yet

[99] *Ibid.,* pp. 352-54.

be a virtuous woman. . . . For none of these things does she *lose caste*. She still retains HER *virtue.*"[100] Fox also took occasion to criticize the English law, which as in the case of Mrs. Siddons, gave the husband full control of the earnings of a talented wife.[101] The reviewer of Bulwer's *England and the English* declared that English reasoning on the subject of marriage did not "turn upon whether a man or woman may not find a mutual agreement for certain purposes to be mutually advantageous; but upon whether, by a certain arrangement, woman does not become to man a better property."[102] Mrs. Mary Leman Grimstone, whose work we shall note in another connection, in her tales and essays labored to advance the cause of woman's education and the adoption of a single standard of morals.[103]

Altogether, the *Repository's* record on the emancipation of women is a distinctly honorable one. For its day it was far in advance of common opinion; no contemporary periodical so consistently advocated an enlightened policy. Though the *Repository's* circulation was small, it was among a select audience. Through that audience it made its contribution to the "mighty stream of tendency" which irresistibly, though at times only inch by inch, was to persist down through the nineteenth and into the twentieth century, to free women from the bondage of ignorance and domestic slavery and to give them their proper share in the concerns of life. Not until 1937 did England adopt a divorce law which at all approached that which Fox had advocated over a hundred years earlier. The *Repository's* part in that movement has of course been forgotten; it is not for that reason the less creditable.

[100] VIII (1834), 536-37.
[101] *Ibid.*, pp. 548-49. [102] VII (1833), 588.
[103] See especially "Acephala," VIII (1834), 771-77; and "Female Education," IX (1835), 106-12.

7: Fox's Repository: "*Those Finer Inlets*"

INTERESTING AS THE *Repository's* political and social criticism is for the light that it throws upon the liberalism of a small but advanced and enthusiastic group of reformers, whatever lasting reputation the magazine has possessed has rested upon its literary and cultural achievements. Fox and his associates worked ardently for political reform, but they never lost sight of the fact that the true progress of a people cannot be maintained through political institutions alone. To them, politics were important but not all-important. Their great concern (to apply to the group what Mill said of W. B. Adams) was "the improvement of the human beings themselves: of which the improvement of their institutions will be a certain *effect,* may be in some degree a *cause,* and is so far even a necessary condition, that until it is accomplished, none of the other causes of improvement can have fair play."[1] Consequently, the *Repository* often devoted its leading articles to political questions but did not neglect to consider the deeper and more fundamental questions of art, music, and literature that inevitably affect the spiritual and intellectual life of a people. The greatest happiness of the greatest number could not be achieved by abolishing the Bread Tax alone. Said Fox in his notable leading article for January, 1835, on "The True Spirit of Reform":

The Suffrage and the Ballot, the House of Lords and the Church, and all the mechanism of legislation and government . . . have, after all, more to do with the clearance of outward and gross impediments to human progress than with the progress

[1]*Monthly Repository,* 2d series, VII (1833), 266. Unless otherwise indicated, all references are to the second series of the *Monthly Repository,* Volumes VI-X, 1832-1836.

itself. Hence real Reformers are deeply interested in whatever belongs to science, art, education, and all the economy of life. They especially desire that the working classes should thoroughly understand their condition, and the means for its improvement. . . . We have ceased to hear of the hard and barren doctrine of utility. The cultivation of a popular enjoyment and philosophy of Art, is amongst the primary objects of real Reformers. They would instil into the people the reality of that taste, of which the semblance is affected as one of the perquisites of Aristocracy. They want not, in the multitude, a mass of brute agency to do their bidding, but men who not only "know their rights, and knowing dare maintain," but who also shall reason, and feel, and derive enjoyment from all those finer inlets which are the access of nature and genius to the human soul.[2]

To the exploration and development of "those finer inlets," especially of literature though not to the exclusion of painting and music, much of the *Repository* was devoted. That chief emphasis among the arts should have been placed upon literature is understandable; then, even more than now, literature was the pre-eminent art among the English, and it was also the art most suitable for refining the taste and enriching the lives of the people. Fox's views of art, literary and otherwise, were essentially utilitarian, but utilitarian in the highest sense of the term. He and his coterie of writers would by no means have agreed with the narrow Benthamite view that pushpin is as good as poetry if it gives the same amount of pleasure. They recognized the importance of the qualitative element which Bentham chose to overlook, but they believed that art must serve, and be judged according as it served, moral and spiritual purposes. The "Victorian morality of art" is discernible before the advent of Victoria.

In the domain of literature, and especially in criticism and poetry, the *Repository* of 1832-1836 takes a high rank

[2] IX (1835), 8.

when compared with contemporary periodicals of its general kind. Its showing is all the more notable for the fact that it was dependent upon voluntary, unpaid contributions; its more popular rivals like *Blackwood's, Fraser's,* and the *New Monthly* magazines were well financed business enterprises which could command the services of the best paid writers of the day. Those who like Carlyle were dependent upon the periodicals for their livelihood could not afford to write for the *Repository.* Fox was fortunately able to attract talented and able amateurs to his cause, and his sympathetic and helpful criticism, as in the case of Harriet Martineau, earned him the services of a few gifted young writers. He himself was one of the ablest of the magazine's writers; in addition to producing the largest share of the political articles, he contributed a number of excellent essays and sketches and most of its best criticism. Not the least of his laurels as a critic were won by his early recognition of the merits of the two great poets of the coming generation; he was the first reviewer to discern the promise of Robert Browning and among the first to praise Tennyson. Just how important was Fox's "fine Roman hand" will be seen when we examine the *Repository* after it was transferred to the editorship of R. H. Horne.

CRITICISM

1. *Literature*

Fox made no pretense of attempting to review every book that came from the presses and on one occasion claimed exemption from "overmuch labour" in reviewing: "We are only an eighteen-pennyworth." The six-shilling Quarterlies "from their Alpine height" might survey the world of literature; the three and sixpenny Monthlies load their columns with periodical criticism; and the weekly Reviews "keep pace with the march of publication": the *Re-*

pository was a Magazine, not a Review. "When we have a hit at authors, it is like sportsmen, not butchers. We are not obliged to cut up calves. We just take a chance shot or two in the season, when we see a tempting book on the wing, and thus make our readers a present of some game by way of civil compliment."[3] Fox was a good shot; unfortunately, game worthy of his aim was sparse. A glance at a chronological table of literary works for the years 1832 to 1836 will reveal how few distinguished books appeared. Most of the great writers of the Romantic period were gone, and the great Victorians were making only trial flights. Dickens was publishing *Sketches by Boz* in 1835, and *Pickwick* was to begin his career in the next year. Thackeray was a hack for *Fraser's*. Carlyle's reputation was largely limited to his periodical articles; his *Sartor Resartus* was not to appear in book form in England until 1838, one year after *The French Revolution*. Tennyson and Browning had each published two works: Tennyson in 1830 and 1833, Browning in 1833 and 1835; but neither had achieved more than a limited *succès d'estime*. Altogether, it is a tribute to Fox's literary acumen that he should have selected for review as many works of lasting importance as he did.

The *Repository's* reviews fall into two classes, major and minor. Major reviews were articles of perhaps ten or a dozen pages, which were interspersed among the original articles. Many of these reviews, especially of non-literary works, were virtually original articles, using the book or pamphlet as a kind of text for the reviewer's own discourse. Of the literary works selected for major review over two-thirds were poetry—an indication of Fox's taste rather than of the public's, it must be admitted. Minor reviews were short critical notices which appeared in a section at the end of most numbers; these notices ranged in length from two

[3] VIII (1834), 677.

or three sentences to two or three paragraphs, or, occasionally, pages. In 1832 and 1833 many of these notices were of religious works; later, the range was wide, from medical treatises to popular novels, and from statistical works to poetry and drama. At one point the magazine resorted to listing a number of current books and supplying in footnotes a few cursory remarks. In general, the minor reviews are of small enough importance to warrant our neglecting them in favor of a fuller consideration of the major reviews of literary works.

Fox's choice of a subject for his first important review was significant both of his interest in poetry and of his concern for the cause of the poor. Entitled "The Poor and Their Poetry,"[4] it was a review of three volumes of verse by Ebenezer Elliott, the "Corn Law Rhymer." Half of the article was devoted to a defense of the thesis that "Poetry is not the privilege of a class, either in its production or its enjoyment." Setting to one side poems which, like Milton's *Paradise Lost* and Gray's Odes, by their classical and historical allusions could appeal chiefly to the educated and wealthier classes, and poems *concerning* the poor but neither by nor for them, like Crabbe's *Borough,* Fox declared that the real poetry of the poor must be made up of something more than observation and sympathy. "It should be the language, not of the observant and pitying gentleman, but of humanity in poverty, pouring forth its own emotions for its own gratification." That the appetite for poetry existed among uncultivated minds could be demonstrated by its rise in the early stages of civilization and by the usual contents of the poor man's library, "his bible, his hymn-book, and the Pilgrim's Progress—all poetry, each in its way, and cherished by him, though he may not be aware of the fact, because they are poetry as well as religion." The poor man's religion in essence is always poetry.

[4] VI (1832), 189-201.

In the past, said Fox, many poets had risen from humble
life, but usually in their elevation they had acquired the
learning, tastes, habits, and feelings of the wealthier classes
and so did not in their poetry speak to the poor. For that
purpose, poetry "must emanate from men who remain surrounded by the scenery, partakers of the privations, subject
to the wrongs, real or imaginary, and animated by the passions and hopes, which belong exclusively to poverty." Admittedly, this could seldom happen, for ordinarily the man
of talent will educate himself and thereby rise in society.
Fox "set no store by the twaddling verses of sundry rhym-
ing laundresses, dairymaids, and butlers, who have been
cockered into a very transitory reputation by the pious
charity of some well-disposed and respectable persons, who
found their milk-and-water effusions congenial with their
own mental and moral mediocrity." Bloomfield and Clare
were the best of this class of writers, but their pictures of
poverty were one-sided. "The genuine poverty of society
does not live in the fields. Its horrors and its passions, in
their sternest form, are city born. Let there be meadows and
mountains, but there must also be streets, alleys, workshops,
and jails, to complete the scenery of the poetry of poverty."
Bloomfield and Clare had been "too merely pastoral" and
their subjects tame.

Robert Burns, according to Fox the only real predecessor of the Corn Law Rhymer, was the first genuine poet
of the poor. His education was not such as to raise him in
society; he seldom indulged in classical or learned allusions;
and his themes—nature, love, and politics—contained the
universal elements of poetry. The emotions which nature
aroused in him were primary, not secondary. "They were
not the *débris* of an old world of poetry." Nor were his
love songs merely conventional, though Fox deplored their
occasional lowering "towards the degraded regions of physi-

cal instinct." Sensitive to beauty, Burns was also sensitive to oppression and social injustice; he set the example of writing on such subjects, "not as the laureate of a party, but as the Tyrtaeus of humanity."

Fox knew nothing of the author of the *Corn Law Rhymes* except that by hearsay he was a workingman in the North, named Elliott. (Actually, Elliott was a small manufacturer, not a mechanic, and he was scarcely poverty-stricken.) At any rate, he filled Fox's prescription for a poet of the poor. The three volumes of his verse which Fox had read treated, in succession, the three great poetic themes of Burns. Intermingled with strong emotions, stern wrath against monopoly and injustice, his poetry was pervaded with "the imagination of a genuine poet." After liberal quoting, Fox concluded with generous praise of Elliott's work as one of the signs of the times:

These "rhymes" are no cold coruscations flitting about, like the northern lights in a dim and distant region, for idle people to gaze at. They are intense flashes of liquid lava from that central fire, which must have vent, or its expansion will shiver to atoms the great globe itself. The intellect of poverty is too powerful, and too impetuous, to be bound within the narrow confines of the condition of poverty. . . .[5]

That Fox's praise of Elliott was over-enthusiastic may be granted; the critic's sympathy for the poor and his hatred of aristocratic monopoly undoubtedly biased his critical judgment—though it will be remembered that a greater writer than Fox, Thomas Carlyle, also paid high tribute to the *Corn Law Rhymes*. Fox's praise netted at least one tangible result for the *Repository:* Elliott, as we shall see, became a contributor.

Since Fox was always on the lookout for evidence of growing intelligence among the masses, he usually accorded

[5] *Ibid.*, p. 201.

favorable review to books by workers. In an editorial postscript at the close of 1833 he expressed the hope that there
would be more of this type of publication:

writings of mechanics, which are not mechanical; more "Independents in Church and State"; works of men, who working
with strong brains as well as brawny arms, shall at length earn
for their class not a drunken "Saint Monday," but the sanctifi-
cation of some portion of every day, for bodily rest, and intellectual activity and enjoyment. No good man should relax his
efforts till this great portion of society is raised to its proper
position. Its recompense, enlightenment, and refinement, are
bound up with the rights of humanity and the progress of
society.[6]

By calling attention to the literary works of the best minds
among the poor, Fox clearly hoped to bring about a better
understanding among the different classes.

The quotation above refers to two "mechanics'" works
reviewed during 1833. The first, a threepenny tract by a
poor Irish journeyman printer,[7] gave Fox an opportunity
to reiterate his own views on church reform, which we have
previously examined. The second reference is to "Saint
Monday" and "The Mechanic's Saturday Night," poems
written "in the vulgar tongue" by an anonymous artisan,
identifiable as one Henry Brown.[8] Here Fox made no extravagant claims for the volumes as literature but rejoiced
to discover a workingman who was writing for working-
men. "It is his want of pretension, his independence of
patronage, his writing more for his own than for any other
class, which excites our interest, and, we think, must interest our readers, when viewed in conjunction with his sturdy
intellect and poetical spirit." Fox rightly believed that

---

[6] VII (1833), 870.
[7] *Ibid.*, pp. 777-84. By one Francis Ross, the tract was entitled "The Examination of an Independent in Church and State."
[8] *Ibid.*, pp. 829-39.

the best teachers for the poor must come from their own ranks; it was greatly encouraging to find that the "producing men" were turning out both politicians and poets.[9] The poems of Robert Nicoll, a Scottish successor of Burns, Fox also reviewed as "poetry of the poor."[10]

Fox welcomed the adaptation of poetry to the cause of social and political reform. "The spirit of utility has seized upon the harp of poetry," he declared in a review of a satirical verse attack on abuses in the Church, entitled *The Village Poor-House,* written by "A Country Curate" (the Reverend James White). "No longer a plaything, or a mere drawing-room ornament," poetry had a useful part to play in the great struggle for human improvement. Poets, like all intelligent men, must labor to rebuild society, to destroy ignorance and class prejudice, and to unite men in the pursuit of common interests. Here was a chance for poets to redeem themselves.

The poets have more to atone for than most people. They have brought on poetry itself the imputation of being frivolous or pernicious, of being essentially feudal, aristocratic, warlike, and superstitious. But the revolution has reached even the La Vendée of literature. The Muses cease from dreaming of the past to prophesy of the future, and begin to pour forth the glowing predictions which are self-fulfilling. Byron scorned the few, though he sympathized not with the many. The purer patriotism of Campbell has ever shone like a bright and steady star; and now the rich metaphysical melodies of Tennyson, and the untameable vigour of Elliot (if Elliot be his name,) are the first fruits of a nobler vintage than has yet been gathered in between the mount of Helicon and the plains of Marathon.[11]

The reference to Tennyson, six months before the appearance of his 1833 volume, corroborates Fox's own state-

---

[9] Briefer review was later accorded to *Sunday,* another poem by Henry Brown.—IX (1835), 623-27.

[10] *Ibid.,* 764-70   [11] VI (1832), 537.

ment as to his early appreciation of the new poet. In his review of Tennyson in January, 1833, Fox related how in the autumn of 1830, when revolution was raging in the streets of Paris and when at home the Spirit of Reform was girding itself "for conflict with the great captain of the age [Wellington] and all corruption's hosts," it had been his fortune

to escape awhile from the feverish and tumultuous scene, with a little book which no flourish of newspaper trumpets had announced, and in whose train no reviewers had waved their banners, but which made us feel that a poet had arisen in the land, and that there was hope for man in powers and principles and enjoyments which flow, a deep and everlasting current, beneath the stormy surface of political changes and conflicts. We profess no indifference to the whirlwind, the earthquake, and the fire, but that still small voice sunk profoundly into our hearts, breathing a calmer and a holier hope. It was the poetry of truth, nature, and philosophy; and above all, it was that of a young man, who, if true to himself and his vocation, might charm the sense and soul of humanity, and make the unhewn blocks in this our wilderness of society move into temples and palaces.[12]

Fox's review of the 1833 volume does more credit to his sensitiveness to poetic beauty than it does to his critical acumen. Declaring that "the true poet is compounded of the philosopher and the *artiste*," he found both qualities in Tennyson to such a degree that in the one the young poet yielded only to Wordsworth and in the other to Coleridge. Full tribute was paid to the music and artistry of the poems: "Some lines, for their soft and easy flowing, others for their stately march, their dancing measure, or their luscious sweetness, might be culled from his writings, which have never been surpassed, and which it would be difficult to match."

[12] VII (1833), 30.

Fox's attempt, however, to make of Tennyson a "mental philosopher" is less felicitous. Here the critic may have been influenced by Bowring's absurd review of the 1830 volume in the *Westminster,* which had sought to raise Tennyson to the dignity of a philosopher worthy of the March of Mind but which had brought crushing rebuke from *Blackwood's.* Bowring, seeking to establish that poetry was no exception to the great law of progress in human affairs, had argued that since poetry depends on "our ever-growing acquaintance with the philosophy of the mind and of man" and since philosophy "advances with the progress of society like all other sciences," ergo, poetry is getting better and better day by day.[13] Fox seems to echo Bowring's line of argument in the following passage:

The first onset of poetry conquered the external world, and erected as trophies descriptions of object and action never to be surpassed: but observation has yielded the foremost place to reflection, in ministering to poetical genius. The classic portrayed human character by its exterior demonstrations and influences on the material objects of sense; the modern delineates the whole external world from its reflected imagery in the mirror of human thought and feeling. This change has taken place not simply because the ground was pre-occupied, but as a necessary result from the stronger light which has been cast on its constitution and operations. . . .

Poetry, in becoming philosophized, has acquired new and exhaustless worlds. . . .[14]

Tennyson's right to the role of philosopher Fox thought was established by "The Confessions of a Second-Rate Sensitive Mind, Not in Unity with Itself" and by "The Palace of Art." From the latter Fox quoted two full pages of excerpts. Less excusable was his reprinting of twenty-two stanzas of

[13] For an excellent discussion of Bowring's review and its effects, cf. G. L. Nesbitt, *Benthamite Reviewing,* pp. 158-62.
[14] VII (1833), 33.

"The May Queen" and its companion piece to show that Tennyson was quite as much at home in a country cottage as in the metaphysical depths. Three stanzas were quoted from "The Miller's Daughter" to show that the poet could create "not merely the enthusiast, the mystic, the poet, or the hero, but good, honest workyday man." Other poems, "Mariana," "Nothing Will Die," "All Things Will Die," "Recollections of the Arabian Nights," and "The Lotus-Eaters," were cited as richly displaying "the action and re-action of mind and matter," but "the best combined display of the author's powers, reflection, and imagination, description and melody" was declared to be "The Lady of Shalott."

Fox in his closing admonitions to the young poet fore-shadows accurately the type of criticism which was to make of Tennyson the bard and prophet of mid-Victorianism. Tennyson's second volume did not show strongly enough marked improvement over his first altogether to please Fox. The poet must remember:

All great intellects are progressive. The mind that only feeds upon itself will not become such "an athlete bold" as the world wants. Mr. Tennyson must have more earnestness, and less consciousness. His power must have a more defined and tangible object. It were shame that such gifts as his should only wreathe garlands, or that the influences which such poetry as his must exercise, should have no defined purpose, and only benefit humanity (for, any way, true poetry must benefit humanity) incidentally and aimlessly. Let him ascertain his mission, and work his work, and realize the aspirations of the sonnet with which this volume commences. ["Mine be the strength of spirit fierce and free."][15]

Three months later (April, 1833) Fox displayed his critical talents to considerably more advantage in his enthusiastic praise of an anonymous poem which had just issued from the press: the poem entitled *Pauline; a Fragment*

[15] *Ibid.*, p. 40.

of a Confession.[16] It is by this review, memorable as the first public recognition of the genius of Robert Browning, that Fox has achieved most reputation as a critic. He did not, however, it must be confessed, discover Browning unaided. We have already mentioned the boy poet's early friendship with Eliza and Sarah Flower and their submission of some of his juvenilia to Fox for criticism. Perhaps the memory of the little preacher's praise of those early poems came back to the twenty-one year old Browning when *Pauline* appeared, or perhaps, if the usual identification of Pauline is correct, the poet naturally thought of Fox because of the latter's close friendship with Eliza Flower; at any rate, Browning wrote Fox requesting the favor of a review in the *Westminster*.[17] Fox expressed interest, accepted twelve copies of the poem for distribution among other reviewers, and proceeded to write his own laudatory criticism for the *Repository*.[18]

He began his review with a discursive and characteristically eloquent defense of psychological poetry, quoting Channing that "the great revelation which man now needs is a revelation of man to himself," and that "the mystery within ourselves, the mystery of our spiritual, accountable, immortal nature, it behoves us to explore." Professional theologians seemed little likely to be of service in this revela-

[16] *Ibid.*, pp. 252-62.

[17] The poet's connection with Fox and the Flowers must have been rather tenuous at this time, since he was evidently not aware of Fox's proprietorship of the *Repository*. For the text of the letters, cf. Mrs. Sutherland Orr's *Life of Browning*, pp. 55 ff.

[18] One of the twelve copies was destined to exercise profound and life-long influence on the poet's art. The copy which Fox gave Mill to review eventually returned to Browning. Mill's criticism of the poet's "intense and morbid self-consciousness" stung Browning with shame at having revealed so clearly his callowness; he resolved never again to expose himself to such humiliation. Henceforth his poetry was to be "dramatic in principle, and so many utterances of so many imaginary persons, not mine." For discussion of Mill's critique, cf. Griffin and Minchin, *Life of Robert Browning*, pp. 59-60; W. L. Phelps, "Notes on Browning's Pauline," *Modern Language Notes*, XLVII, 292-99; and W. C. DeVane, *A Browning Handbook*, pp. 12-13, 43-45.

tion, but here and there a poet or philosopher, such as a Channing, a Bailey, a Tennyson, or a Coleridge, "knows what is in man, and makes it visible." The anonymous poet of *Pauline* could now be added to the select list. The poem, "though evidently a hasty and imperfect sketch, has truth and life in it, which gave us the thrill, and laid hold of us with the power, the sensation of which has never yet failed us as a test of genius. Whoever the anonymous author may be, he is a poet." One could not always with certainty judge of a scientist by a brief sample of his work, but one could detect the poet in a few pages or even a few lines. "We felt certain of Tennyson, before we saw the book, by a few verses which had straggled into a newspaper; we are not less certain of the author of Pauline."

Fox labeled the poem as "purely confessional" and its composition wholly of the spirit.

The scenery is in the chambers of thought; the agencies are powers and passions; the events are transitions from one state of spiritual existence to another. And yet the composition is not dreamy; there is on it a deep stamp of reality. Still less is it characterized by coldness. It has visions that we love to look upon, and tones that touch the inmost heart till it responds.

After a running summary of the main sections of the poem, interspersed with very generous quotation—the ten-page article contains five pages of excerpts—Fox warned the poet not to expect to make a popular hit; Tennyson, though the variety of his published work was better designed to gain popularity, was making only slow headway with the public; "and the common eye scarcely yet discerns among the laurel-crowned, the form of Shelley, who seems (how justly we stop not now to discuss,) to have been the god of his [Browning's] early idolatry."

Fox unerringly identified Shelley as the poet's "adoration and inspiration" and quoted at full length the magnificent "Sun-treader" passage. Two months later in "Local Logic," a description of a day in the woods, Fox wrote:

Shelley and Tennyson are the best books for this place. They sort well with the richness, richness to every sense; with the warm mists, and the rustling of the woods, and the ceaseless melody of sound. They are natives of this soil; literally so; and if planted would grow as surely as a crow-bar in Kentucky sprouts tenpenny nails. *Probatum est.* Last autumn L— [Eliza] dropped a poem of Shelley's down there in the wood, amongst the thick, damp, rotting leaves, and this spring some one found a delicate, exotic-looking plant, growing wild on the very spot, with "Pauline" hanging from its slender stalk. Unripe fruit it may be, but of pleasant flavour and promise and a mellower produce, it may be hoped, will follow. It would be a good speculation to plant a volume of Coleridge."[19]

Fox conceded that there were blemishes in *Pauline* but brushed over them as of little account. "In recognizing a poet we cannot stand upon trifles, nor fret ourselves about such matters. Time enough for that afterwards, when larger works come before us. Archimedes in the bath had many particulars to settle about specific gravities, and Hiero's crown, but he first gave a glorious leap and shouted *Eureka!*"[20]

Fox's enthusiastic review brought grateful thanks from the poet—"I shall never write a line without thinking of the source of my first praise"—but neither it nor Allan Cunningham's favorable notice in the *Athenaeum* for April 6 persuaded anyone to purchase *Pauline.* Not a copy was sold, and the unbound sheets were eventually trundled off to the Browning attic. By fall the poet could write in Mill's copy, "Only this crab remains of the shapely Tree of Life in this Fool's Paradise of mine."

Browning's next publication, *Paracelsus,* though it sold only less badly, received a good deal of critical acclaim. Fox

[19] VII (1833), 421.   [20] *Ibid.,* p. 262.

this time was not nearly so alone in discovering the poet's merits. John Forster wrote enthusiastic reviews in both the *Examiner* and the *New Monthly,* and Leigh Hunt praised it in his *London Journal.* Fox was perhaps entitled to a fatherly interest in the poem, for he had persuaded Effingham Wilson, the ultra-liberal publisher, to bring it out. His review did not appear so promptly this time, not until November, 1835, three months after publication.[21] Exposition rather than criticism Fox conceived to be his task, and he set himself to the performance with evident joy.

The first paragraphs boldly seized the nub of the difficulty that had troubled some superficial critics, like the *Athenaeum's,* who had charged mysticism, obscurity, and vagueness against the poem. Said Fox: "This poem is what few modern publications either are, or affect to be; it is A WORK. It is the result of thought, skill, and toil. . . . It was not written, nor is it to be read, extempore." Like any poem that aspired to more than transitory fame, *Paracelsus* had a great purpose, the solution of one of the great enigmas of human life; it was a poem which required intelligence to create and intelligence to comprehend. "Truly here is something for the mind to grapple with, but the labour is only of that species which accords with the proper enjoyment of poetry, and which raises that enjoyment to its due degree of loftiness and intensity."

Most of the review Fox devotes to an orderly exposition of the purpose and plan of the poem; fully half of the article consists of long quotations. Fox was probably right in choosing to explain rather than to judge; understanding would bring appreciation. "To take up a book, and that book a poem, with real mental matter in it, is a novelty which calls more for announcement than for criticism." The poem could speak for itself. Fox fancied it coming forth,

[21] IX (1835), 716-27.

"as Brutus did into the rostrum, with the appeal, 'Censure me in your judgments; and awake your senses that you may the better judge.' "

Fox's other reviews of literary works are of less importance than those that we have considered, but they may be of interest to notice briefly. Two reviews of books by Leigh Hunt reveal Fox's sympathy with the veteran who had suffered in the cause of Radicalism. In his review of the 1832 collected edition of Hunt's poetry,[22] his admiration for the man colored his appreciation of the poet, though he was not altogether blind to deficiencies. He conceded that Hunt was not of the first rank of poets, that he was "a poet not by necessity but by choice." His apparent originality Fox attributed to imitation of the older poets. "If he is not a giant himself, he has breathed the air of the giant world." And, greatly to his credit, in "an age of versifiers and poetasters," Hunt had "not consulted the sale of his productions, the attainment of ephemeral reputation and hot-pressed morocco-gilt glory, at the expense of that which every true poet would seek for, though he knew he was to be a loser in immediate profit and praise." Disgraceful and vituperative literary persecution he had suffered because of his political views; now he had lived to see his heresies gradually becoming recognized as truths. One could forgive Fox his praise of Hunt as a man; it is more difficult to forgive his enthusiasm for that sugar paste-and-water concoction, *The Story of Rimini*.[23] In the following year a brief review of Hunt's *Indicator* and *Companion* essays was somewhat more critical.[24] Fox here shows an awareness of

[22] VII (1833), 178-84.

[23] Mill's protest to Fox that he had overpraised Hunt contains a remark that may be fairly applied to much of Fox's criticism: "I think you often overpraise, and the cause is the keen sense of enjoyment which all things give you, that have anything of good and beautiful in them."—Garnett, *Life of W. J. Fox*, p. 104.

[24] VIII (1834), 101-3.

Hunt's tendency to affectation and his self-consciousness: "We would rather that when the author feels like a boy, he did not stop to think and say, 'How like a boy I do feel!'" This review, too, ends on a note of indignation for the malignity of the political and literary persecution to which Hunt had for so long been subjected. One may suspect that sympathy was a prime factor in Fox's eventual gift of the *Repository* to Hunt.

One brief review of Wordsworth's *Yarrow Revisited,* which cannot definitely be identified as Fox's work, is worthy of mention if only for its testimony to the height of Wordsworth's reputation by 1835.[25] The reviewer begins with an acknowledgment of the host of difficulties and prejudices which Wordsworth had lived and written down.

This is the course of greatness. We do it reverence; and not the less fervently for perceiving that there is some lack of discrimination in the homage which all now render, as there was in the laugh which all aforetime echoed. Genuine poetical criticism is the next rarest, and perhaps next best thing in the world to genuine poetry.

In the midst of the universal chorus of critical admiration, this reviewer dares to turn against the poet the compliment that had been paid to him, that he was the most philosophical of poets and the most poetical of philosophers. Says the reviewer:

. . . to us it does seem that Wordsworth is frequently philosophical at the expense of his poetry, and poetical at the expense of his philosophy. His powers play at cross-purposes. . . . The process that belongs to the one is often conducted in the other, and his admirers require of us that we shall not repine at the want of beauty or adornment because the poem is a philosophy, and yet that we shall not question the truth of facts, positions, or influences, because the philosophy is a poem. The two classes of

[25] IX (1835), 430-34.

qualities, the poetical and the philosophical, approach too near to a perfect equality in Wordsworth. Their happiest combination requires the decided predominance of one or the other.[26]

But withal, the reviewer concedes the new volume to be one of the most beautiful published in many a year. His criticism had been provoked not by the volume itself but by "the superficial and unmeaning praise, from pens that a few years ago would have censured as mechanically." The new volume bore few traces of what had once been thought characteristically Wordsworthian. "But every one gifted with any portion of the faculty of appreciation, may note in its contents those attributes of the great reflective poet which have established for him not only a school of disciples whose admiration approaches to fanaticism, but a silent, mighty, pervading, and enduring influence over the mind and heart."[27]

Few of the remaining *Repository* reviews of literary works merit any close examination, in part because few works of lasting importance were published during the period. Landor's *Examination of William Shakespeare Touching Deer-Stealing* was praised for having told more of Shakespeare's youth "than antiquarianism has ever yet poked out of mouldy records," and very generous excerpts were quoted.[28] This notice, possibly written by R. H. Horne, was, according to Crabb Robinson, "the one review without which the book would have fallen dead." Charles Cowden Clarke was a favorite of Fox and several of his books were given enthusiastic praise, notably his *Adam the Gardener* and *The Riches of Chaucer*.[29] Clarke, in gratitude, contributed a letter from Charles Lamb.[30] In a notice of *The Revolutionary Epic,* Fox labeled Disraeli as a child of

[26] *Ibid.*, p. 431.
[27] *Ibid.*, p. 432.
[28] *Ibid.*, pp. 44-56.
[29] VIII (1834), 139-55, IX (1835), 78-80.
[30] Entitled "Musical Commentaries and Correspondence of the Late Charles Lamb."—IX (1835), 234-37.

genius, but a spoiled child—"spoiled by that cleaving curse of our country, the spirit of aristocracy." Possessed of great powers, Disraeli was "in danger of being a failure," but Fox did not wholly despair of him: "Let him go into parliament; let him fall in love; let him be converted, and go out into heathen lands as a missionary; . . . let him do, be, or suffer anything that will give singleness of aim, concentration, intensity, to his great and varied faculties, and he will then be redeemed to the high destiny to which he was born."[31] Few novels were reviewed; Bulwer was on several occasions called "the prince of living novelists," but only his *Rienzi* was noticed at any length.[32]

Books by *Repository* writers, of course, received favorable notice. This might be thought to have been one way of recompensing contributors, except for that fact that in a number of instances the reviews preceded the contributions; such was the case in the reviews of Elliott's, Nicoll's, and Browning's poems and one of Mrs. Leman Grimstone's novels. The review of Thomas Wade's *Mundi et Cordis Carmina*[33] did, however, follow the publication of a number of the poet's verses, though the praise was temperate enough to avoid suspicion of puffery.

In addition to reviews of current books, the *Repository* also printed some interesting, and in several instances important, pieces of literary criticism. Most notable of these are Crabb Robinson's series on Goethe and John Stuart Mill's essays on poetry.

Robinson, as we have noted earlier, had supplied some verse translations to the first number of the *Repository,* but thereafter during the active years of his legal career he had contributed only infrequently. Crabb was a loyal but not aggressive Unitarian; he seems to have taken very little part in the activities of the denomination. Any lack of zeal

[31] VIII (1834), 378.
[32] X (1836), 47-53.   [33] IX (1835), 453-59.

for things theological, however, was more than made up for by his almost overweening enthusiasm for German literature. As a young man he had spent over five years in Germany (1800-1805), much of the time as a student at the University of Jena; among German literary circles he had made many acquaintances, the most prized of whom was Goethe. Despite the fact that Goethe seems at this time to have paid little attention to the young Englishman, whose literary talents (despite his aspirations) were mediocre, Robinson became an ardent worshipper of the great German. When Crabb returned to England, he set himself to work to popularize German literature among his countrymen through the medium of translations and critical essays.[34] His ambitions were frustrated by his own lack of a gift for writing and by the public's indifference to German literature. After a few years spent in Sweden and Spain as foreign correspondent for the *Times,* he returned to England once more, set aside his literary ambitions to read for the bar, and in 1813 became a barrister. In this profession he achieved enough success to enable him to retire in fifteen years. Thereafter, having achieved a competence, he was able, for the nearly forty years of life that remained to him, to indulge in the pursuits he loved best—literature and literary conversation with the great and near great.

Even through the years of his bondage to the legal profession, Robinson maintained his interest in German literature, but it was largely expressed in conversation rather than in writing. His admiration for Goethe assumed almost the proportions of a monomania, and his good friends Lamb and Wordsworth, who disliked Goethe, were sometimes hard pressed to steer him off the subject. In 1829 he returned to Germany for a stay of some length, and this time Geothe

[34] For an account of Robinson's essays and translations, cf. J. M. Carré, "Un ami et défenseur de Goethe en Angleterre, Henry Crabb Robinson . . . ," in *Revue Germanique,* July-August, 1912, pp. 386-92.

seems first to have become interested in his English admirer. Robinson basked in the condescension of the great poet.

Crabb returned to England in October, 1831. On April first of the following year he heard of Goethe's death, an event which was to bring to Robinson some unexpected literary employment. Three days later he received a letter from Fox, opening the columns of the *Repository* to him for an article on the poet. Crabb could not refuse such an opportunity, apparently the first real one he had had in thirty years, to publish his views on German literature. He at once plunged into the task, and his commemorative article on Goethe appeared in the May number.[35] Fox was pleased enough with the paper to invite Robinson to supply a *Catalogue raisonné* of Goethe's works, an invitation he later regretted when the *Catalogue* extended to nine numbers.

Robinson's series merits credit for the fact that it was the first systematic survey of Goethe's work to appear in England; the series achieved some slight contemporary reputation, was republished by the Diffusion Society, and has been frequently mentioned in discussions of Anglo-German literary relationships. Viewed objectively, however, Crabb's survey falls considerably short of success. Just how short may be seen in F. Norman's excellent study, *Henry Crabb Robinson and Goethe*.[36] Mr. Norman, in maintaining his thesis that Robinson's influence has been greatly over-rated, may tend to judge rather severely, but for the most part his criticism, of the *Repository* articles at least, is just. The commemorative article he declares to be "only eulogy eked out by an account of the incidents of Goethe's life compounded from ordinary works of reference . . . and an uncritical acceptance of stories from *Dichtung und Wahrheit*."[37] The extrava-

[35] VI (1832), 298-308.
[36] In *Publications of the English Goethe Society*, New Series, VI (1930) and VIII (1931). Pages 36-65 of Vol. VIII are devoted to the *Repository* series.
[37] *Ibid.*, VIII, 37.

gance of one sentence in Robinson's opening paragraph is, as Mr. Norman remarks, more than most Germans of the time would have dared: "It is literally true, that there is no one form of poetry, or of composition allied to poetry, appertaining either to ancient or modern literature, in which he has not produced a work that, by the common consent of the learned of his country, is considered as a masterpiece." Though in his letters and his voluminous diaries Crabb found many things to criticize in Goethe, in his article he displays no critical independence.

The *Catalogue raisonné*, which appeared in nine monthly numbers, from June, 1832, to April, 1833, professed to be no attempt at criticism but simply an orderly account of the forty volumes of Goethe's published writings, exclusive of his scientific works. Robinson does, however, frequently indulge in criticism. No summary of the contents of the series need be made here, for that has been done well and at some length in Mr. Norman's study, already cited. Mr. Norman concludes that the criticism in the articles has no leading idea or discernible principle. Indiscriminate eulogy is intermingled with depreciation of some of Goethe's best works such as *Faust* and *Wilhelm Meister,* chiefly on moral grounds. "Unversed in the art of literary composition, he [Robinson] follows the lead of the reviews and adopts their pompous manner of pronouncing judgment. His articles show high admiration of Goethe, but they also show little understanding. Crabb was willing though unintelligent."[38]

The Goethe series caused Robinson much mental anguish and his relations with Fox became strained as a result of the latter's impatience when the series dragged out too long. Crabb's Diary for 1832-1833 contains a good many references to the subject, and there are extant a number of his letters to Fox.[39] On June 16 he recorded in his Diary his

[38] *Ibid.,* p. 65.
[39] Cf. A. B. Benson, "Fourteen Unpublished Letters by Henry Crabb Robinson," *Publications of the Modern Language Association,* XXI (1916), 395-420.

annoyance at Fox's declining to print one of his translations (evidently the "Amor als Landschaftmaler") and intimated that he might terminate the series if Fox did not relent. The threat was probably bravado, for Crabb at this stage would have hated to give up his beloved mission. In September Fox thought well enough of the articles to propose that they be reprinted; Crabb, by now increasingly at odds with the editor, wrote in his Diary that he must first have encouragement "from some persons of some other sort of taste and knowledge of philosophy than Fox has."[40] On October 3 Crabb's vanity was mortified by Fox's request that the articles be shortened and the series completed in the number following the discussion of *Faust*. Crabb indignantly protested and Fox temporarily relented. In January came a request that the series be completed in three more numbers, and this time Robinson gave in. The disappointed literary aspirant wrote in his Diary on February 17, 1833: "I have but one more to write and shall be glad when I have finished, since I find no one cares anything about what I write and I have no confidence in what I do myself." The series ended with the April number. Crabb's disappointment was somewhat assuaged by the compliments of Sarah Austin, in her day one of the more able students and translators of German literature. Crabb supplied a few notes to her *Characteristics of Goethe*, largely a translation from the German of J. D. Falk, and he became once more a contributor to the *Repository* in order to review her book.[41] Robinson's sense of injustice at the hands of Fox may have contributed to his harsh verdict on Fox's marital difficulties, but it is more probable that the increasing radicalism of the magazine was the determining factor. Crabb later became a fairly frequent contributor to Aspland's new series of the *Christian Reformer*, the real continuation of the old *Repository*.

[40] Typescript Diary, 20 Sept., 1832.   [41] VIII (1834), 177-89.

The critical contributions of John Stuart Mill to Fox's magazine were less ambitious in extent and purpose than Crabb Robinson's but succeeded somewhat better. Mill supplied four such articles. The first, an essay "On Genius," has already been mentioned as the earliest of his contributions to Fox's magazine; it appeared in the October, 1832, issue.[42] In form it was cast as a letter addressed to the unidentified author of two articles that had appeared in the two previous months: "Some Considerations respecting the Comparative Influence of Ancient and Modern Times on the Development of Genius," and its continuation, entitled, "On the Intellectual Influences of Christianity."[43] The unknown writer argued against the notion then prevalent (he found it also in Carlyle's "Characteristics") that the age was hostile to genius—"that we are fast settling down to a dead level of intellect; a tolerably high level perhaps, but still a level;—that the mind cannot grow and thrive on the unnumbered medicaments which modern civilization drugs it with. . . ."[44] Though he granted that ancient civilization was in certain respects more favorable to the rapid development of the inventive powers, he maintained that modern civilization did not frustrate genius because the materials and the knowledge with which genius must work were greatly multiplied. The only question lay in whether modern intellect had the requisite vigor to make use of those materials and that knowledge.

Mill's essay was not so much a refutation of the anonymous articles as a correction and expansion. He began with a compliment to the writer for seeing the importance of so fundamental a problem in human society. The compliment reveals Mill himself:

You do not look upon man as having attained the perfection of his nature, when he attains the perfection of a wheel's or a

[42] VI (1832), 649-59.
[43] *Ibid.*, pp. 556-64, 627-34.   [44] *Ibid.*, p. 556.

pulley's nature, to go well as a part of some vast machine, being in himself nothing. You do not esteem the higher endowments of the intellect and heart to be given by God, or valuable to men, chiefly as means to his obtaining, first, bread; next, beef to his bread; and, as the last felicitous consummation, wine and fine linen. . . . You judge of man, not by what he does, but by what he is. For, though man is formed for action, and is of no worth further than by virtue of the work which he does; yet (as has been often said, by one of the noblest spirits of our time [Goethe?]) the works which most of us are appointed to do on this earth are in themselves little better than trivial and contemptible; the sole thing which is valuable in them is the spirit in which they are done. Nor is this mere mysticism; the most absolute utilitarianism must come to the same conclusion. . . . Whether, according to the ethical theory we adopt, wisdom and virtue be precious in themselves, or there be nothing precious save happiness, it matters little; while we know that where these higher endowments are not, happiness can never be, even although the purposes for which they might seem to have been given, could, through any mechanical contrivance, be accomplished without them.[45]

Much of Mill's article is concerned with a discussion of what constitutes genius. His predecessor on the subject had too much limited the province of genius to the "discovery of truths never before known, or the formation of combinations never before imagined." Mill preferred to identify genius with the faculty of thought itself, not as a "peculiar mental power, but only mental power possessed in a peculiar degree."

Philosophic genius is said to be the discovery of new truth. But what is new truth? That which has been known a thousand years may be new truth to you or me. There are born into the world every day several hundred thousand human beings, to whom all truth whatever is new truth. What is it to him who was born yesterday, that somebody who was born fifty years

[45] *Ibid.,* pp. 649-50.

ago knew something? The question is, how *he* is to know it. There is one way; and nobody has hit upon more than one— by *discovery*.

This discovery, however, cannot be vicarious; one cannot passively receive a truth from someone else. One may be told a truth and learn to parrot it; but if one would *know* a truth he must make the thought his own thought, verify it by his own observation, or by interrogating his own consciousness.

Mill equates originality and genius; by originality he means "the capacity of extracting the knowledge of general truth from our own consciousness, whether it be by simple *observation*, by that kind of self observation which is called imagination, or by a more complicated process of analysis and induction." The man who achieves his convictions by his own faculties, and not by passively receiving them from someone else, that man is an *original thinker*, or a *man of genius*.

Having thus established that "the genius which discovers is no peculiar faculty," Mill proceeds to show that "neither is the genius which *creates*." The faculty which *comprehends* great creative works is also genius.

Without genius, a work of genius may be felt, but it cannot possibly be understood. . . . To transport ourselves from the point of view of a spectator or reader, to that of the poet or artist himself, and from that central point to look around and see how the details of the work all conspire to the same end, all contribute to body forth the same general conception, is an exercise of the same powers of imagination, abstraction, and discrimination (though in an inferior degree) which would have enabled ourselves to produce the selfsame work. Do we not accordingly see that as much genius is often displayed in explaining the design and bringing out the hidden significance of a work of art, as in creating it?[46]

[46] *Ibid.*, p. 653.

Since in Mill's view, genius is "nothing but a mind with capacity to know," there is no reason to believe that the progress of civilization must hinder the development of genius. Even at the pinnacle of attainable civilization there will be room for and need for genius; "it will still remain to distinguish the man who knows from the man who talks upon trust—the man who can feel and understand truth, from the man who merely assents to it, the active from the merely passive mind."

The real difference between ancient and modern times with reference to the development of genius lies in the failure of the moderns to cultivate so highly as the ancients the faculty of thought. Unlike the ancients, the moderns have tended merely to *remember* and *imitate; genius* has accordingly suffered. The chief reason for this tendency has been defective education. Mill believes that modern education suffers badly in a comparison with ancient.

Education *then* consisted not in giving what is called knowledge, that is, grinding down other men's ideas to a convenient size, and administering them in the form of *cram*—it was a series of exercises to form the thinking faculty itself, that the mind, being active and vigorous, might go forth and know. . . .

Modern education is all *cram*—Latin cram, mathematical cram, literary cram, political cram, theological cram, moral cram. The world knows everything, and has only to tell its children, who, on their part, have only to hear, and lay it to rote (not to *heart*). Any purpose, any idea of training the mind itself, has gone out of the world. . . . Those studies which only train the faculties, and produce no fruits obvious to the sense, are fallen into neglect. . . . Even the ancient languages . . . are insensibly falling into disrepute as a branch of liberal education. Instead of them, we are getting the ready coin of modern languages, and physical science taught empirically, by committing to memory its results. Whatever assists in feeding the body, we can see the use of; not so if it serves the body only by forming the mind.[47]

[47] *Ibid.,* pp. 656-57.

With such education it could scarcely be a matter of wonder that genius had declined. The wonder was that there should have been produced as much genius as there had been. The modern age had produced a few true philosophers, a few genuine poets, and two or three great scientists; "but in almost every branch of literature and art we are deplorably behind the earlier ages of the world." The remedy lay in recognizing that the purpose of education is "not to *teach*, but to fit the mind for learning from its own consciousness and observation."

Let the education of the mind consist in calling out and exercising these faculties: never trouble yourself about giving knowledge—train the *mind*—keep it supplied with materials, and knowledge will come of itself. Let all *cram* be ruthlessly discarded. . . . Let the feelings of society cease to stigmatize independent thinking, and divide its censure between a lazy dereliction of the duty and privilege of thought, and the overweening self-conceit of a half-thinker, who rushes to his conclusions without taking the trouble to understand the thoughts of other men. Were all this done, there would be no complaint of any want of genius in modern times.[48]

This first *Repository* essay of Mill's has here been summarized at length and generously quoted not only because of its autobiographical significance but also because the essay seems hitherto to have gone unnoticed. The same justification cannot be claimed for examining in detail Mill's other critical essays in Fox's magazine, since the two most important, "What is Poetry?" and "The Two Kinds of Poetry,"[49] Mill later reprinted in his *Dissertations and Discussions*. Under the title "Thoughts on Poetry and Its Varieties," the two essays are sufficiently well known to those at all acquainted with Mill's work as to make summary here superfluous.

[48] *Ibid.*, p. 659.   [49] VII (1833), 60-70, 714-24.

In republishing the essays, however, Mill made certain changes and excisions, one or two of which it may be of interest to note. Most of the changes were slight: alterations of punctuation and wording, and removal of illustrative references which would have been clear to a reader of 1833 but not to one of a later generation. Some of the omitted passages reveal a change in Mill's own taste in the course of a quarter of a century. For instance, in the passage on painting, he has deleted a reference to the painter Lawrence, shortened a reference to Turner, and added one to Titian and Vandyke.[50] On the same subject Mill omitted this paragraph:

> The poetry of painting seems to have been carried to its highest perfection in the Peasant Girl of Rembrandt, or in any Madonna or Magdalen of Guido; that of sculpture, in almost any of the Greek statues of the gods; not considering these in respect to the mere physical beauty, of which they are such perfect models, nor undertaking either to vindicate or contest the opinion of philosophers, that even physical beauty is ultimately resolvable into expression; we may safely affirm, that in no other of man's works did so much of soul ever shine through mere inanimate matter.[51]

In the reprinting of "What is Poetry?" nearly two pages have been cut from the end of the original version in the *Repository*. The most important part of the excised material contains a discussion of what Mill calls "the poetry of architecture," unfortunately a passage too long for quotation here. Also cut is Mill's apologetic conclusion with its interesting reflection on the contemporary state of the fine arts in England.

The above hints have no pretension to the character of a theory. They are merely thrown out for the consideration of thinkers, in the hope that if they do not contain the truth, they

[50] Cf. *ibid.*, p. 67, and *Dissertations and Discussions*, I (1873), 101.
[51] VII (1833), 67-68.

may do somewhat to suggest it. Nor would they, crude as they are, have been deemed worthy of publication, in any country but one in which the philosophy of art is so completely neglected, that whatever may serve to put any inquiring mind upon this kind of investigation, cannot well, however imperfect in itself, fail altogether to be of use.[52]

The second part of the reprinted essay, originally "The Two Kinds of Poetry," memorable for its comparison of Wordsworth and Shelley, has been subjected to no significant revision.

Mill's fourth and last critical essay, entitled "On the Application of the Terms Poetry, Science, and Philosophy,"[53] is perhaps of chief interest as a supplement to his discussion of the nature of poetry. Quotation of two sentences will reveal that his definition of poetry had not undergone alteration: "The radical idea, involved in the term Poetry, is the vivid reproduction of feelings and impressions previously experienced";[54] and, "Wherever a strong emotion is excited by revived impressions of reality, provided the emotion be so far tempered and idealized by art, as to become predominantly pleasurable, and to exclude all such associations as would defeat the general effect contemplated—there is Poetry."[55] Science he defines as "the classification of individuals, the comprehension of general facts"; its object is, "through the medium of general propositions, to furnish knowledge, and to grasp as many particulars at once as possible."[56] Philosophy is defined as "an inquiry into the reason of things," and in the term "there is always an implied reference to purpose and tendency, an inquiry into the *why* and the *wherefore* of the phenomenon under consideration."[57] In one passage in the article Mill contrasts Poetry and Science:

[52] *Ibid.*, p. 70.
[54] *Ibid.*, p. 324.
[56] *Ibid.*, p. 327.

[53] VIII (1834), 323-31.
[55] *Ibid.*, p. 325.
[57] *Ibid.*, p. 329.

Poetry exhibits nature in detail, as it strikes the sense or acts upon the feelings: Science, as it is grasped and mastered by the reflective faculties of the mind: Poetry presents us with partial sketches, and transient glimpses of nature as it really exists; Science is the effort of reason to overcome the multiplicity of impressions, with which nature overwhelms it, by distributing them into classes, and by devising forms of expression, which comprehend in one view an infinite variety of objects and events.[58]

Mill's remaining important literary contribution to the *Repository* in one sense partook of the nature of what Crabb Robinson attempted in his series on Goethe; as Robinson sought to dispel widespread ignorance of Goethe, so Mill by his "Notes on Some of the More Popular Dialogues of Plato" tried to encourage the reading of Plato. The circumstances were somewhat different, however. Plato possessed an "almost boundless" reputation among scholars and even among many of the less learned, but, according to Mill, "of the great writers of antiquity, there is scarcely one who, in this country at least, is not merely so little understood, but so little read." This neglect gave Mill an opportunity for a characteristic onslaught against Oxford and Cambridge:

Our two great "seats of learning," of which no real lover of learning can ever speak but in terms of indignant disgust, bestow attention upon the various branches of classical acquirement in exactly the reverse order to that which would be observed by persons who valued the ancient authors for what is valuable in them: namely, upon the mere niceties of the language *first;* next, upon a few of the poets; next, (but at a great distance,—) some of the historians; next, (but at a still greater interval,) the orators; last of all, and just above nothing, the philosophers.[59]

[58] *Ibid.,* pp. 327-28.   [59] *Ibid.,* p. 89.

A recent English edition of Plato by a German scholar had helped to bankrupt its publisher; and, except for the editing of two dialogues, neither of the "impostor-universities" had done anything "to facilitate the study of the most gifted of Greek writers." Mill thought it unlikely that as many as six university honors graduates in ten years had even looked into Plato's writings. If such was the neglect at the universities, little could be expected elsewhere. "The consequence is," said Mill, "that there are, probably, in this kingdom, not so many as a hundred persons who ever *have* read Plato, and not so many as twenty who ever *do.*"

In an attempt to remedy this neglect Mill offered to the *Repository* very full abstracts, with explanatory notes, of four dialogues: the *Protagoras,* the *Phaedrus,* the *Gorgias,* and the *Apology.*[60] These notes and abstracts had been written three or four years earlier in the course of Mill's studies. As published, their object was "not to explain or criticize Plato, but to allow him to speak for himself." The translator aimed at fidelity, though because of the need of abridgment he was not always able to retain all of "the dramatic excellences of the dialogues." The high points of each dialogue, however, are little curtailed, and the translation is as nearly literal as Mill could make it and still keep it readable English. The *Apology* is practically a complete translation rather than an abstract. Altogether, Mill performed this task well; his notes and explanatory paragraphs are informative, interesting, brief, and to the point. The series constitutes one of the most interesting features of the *Repository;* Mill in his *Autobiography* remarks that he had afterwards found that they had "been read, and their authorship known, by more people than were aware of anything else which I had written, up to that time."[61]

While the *Repository* devoted its chief efforts in the field

[60] Cf. Appendix, p. 418, for complete listing of pages.
[61] *Autobiography,* Columbia ed., p. 138.

of criticism to the encouragement and development of literature, particularly poetry, it did not neglect drama, music, and painting. Less of its space was given to these arts, it is true, but not because its writers regarded them as of inferior importance. In fact, so important did drama, music, and painting seem to this small group of radicals that they sought reforms designed to free the arts from obstructive forces that denied their freest development and prevented the mass of the people from enjoying them. More of the *Repository's* space was therefore devoted to urging the importance of these arts than to criticism of existing examples. In a day when art was still compelled to struggle for its right to exist—against the Evangelical code of morality which viewed art as inimical to the pursuit of the godly life and against the narrow middle-class utilitarianism which looked upon art as little conducive to the pursuit of the main chance—the *Repository's* stand reflects considerable credit upon the vision and even the courage of its writers.

2. *Drama*

Drama, after poetry, was the art which held the greatest appeal for the magazine's contributors; at least six of the regular writers had a deep interest in the stage. Fox, as we have seen, in his student days at Homerton, had risked breaking academic rules to indulge his fondness for the theatre; this predilection he never lost, and for a time after the collapse of the *Repository* he became a dramatic critic. W. B. Adams was an enthusiastic devotee of the stage. Sarah Flower, who became his wife in 1834, dreamed of a career as an actress and even made a few professional appearances. Charles Reece Pemberton was an actor by profession. R. H. Horne and Thomas Wade had written plays which had been produced with some degree of success. The interest of such an array of writers was a guarantee that the *Repository* would not overlook the drama.

Of the group, Sarah Flower was the first to protest the Evangelical prejudice against the drama. In 1832 when the *Repository* was still at least vestigially a religious magazine, she wrote a short piece entitled "Archdeacon Glover and the Bottle Imp,"[62] which reproved the Evangelical *Record* for its animadversions on the theatre and on any cleric who had the effrontery to endorse, even by his presence, any dramatic representation. Archdeacon Glover had dared to request the performance of a romantic melodrama called "The Bottle Imp"; such conduct the *Record* felt duty bound to reprobate. Sarah Flower's protest against this bigotry is itself, however, tinged with moral fervor. She holds no brief for the corruptions of the theatre but maintains that the drama can never be purified if religious folk simply shun it. Let playwrights lead, not follow the tastes of the public, let actors love "the art for the sake of its power for good," let audiences purify the theatre from the corruptions within its walls; "then would the drama become what it ought and will become, one of the highest means for promoting the virtue and happiness of mankind." The continued war against the theatre served only to keep away virtue and talent. "How is the stage to become pure while the outcry is kept up? The moment an actress treads the boards there is the serpent's tooth of scandal at her heel, and it requires all the energy of a Siddons, or the courage of her high-souled and talented niece, to 'crush the reptile ere it deeply wound.'"[63] The reference to the ill repute of actresses no doubt had importance for Sarah Flower: it was one of the barriers to a stage career for a person like herself. Three years later Sarah, by then Mrs. Adams, was to write for the *Repository* a moving, though somewhat oversentimental novelette, "The Actress," portraying the triumph of a beautiful and virtuous girl over the social ostracism accorded to actors.[64]

[62] VI (1832), 406-9.   [63] *Ibid.*, pp. 408-9.
[64] IX (1835), 460-75, 514-30, 571-91.

One of W. B. Adams' early articles for the *Repository,*
"On Theatrical Reform,"[65] attempted to survey the condition of the theatre, to defend the moral utility of the drama,
and to propose reforms which would remove abuses and
promote a renaissance of dramatic art. Adams began by
challenging the validity of the stock phrase, "the decline of
the stage," which was so frequently heard; despite the financial difficulties of the large patent theatres, he claimed
that there had been an increase in the number of smaller
theatres, especially in the provinces. In London the monopoly enjoyed by the patent theatres had been productive
of many evils: theatre buildings too large for the production
of anything but gaudy spectacles, wasteful expenditures
which kept admission prices too high, and a deterioration
in the quality of plays selected for performance. Here, as
in the economic life of the nation, monopoly was the root
of evil.

But while the decline of the patent theatres was no proof
of general decline, the improvement of the stage had "not
kept pace with the improvements in other branches of art."
The proscription of actors had operated to the detriment
of their profession. As a result, actors had to be recruited
too often from the needy, vicious, or idle classes, rather
than from the refined and educated. Removal of society's
ban on the actor would encourage the educated and talented
to enter the profession and thereby raise its standards. There
was nothing in the art of acting itself to foster immorality;
it might even be doubted that actors were "any more immoral than the rest of the community." Nor was anything
necessarily immoral in the theatre itself. "Are not the
lights of a theatre as good and wholesome lights as the
lights of a chapel or church?" Morality could be taught
within other than consecrated walls. From its most ancient
days the drama had been "a moral instructor for the com-

[65] VII (1833), 551-60, 616-23.

munity." If rightly guided, it might once again exert enormous influence for good. Adams, like many of the Philosophic Radicals, believed that it had not had such influence because of "the odious, the accursed, the mischievous, the suicidal monopoly."[66]

Adams' program of reform, based upon the abolition of the monopoly, contained some sound proposals, though few of them have been adopted. Once the monopoly was abolished, a number of small theatres should be erected in various parts of the city. There should be no censor, and perhaps even no licensing requirement. The price of admission should be low, and uniform for all parts of the house. Each theatre should specialize in one type of drama. Government should foster and, if necessary, subsidize the theatres. And the audience for this revitalized drama? It was to be found in "the great body of the working classes,—the mechanics."

Fox, despite his attachment to the theatre, did not contribute much to the *Repository* on the subject. In his review of Campbell's *Life of Mrs. Siddons*,[67] however, he took occasion to declare his belief that "the theatre is one of the necessaries of civilized life. . . . The form may have varied, but society has seldom arrived at a condition which was worthy of that name, without something that was, essentially, dramatic representation." Unfortunately, "though religion generated the drama, she has not been overkind to her progeny." In England, the pulpit and the playhouse had come to be regarded as "natural belligerents," largely because of the reputed tendency to immorality in the theatrical profession. Yet there were other professions, notably the legal and the military, which were basically far more immoral. And as for the haughty clergyman, look at "the

[66] The Radicals' diagnosis of the theatre's malady was faulty: the monopoly was abolished in 1837, but the English drama languished for nearly fifty years thereafter.   [67] VIII (1834), 533-50.

moral tendency of *his* profession. We will cast no doubts on his being 'moved by the Holy Ghost,' but it is unfortunate that he is obliged to say so; it is unfortunate for the morality of a profession that it holds out strong inducements for those to say so who are not sure of it." A clergyman must give assent to hundreds of propositions upon which he cannot have formed an honest opinion. Does not the clergyman's office resemble that of the actor?

On certain days, nay, at certain hours, and even minutes, he is bound publicly and solemnly to tell his God that he is in a particular state of mind and feeling, when perhaps he is in a very different state of mind and feeling. He modulates his voice, as he reads the liturgy, to the emotions of reverence, contrition, supplication, thanksgiving, sympathy, etc.; but who is so totally ignorant of the human mind as to imagine that these emotions either do or can arise within him at his bidding, and in their prescribed order of succession?[68]

Fox did not deny that the dramatic profession had its demoralizing tendencies, but he doubted whether they were worse than those of other professions which were in better odor. Actors might be improvident and actresses unchaste; so were men and women in many other walks of life. It is at this point that Fox, by implication at least, assails the idea of chastity being the sole virtue requisite in woman; the gist of his remarks has been quoted in the preceding chapter. Fox closes his general discussion of the theatre with the usual attack upon the "infamous monopoly."

R. H. Horne, two years later, was still echoing that theme.[69] And the reviewer of Bulwer's *England and the English,* in his attack on the principle of aristocracy, gave a passing sideswipe at both monopoly and aristocratic patronage:

Aristocracy has overlaid the drama, making the theatres as much of a job and more a monopoly than the Royal Academy. . . .

[68] *Ibid.,* p. 535.   [69] X (1836), 329.

No patronage is needed, only allowance, for the drama in this country to become a rational and refining agency, full of good, reaching those whom no other influence is likely to reach. This easy allowance, this niggard boon, is refused by the aristocracy. For the complete popular enjoyment of works of art by the people, . . . we must look back to the democracies of antiquity.[70]

The *Repository* during Fox's editorship only rarely criticized either published or acted drama; later, under Horne, more space was given to such criticism. Fox made occasion, however, to insert praise of his favorite actor, Macready, who was then acting little but Shakespeare; "and little but Shakespeare *should* be enacted," said Fox, "by a man of mind so philosophic, of conception so just, of taste so delicate; with critical faculties so acute, and the sense of poetical appreciation so strong; and whose powers of personation and expression (though with some physical drawbacks) are so vast and varied."[71] Fox became a good friend of Macready and later as dramatic critic of the *Morning Chronicle* lent his aid to the actor in the revival of the poetic drama. More deserving of praise were Macready's reforms in the staging of Shakespeare and his restoration of the genuine text. The *Repository* offers other tribute than Fox's, however, to the ability of Macready. Sarah Flower Adams wrote a beautiful appreciation in verse, "Lines suggested by Macready's Hamlet";[72] and Charles Reece Pemberton, himself a Shakespearean actor, contributed two encomiastic analyses of the actor's performances in *Coriolanus* and *King John*.[73]

The revival of *Coriolanus* occasioned one series of articles which demonstrated not only that the writer took his Shakespeare seriously to heart but also that political sympathies could still affect literary judgments. W. B. Adams' "Coriolanus no Aristocrat"[74] endeavored with all that

[70] VII (1833), pp. 599-600.   [71] VIII (1834), 549.
[72] IX (1835), 749-50.   [73] VIII (1834), 76-81, 114-21.
[74] *Ibid.*, pp. 41-54, 129-39, 190-202, 292-99.

writer's usual vehemence "to destroy an ancient Tory fallacy." The Tories had made Coriolanus all their own as an exemplar of arbitrary power; the Duke of Wellington was figured in prints adorned in a Roman garb. This was manifestly unfair, thought Adams; if Coriolanus were alive, "he would have been a heart-whole leader in the great cause of human nature, which has been espoused by those who are best described as philosophic radicals."[75] Coriolanus was no aristocrat in the modern English sense of the term; he was an aristocrat only in the noble sense. This thesis Adams elaborates in a scene-by-scene analysis of the play. Perhaps the high point of the articles is his comparison of Coriolanus and the Duke of Wellington; the Great Duke, needless to say, does not profit by the comparison![76]

Altogether, for its sympathetic and appreciative treatment of the drama, even though the space it allotted to the subject was not large, Fox's *Repository* must be accorded a high place among the journals of its period. In the months when Fox was more and more relinquishing control to R. H. Horne, the latter printed short critiques of several current plays. These critiques are chiefly of importance as revealing Horne's advocacy of the new school of poetic drama, which by its high-flown moral eloquence appealed to the Philosophic Radicals. One wonders if the insistence of Fox and his friends upon the high moral utility of the drama was not, perhaps unconsciously, a way of combatting Evangelical prejudice. Or was it, also unconsciously, a product itself of Evangelicalism?

3. The Fine Arts

The same insistence upon moral purpose is seen in the *Repository's* occasional criticism of painting. The first essay of this sort was a description by Fox of an exhibition of

---

[75] *Ibid.*, p. 43.   [76] *Ibid.*, p. 137.

paintings illustrative of sacred history.[77] The exhibition Fox thought not particularly successful, yet he hailed it "as a promise of future efforts of a similar description, which will eventually lead to a perception of the moral power of art amongst many who have not hitherto been trained to appreciate its productions." There was even hope that under the spell of art, religious bigotry might relax. "Let Calvinism fairly take to the study and the enjoyment of the works of art, and we shall hope that its roughness and hardness will wear off, and that the rigid tension of its faith and feeling will relax under the bland influence of the purest enjoyment of sense." Fox saw the absurdity of limiting an exhibition of paintings to scriptural subjects but conceded that ignorance and narrow-mindedness might thus for a while have to be propitiated. The admission of a few "popish" subjects to the exhibition raised hope that squeamishness against Catholics and their art might soon be abated. The "strange insensibility" of Protestants to the high utility of art Fox thought had been occasioned by "the abuse of painting by the Catholic church, to many of its own selfish purposes." But the Protestants by their insensibility and even aversion to art, had tended to deprive themselves of one of the great elevating forces in human life.

W. B. Adams in his first *Repository* essay, "On the State of the Fine Arts in England,"[78] ascribed the lamentable condition of the fine arts, especially painting and sculpture, to the fact that English society provided insufficient motives for artists to strive for excellence.

In modern times, and more especially in England, the thing sought for, above all others, is money—because the possessor of money can command thereby the possession of all sensual and most mental gratifications: in short, money is power, according to the present construction of English society—and power ever was, and ever will be, the source of consideration. . . .

[77] VI (1832), 338-45.   [78] VII (1833), 1-13.

In a civilization in which, like that of the ancient Greeks, "the only road to power was intellect," the arts could attain their proper development because men of talent would have the proper incentive to excel. Before such a civilization could be attained, however, there must be widespread education of the people. At present the artists, themselves often too poorly educated, must fight, "under the influence of poverty, against the sparsely-scattered judgment of an uneducated public." The prospects for painters and sculptors of the highest class were discouraging; the church or royal patrons of the Middle Ages were no more, private patronage was insufficient, and the public was "not yet sufficiently refined for the establishment of national galleries in all the cities." Adams was as confident as most of his fellow-reformers that when education should be made universal some sort of millenium would arrive, in art as well as in other domains of human life. Meanwhile, in the development of the art of engraving he found chief encouragement for the spread of a taste for art among the people.

Only one other contributor to the *Repository* in these years, Sarah Flower, gave tangible evidence of her appreciation of the value of art to human life. Her essay entitled "A National Gallery"[79] is an impressionistic description of a visit to the Louvre; the essay makes no attempt at a catalogue or at technical criticism, but its description of perhaps half a dozen pictures, ranging from David to Rubens, is attractive as a revelation of Sarah Flower's sensitivity to beauty. The essay ends with a plea for the English to take a lesson from the Louvre and establish their own National Gallery. A similar later essay, "The Luxembourg,"[80] declared that "the highest task of a painter is to create a love for moral and intellectual beauty by depicting moral and intellectual beauty; rather than the more indirect way of creating a loathing for vice by painting it in all its de-

[79] *Ibid.*, pp. 840-45.   [80] VIII (1834), 54-63.

formity." The last, and perhaps best, of Sarah Flower's essays on art, "Buy Images," [81] is a delicate and beautiful embroidery on the theme "that a thorough appreciation of art of every kind is one of the surest safeguards of the spirituality of a people." "Buy Images" takes its title from the street cry of Italian vendors of plaster-cast figures. Sarah's comparison of the itinerant Italian boy with his English counterpart is a telling point in her case for developing an appreciation of art among the masses:

Look at the faces of the Italian boys; watch their glances of expressive admiration—nay, affection—for the objects of their occupation; hear their eloquent description of the different works of art with which they are familiar; and then compare them with the ragged urchins who infest your gates, with thievish eye and harsh voices, crying "h-a-arth-stone!" till your "hearth-stane" is no longer a quiet place of refuge,—and in that contrast you will have the whole difference between the marble of the sculptor and the rough stone of the quarry,—a nation with or without the influence of the master spirit which lives and breathes throughout the creations of glorious art.[82]

Sarah Flower refused to believe that the great days of the arts had passed forever; she looked forward to a time when their universal influence might become a reality.

And there is yet another day beyond—when art shall have fulfilled its mission; when the whole world shall be one vast spectacle of moral, intellectual, and physical beauty; when the forms that as yet live but in the far-sighted glimpse of the poet, shall be seen breathing in triumphant life; when universal love shall have wrought out universal beauty—beauty glowing in a reality of existence, that shall make the noblest statue of the noblest sculptor seem cold and corpse-like, when compared with the power of warm life, when linked in glorious union with the divinity that dwells within us![83]

[81] Ibid., pp. 756-62.
[82] Ibid., p. 756.
[83] Ibid., p. 762.

To music the *Repository* devoted little space, probably more because of the lack of qualified contributors than because of any intentional neglect. One wonders why Eliza Flower was not persuaded to contribute; if she could have written anywhere nearly so well as her sister, her criticisms in the field of her chosen art would have been valuable. Her views, however, are probably reflected in the music articles which Fox contributed. In all, the *Repository* printed only five articles on music; three can be identified as by Fox, and the other two are probably his also. But if Eliza could not or would not contribute criticism, she could supply some of her own compositions. A feature of the best year of the magazine, 1834, was her series of twelve "Songs of the Months." Each month in that year Fox presented his readers with the score of one of Eliza's songs, placed as a kind of frontispiece to the number. The verses for this music were supplied by various writers for the *Repository*, notably Sarah Flower, C. R. Pemberton, Alexander Hume, and Harriet Martineau. Both poems and music set a relatively high standard; in that day for a magazine to print music was something of an innovation.

The first of the articles on music took its departure from the publication of Novello's edition of Purcell's Sacred Music.[84] No attempt is made to offer a criticism of Purcell; instead, the writer (almost certainly Fox) devotes much of his article to a discussion of the need of a national system of education by which musical and other talent might be early discovered and fostered. Circumstances had been favorable to the development of Purcell's genius, but far too many talented young people were deprived of their chance by rank, financial necessity, or misfortune. "What events did for Purcell it were well that social wisdom should do, as far as possible, for all." Existing conditions were dis-

[84] VII (1833), 289-97.

tinctly unfavorable for the development of musical talent. Even in music, monopoly reared its ugly head. Said Fox,

It is no wonder that we have no Purcells. Every department is a monopoly, teachers of schools and families are compelled to eke out their scanty and precarious remuneration by the sale to their pupils of music, specially adapted for that purpose. . . . Cathedrals stick to the old established anthems, as an integral portion of the old established faith; and Dissenters must have only what is bald enough and bad enough for the whole congregation to sing with their "most sweet voices," and most exquisite skill. Concerts borrow the *stars* from the Opera, and they will sing nothing new, while money is to be had for the old. . . . And as to music, the theatres are a monopoly within a monopoly. "In the lowest deep, a lower still."[85]

If music was to fulfill its appointed mission, obstacles must be removed which prevented its widest dissemination among the people. As Fox remarked in his "Utilitarian Reflections on the Norwich Musical Festival"[86] music should not be "an aristocratical luxury." The ability to enjoy and appreciate music was dependent not on station, fortune, or education; the opportunity of enjoying it should be open to all. Fox distinguishes between two species of musical enjoyment, one that might be called a technical, the other a poetical enjoyment. He depreciates the former of these, and it is evident that his own appreciation was almost wholly of the poetical variety. His impressionistic essay on Mary Kingston's Fantasia on the national air of "Rule Britannia" is a delightful prose poem evoked probably by Eliza's performance of the composition.[87] Fox's brief article "The Amateur Musical Festival[88] hailed an amateur exhibition as a triumph for the "voluntary principle" in art and as a promise of "reformation in the musical world."

[85] *Ibid.*, pp. 293-94.
[86] *Ibid.*, pp. 751-60.
[87] *Ibid.*, pp. 450-53.
[88] VIII (1834), 883-84.

Music, as well as the other arts, must serve the needs of the whole people.

The *Repository's* attitude toward the whole problem of the improvement of society may be seen in Fox's review of Francis Place's tract on the "Improvement of the Working People."[89] Instruction could do much towards accelerating the improvement of the masses, but it could not do all that was necessary. Something must be done "for the existing generation, to render their burdens less grievous and supply them with the means, not only of direct instruction, but of appropriate and wholesome joyousness." There should be reading rooms "as comfortable as the public house, and as splendid as the gin-temple"; working people should be admitted free to Westminster Abbey, the British Museum, and the promised National Gallery; the Zoological Gardens should be open on Sundays; lectures and theatrical amusements, public walks and gardens, should be provided for the poor. Such a course of action, Fox advised the religionists who were bewailing the brutality and drunkenness of the lower classes, was the shortest cut, even for the religionists' purposes.

You cannot make a railroad from the tavern to the church. You cannot send a pressgang to clear out the taproom and man the conventicle. The distance will never be got over without resting by the way. The best chance for the mechanic's accomplishing the journey from animal pleasures to spiritual exercises, is by opening for him the half-way house of rational enjoyments. If that will not draw him, you cannot force him further, nor ought you to be allowed to torment him by trying.[90]

ORIGINAL LITERATURE

1. *Fiction*

Despite the emphasis in the foregoing pages on the *Repository's* critical views and policies with relation to the arts

---

[89] *Ibid.*, pp. 625-31.   [90] *Ibid.*, p. 631.

of poetry, drama, painting, and music, it must not be forgotten that Fox's periodical was properly a Magazine, not a Review. In addition to political articles and social and literary criticism, it contained a variety of original literary material, fiction, essays and sketches, and poetry. It is to this side of the magazine that we must now turn.

Relatively little fiction was published and its quality was no higher than the bulk of that which appeared in contemporary magazines. The art of the short story was then as yet very imperfectly realized; and while the absence of the almost machine-like technique of the modern popular magazine story is refreshing, the rambling structure and the obtrusive moralizing and sentimentality of most of these stories make unattractive reading. Many of them were properly tales or condensed novels rather than short stories. Imperfectly developed characterization, unconvincing dialogue, frequently too summary narrative, were faults noticeable in the *Repository's* fiction as well as in that of its rival periodicals.

Nearly half of the *Repository's* fiction was dominated by didactic purpose. Harriet Martineau's "Liese; or The Progress of Worship," which we have noticed earlier, was quite as didactic in intent as her Political Economy Tales. Harriet's management of narrative and characterization, however, was considerably more skillful than the technique of Mrs. Leman Grimstone, who contributed a series of nine "Sketches of Domestic Life" in 1835-1836. Mrs. Grimstone, an ardent social reformer and feminist, had published several novels, *Character; or Jew and Gentile,* and *Cleone, A Tale of Married Life,* to which Fox had given favorable reviews. The congeniality of her opinions with those of the *Repository* on questions relating to the condition of women, made her a welcome contributor. Her attempts to sugar-coat her moral and social views in verse and fiction, however, provide less palatable reading today than the straightforward argumentative discourses of Fox, Adams, and Mill. The "Sketches of Domestic Life" were rather too obviously manufactured tales designed to illustrate and reprobate various undesirable female traits. Some of the titles will indicate sufficiently the types of faults aimed at— all of them, of course, faults primarily traceable to woman's imperfect education and dependent status: "The Fashionable," "The Coquette," "The Sentimental," "The Insipid," and "The Gossip."[91] One need not quarrel with Mrs. Grimstone's analysis of the faults or with her advocacy of improved education and opportunity for women; but it is difficult to appreciate her inept blending of sense and sentimentality, of realism and melodrama, even if Fox did compare her with Jane Austen.[92]

Much better, though far from perfection of form, were three tales contributed by Sarah Flower Adams. The first, entitled "The Welsh Wanderer,"[93] is chiefly of interest as a kind of early Wordsworthian tale of a beautiful country girl who, driven mad by the desertion of her faithless lover, wanders about the countryside singing songs to her bastard child. The story is artlessly told, even ineptly, but the author has enough of a poetic vein to lend it some charm; the one song that the wild mother sings to her child was provided with a musical score by Eliza Flower. Sarah's second tale, "The Three Visits"[94] compresses into nine pages the outline of a story which would take the length of a novel to do proper justice. The uneventful story of a simple, obscure, but noble woman, it was intended to demonstrate the true power of woman's heart, strength, and intellect, when not hampered by imperfect education. Sarah's third tale, "The Actress," has been mentioned earlier.

[91] IX (1835), 145-53, 225-34, etc.; X (1836),-14-25, etc.
[92] VII (1833), 546.
[93] VIII (1834), 514-20.   [94] *Ibid.*, pp. 724-33.

The remainder of the *Repository's* fiction may be disposed of even more summarily. An example of the once popular Oriental tale may be seen in R. H. Horne's "Akiba: A Hebrew Story,"[95] no better and perhaps no worse than hundreds of its sort written both before and since. Somewhat more interesting is the same writer's satirical dialogue, "High Church and Conventicle";[96] Horne displays enough skill in handling the dialogue between a pompous rector and his Methodized cook to make one wonder if the dramatist of *Cosmo de'Medici* and *The Death of Marlowe* could not have written good comedy if the dramatic auspices of the times had been more favorable. Another contributor of fiction to Fox's magazine it has not been possible to identify; his five stories are all signed W.L.T. Labeled as "Fantasy Pieces after Hoffman," they are free translations and abridgments of tales of the popular German writer. Their fantastic, fairy-story quality, as seen in "The Magic Snuff-Box"[97] and "The Nutcracker,"[98] sounds an incongruous though not unwelcome note amid the usual sharper, more solemn tones of the magazine.[99]

Only one item of the *Repository's* fiction has deserved, and received, a modern reprinting: Charles Reece Pemberton's fragmentary *Autobiography of Pel. Verjuice,* which appeared in eleven installments in 1833 and 1834.[100] We classify it as fiction, though it is probably a fairly accurate record of Pemberton's early years. So little is known of his childhood and youth that it is impossible to separate the fact from the fiction, if fiction there be. At any rate, it is

---

[95] *Ibid.*, pp. 646-53.
[96] IX (1835), 237-46.
[97] VIII (1834), 844-53.
[98] IX (1835), 9-29.
[99] The other three of the series include "The Sanctus," IX (1835), 81-90; "The Choice," *ibid.*, 179-93, 247-58; and "Gluck," *ibid.*, pp. 805-9.
[100] It has been reprinted three times: once in a cheap abridgment; second, in *The Life and Literary Remains of Charles Reece Pemberton*, edited by John Fowler (London, 1843); and most recently by the Scholartis Press in its "Nineteenth-Century Highways and Byways Series," a handsome limited edition, with an introduction by Eric Partridge (London, 1929).

the only piece of exciting narrative to be found in the *Repository*.

Pemberton himself is an interesting enough person to warrant our digressing briefly to outline his career. He was born in 1790 in Wales of English and Welsh stock, educated in Birmingham at a Unitarian Charity School, and at fifteen apprenticed as a clerk in his uncle's business. A warm-hearted, imaginative youngster, fond of reading romantic adventure and travel books, he soon found the routine of business unbearable. After two years of it, he ran away and at Liverpool was seized by a press gang. For the next seven years (1806-1812) he traveled the seas as a member of His Majesty's Navy; his descriptions in the *Autobiography* of the brutality and cruelty with which the enslaved seamen were treated, are based upon observed facts. The details of his life for the next sixteen years are obscure. Much of the time he was evidently a wanderer in remote areas of North and South America. For a while he was an actor and manager in the West Indies, but when his marriage was wrecked by his wife's affair with the governor of the island, he set out once more on his wanderings. Not until 1828 did he return to England. For a time he toured the provinces, lecturing and acting. Talfourd, after witnessing one of his performances, published a long and appreciative criticism in the *New Monthly* and persuaded Charles Kemble to engage him for Covent Garden performances in March, 1829. Though praised by some critics, he did not achieve enough success to warrant continuance in London. In the provinces he was more successful. Soon, however, he gave up the stage for the lecture platform. His lectures on Shakespeare and poetry, interspersed with dramatic readings, gained popularity, especially at various mechanics' institutes, and he was soon much in demand in London and elsewhere.

It was at this period that his acquaintance with Fox began. The immediate occasion was Fox's essay "The Victim," which we have earlier noticed. The article moved Pemberton's sympathies deeply, and he at once offered his services to the *Repository*. The first installment of *Pel. Verjuice* appeared two months later, in May, 1833, and continued intermittently until late in 1834. He also contributed a number of poems and essays, most of them signed "P.V."

In 1836 when his health broke, his friends raised a subscription to send him to the Mediterranean, where he remained for most of the next three years. He returned to England late in 1839, and died at Birmingham in March, 1840. Fox delivered a commemorative address at South Place Chapel, and a tribute by Ebenezer Elliott was read. Three years later Fox contributed a warmly appreciative sketch of Pemberton to the published edition of his *Remains*. On the list of subscribers may be found the names of Dickens, Macready, Talfourd, Elliott, Bowring, Moore, William Howitt, G. J. Holyoake, and Samuel Smiles.

Pemberton was a thorough-going Radical; not even Junius Redivivus could outdo Pel. Verjuice in the bitterness of his scorn of aristocratical privilege, his hatred of social injustice, and his contempt of cant and humbug. He burned with indignation when Parliament refused to abolish the notorious evils of impressment which he had observed at first hand;[101] he lashed with irony and satire a pompous parson who sought to convince the poor that their salvation and security rested in obedience to authority in Church and State;[102] and in his delightfully humorous "John Bull, Esquire, of Wheedle-Hall"[103] he deftly annihilated the cultural pretensions of the ignorant *nouveau riche*. With his acute social consciousness was blended what his friend Holyoake

---

[101] Cf. "The XV of August, MDCCCXXXIII," VII (1833), 652-57.
[102] Cf. "Social Evils and Their Remedies," *ibid.*, pp. 733-43.
[103] *Ibid.*, pp. 708-14.

described as "a sensitive, poetic, and dramatic temperament."
Fox observed that his self-imposed descriptive pseudonym,
Verjuice, was a misnomer: "There was no real verjuice in
his composition; what he mistook for it was only the milk
of human kindness soured by circumstances."

The sum of his qualities is best to be seen in *Pel. Verjuice,* a distinctly unusual autobiography. Richard Garnett
has called it an "artless but riveting narrative in the manner of Trelawny's *Adventures of a Younger Son.*" It is
that and more. Passages of vivid narrative are interrupted
by both poetic and satiric digressions; diatribes against injustice, cruelty, and hypocrisy vie for attention with beautiful descriptions of scenery, sharply etched characteriza-
tions, and stirring recitals of naval battles with the French.
The style is full of life and dramatic energy, somewhat
lacking in restraint, perhaps, but at least never dull. It is
to be regretted that the *Autobiography* was never finished,
though, as Fox remarks, Pemberton's life too was fragmentary. Nine chapters of the narrative, covering his life
up to his eighteenth year, form a consecutive sequence; the
other chapters deal with later episodes of his *Wanderjahre.*
The truth of Pel. Verjuice's *Autobiography* is not only
stranger than Captain Marryat's fiction; it is vastly more
interesting.

2. *Essays*

Although the *Repository* did not publish many of what
may be called essays or sketches, seldom more than three or
four a year, their general level of excellence is higher than
that of the magazine's fiction. The looser form of such
essays was evidently better suited to the abilities of the
writers, and the pieces themselves date much less than the
fiction. Their range of subject matter is varied: from descriptions of the London scene, excursions into the country,

reveries on nature and the seasons, to the delightful recollections of an evening spent in the company of Lamb and
Coleridge. If one were to add some of Leigh Hunt's writings from the period of his brief editorship of the magazine,
a very pleasant volume could be made up of the *Repository's* essays.

The best of these can be identified as the work of Fox
and Sarah Flower. Fox's "Sandown Bay"[104] we have earlier
cited for the light that it throws upon his nervous breakdown soon after his marriage. Written as a chapter of autobiographical recollections, it describes in moving poetical
prose the beauties of the Isle of Wight's natural scene that
brought to him relief from the demons of hypochondriasis.
His "Autumn in London"[105] pleasantly records the joys to
be found in the metropolis in the "off-season," when those
not bound to their work betake themselves to the country;
Crabb Robinson was so delighted with the anonymous essay
that he declared that it could be the work of no other than
Talfourd. "Local Logic"[106] was a favorite with Mill; it is
a charming description of a May Day picnic in the woods
in connection with Carolina Southwood Smith's Pestaloz-
zian school. Fox's genuine vein of poetry is little given to
romantic melancholy; his sense of humor saves his occasional poetic rhapsodizing from extravagance. The poet-
izing of "Local Logic" ends with a summary of principles
illustrated, by way of a genial take-off on Harriet Martineau's Political Economy tales. Best illustrative of Fox's
humor is the short squib "Mrs. Thomson, You Are
Wanted,"[107] occasioned by overhearing a boy paging that
unknown lady at a coach station. A brief quotation can
give only a little of the flavor of the essay:

I go about repeating, "Mrs. Thomson, you are wanted?" Of
whom else one dare make such an affirmation? Who is wanted

[104] VI (1832), 271-80. [105] *Ibid.*, pp. 660-67.
[106] VII (1833), 413-26. [107] VIII (1834), 282-85.

in this world? Who, but *she?* The Whigs are not wanted. The poets are not wanted; for, as Kirk White says, "Fifty years hence, and who will think of Henry?" Kings are not wanted; when once that grim groom death trots them out, how soon it is
                  "For O, and for O, the hobby horse is forgot."
Nay, even, according to Malthus, people are not wanted. And is it not something, then, to know that *Mrs. Thomson is wanted?*[108]

Altogether, Fox's few essays of this sort are so pleasant as to make one wish that *he* had not been wanted in so many other fields of endeavor that he could not write more in this vein.

For its literary associations as well as for its own sake, the most interesting of Sarah Flower Adams' essays is "An Evening with Charles Lamb and Coleridge."[109] Bertram Dobell reprinted this in 1903 in his *Sidelights on Charles Lamb,* but was unable to identify the writer. Of the essay Dobell remarked: "It is true that we are rich in pen-pictures of Coleridge and Lamb; but were our knowledge of them, as gained from the writings of their contemporaries, ten times more copious than it is, we should still have reason to welcome such accessions to it as we find in S.Y.'s paper." Sarah's other essays, even without the magic of great names, still make pleasant reading. "A Chapter on Chimnies"[110] reflects her husband's ideas on household management; earlier in the *Repository* he had contributed a long article on "Housebuilding and Housekeeping"[111] in which he attacked the waste of time and energy in the usual domestic arrangements and advocated the building of what we should call apartment houses, with provisions for communal kitchens and laundries and running hot water! Sarah's third essay, entitled "An Odd Subject,"[112] takes its point of de-

[108] *Ibid.,* p. 285.
[109] IX (1835), 162-68.
[111] VIII (1834), 485-94, 572-84.

[110] *Ibid.,* pp. 57-59.
[112] IX (1835), 795-802.

parture from a flea circus. Using as the central figure of the
essay the little boxes in which fleas are taught to submit to
captivity, she develops the theme that human beings too
are confined to torture boxes.

There is a box of Toryism, and a box of Episcopacy; and there
is a box of Legal injustice, and a box of Social law, which is the
most cruelly oppressive box of all. Into all these wrong boxes,
or boxes of wrong, many find their way without the hope of
extrication, awhile to struggle with the circumstances around
them, to "kick against the pricks," that is, to leap against the lid,
and then to be turned out to perform a part in life, so fan-
tastically untrue to the nature that should show forth in the
glorious human creature, as to make the "angels weep" and
demons shout!

The worst box of all, according to Sarah, is the box of marriage—"and for this reason, that it is the evil of all others
which inflicts the deepest injury on posterity." Society demands that a married couple be bound for life, no matter
how unsuited to each other husband and wife may turn
out to be. The world, "by perpetuating the error of a mistaken marriage, changes it into a crime against society of
the worst possible consequences."

Sarah's essay, "York Minster and the Forest Bugle,"[113]
reveals less of the reformer, more of the poet. Attending
a service in the great cathedral, she falls into a reverie as
her eyes rest upon a forest bugle that hangs upon the wall.

In one moment the whole cathedral had vanished. Instead of
the lofty pillars, trees of a thousand years uprose in giant majesty,
their wide arms spreading in stately arches, their multitudinous
leaves mingling overhead in forest fretwork. . . . The drowsy
murmur of the preacher melted into the music of a brook, that
went on its cheering way leaping and laughing at the pebbles
that threw themselves across its path. The sound of the organ
was lost in the myriad united voices of the mighty winds, swelling

[113] X (1836), 38-43.

forth hymns of praise amongst the lofty tree-tops; the voices of the choristers were mute in the upspringing of a thousand woodland throats fraught with sweet unbought thanksgiving; while a universal voice seemed to utter forth, "He dwelleth not in temples made with hands."

But when the reverie is broken by the close of the service, Sarah does not forbear to show her appreciation of the beauty and majesty of the man-made temple which is York Minster.

Of the remaining *Repository* essays none quite comes up to the standard set by Fox and Mrs. Adams, though a few are worthy of brief mention. One short essay by Harriet Taylor, "The Seasons,"[114] is of especial interest for the gleam of light it throws upon the nature that inspired John Stuart Mill to adulation. Mrs. Taylor's eleven brief and anonymous contributions to Fox's magazine seem to be the only extant first-hand evidence by which to estimate the truth of Mill's praise. He, it will be remembered, compared her to Shelley: "but in thought and intellect, Shelley, so far as his powers were developed in his short life, was but a child compared with what she ultimately became." Perhaps Mrs. Taylor in 1832 was not what she ultimately became—it reflects no discredit upon her if she never became all that Mill thought her—but her *Repository* contributions do not show much more than sensitivity to beauty and poetry, a highly wrought temperament, and an intelligence, it is true, of more than average ability. "The Seasons" is a brief embroidery on the old theme: "Which is the most enjoyable of the seasons?" Answer: "Each hides some delight." The writer reveals a poetic nature, but more by her retention of the poetry of others than by her own original expression:

All the enjoyments of winter are of the kind which can the most easily be brought within the compass of the individual will.

[114] VI (1832), 825-28.

If they are in their nature less spiritual than those of spring and autumn, they admit of being made the most perfect of their kind. A thousand checks of custom or convenience may and do arise to prevent our having, in the right mood and with the right society, the breath of morning, newly alighted on a heaven-kissing hill; whence, in the devout stillness of the blue and dewy air, we might look down on "the kingdoms of the world and the glory thereof"; intense admiration of "the world" which "is all before us," making it hard to bear that it is not for us "to choose where." But in winter the eye *is* "satisfied with seeing and the ear with hearing," when for the one there is a bright fire, and for the other a voice we love.[115]

The comparison is probably unfair, since based only upon single instances, but W. B. Adams' essay "Beauty,"[116] a striking description in poetic prose of a voyage off South America, and C. R. Pemberton's "A Peep into Sherwood Forest"[117] show more truly original poetic perception than Mrs. Taylor's rather bookishly obscured vision. Her feeling for poetry was nevertheless genuine, and on at least one occasion, as will be seen, she was to write a true poem.

3. *Poetry*

In the generally high level of its poetry the *Repository* of these years compares very favorably with its best contemporaries. None of its verse is to be ranked in the highest order of nineteenth-century poetry, but it did publish a good deal that rises well above mere respectability. That it was the first magazine to give recognition to the genius of Robert Browning and to publish a few of his poems is not its only distinction; the *Repository* became, as Richard Garnett has pointed out, almost "the rallying point of the young writers by whom the impulse originally received from Shelley was propagated throughout English litera-

[115] *Ibid.*, p. 826.
[116] VII (1833), 89-96. [117] VIII (1834), 424-35.

ture." Also notable was its attempt to encourage the writing of what today might be termed proletarian poetry, aimed at the stimulating of the masses in their struggles for economic emancipation.

In the four years and a half of Fox's management, the periodical published nearly 150 original poems by perhaps two dozen authors. The writers of about nine-tenths of the poems can be identified. Space will not permit, even if the calibre of all the poems warranted it, to examine the whole number in detail. We shall have to content ourselves here with noticing briefly the work of a few of the more important poets.

Browning's contributions, of course, are well enough known as to make comment unnecessary. Of the five poems he supplied (over the signature "Z") only two were republished by the poet essentially as they appeared in the *Repository*, "Porphyria" and "Johannes Agricola"; even here the titles and a few lines have been modified. The first to appear (October, 1834) was the sonnet "Eyes, calm beside thee," which Browning never thought well enough of to include in his collected works. Edmund Gosse first discovered it and reprinted it in the Browning Society Papers; it is now usually published in complete editions, though not on the basis of merit. The sonnet was a form little suited to Browning, as the poet evidently realized. "The King," published a year later in the same number as the review of *Paracelsus,* was inserted in Part III of *Pippa Passes,* in an extended and greatly altered form. And the last, entitled "Lines" (beginning "Still ailing, wind?") became the first six stanzas of Section VI of "James Lee's Wife," with a few changes in wording and punctuation.[118] Although it is fair to say that the *Repository's* distinction in its connection with Browning lies rather in its reviews of *Pauline* and *Paracelsus*

[118] An account of each of the poems may be found in W. C. DeVane's *Browning Handbook.*

than in the verse of his that it published, nevertheless at least two of these poems, "Porphyria" and "Johannes Agricola," for their highly wrought art in style and content, can be read with real interest and pleasure—which is more than can be said of most poems printed in magazines before 1840.

Ebenezer Elliott was the most voluminous of the poets represented in the *Repository* in these years; in all he supplied about thirty poems, most of them in 1836 in a series entitled "Songs for the Bees." Though the *saeva indignatio* of the Corn Law Rhymer is interesting as a sign of the times, his often crude verses have little permanent appeal. One can sympathize with their denunciation of heartless landlords, of oppressive laws and selfish aristocrats, without according the verses high rank as poetry. Elliott's indignation was sincere, but, despite the classical adage, it takes more than indignation to make verses. For those who are unfamiliar with Elliott's poems one or two samples from the *Repository* may be of interest. This stanza from Number XVII of "Songs for the Bees" is one of his mildest "Free Trade" poems:

> Let idlers despair! there is hope for the wise,
>   Who rely on their own hearts and hands;
> And we read in their souls, by the flash of their eyes,
>   That our land is the noblest of lands.
> Let knaves fear for England, whose thoughts wear a mask,
>   While a war on our trenchers they wage:
> Free Trade, and no favour! is all that we ask;
>   Fair play, and the world for a stage.[119]

Number VIII of the same series is more characteristic of Elliott's mingled anger and sympathy:

> Thick Dick can read, but signs his mark;
> He likes a spree, when nights are dark,

[119] X (1836), 286.

And sometimes drinks his wages:
Blue Jem can neither read nor write,
But starves his wife, and loves a fight:
    What beasts are bards and sages!

Dick poaches when his work is done;
Jem fuddles at the "Dog and Gun,"
    And laughs at bards and sages:
With stolen brass Dick's boy buys gin;
In lampless lanes, Jem's daughter, thin,
    Earns prostitution's wages!

.   .   .   .

To clothe the squire, they waste their lives;
They rob their children, starve their wives,
    To pay his footmen's wages:
They cannot write, they will not think;
To feed their foes, they work and drink,—
    What beasts are bards and sages!

See, Palaced Brutes, that feed on brutes!
And curse Mechanics' Institutes,
    Because ye want their wages!
See, how they reel from street to street,
Where brawls my lord, and ruffians meet!
    You're safe if these are sages![120]

Elliott supplied more "reform" poetry than any of the other contributors, but he was not the only one to enlist verse in the cause. In the year of the Reform Bill, even Harriet Martineau, who was scarcely a revolutionary, was moved to militant song. Her "Reform Song" (to the tune of "Scots, wha hae") was worthy of a greater cause than merely the enfranchisement of the middle classes:

Now's the day, and now's the hour!
Freedom is our nation's dower,
Put we forth a nation's power,
    Struggling to be free!

[120] *Ibid.*, p. 91.

Raise your front the foe to daunt!
Bide no more the snare, the taunt!—
Peal to highest heaven the chaunt,—
   "Law and Liberty!"[121]

And when the Bill had passed, both Fox, in "The Barons Bold on Runnymede,"[122] and Harriet, in "Lion of Britain,"[123] in their rejoicing over the victory of the people urged continued and united effort:

O! lie thou not down till thy last foes are fled!

R. H. Horne several years later in "A Political Oratorio"[124] demonstrated his radical sympathies in bold language. Sings the chorus of workers led by Poet Clinker:

Off with the poor man's tax;
Descending multiplied by's poverty!
   Are we like nacker's hacks,
Working for hounds of aristocracy?
      Shame, with a tongue of flame,
      Blister the noble's name
      Who advocates this game,
Curs'd by the past and present times—and to posterity![125]

By no means was all the *Repository's* poetry of the revolutionary or proletarian order. Nature and love were the themes most frequently treated, and in a manner usually suited to a popular audience. One wonders, however, just how well pleased was a popular audience with the often obscure verses of Thomas Wade, who was, next to Elliott, the *Repository's* most faithful poet. Wade, like the young Browning, was an heir of Shelley, but unlike Browning he never developed a manner of his own. Among minor poets he is perhaps the purest example of direct Shelleyan influence. Wade has not been without a few admirers, but

[121] VI (1832), 371.
[122] *Ibid.*, p. 459.
[124] IX (1835), 37-44.
[123] *Ibid.*, p. 492.
[125] *Ibid.*, p. 39.

as one of them (H. Buxton-Forman) has phrased it, "with the sole exception of Thomas Lovell Beddoes, no nineteenth century English poet whose merit equals that of Thomas Wade has been so liberally neglected."[126] The reasons for the neglect are evident in his *Repository* poems, though it may be admitted that these do not include some of his best work. One can perceive, even in the close imitations of Shelley, a genuine and original poetic feeling, a sensitive and passionate nature. But the poetry itself suffers from obscurity, extravagance, turgidity, poor form, and lack of melody. Often good enough to arouse interest, it soon disappoints by a faulty line or an unwarranted obscurity.

The Shelley influence is unmistakable in Wade's *Repository* poems. "To a Glowworm," for instance, is directly modeled upon "To a Skylark":

> Drop of dewy light!—
> Liker dew than fire,
> Lit to guide the flight
> Of thy mate's desire,—
> Thou look'st a fairy robed in a moonbeam's attire.

And the last two stanzas:

> Round thee wild winds howl,
> Dashing thee to earth,
> Where thy tranquil soul,
> With unalter'd mirth,
> Gleams—as in our fierce world, sweet innocence and worth.

> Thro' the tempest loud
> Thou dost calmly pierce,
> From the perfumed shroud
> Which thy beams immerse,—
> As thro' the storms of time the poet's balmy verse.[127]

---

[126] W. R. Nicoll and T. J. Wise, *Literary Anecdotes of the Nineteenth Century*, I, 45.
[127] VIII (1834), 571-72.

"To a Water Drop"[128] adopts the form and the device of personification used in Shelley's "The Cloud." Buxton-Forman traces the "profound humanness" of "The Life of Flowers"[129] to the address to the animal creation in "Alastor." Other resemblances could be traced, but to detail them is beyond our need here. As a final excerpt from Wade, we shall quote his sonnet to Shelley, which Fox reprinted in his review of the now rare 1835 volume *Mundi et Cordis Carmina*.[130] The false touch in the last line illustrates Wade's frequent inability to turn out a completely finished poem.

> Holy and mighty poet of the Spirit
> That broods and breathes along the Universe!
> In the least portion of whose starry verse
> Is the great breath the sphered heavens inherit—
> No human song is eloquent as thine;
> For, by a reasoning instinct all divine,
> Thou feel'st the soul of things; and thereof singing,
> With all the madness of a skylark springing,
> From earth to heaven, the intenseness of thy strain,
> Like the lark's music all around us ringing,
> Laps us in God's own heart, and we regain
> Our primal life ethereal!—Men profane
> Blaspheme thee: I have heard thee *Dreamer* styled—
> I've mused upon their wakefulness, and smiled.[131]

Of the other young poets of the time who were trying their powers, R. H. Horne, later the author of the famous "farthing" epic, *Orion,* also contributed some verse to the *Repository,* but none of it is of much consequence. In addition to several of his juvenilia, he supplied "The Age of Steam, A Hudibrastic Poem"[132] and "The Great Unbled,"[133] the latter a long satirical allegory on the Church of England,

[128] *Ibid.,* pp. 19-21.
[130] IX (1835), 453-59.
[132] VIII (1834), 877-82.
[129] *Ibid.,* p. 711.
[131] *Ibid.,* p. 455.
[133] IX (1835), 293-305.

written in free octosyllabic couplets. William Leman Rede, a minor dramatist, contributed "Dreams" and a poem on "Chatterton."[134] Alexander Hume and Robert Nicoll, followers of Burns, sent a few poems in Scottish dialect. And both Junius Redivivus and Pel. Verjuice contributed poetry as well as prose. Adams' "Patriot Warrior to his Dead Barb"[135] is amusing for its attempt to provide a catalogue of South American customs and natural history; for instance, to the line

On thy flesh shall no ravening puma prey,

he appends a footnote: "The *puma* or silver lion prefers horse to all other flesh." Adams' poetry was better in prose. Pemberton's gift is best revealed in three of the poems he contributed to Eliza Flower's "Songs of the Months" series.[136]

Of the women who contributed verse, Sarah Flower maintained the best general level of performance, though Harriet Martineau, oddly enough, wrote the best single poem in her song for Eliza's series, "The Harvests of all Time."[137]

Beneath this starry arch
　　Nought resteth or is still;
But all things hold their march
　　As if by one great will.
　　　Moves one, move all;
　　　Hark to the footfall!
　　　On, on, forever.

Yon sheaves were once but seed;
　　Will ripens into deed;
As cave-drops swell the streams,
Day thoughts feed nightly dreams;
　　And sorrow tracketh wrong,
　　As echo follows song.
　　　On, on, forever.

[134] VII (1833), 788; VIII (1834), 737.　　[135] VII (1833), 160-64.
[136] "St. Valentine's Day," VIII (1834), 99; "Tears and Smiles," *ibid.*, p. 291; "December," *ibid.*, p. 828.　　[137] *Ibid.*, p. 533.

By night, like stars on high,
  The hours reveal their train;
They whisper and go by;
  I never watch in vain.
    Moves one, move all;
    Hark to the footfall!
    On, on, forever.

They pass the cradle head,
  And there a promise shed;
They pass the moist new grave,
  And bid rank verdure wave;
They bear through every clime,
The harvests of all time.
    On, on, forever.

Sarah Flower contributed three beautiful songs to Eliza's series and a number of other poems, but her best lyric, despite a few imperfections, is her "Morning, Noon, and Night," written soon after her marriage.[138] Emily Taylor, Jane Roscoe, Mary Howitt, and Mrs. Leman Grimstone were among the other women poets who wrote for the *Repository,* but we shall pass them by to excerpt one poem by Harriet Taylor. She printed three in the *Repository* but this is the only one that comes near to justifying Mill's estimate of her "eminently poetic nature." Imperfect as the poem is, one can hear a poet.

To the Summer Wind

Whence comest thou, sweet wind?
Didst take thy phantom form
'Mid the depth of the forest trees?
  Or spring, new born,
  Of the fragrant morn,
'Mong the far-off Indian seas?

---

[138] IX (1835), 562. Reprints of it are to be found in B. Dobell, *Sidelights on Charles Lamb,* and H. W. Stephenson, *The Author of Nearer, My God, to Thee.*

Where speedest thou, sweet wind?
Thou little heedest, I trow—
Dost thou sigh for some glancing star?
    Or cool the brow
    Of the dying now,
As they pass to their home afar?

What mission is thine, O wind?
Say for what thou yearnest—
That, like the wayward mind,
    Earth thou spurnest,
    Heaven-ward turnest,
And rest canst nowhere find![139]

In conclusion it may be noted that the *Repository* in these years, unlike the first series, printed few translations: one piece by Bowring, the translations of Goethe by Crabb Robinson, and two specimens from the Italian of Manzoni and Ugo Foscolo.[140] Religious and occasional verse also tended to disappear from its columns. And the evident modeling of its poetry on the practice of the Romantic poets rather than on that of the eighteenth century testifies to the completeness of the revolution that had been wrought in poetic taste by Wordsworth, Coleridge, Byron, and Shelley. In its poetry and criticism, as in its political and social views, Fox's *Repository* was not only abreast of the times, it was in the van.

CLOSE OF FOX'S EDITORSHIP

Had it not been for events in his personal life, Fox might well have continued the *Repository* for some years. By his own talents and those of the able contributors he had attracted to the magazine, he had raised the once sectarian periodical to a high place in the esteem of intelligent readers. James Grant, an observant newspaperman, writing on contemporary periodicals in his *The Great Metropolis*

[139] VI (1832), 617.   [140] X (1836), 226-29, 298-99.

(1836), notes that the *Repository* was "admired by all who read it, and was perhaps more liberally and generally praised by the newspapers than any of its contemporaries."[141] John Stuart Mill in the liberal *Examiner* in 1834, when the *Repository* was attaining its zenith, declared: "It stands conspicuous among the periodicals of the day, not less in the comprehensiveness of its objects and views, than in its progressive and rapid improvement in point of literary merit."[142]

But then as now the critical acclaim of intelligent and liberal readers did not necessarily mean extensive circulation. Grant is probably correct in his statement that the circulation at its highest never exceeded a thousand copies. And when Fox relinquished the editorship it was down to about eight hundred, even after the expedient had been resorted to of dropping the price from 1s. 6d. to a shilling. Lest in this day of astronomical circulation figures reaching hundreds of thousands and even millions, a sale of one thousand be thought despicable, one should compare Grant's figures for the *Repository's* contemporaries. He estimates the *Quarterly Review* sale in 1836 as nine thousand copies; the *Westminster Review,* once at the height of three thousand copies, had fallen to one thousand, and after its merger with the *London Review* to no more than fifteen hundred; the *Foreign Quarterly Review* had under twelve hundred. Of the magazines, the *New Monthly* had fallen from its high of five thousand in 1831-1832, *Fraser's* and the *Metropolitan*

---

[141] *The Great Metropolis,* II, 327.

[142] *The Examiner,* Jan. 12, 1834, p. 21. Other brief reviews of monthly numbers of the *Repository* may be found in the *Examiner* for Mar. 17, Apr. 14, June 16, Sept. 8, and Dec. 15, 1833. That all these notices were by John Stuart Mill is established by a manuscript bibliography of Mill's writings compiled by Mill himself. This manuscript, now owned by the British Library of Political and Economic Science, was discovered by Professor James McCrimmon in 1935. See his "Studies Towards a Biography of John Stuart Mill," an unpublished dissertation at Northwestern University, 1937. The manuscript is reproduced in John Robert Haind's "John Stuart Mill's Views on Art," also an unpublished Northwestern dissertation, 1939.

each sold about fifteen hundred. Since these latter magazines were financial ventures which aimed at popularity and profit, and paid good rates to contributors, the *Repository* does not suffer by comparison. Fox seems to have been able to conduct it without loss and may even have made a small profit, but he did not reach the hoped-for point where he could remunerate contributors. For both editor and contributors the *Repository* was chiefly a labor of love.

The events in Fox's personal life in 1834-1835 made the undertaking increasingly difficult. The publicity over his marital difficulties and his resultant expulsion from the London association of Unitarian ministers, together with the establishment of the new series of the *Christian Reformer,* undoubtedly tended to reduce further the number of Unitarian subscribers. The possibilities of increase in other directions were limited by the nature of the magazine's policies. It was too radical to be popular among the conservative middle classes, too expensive and too intellectually advanced to meet the needs of more than a small segment of the working classes.

Faced with the necessity of maintaining two establishments after the separation from his wife, Fox could not much longer afford to devote his time to the *Repository*. The secession of a number of the members from South Place Chapel probably cut his income from that source. Financial necessity, therefore, as well as his desire to exercise a wider influence by his writings, led him to turn to newspaper work. When Daniel Whittle Harvey purchased the *True Sun* in the summer of 1835, Fox became the leading editorial writer, and thereafter on one newspaper or another he was for many years a member of the working press.

The effect of Fox's new responsibilities was soon evident in the *Repository*. A decline is noticeable by the beginning of 1836, and increasingly the direction of the magazine was turned over to R. H. Horne. In February Horne proposed that Fox relinquish the management to him and Mary Gillies, sister of the painter Margaret Gillies; by this proposal Fox was to guarantee the new editors against loss for three months, to write half a sheet monthly when requested, and to share any profits over £20 a month. Whether these are the actual terms finally agreed upon is not known, but it is clear that Fox promised to continue as a contributor, a promise which proved impossible for him regularly to keep. In June, 1836, Horne assumed the editorship, and the July number was published over his name. The *Repository* was to linger on for nearly two years, but despite the efforts of Horne and Leigh Hunt, its interest and influence steadily declined. It seems fair to conclude that Fox's articles and the force of his personality, which had attracted a loyal corps of talented writers to his aid, were the factors that had enabled the magazine to gain distinction.

The *Repository* under Fox is a rare instance of a magazine maintained on a high level of excellence over an appreciable period of time by voluntary, unpaid contributors. Dr. Johnson once remarked that anyone was a fool to write for anything but money; the *Repository* was an exception to that rule, if rule it be. One cannot establish that the magazine exercised great or immediate influence, but its efforts on behalf of social and political reform and for the improvement of the taste and culture of the English people cannot have been wholly unavailing. In the years at the threshold of the Victorian era it takes a high and honorable place among the works of a small but enlightened group whose ideas were gradually to become a part of the English heritage.

8: Epilogue

THOUGH ONLY thirty-three years of age when he became editor of the *Repository,* Richard Henry (later Hengist) Horne had already experienced enough adventure to last the average man a lifetime. Born in London in 1803, he had been educated at Enfield and Sandhurst. As the result of expulsion from Sandhurst for insubordination, he failed to receive the appointment to the East India Company's service for which he had been preparing. In 1825 he enlisted as a midshipman in the Mexican Navy and saw active service in the war against Spain. He was at the siege of Vera Cruz, and later as a Spanish prisoner narrowly escaped being shot. After gaining his release, he proceeded to the United States, where he spent some time in travel. Adventure still followed him; he lost his money to some sharpers, broke two ribs trying to swim the Niagara on a wager, and was shipwrecked in the St. Lawrence. The crew of the lumber ship on which he worked his passage back to England mutinied, and the ship itself was nearly destroyed by fire. After such adventures a literary life must have seemed tame indeed.

The year 1828 saw the beginning of Horne's literary career when the *Athenaeum* published a poem of his entitled "Hecatompylos." Little is known of his activities during the next few years until his publication in 1833 of *The Exposition of the False Medium and Barriers Excluding Men of Genius from the Public.* This was a scathing attack upon critics, publishers, and theatre managers for their treatment of artists, literary and otherwise. One touch in the anonymous work reveals something of the egotism of the writer: he discusses as an example of neglected genius his own poem, "Hecatompylos." The *Exposition* made no great stir but aroused some animosity among critics. A mélange of prose and verse dramatic scenes, called *The Spirit of Peers and People* (1834), also attracted little attention, though the *Repository* labeled it as the work of a writer "of originality and genius."

Perhaps the brief though flattering notice encouraged Horne to offer his services to the *Repository;* at any rate, his first contribution, "Correspondence Between A Country Curate and the Bishop of a Diocese,"[1] designed to reveal the "heartless insensibility" of the higher clergy towards the downtrodden curates, appeared as the leading article in the July, 1834, number. Thereafter, Horne was a frequent contributor of fiction, of satirical sketches and verse (chiefly directed against the Church and the aristocracy), and of critical essays and reviews. None of this work was of a particularly high order, but it revealed cleverness, imagination, facility, and a good deal of vigor. All of his writing at this time may fairly be considered apprentice work, and it was not until about 1837 that he began to find his proper medium in poetry and the drama. He is today remembered chiefly as the writer of the allegorical epic, *Orion,* which appeared in 1843. In the drama he was an exponent of that "Elizabethan" school which flourished for a brief period in the 1830's and 40's; his short play, *The Death of Marlowe,* which Leigh Hunt published in the *Repository* in 1837, does succeed in capturing something of the Elizabethan spirit, though the legend upon which the play is based has been exploded by modern scholarship.

Horne's reputation has never been great, and in 1836, when he assumed control of the *Repository,* he was little

[1] *Monthly Repository,* 2d series, VIII (1834), 461-67. Unless otherwise indicated, all references in this chapter are to Vols. X and XI (1836-1837) of the second series of the *Repository* and to Vols. I and II (1837-1838) of the Enlarged Series.

known. His writing had been published anonymously and none of it was of much consequence. Without reputation or influence, therefore, he was scarcely well chosen to head a periodical which depended for its materials upon the personal friends and the prestige of its editor. Fox, however, by now anxious to be rid of the burden of the editorship because of his newspaper work, accepted Horne's offer to assume responsibility for the direction of the magazine.

The new editor made no changes in the format or general policy. His chance allusion to "the philosophic reformers—to whom this Magazine is chiefly addressed,"[2] reveals more explicitly than any statement by Fox just what audience the *Repository* still tried to reach. But philosophic reformers could soon observe that less attention was being paid to political and social questions, and that more space was being given to rather ordinary miscellany. This was not altogether the fault of Horne. Fox had promised to supply political articles, but he soon found it impossible to keep the promise. Others of his best writers also withdrew their support. Mill had earlier ceased to contribute, soon after the establishment of the *London Review,* of which he became the virtual editor. Sarah Flower Adams wrote no more for the magazine; her husband and Charles Reece Pemberton each contributed only one further article. A few remained loyal: Mrs. Leman Grimstone and some of the poets, notably Thomas Wade, Ebenezer Elliott, and Robert Nicoll. Of the new hands evident it has been possible to identify only one or two. "M.," the writer of a number of reviews, is quite possibly Mary Gillies, who was associated with Horne in the management of the periodical. Several pieces of fiction, signed "By the Author of 'Jerningham,'" are identifiable as by John William Kaye, a young soldier novelist, who years later was to be knighted by Victoria for his services in the management of East Indian affairs.

[2] XI (1837), 129.

The *Repository's* politics continued to follow the Radical program which Fox had so vigorously upheld, but, with the exception of one or two of his, none of the political articles is of any lasting interest. As the reviewer (probably Horne) of Albany Fonblanque's *England under Seven Administrations* remarked: "To write continuously on political subjects in a style which shall be at once instructive and entertaining, original, appropriate, and permanent, is the most difficult of all literary labours."[3] That Horne himself found it so may be guessed from his own political articles, and from the fact that he was not able to locate a satisfactory substitute for Fox.

The slashing vigor of Fox's leading article for Horne's first number, "Politics of the Common Pleas,"[4] is nowhere else matched in the year of Horne's editorship. The occasion was the notorious civil suit of the Honorable George Norton against the Prime Minister for the alienation of the affections of the talented writer Caroline Norton. The whole affair was later to furnish the background for George Meredith's novel, *Diana of the Crossways.* It was a subject ideally suited to Fox, for it enabled him at one time to vent both his hatred of the Tories and his scorn of the hypocrisy and shame of the English divorce laws. That Mrs. Norton was a gifted woman tied by law to a worthless husband was bad enough; that for obvious political purposes she should be subjected to a prurient public inquisition was unbearable. Fox was never moved to more bitter language than on this occasion. To him the trial of Melbourne was obviously a maneuver of the Tories to break up the Whig administration and restore themselves to power. "The dirty dogs; and as ravenous as they are dirty, and as blind as they are ravenous." If the nation must once more be subjected to the "degrading and rapacious domination" of a Tory government, "let it be by royal vacillation, by Whig im-

---

[3] *Ibid.*, p. 301.   [4] X (1836), 393-400.

becility, by fanatic wrong-headedness, by lordly perversity, by unblushing bribery, or by the bare sword of hireling soldiers; any way but through the sacrifice of an intelligent and lovely woman on the altar of Hypocrisy, repeating his filthy ritual of cant and slander." And such a move had emanated from the élite of the aristocratic party, a party which prided itself on its adherence to the age of chivalry! Fox in his anger attributed to the aristocracy, it would seem, blame for half the misery of society: for prostitution, the ignorance of the masses, and the mercenary spirit which corrupted even men of intelligence and talent. "To have gained a party point by crushing an erring woman, would have been disgraceful enough; the descent has been effected into a lower deep of infamy by a baffled conspiracy against an innocent woman."

Having thus paid his respects to the Tories, Fox proceeded to hand out like measure to English law. The penal code of the nation did not recognize the crime of adultery;

it is only taken cognizance of in the Ecclesiastical Courts, where it is called a sin, but dealt with as a virtue, and rewarded by the privilege of divorce; which must, under the circumstances, be no slight privilege to the parties. The civil proceeding [as in Norton's suit against Melbourne] is merely to repay the plaintiff in hard cash for the damage done to his female property.

But what of the wrong to the woman, whether innocent or guilty? "For a woman's having loved another man besides her husband does not unhumanise her; it does not make her a wild beast, to be beaten, and pelted, and hunted, and mangled." Even if she has been *"as bad as a man,"* it is a pernicious practice for society to subject her private life to judicial investigation.

And what should be Mrs. Norton's course now that her husband had lost his suit—hope that he might change his mind and take her back?

A Tory newspaper, a mighty support of our "holy religion," protestant principles, social order, and glorious constitution, . . . recommends the husband to banish from his mind all the unworthy suspicions which had been infused into it; and then, we suppose, to recall Mrs. Norton, and tell her to be sure and love, honour, and obey him, till death shall them part—a very moral and magnanimous mode of closing the transaction.

Yet if one were to raise the question whether she should not be permitted a divorce, the judges, the bishops, and the Tories "who flung her reputation at Lord Melbourne's office" would "cry out on the immorality."

Man and wife they are, and so they must remain, in spite of the cruelty, the injustice, the grossness, or the utter falsehood, involved in the assumption of such continued mutual relation. And all because the clergy have not sense and learning enough to discover, or not honesty enough to tell, the true meaning of a text in the New Testament, which has just as much to do with the morality of a public law of divorce, on reasonable grounds, as it has with the commutation of tithe for hop-gardens, or with the adoption of poor laws for Ireland.

Fox closed his article with some not unmixed praise of Melbourne. The nation was to be congratulated that the Prime Minister had escaped the Tory trap, for not until thorough reform of Parliament had been accomplished could the nation expect to see a better man at the head of the government.

He deserves to be a Radical, for he feels and acts like a man, although he is a Whig Lord. When the Church is dallied with, and the Ballot is burked, and a newspaper stamp retained, we would fain forget that he is implicated in the feeble policy of his party. It is pleasanter to remember that he has led them further than they ever went before. Let us thank him for that, and look to ourselves.[5]

[5] *Ibid.*, p. 400.

Promising as this article was that the *Repository's* political writing would continue to be as vigorous as ever, none that followed measured up to it. Fox contributed only a few more short articles: one a thrust at the Tories in a review of Disraeli's *Letters of Runnymede,*[6] a short piece on Britain's foreign policy,[7] and one reproving O'Connell for accepting "installment" or piecemeal reforms.[8] Horne himself tried his hand at political articles, usually without notable success; perhaps his best effort is to be seen in his leading article for January, 1837,[9] which attacked the failure of Parliament to reform the Church, provide for National Education, abolish the impressment of sailors, remove the taxes on the Press, repeal the Corn Laws, and, most important of all, grant the Ballot. Horne was also interested in the English policy with regard to the Civil War in Spain; he attacked England's interference in the war[10] and printed several eye-witness accounts of the activities of the British Auxiliary Legion.[11] The other writers of political articles it has not been possible to identify. One anonymous contributor quoted heavily from Mill's *London Review* to support his argument for establishing the English Poor Law system in Ireland.[12] A certain J.C.S. attacked the Whigs for their derelictions;[13] Z.Q. argued for international free trade;[14] and another anonymous writer claimed that more real reform had been achieved in the five years before the Bill of 1832 than in the five following—chiefly because of the failure to secure the ballot.[15] None of these articles is of much interest, however, except as an indication of the *Repository's* continued advocacy of Radical Reform. For-

[6] *Ibid.,* p. 540.
[7] XI (1837), 54-56.   [8] X (1836), 769-73.
[9] "Our Representatives," XI (1837), 1-12.
[10] "The Innocent Debates on Spain," *Ibid.,* pp. 305-14.
[11] "The Civil War in the North of Spain," XI (1837), 129-38.
[12] X (1836), 510-19.   [13] *Ibid.* pp. 572-75.
[14] *Ibid.,* pp. 733-38.   [15] XI (1837), 257-69.

tunately for the Radical cause, in view of the *Repository's* general ineffectualness at this time, the *London Review* was carrying on vigorously under the direction of John Stuart Mill.

Horne's magazine showed no change in policy with regard to social reforms except that it devoted much less space to such topics than had Fox's. One unidentified writer attacked the prevailing double standard in education and morality: "Inconstancy in a man is regarded with rather a jocular eye; in a woman it is a heinous crime. In either case her heart may be broken; if through the former, the world merely says, 'poor thing!'—if through the persecution attending the latter, the world's jury brings it in 'served her right.' "[16] The writer of an article on "The Factory Bill"[17] was only slightly more favorable to increased governmental interference in behalf of child workers than the *Repository* had earlier been. Mrs. Leman Grimstone continued the campaign to secure the development of rational amusements for the poorer classes.[18] Other than these few articles, Horne's magazine has little to offer as evidence of the social views of the Philosophic Reformers.

In place of extensive discussion of political and social reform Horne, perhaps perforce, substituted a good deal of rather mediocre miscellany. Resort was made to the practice familiar in that day of filling up pages with summaries and excerpts of volumes of history and travel; in successive months such articles were compiled on China, Brazil, Madrid, and Norway.[19] Of several original articles on travel experiences, the most interesting were three "Mexican Sketches" in which Horne related some of his early adventures.[20] One other bright spot among the miscellany was

[16] X (1836), 429.   [17] *Ibid.,* pp. 450-57.
[18] "Amusements," X (1836), 747-55; "On the Love of the Hideous," XI (1837), 357-60.
[19] X (1836), 409-17, 478-83, 525-39, 653-67.
[20] *Ibid.,* pp. 608-16, 675-79; XI (1837), 22-28.

the posthumous publication of the "Analytical Disquisition on Punch and Judy,"[21] found among Charles Lamb's papers. Charles Reece Pemberton's "Fourteen Days at School"[22] was a refreshing description of a new type of progressive school. Tribute to Jeremy Bentham was paid in a brief biographical article, accompanied by an engraving "drawn from the preserved figure confided to the care of Dr. Southwood Smith."[23] None of the magazine's fiction was distinguished, though John William Kaye's "Sheep-dog" and "Stephen Cameron" were fairly interesting character sketches.[24]

The only satirical piece of any merit was an anonymous description of "The Royal Suitors," who were flocking to England to seek the hand of the Princess Victoria.[25] James Grant in *The Great Metropolis* reported that the authorship of the squib was widely attributed to Thomas Love Peacock, but Horne expressly contradicted this.[26] The tone of the anonymous writer's satirical catalogue can be revealed by brief quotation. Prince Alexander of the Netherlands was described as neither wealthy nor witty; but John Bull was rich and the latter deficiency was "of no consequence to a head that aspires to a corner in the English crown, since the whole of it may be worn without the slightest pretensions to that or any other mental quality." The Prince of Hesse Homberg was tall, stout, and the owner of fine mustachios.

He is a sovereign prince; has sixteen quarterings in his arms; possesses a fine development of the organs of self-love and ambition, and maintains a standing army of 200 men. He rides well; sings with some taste, by means of a voice that can be tolerated; shoots skilfully, and is allowed to be the largest eater

---

[21] XI (1837), 39-42, 113-17.   [22] *Ibid.*, pp. 117-23.
[23] *Ibid.*, pp. 16-21. Cf. also Fox's eye-witness account of the dissection of Bentham, with extracts from Dr. Southwood Smith's address on the occasion.— VI (1832), 450-58.   [24] XI (1837), 139-47, 368-76.
[25] X (1836), 469-76.   [26] XI (1837), 184.

of sour-crout of any crowned prince in Europe. He loves the princess for herself alone, and deeply regrets that she will ever be sovereign of England, as his motives may perhaps be misinterpreted. For her he will gladly sacrifice everything. . . . To her exclusive service he is ready to devote himself, his love, his 200 men, and those talents aforesaid, which would have raised Homberg to an equality with the most flourishing empires in the world.

In conclusion, the foreign suitors are admonished in the words of the "old Latin proverb of *Knee-suitor ultra crepidam;*—Go and kneel to your own princesses!"

In criticism also the magazine lagged behind the standard set by Fox. Few novels were reviewed; Mrs. Shelley's *Falkner* was praised as her best book since *Frankenstein,*[27] and J. W. Kaye's *Doveton*[28] lauded for its style "at once elegant and familiar." Most of the reviews of fiction are signed "M." (perhaps Mary Gillies); they reveal no profundity of critical judgment and are heavily loaded with excerpts. One unsigned review alone, that of Carolina and Henrietta Beauclerk's *Tales of Fashion and Reality,*[29] is of any interest, and that more for its attack upon the aristocratic society portrayed in the fashionable novels than for its critical acumen.

These low-minded productions are not, however, without their value to the progress of society. They all aid, more or less, to show the kind of power which is behind, before, and underneath the throne. They are the revelations of aristocratic intellect, wit, morality, manners, and accomplishments, and will serve as astounding historical records for future times, of the intellect and principles of that class which considers itself born to legislate for a great nation, and in which preposterous assumption the said nation has coincided for so long a period with a fund of patience so truly marvellous.

[27] XI (1837), 228-36.
[28] *Ibid.,* p. 290.
[29] X (1836), 401-8.

That such novels often seemed to satirize the levity and folly of the aristocracy was nothing but affectation; it was usually evident that the writers were deprecating a life to which they themselves were wedded.

Only in its dramatic criticism did Horne's volume of the magazine show improvement. Here he was on familiar ground, for at the time he himself was engaged in writing plays. The first play noticed was Thomas Noon Talfourd's *Ion*, which had achieved considerable success.[30] This time "M." revealed more discernment than on other occasions Though declaring the tragedy to be "a creation of beauty and grace" without a "blemish on the pervading sweetness of the poetry" or on "the uniform smoothness of the action," nevertheless it was a "graceful structure without a solid foundation; a sport of the fancy, not a great work of art, or the result of the nobler powers of the imagination." Even as imitation it failed. "*Ion* is not like a Greek play. It matters not that the unities are preserved, that the plot, the scene, the characters, are Grecian."

Horne and several of the other writers on the drama aligned themselves with the Elizabethan school. Horne in reviewing Chateaubriand's *Sketches of English Literature*[31] almost exploded when he discovered that the French critic had only named eight or nine of Shakespeare's contemporaries, and had not even mentioned Webster, Marlowe, Massinger, Ford, and others! Some of Chateaubriand's criticism of Shakespeare's heroines was labeled as absurd, but Horne had to admit that the Frenchman had scored in this passage:

"In theory, the English are unreserved admirers of Shakespeare: but in practice their zeal is much more circumspect. Why do they not act the plays of their deity in a perfect form? By what presumption do they venture to abridge, mutilate, alter, and transpose the scenes of *Hamlet, Macbeth, Othello,* the *Merchant*

[30] *Ibid.*, pp. 446-50.   [31] X (1836), 589-96.

of Venice, Richard III? Why have these sacrileges been committed by the most enlightened critics of the three kingdoms?"

This theme was taken up in the same month in an article on "Stage-Profanation of Shakespeare,"[32] signed L.D. This critic proposed "a representation of Shakespeare's plays without any curtailment—all mere grossness, of course, excepted."

Dramatic composition is necessarily elliptical. When the actor fails in the filling up of the mere visible scene, how miserable a set of half-covered dry bones are set in motion! but when the case is aggravated by omissions of whole scenes and half scenes—whole speeches and half speeches—to what tatters—to what very rags, is the course of a passion torn!

To this critic the life of acting was dependent upon the actor's ability to harmonize "the whole series of the poet's words into one living expression of a consistent, intelligible, natural sequence of psychological causes and effects." Actors who cut out sections rendered disservice to the poet. Even Macready had been guilty, for in professing to restore *Lear,* he had omitted the Fool. This version, declared the critic, "should not have been put forth as Shakespeare restored; it was, after all, only Tate demolished." The critic made practical proposals for the reviving of an uncut text. The cost of such a production would be high and should therefore be met by subscription. No applause or disapprobation should be allowed during the performance. Numerous rehearsals should be provided, and adequate costume and scenery. A play should be made the whole evening's entertainment; the resultant effect would be thereby enhanced, since "attention would be more concentrated."

With the exception of a short essay on "Iago,"[33] the *Repository's* remaining critical articles dealt with the modern poetic drama. In February, 1837, Horne explained why

[32] *Ibid.,* pp. 623-30.   [33] XI (1837), 212-20.

in recent months he had been comparatively silent on the subject.

As no fresh production of sufficient note, except "Ion," had issued from the press, and as the theatres remained in the same Augean state of managerial sensuality and ignorance, we felt indisposed to vex our readers or ourselves by fruitless repetitions and monotonous accounts of abortive plays and bear-garden vulgarities.[34]

But there were once more signs of hope for the drama. Sheridan Knowles had long stood alone "in the long dull gap between the Drama and the Beast." Talfourd had come to his aid, and a number of critics also. Now Bulwer, "versatile, accomplished, and certainly the most popular author of the day," had appeared to help revive Dramatic Genius. "The rise of dramatic literature must reform the Stage, and the stage will then become an important means of refining the intellect, elevating the feelings, and inciting the nobler energies of all classes of the nation. Such is the faith the *Monthly Repository* has always held. . . ."[35]

Grateful as Horne was for Bulwer's service to the drama in writing *The Duchess de la Vallière,* he did not find the play without fault; there were peculiarities of construction, the heroine was too weak a character for a tragic role, and numerous feeble speeches, colloquialisms, and hackneyed allusions needed revision. Horne's chief objection was registered against the morality of the play.

Far be it from us to trouble our readers with the old vulgar nonsense about *the* moral and *a* moral, which, even at the present day, many of the critics so gravely discuss, though we had hoped it was at length generally exploded from all discussions on works of Art. The *moral tendency,* the broad abstract principles of humanity, constitute the only true morality of such works.

[34] *Ibid.,* p. 65. [35] *Ibid.,* pp. 65-66.

In this respect Bulwer had unfortunately "ranged himself on the side of the remorseless stupidity of conventional selfishness" in that he evidently regarded La Vallière's conduct as immoral. Horne maintained that "the tenour of her conduct was real morality. If she had married *Bragelone*, whom she never loved, she would have been made 'an honest woman,' according to the moral of this play— but in reality a prostituted, instead of a betrayed, victim."

The same article also contained a brief review of Sheridan Knowles's play *The Daughter*. Knowles, according to Horne, combined "more dramatic excellences than any of his contemporaries," probably because of them all he knew the stage best. Knowles

has not the refined pathos and classicality of Barry Cornwall, or Mr. Serjeant Talfourd,—the fine poetry contained in the dramas of Shelley, Byron, nor in those of the authors of "Joseph and his Brethren," "The Jew of Arragon," and "The Bride's Tragedy": in some respects he is inferior to Jerrold; but as one who can write good sterling poetry of nature, originating in action, and suited to the physical cravings of a theatrical audience, he has no equal.[36]

To the three plays just mentioned "M." devoted an article entitled "Dramatic Recollections" in the following month.[37] The article is less notable for its criticism than for its selection of these plays to refute charges that there was no dramatic talent in the land. These three, all works by very young poets (Charles Wells, Thomas Wade, and Thomas Lovell Beddoes, respectively) and all published between 1822 and 1830, were to the writer evidence enough that nothing "but the total absence of encouragement or countenance could have prevented [their power] from being developed to the most complete results." Monopoly and the stupid management of the theatres, not the lack of dramatic genius, were responsible for the low state of the drama.

[36] *Ibid.,* p. 73.   [37] *Ibid.,* pp. 148-63.

In its original poetry Horne's volume of the *Repository* compares favorably with those edited by Fox. Four poems by Ebenezer Elliott are of about the same quality as his earlier work;[38] and two by Robert Nicoll[39] reveal again the Scottish poet's talent for song. Thomas Wade continued to contribute generously; some of his best sonnets appeared in this volume and in the succeeding one edited by Leigh Hunt.[40] His irregular sonnet "The Fallers-Short" is interesting for its evidence of his allegiance to Reform; like many of the Philosophic Radicals he mourned to see leaders acting unworthily of their powers.

> When Great Men are not great, we needs must mourn,
> More than for all the pranks of Littleness;
> For that short-falling doth increase the weight
> Our spirits bear beneath this dust forlorn.
> Great men are solid harbour-holding banks
> Bounding the weltering waves of Life's distress;
> And when they sink and fail us, we are left
> Upon a shoreless ocean, hope-bereft.[41]

Wade's ballad "The Wedding Ring"[42] is notable for its echoes of Keats and Coleridge in place of the more usual reminiscences of Shelley. Horne himself in one long poem, "The Ballad of Delora; or, The Passion of Andrea Como,"[43] also reflects influence from Coleridge, even to the adoption of marginal glosses after the manner of those in "The Ancient Mariner." The first and last stanzas will perhaps sufficiently illustrate the ballad. The repetition of the open-voweled "Delora" as a refrain recalls some of Edgar Allan Poe's verse; Poe, it will be remembered, was an enthusiastic admirer of Horne's work.

---

[38] See Appendix (p. 405) for listing.
[39] "Life's Pilgrimage," X (1836), 546; "Song for a Summer Evening," XI (1837), 668.
[40] See Appendix (p. 424) for listing.   [41] XI (1837), 278.
[42] *Ibid.*, pp. 12-15.   [43] X (1836), 717-32.

Long years are gone, and I am old:
My locks once wore the lion's gold;
Life's winter now, with double smart,
Sheds frost upon my head and heart;
And thus I stand a lonely tree
All bare and desolate to see,
And worse within, since 'reft of thee;
   Delora!

Andrea Como, standing in utter desolation and solitude, poureth forth the impassioned history of his soul.

Cold are the winds on northern lea;
Cold is the wind o'er the sea:
Howl, winds! gripe, winter! shatter, wave!
Mankind, do all!—behold this grave!
Seasons roll on, as morn on morn;
So ages pass: oh, world forlorn!
The dead smile at thy scorn.
Time, ever childless and heart-bare,
Begins to mourn, and crave an heir.
Andrea Como sleeps—sleeps where?
   Delora![44]

Even Time sorroweth o'er the grave of one whom he had almost thought destined to survive him, and that he himself at last should rest. But Andrea Como sleepeth with Delora in celestial passion, beyond the Father of Years.

Horne may have contributed more poetry to the volume than can be identified with certainty as his. There is a good deal of anonymous verse, and in one instance an unsigned "Sonnet to Wordsworth"[45] is signed in the Table of Contents, R.H.H. Horne was probably also the author of a sonnet to Sir William Molesworth, the wealthy backer of the *London Review*.[46] One would like to be able to identify the authors of some of the anonymous poems, such as "The Water Lily,"[47] signed Pauline, and the "Stanzas"[48] beginning "Awake the myriad choir—bid music sound!" which are signed "V." (possibly Harriet Martineau), but unless there is in existence somewhere a marked file of the 1836-1837 issues, identification is probably impossible.

[44] For complete text, cf. Nicoll and Wise, *Literary Anecdotes of the Nineteenth Century*, Vol. I.
[45] X (1836), 424.
[46] XI (1837), 22.
[47] X (1836), 553.
[48] XI (1837), 289.

In summary, it may be said that Horne seems to have made a valiant effort to keep the *Repository* up to the level which Fox had maintained. That he did not succeed was not wholly his fault; in addition to the loss of some of its best writers, the *Repository* still bore the onus of its Unitarian past. As Horne wrote to Fox: "We are still perseveringly considered a Unitarian magazine by the public, who persist in not reading us to see the absurdity of their opinion; and of course we have lost all the Unitarian connection, with lots of all other dissenters to boot, by being beyond all sectarianism."[49] It is possible that Fox's venture might have achieved greater success if the changes he had made had included a change of title; the association of his periodical with the earlier series may have been an advantage at first in supplying an assured list of subscribers, but later on it was a decided disadvantage.

Finally in April, 1837, Horne wrote to Fox advising him that he must give up the struggle to keep the *Repository* afloat.

I intend to lay down the bâton at the end of the half year, the number for June being my last. Private circumstances . . . would make me regret that we cannot stop at once. But this ought never to be. After all your past labours, and the labours of others, to sneak out of existence, or to drop like a pill into the maw of Time (however good a pill), would be as painful as unbecoming. We must have time to arrange the mantle and ascend with decency.[50]

HUNT'S REPOSITORY

The *Repository's* end was not quite yet, however; one more editor was to try his hand. Fox, after conferring with Horne and several friends who had been interested in the magazine, decided to offer it as a free gift to Leigh Hunt,

[49] Quoted in Garnett, *Life of W. J. Fox*, p. 96.
[50] *Ibid.*, p. 174.

who was then without any other editorial responsibilities. Hunt, after some deliberation, accepted the offer jointly with Charles Reynell, the printer. And in July, 1837, appeared the first number of Volume I of a new and "enlarged" series.

One might have expected that the new proprietorship would prosper. Leigh Hunt had been before the public for a good many years in the role of reformer, poet, and essayist. He had by now succeeded in living down most of the bad reputation he had acquired as a youthful firebrand; his having suffered imprisonment for libeling the Prince Regent was now almost an enviable distinction, and even those who had fiercely attacked him as the leader of the "Cockney School" in poetry were willing to let bygones be bygones. He was an experienced writer for the periodicals and had edited a number of his own; the *Repository* was the tenth that he had directed. His reputation as a martyr in the liberal cause should have made him acceptable to the Radicals; his religious views, though liberal, were not of any sect; and his known literary talents, coupled with his wide literary connections, offered promise that that side of the *Repository* would not suffer. Why, with all these things in his favor, Hunt failed so quickly, will presently appear.

Hunt began the new venture with his characteristic vivacity and with all the delight of a child in a new toy. So full of light matter was the first number, in fact, that the new editor in his introductory address felt obliged to apologize on the grounds that the suddenness of the new responsibility had not permitted him to assemble his contributors. The next number, he promised, would have a "greater mixture of seriousness, and be more properly our SPECIMEN NUMBER." In general character, he explained, the new series would extend the "*anti-sectarian* philosophy of the two Editorships preceding."

The *Monthly Repository* was for a long time in the hands of a most respectable and liberal sect, but still a sect; and it was with great difficulty it partly extricated itself from the consequences. Mr. Fox boldly broke the chain, and may be said to have tried the numerous friends who remained with his Editorship in truly golden fires (we hope to have the honor of retaining them.) Mr. Horne, his successor, having never been connected with any sect, was enabled still farther to throw open the speculative character of the Magazine; and he brought to it new zeal for his own departments of literature, which thus extended it in fresh quarters. For ourselves, we may venture to say, that it is with the approbation of our predecessors, and, we hope, the good wishes of increasing multitudes of men, that we openly profess a Christianity not inimical to any sect, but desirous of merging them all into one great unsectarian brotherhood of placid differers in opinion (as long as they must needs differ) and exalters of the spirit above the letter. . . .

The *Monthly Repository* then will be very unsectarian, very miscellaneous, very much given to literature and unlimited enquiry, a great lover of all the wit and humour it can bring into it, and an ardent Reformer, without thinking it necessary to mistake brick-bats for arguments, or a scuffling with other people's legs for "social advancement."[51]

Enough of a change was made in the format to mark off the new series distinctively from its predecessor. The page was divided into two columns and shortened by a few lines, but what was lost in this way was made up for by the addition of eight pages to each number. Hunt in typical fashion devoted three pages to a versified defense of the change: "Doggerel on Double Columns and Large Type."[52]

> Look at the fact. All monthly, publi-
> cations that have been colum'd doubly,
> Have always hit the public fancy
> Better, and with more poignàncy
> Than your platter-fac'd, broad pages.

[51] I (July, 1837), 1-2.   [52] I (1837), 86-88.

Far more marked than the changes in appearance were the alterations in content. The first number proved to be reasonably typical of what was to come, despite Hunt's promise of more serious matter for later numbers. The *Repository* acquired a completely different style and manner—and it was, of course, the style and manner of Leigh Hunt. His personality, taste, and preferences completely dominated, and his writing filled the largest share of the pages. At least fifty of the seventy-two pages in the first number were his, and of the seven hundred-odd pages published during the ten months of his editorship close to three hundred can be identified as his. In addition, his son Thornton contributed a number of articles. The periodical should have been entitled *Hunts' Repository*.

From Hunt Senior's pen in the first number came these articles: "Female Sovereigns of England When Young," appropriately reviewing the careers of earlier princesses at a time when the English were speculating about the character of their new queen; "Vicissitudes of a Lecture," an amusing light essay on the platform difficulties of "poor Ned Pounchy"; "Her Majesty's Name; and a Caution Thereon," a *jeu d'esprit* ransacking literature for puns on Victoria; "Blue-Stocking Revels; or the Feast of the Violets," a long poetical catalogue of England's women writers, in the manner of Hunt's earlier *Feast of the Poets*.[53] Hunt probably also wrote most of the brief critical notices. Thornton Hunt wrote two short articles: "Mr. Serjeant Talfourd's Copyright Bill" and "Universal Penny Postage."

In later numbers some of Hunt's friends were prevailed upon to contribute. Thomas Carlyle supplied two short poems, and Horace Smith, of *Rejected Addresses* fame, two sets of satiric verses. Walter Savage Landor, back from Italy somewhat less than a year, contributed "High and Low Life

[53] The *Revels* had originally been intended for the *New Monthly* but had been held back because of Hunt's dislike of the latter's new editor.

in Italy," in installments stretching over nine months. Thomas Wade continued to send in his verses, and Horne gave his short play, *The Death of Marlowe,* and at least one short essay. Hunt seems always to have gathered about him a circle of talented young men, and a few of these now came forward with their writings: Egerton Webbe, William Bell Scott, and George Henry Lewes. These are all who signed their contributions or who can be identified. Horne, reminiscing about Hunt some years after his death, thought that Robert Bell, and probably Browning, Harriet Martineau, and Mrs. Jameson had been among the contributors,[54] but if so, it seems impossible to identify their work with certainty.

Altogether, from the array of contributors, one might expect a more interesting magazine than Hunt's *Repository* actually turned out to be. It was pleasant and sometimes amusing, but rather lacking in what one might call, for want of a better word, character. The two former series of the magazine had never been very sprightly, to say the least, but even in the days when it had been a loosely-knit sectarian miscellany there had always been a kind of unity of purpose which gave it strength. Now, under Hunt, despite its generally liberal views it seemed by contrast a purposeless and flabby miscellany.

Among the best of that miscellany must be mentioned a number of Hunt's essays, ever the field in which he shone to advantage. Despite his long course of domestic and financial woes, Hunt could still turn out pleasant, informal

[54] S. R. T. Mayer, *Letters of Elizabeth Barret Browning Addressed to Richard Hengist Horne,* II, 280-84. No one of these four is named in Leigh Hunt's presentation copy in which he identified most of the writers (cf. Appendix, p. 425). Since Horne was writing more than thirty years after the *Repository* had expired, his recollection may have been confused. William Bell Scott might, for instance, have been confused with Robert Bell, although it is perfectly possible that the latter, then a young radical journalist, may have contributed. If Mrs. Jameson was a contributor, one might guess that "The Tale of the Garden Bower at Amalfi" (II [1838], 39-45) was hers.

essays, full of deft trifling and good humor. None of his *Repository* essays perhaps ranks among his best work in this sort, but the "Vicissitudes of a Lecture,"[55] "Inexhaustibility of the Subject of Christmas,"[56] and "Soliloquy During a Walk Home at Night"[57] may still please his admirers. Of more substance are his articles on old books which he included under the heading "Retrospective Review."[58] An inveterate bookworm, Hunt could ramble on enthusiastically about old and rare books, bookshops and booksellers, for pages on end. His long essay entitled "Duchess of St. Albans; and Marriages from the Stage"[59] combines his love for the theatre and his fondness for the chit-chat and gossip of memoirs. "Of Statesmen Who Have Written Verses"[60] is a rapid survey in Hunt's "dear-reader" style, with excerpts from the statesman poets.

Most of the other miscellany is of no permanent interest. Thornton Hunt, later to become a successful journalist, was apparently assigned current topics for short "filler" articles: "Steam-Boat Accidents and Their Prevention," "Universal Penny Postage," "The Colonization of New Zealand," and the like. Horne wrote an essay which began with a fishing expedition and ended with a tour of the "Harefield Copper Works." Of better quality were "Hints Towards a Right Appreciation of Pictures,"[61] by the young artist and poet, William Bell Scott, later to be heard of in connection with the Pre-Raphaelites, and L.D.'s "Analysis of Laughter."[62] Three of the young writers, Webbe, Lewes, and Thornton Hunt, tried their skill on a philosophical subject: "Of the Sufferings of Truth," "Hints Towards an Essay on the Sufferings of Truth," and "Of the Alleged Sufferings of

[55] I (1837), 25-29.
[56] *Ibid.* pp. 391-94.   [57] II (1838), 127-30.
[58] See Appendix (p. 426) for listing of titles.
[59] I (1837), 154-76.   [60] *Ibid.*, pp. 279-83, 410-16.
[61] *Ibid.*, pp. 265-73.   [62] *Ibid.*, pp. 16-25.

Truth."[63] The second of these is probably the first appearance in print of Lewes.[64]

Most miscellaneous of the major contributions to Hunt's *Repository* was Walter Savage Landor's "High and Low Life in Italy, exhibited in letters and memoirs collected by the late J. J. Pidcock Raikes, Esq., and now first published by his nephew, Sir Rodney Raikes, with several material additions."[65] This is an odd mixture of letters, journals, dialogue, verse, and commentary, strung together on a very slender thread of story. There are some delightful insights into Italian life and character, especially on the seamier side, but in the aggregate it is a confused, rambling sketch. The *Repository's* readers may well have been puzzled if not annoyed. Hunt supplied a footnote introduction to the eighth installment, evidently to answer objections:

> As readers not intimate with Italian manners appear to be occasionally mystified with these masterly papers of Mr. Landor, which we will venture to say contain not a syllable without its weight and significance, whether the subject be grave or gay, we think it may be as well to remind them, that the said manners are here painted to the very letter as well as in spirit, including specimens even of idiom, and of the phraseology of obsequious intercourse. . . .[66]

"High and Low Life in Italy," in spite of Hunt's praise, can scarcely be considered one of Landor's best works. Posterity has seen fit to reprint it only once, and that in an edition which sought to be complete.[67] Hunt was so determined

---

[63] *Ibid.*, pp. 116-22, 311-19, 403-9.

[64] Anna T. Kitchell in her *George Lewes and George Eliot* (New York, 1933) overlooks Lewes' signed contributions to the *Repository*. She says (page 20), "The earliest published work that we can definitely attribute to Lewes is an article in the *Westminister Review* for September, 1840." Lewes also contributed to the *Repository*: "A Companion for the Fragment of Simonides," I (1837), 401-3; and "Thoughts for the Thoughtful," a youthful attempt at aphoristic wisdom, II (1838), 56-58, 130-32.

[65] See Appendix (p. 000) for paging.   [66] II (1838), 163.

[67] Vol. XI, *The Complete Works of Walter Savage Landor,* edited by T. Earle Welby. London, 1930.

not to cheat his readers of any of these sketches by Landor that he devoted two thirds of the final number of the *Repository* to the ninth and last installment.

Poetry in the *Repository* under Hunt's direction continued to maintain a fairly high level. Much more space was given to light verse. The *Blue-Stocking Revels* is in the manner of Hunt's earlier *Feast of the Poets,* but in dealing with feminine writers he is more careful to avoid offense. The writers and poetesses are arranged alphabetically to avoid distinctions, and the criticism is tempered with a good deal of mercy. Some advice was administered gratis, as in the lines on Elizabeth Barrett:

A young lady then, whom to miss were a *caret*
In any verse history, named, I think, Barrett,
(I took her at first for a sister of Tennyson)
Knelt, and receiv'd the god's kindliest benison.
—"Truly," said he, "dost thou share the blest power
Poetic, the fragrance, as well as the flower;
The gift of conveying impressions unseen,
And making the vaguest thoughts know what they mean.
Only pray have a care, nor let Alfred beguile
Admiration too far in manner and style;
Nor divide with the printer your claims to be read
By directing our faculties when to say *èd.*
Such anxieties do both your Geniuses wrong;
Tend to make things too verbal, the mind not so strong;
And besides, my dear, who has not read an old song?"[68]

The lines on Harriet Martineau gently satirized her Malthusianism:

Ah! welcome home, Martineau, turning statistics
To stories, and puzzling your philogamystics!
I own I can't see, any more than dame Nature,
Why love should await dear good Harriet's dictature!
But great is earth's want of some love-legislature.[69]

[68] I (1837), 39.   [69] *Ibid.,* p. 44.

Except for "Bodryddan,"[70] most of Hunt's other verse consisted of translations from the Greek, such as "On a Cultivator of the Ground" from the Greek Anthology, or from Italian and French light verse, such as Giovanni de la Casa's "A Deprecation of the Name of John" and the Chevalier de Boufflers' "An ABC for Grown Gentlemen." Thomas Wade contributed his "Curse of the Flowers" and a number of sonnets. Horne gave his notable short play "The Death of Marlowe" for its first publication. Horace Smith supplied a squib on "Church Rates" and an allegory called "The Quarrel of Faith, Hope, and Charity." More interesting in that it seems in some ways a kind of *pre*-Pre-Raphaelite poem, is W. B. Scott's "Rosabelle,"[71] a long narrative of a country maiden who follows the road to ruin. Thomas Carlyle's verse is unfamiliar enough to warrant quoting one of the two poems he gave to Hunt.

LILLIPUTIAN

So here hath been dawning
Another blue day:
Think wilt thou let it
Slip useless away.

Out of Eternity
This new day was born;
Into Eternity,
At night, will return.

Behold it aforetime
No eye ever did:
So soon it for ever
From all eyes is hid.

Here hath been dawning
Another blue day:
Think wilt thou let it
Slip useless away.[72]

[70] *Ibid.*, p. 243.
[71] II (1838), 112-17; 189-96.   [72] I (1837), 85.

There is no evidence that Browning submitted any of his poetry to Hunt, but one cannot help speculating whether the Z. addressed in the following note to correspondents in March, 1838, was directed to Browning, especially since Z. had been his usual signature. Even if no connection with Browning is warranted, the note and its sequel are interesting as examples of Hunt's advice to young poets.

There is so much power in the sonnets of Z. that we are grieved to see it struggling, half in fancied scorn, and half in ter-ror and despair, with the deformities or mistakes of things, instead of exercising the poet's true office, and showing how we are to overcome and supersede them with the good and the beautiful. We beg him to read the beautiful poem of "Brain and Heart" in our present number, and recognize the *right* process there.[73]

One month later (April, 1838) Hunt wrote:

Z. has sent us a very welcome and sensible letter, in which he deprecates the "fancied scorn" we imputed to the melancholy of his sonnets, and his letter is accompanied with some more compositions of the same class, which we regret came too late for the insertion of even one of them. He is in the right road; and may God speed him in it;—always premising, that he does not seek fortune as well as consolation in it,—poets, as such, having no business with the desire of anything but the cultivation of the beautiful for its own sake.[74]

The weakest department of Hunt's *Repository,* as with Horne's, was the political. Hunt's radicalism had mellowed through the years into a kind of sentimental idealism. No longer the ardent young radical who had excoriated aristocracy and throne in the *Examiner,* he was now disposed to see good on both sides of the political fence. As Hunt himself phrased it in his essay on "The Examiner Twenty Years Ago": ". . . the sharp taste of suffering has rendered

[73] II (1838), 216.   [74] *Ibid.,* p. 288.

us less willing to inflict pain, and we have learnt to know that enemies may be as good men as others, and that the great point is, to lift the whole world if you can, and trample on nobody."[75] This was all very admirable but it did not make for good stirring radical articles such as the *Repository's* readers had been used to under Fox. Though Hunt maintained that he had thought it his duty to carry on the spirit of the magazine's politics, he was now incapacitated by temperament and inclination for performing that duty effectively. In all sincerity he called for the Ballot, Household Suffrage, and National Education, but his voice was modulated to the tone of a gentlemanly and unheated conversation. His political articles are more the work of a philosophical and almost disinterested spectator than of a conductor of a Reform periodical.

It was to this weakness in the political department, one may suspect, that the *Repository* owed its demise. A letter written in January, 1838, would seem to indicate that the magazine was progressing satisfactorily,[76] but an undated letter to John Forster announces that

the poor *Repository* is about to die; or at all events to transmigrate into some other shape, altogether unpolitical. I think I have suffered enough in my time, and may finally be laid up, and try to recover of my "scars upon scars," especially as by *silence* on politics I shall compromise no principles, and reform, thank God, must progress somehow or other.[77]

In his final address to the reader in the April, 1838, number, Hunt announced that if the periodical should continue in any shape it would contain no politics and would appear under another title, since its sectarian associations still hampered it. Hunt in effect confessed his inability any longer to write on political subjects.

[75] I (1837), 226.
[76] To J. W. Dalby.—*Correspondence of Leigh Hunt*, I, 295-96.
[77] *Ibid.*, p. 277.

I must therefore end life as I began it, in what is perhaps my true vocation, that of a lover of nature and books;—complaining of nothing,—grateful, if others will not complain of me,—a little proud perhaps (nature allows such balm to human weakness) of having been found not unworthy of doing that for the good cause by my sufferings, which I can no longer pretend to do with my pen,—and possessed of one golden secret, tried in the fire, which I still hope to recommend in future writings; namely, the art of finding as many things to love as possible in our path through life, let us otherwise try to reform it as we may.[78]

The *Repository* had cost him time and anxiety, but he took pleasure in the friends he had thereby acquired; "and if I owe an apology for being the unwilling terminator of its existence to them, and to the estimable ghosts of the Vidlers and Priestleys, their good nature will not refuse me its forgiveness, seeing that I have neither sullied its reputation for sincerity, nor restricted the contemplated expansion of its sympathies."

It remained for Horne years later to pronounce the final benediction on the *Repository:*

It flourished for a season; but so absorbent and reticent is public opinion that this always valiant, intellectual and energetic pioneer of most of the leading ideas and principles of progression in our present day, having once been,—in the memory of the oldest living inhabitant—the chief organ of a dissenting sect, that early fact still hovered and vapoured around it with a smothering atmosphere, and finally poor Leigh Hunt discovered that it was "labour in vain," and so the brave little *Repository* died in his editorial arms; about as happy and honourable an end as it could have had.[79]

[78] II (1838), 218.
[79] S. R. T. Mayer, *Letters of Elizabeth Barrett Browning,* II, 280-84.

Appendix: *Identification of Authorship*

As has been pointed out in Chapter III, the great majority of contributions to the first series were anonymous or signed only with pseudonyms or initials. Identification of authorship is therefore difficult, and in many instances apparently impossible. There may be in existence somewhere an editorial key with contributors marked, but even this would not be complete, since it is evident that Aspland himself often did not know the identity of some of the writers. Not until after the death of Mrs Barbauld, for instance, did Aspland learn that she was the author of several anonymous poems he had printed.

From various sources, however, a number of identifications can be made. R. B. Aspland's *Memoir* of his father (pages 183-92) contains a list of many writers in Volume I. Various published memoirs of Unitarian worthies, including obituary sketches in the *Repository* itself (for example, Crabb Robinson's obituary of Anthony Robinson) and in the *Christian Reformer,* supplement Aspland's account. Alexander Gordon in many articles on Unitarians in the *Dictionary of National Biography* names various *Repository* writers, as do Robert Spears' *Record of Unitarian Worthies* and Herbert McLachlan's *Unitarian Movement in the Religious Life of England.*

It has seemed advisable not to attempt an elaborate listing of all the identifiable articles, many of which are of no consequence. Instead, a list is herewith printed of contributors who are the subjects of biographical articles in the *Dictionary of National Biography* and, in a few instances, in the *Dictionary of American Biography.* The list also includes the names of a small number of more or less regular contributors who are thought to be of some importance, even though they have not been included in the *D.N.B.;* the names of such persons are starred in this list. No pretense to completeness can be made for the list; and the presence of a name does not necessarily mean that the person was a *regular* contributor.

In addition, an attempt has been made to list the writings of four contributors who are still of at least some slight literary importance: Anna L. Barbauld, Harriet Martineau, Henry Crabb Robinson, and Thomas Noon Talfourd. Also, we have reprinted from the Aspland *Memoir* identification of the Non-Con Club papers referred to in Chapter III.

I. Some Contributors to the First Series. (*Except* for names preceded by an asterisk, biographical sketches for all of the following will be found in the *D.N.B.*, or, in a few instances, the *D.A.B.*)

Acton, Henry
Aikin, Arthur
Aikin, Dr. John (1747-1822)
*Allchin, R.
*Anstis, Matthew
Aspland, Robert
Baker, Franklin
Barbauld, Anna L.
Barham, Thomas Foster
Belsham, Thomas
Bowring, John
Bransby, James Hews
Bretland, Joseph
Brettell, Jacob
Browne, Theophilus
Bruce, William (1757-1841)
Buckingham, James Silk
Butcher, Edmund
*Cappe, Catherine
Carpenter, Lant
Christie, William
Cogan, Eliezer
Cogan, Thomas
Cornish, Joseph
*David, Job

*Dewhurst, John B.
Disney, J. Alexander
Dyer, George
*Eaton, David
Estlin, J. P.
Evans, John (1767-1827)
Flower, Benjamin
Flower, Richard (in *D.A.B.*)
*Foster, Thomas
Fox, W. J.
Frend, William
*Fry, Richard
*Fullager, John
Grundy, John
*Hazlitt, William, Sr.
Higginson, Edward
Hincks, Thomas D.
Hincks, William
Holden, Lawrence (1752-1844)
Holland, John (1766-1826)
Horsfield, Thomas Walker
*Howe, Thomas
*Hughes, Mary
Hunter, Joseph (1783-1861)

James, John Angell
*Jevons, Joseph
*Johns, John
Johns, William
Jones, John (1766?-1827)
Joyce, Jeremiah
Kenrick, George
Kenrick, John
Kentish, John
LeGrice, Charles Valentine
Lloyd, Charles (1766-1826)
*Luckock, James
*Madge, Thomas
*Manning, James
*Mardon, Benjamin
*Marsom, John
Martineau, Harriet
*Maurice, Michael
*Moggridge, John H.
*Morell, John
Nightingale, Joseph
Palmer, Samuel (1741-1813)
Parkes, Samuel
Platts, John
Probert, William
Rees, Thomas
Richards, William (1749-
1818)

Robberds, John G.
Robinson, Anthony
Robinson, Henry Crabb
Rutt, John Towill
Scargill, William Pitt
Simpson, John (1746-1812)
Smith, Sir James E.
Smith, John Pye
Smith, T. Southwood
Stockdale, Percival
Stone, Francis
Sturch, William
Talfourd, Thomas Noon
Taylor, Edgar
Taylor, Edward
Taylor, Emily
Toulmin, Joshua
*Townsend, Josiah
Turner, William, II
Turner, William, III
Van der Kemp, Francis A.
   (in *D.A.B.*)
Wallace, Robert
Wellbeloved, Charles
Wilson, Walter
Worsley, Israel
Wright, Richard
Yates, James

II. Contributions by Mrs. Barbauld, Harriet Martineau, Crabb Robinson, and Thomas Noon Talfourd

Abbreviations: [P], Poetry; [R], Review; [Tr.], Translation. A question mark preceding an entry indicates that the ascription is conjectural.

ANNA LETITIA BARBAULD

The Pilgrim [P], II, 261
Memoir of the Rev. Rochemont Barbauld, III, 706-9
On the King's Illness [P], VI, 608
Vindication of the Dialogue on the Scriptures in reply to Mr.
   Sturch, VIII, 738-41

The Death of the Righteous [P], IX, 243
Memoir of the Rev. John Prior Estlin, XII, 573-75
A Thought on Death [P], XVII, 636; 679
To the New Year [P], XVIII, 49
HARRIET MARTINEAU [Discipulus, H. M.] See also 2d Series, page
    414.
Female Writers on Practical Divinity, XVII, 593-96; 746-50
On Female Education, XVIII, 77-81
Lines Occasioned by the Controversy on the Origin of Evil,
    XIX, 43-44
On the Death of Lieutenant Hood [P], XIX, 44-45
Defense of Metaphysical Studies, XIX, 268-73
Reply to Difficulties in the Unitarians' Scheme of Atonement,
    XIX, 598-600
HENRY CRABB ROBINSON [Viator, H. C. R.] See also 2d Series, page
    421.
Translations from the German: A Fragment of a Hymn to
    Cecilia (Herder); The Spirit's Greeting (Goethe); Va-
    pours (Herder), I, 55
A Parable from the German of Lessing [Tr.], I, 183-85
The Education of the Human Race (from the German of
    Lessing) [Tr.], I, 412-20; 467-73
? A Theological Conversation, II, 580-84
Remarks on the Genius and Writings of Herder, III, 173-79
Paramythia: from the German of Herder: Aurora; Flora's
    Choice; Echo; The Dying Swan; The Lily and the Rose;
    Sleep [Tr.], IV, 142-45
? Use of the Improved Version in Public Worship, VI, 539
? Sunday Schools of Catholic Origin, IX, 93-94
? Deaf and Dumb Institutions, Paris, IX, 738-40
THOMAS NOON TALFOURD [T.N.T., and possibly S.N.D.]
Consolations of Universal Restoration [P], VII, 333-34
? On Poetical Scepticism, XI, 157-59; 216-20; 278-80; 383-85;
    508-10. Signed S.N.D.
A Tribute to the Memory of Joseph Fox [P], XI, 295-96
Obituary: Joseph Fox, XI, 297-98
A Tribute to the Memory of the Rev. William Vidler [P], XI,
    550-51

? To S. T. Coleridge, Esq., on the Attack on Unitarians Contained in his Second Lay Sermon, XII, 213-16, 268-72. Signed S.N.D.

Sonnets Supplementary to Wordsworth's Sonnets to Liberty [P], XII, 370-71

Thomas Chalmers' A Series of Discourses on the Christian Revelation, Viewed in Connection with Modern Astronomy [R], XII, 418-26

On the System of Malthus, XII, 471-74; 532-35; 660-65

On the Execution of General Lacey . . . [P], XII, 489

Legality of a Quaker's Affirmation, XII, 654-55

Latin Epigram, with a Translation, on Two Brothers . . . , XIII, 63

Sonnets to Fame [P], XIII, 209

Prologue to Cato [P], XIII, 523-24

Obituary: Sir Samuel Romilly, XIII, 720-22

Sonnet on the Death of Her Majesty, the Queen [P], XVI, 732

See also Nos. 8 and 16 of the Non-Con Club Papers

THE NON-CON CLUB PAPERS, 1818-1826

Since there are mistakes in the *Repository's* numbering of this series of papers, the following numbering does not in all cases agree with that published.

1. Robert Aspland, A Vindication of the Two Thousand Ejected Ministers, XIII, 42-45

2. John Bowring, On the Opinions of the Puritans Respecting Civil and Religious Liberty, XIII, 114-22

3. W. J. Fox, On the Conduct of the Quakers as Distinguished from that of other Nonconformists in the Reign of Charles II, XIII, 172-76

4. Samuel Parkes, On the General Prevalence of Superstition, XIII, 260-64, 309-15

5. Thomas Rees, Faustus Socinus and Francis David, XIII, 382-85

6. C. Richmond, The Cause of Nonconformity as Connected with the Interests of General Literature, XIV, 24-30

7. G. Smallfield, The Principles and Conduct of the Baptists respecting Civil and Religious Liberty, XIV, 92-100

8. T. N. Talfourd, The Intolerance of the Dissenters usually Denominated "Orthodox," as Compared with that of the Established Churches, XIV, 171-74

9. Edgar Taylor, Memoir of Wetstein, XIV, 248-56

10. Richard Taylor, On High-Church Infidels, XIV, 308-12

11. John Bowring, Sketch of the History and Literature of the Spanish Jews, XIV, 345-52

12. Robert Aspland, On the Corporation and Test Acts, XIV, 426-30

13. W. J. Fox, On the Controverted Clause in the 20th Article of the Church of England, XIV, 461-65

14. Samuel Parkes, Life and Character of Hugh Peters, Chaplain to Oliver Cromwell and the Parliament, XIV, 525-32, 602-7

15. Thomas Rees, The Sentiments of the Early Continental Reformers respecting Religious Liberty, XIV, 680-84, 735-43

16. T. N. Talfourd, On the Supposed Affinity of the Poetical Faculties with Arbitrary Power and Superstitious Faith, XV, 95-99

17. C. Richmond, On the Patronage of Religion by the Civil Power, XV, 223-28

18. Edward Taylor, On Mahometanism: Its Church Establishment and Treatment of Nonconformists, particularly the Wahabites, XV, 257-66, 348-56

19. John Bowring, Ultra-Catholicism in France, XV, 325-32

20. Robert Aspland, Inquiry into the Operations of Mr. Brougham's Education Bill as far as regards Protestant Dissenters, XVI, 25-33

21. Richard Taylor, An Inquiry respecting Private Property and the Authority and Perpetuity of the Apostolic Institution of a Community of Goods, XVI, 88-101

22. M. D. Hill, On Freedom in Matters of Opinion, XVI, 452-63

23. William Hincks, The Old Crab-Stock of Noncomformity, XVI, 660-64

24. Thomas Rees, On the Attempts that were made towards the Reformation of Religion in Italy in the 16th Century, XVII, 1-6, 86-93
25. C. Richmond, The Existing Disabilities and Inconveniences which Attach to Dissent from the Church of England, XVII, 129-40
26. Southwood Smith, Plan of an Institution for Acquiring and Communicating an Accurate Knowledge of the Scriptures without Expense, XVII, 419-25
27. Edgar Taylor, Mahometan Influence on Christian Literature and Opinions, XVIII, 1-8
28. Henry Acton, On the Maxim that Christianity is Part and Parcel of the Law of the Land, XVIII, 222-26
29. Walter Wilson, On the Causes of the Decline of Nonconformity, XVIII, 341-46, 388-95
30. Richard Taylor, On Religious Prosecutions, XVIII, 368-72
31. John Bowring, State of Religion in Sweden, XIX, 193-200
32. Benjamin Mardon, The Principle of Subscription to Human Formularies of Faith, XXI, 129-39

Second Series, 1827-1837

The problem of identification of authorship in the second series is much simpler than in the first. In the British Museum is a manuscript key to the writers of Volumes IV through X (1830-1836). The essential information of this key, corrected and supplemented by evidence from other sources, is here printed for the first time.

Though British Museum officials seemed unable to supply the present writer with information as to the origin of this key, Principal Herbert McLachlan's statement in *The Unitarian Movement in the Religious Life of England* is probably correct that it was compiled from Fox's notes by his daughter, Mrs. E. Bridell-Fox. The latter supplied Richard Garnett with materials for his biography of her father, and since Garnett was an official of the British Museum, it seems likely that the key came into the possession of the Museum through his hands.

The key is not complete and in a few places seems to be inaccurate. (See John Stuart Mill and John H. Moggridge, below.) In the following list some identifications have been added for Volumes I, II, III, and XI. Wherever the manuscript key itself is doubtful about the ascription to a given writer, a question mark precedes the entry. Where the identification has been made on the basis of other evidence, the source has been indicated; where it has been made on the basis of internal evidence or of the usual initialing of a given writer, the entry has been marked: [In.]. Other abbreviations have been used as follows: [P], Poetry; [Tr.], Translation; [R], Review.

SARAH FLOWER ADAMS [S.Y.]
A Dream [P], VI, 257-59
Archdeacon Glover and the Bottle Imp, VI, 406-9
What Constitutes a Bishop? [P], VI, 475
A National Gallery, VII, 840-45
The Luxembourg, VIII, 54-63
Songs of the Months [P], VIII, 203, 717, 762
The Welsh Wanderer, VIII, 514-20
The Three Visits, VIII, 724-33
Buy Images, VIII, 756-62
A Portrait [P], IX, 56
A Chapter on Chimnies, IX, 57-59
Charade Drama, IX, 122-33
An Evening with Charles Lamb and Coleridge, IX, 162-68
Ruth [P], IX, 204
To an Invalid, with some Violets [P], IX, 258-59
The Actress, IX, 460-75, 514-30, 571-91
Morning, Noon, and Night [P], IX, 562
The Dead Grasshopper [P], 675
Lines Suggested by Macready's Hamlet [P], IX, 749-50
An Odd Subject, IX, 795-802
York Minster and the Forest Bugle, X, 38-43
Valentine's Day, X, 94-106

WILLIAM BRIDGES ADAMS [Junius Redivivus]
On the Conduct of the Monthly Repository, VI, 793-94
On the State of the Fine Arts in England, VII, 1-13
Beauty, VII, 89-96

REV. ROBERT ASPLAND
Religious State and Prospects of France, III, 777-80. (Cf. *Memoir*, p. 505)

THOMAS FOSTER BARHAM [T.F.B., Filaret]
On the Use of the Term Unitarian, I, 408-10 [In.]
On Mr. Elton's "Second Thoughts," I, 553-56, 818-21 [In.]
Illustrations of Passages in the Epistle to the Hebrews, II, 376-80 [In.]
On the Atonement, II, 489-91 [In.]
On the Proem of John's Gospel, III, 713-16 [In.]
On Extempore Preaching, IV, 129-31
Middleton on the Greek Article, IV, 412-14
An Important Simplification in Greek Grammar, V, 559-60

REV. JOHN RELLY BEARD [J.R.B., The Watchman, B.]
The Watchman, III, 183-94, 261-76, etc.; IV, 30-44, 173-81, etc.
State of the Curates of the Church of England [R], III, 225-37
Whately's Essays on the Writings of St. Paul [R], 526-39, 607-18
Higgins' Apology for Mohammed [R], IV, 234-39
Lord Byron's Theology [R], IV, 605-13
Correspondence . . . on the Church Establishment [R], IV, 693-98
Critical Notices
  Nos. 6, 7, 9, 11, IV, 706-11   Nos. 2, 9, V, 533-36, 545-46
  No. 3, V, 54   No. 1, V, 852-53
  Nos. 1-3, V, 116-20   No. 6, VI, 56-57
  Nos. 1-2, V, 485-89   No. 1, VI, 134-36
Confessions of a Member of the Church of England [R], V, 25-30
On Home Missions, V, 78-82
Ellis's Polynesian Researches [R], V, 91-95
Sir Isaac Newton an Antitrinitarian, V, 153-59
The History and Mystery of Church Property [R], V, 299-305
Christianity an Intellectual Good, V, 440-44
Thorne Unitarian Controversy [R], V, 477-80
Why Does a Unitarian Take the Lord's Supper? V, 624-27
Dr. Channing and the British Critic [R], V, 761-63
Offering of Sympathy to Parents [R], V, 809-11

The Question between the Nation and the Church, V, 824-31; VI, 98-106

The Rise and Progress of the Doctrine of the Trinity, VI, 15-23, 109-15, 259-66, 315-23

Sunday School Education, VI, 161-65, 234-38

Rise of Unitarianism in America [R], VI, 210-11

G. R. Noyes' New Translation of the Psalms [R], VI, 349-51

A Discourse . . . by Simon Clough [R], VI, 499-500

Blasphemy, What it is and on whom Chargeable [R], VI, 352

On the Prevailing Forgetfulness of God [R], VI, 501-2

On the Study of Paul's Epistles [R], VI, 670-77

Tucker's Expostulary Letter . . . [R], VI, 791-92

JOHN BOWRING [A., B., J.B.]

Transylvanian Unitarians, I, 243 [In.]

Reported Burning of a Jew, I, 264 [In.]

Hungarian Literature [with translations], I, 556-57 [In.]

Secret Worship [P], II, 102 [In.]

From the German of Novalis [P], II, 154-55 [In.]

Hymn ("When bitter thoughts and things intrude"), II, 367 [In.]

2 Samuel VII. 12 [P], II, 383 [In.]

Consistency [P], II, 697 [In.]

Ecclesiasticus [P], III, 48 [In.]

Translation. To the Redbreast [P], III, 167 [In.]

From the Dutch of Withuys [P], III, 254 [In.]

The Eagle's Death [P], III, 260 [In.]

Cantate. By Lamartine [P., Tr.] IV, 154-58

Rejoice with Trembling [P], IV, 243

St. Leonard's Chapel, IV, 450-51

The Bible Illustrated by Shakespeare, VI, 555 [In.]

? The Moderate Whig, VII, 851-54

REV. JACOB BRETTELL [J.B.]

On the Character of Moore as a Poet and Translator . . . , I, 648-51 [In.]

On the Poetry of Byron, I, 868-70 [In.]

Anecdotes of Milton, Descriptive of his Feelings and Conduct, Related by Himself, IV, 673-90

A Glimpse of the Future [P], X, 477
The Broken Heart [P], X, 685
The Rights of Despots [P], X, 760

JOHN FISHER

The French Sect of Saint Simonites and the "New Christianity" of its Founder, V, 82-88, 181-89, 279-81

WILLIAM JOHNSON FOX

In the British Museum's key to writers in the *Repository* a number of articles are listed as of uncertain authorship but possibly by Fox. These (with the exception of a few which, from other evidence, have been attributed to other authors) have been listed below along with Fox's known contributions, but with a prefixed question mark.

Critical Notices

Nos. 1-13, 16-17, IV, 45-62
Nos. 4-5, IV, 184-87
Nos. 11, 13, IV, 332-33
Nos. 1, 8-12, IV, 624, 631-32
No. 1, IV, 783-85
Nos. 1-4, 9, IV, 846-57
No. 8, V, 57
Nos. 5-14, V, 120-23
No. 1, V, 197-98
Nos. 1, 3-7, 10-11, V, 533-51
Nos. 1-4, V, 645-48
No. 1, V, 781-82

Nos. 2-9, V, 853-56
Nos. 1-6, 8-12, VI, 47-61
Nos. 2-4, VI, 136-44
Nos. 1-6, VI, 204-9
Nos. 8-11, VI, 211-13
Nos. 2, 4-5, VI, 351-53
Nos. 1-4, VI, 424-32
Nos. 1, 4, 5, 8, VI, 498-504
Nos. 1-7, VI, 573-76
Nos. 1, 3-9, VI, 642-48
Nos. 2, 4-6, VI, 714-20
Nos. 1-4, VI, 849-54

On the Character and Writings of the Rev. T. Belsham, IV, 73-88, 162-72, 244-53
Humanity to Animals [R], IV, 315-25
Sunday in London [R], IV, 389-95
On the Reign of George the Fourth, IV, 505-11
Traditions of Palestine [R], IV, 521-29
France, IV, 620-24
Trinitarian Alarms and Combinations, IV, 721-23
Public Intelligence, IV, 871-72
Lady Hewley's Fund, V, 72
The Conversations of Ebion Adamson and his Friends, V, 190-97, 273-77, etc.
Parliamentary Reform, V, 284
The Elections, V, 431-32

Joanna Baillie on the Nature and Dignity of Christ [R], V, 505-16
The Church Establishment Founded in Error [R], V, 517-26
? Politics of the Month, V, 703-11 [In.]
Coronation Sermons [R], V, 725-33
The Bishop of Salisbury's Reply to Mrs. Joanna Baillie [R], V, 754-56
On the Present State of the Reform Question, V, 775-79
On the State and Prospects of the Country . . . 1831, VI, 1-11
Beard's Family Sermons [R], VI, 79-85
The Invalid Exile [P], VI, 106
Religion Without Taxation [R], VI, 116-24
Who Killed Colonel Brereton? VI, 130-34
The Fast Day and the Cholera, VI, 145-53
The Poor and their Poetry [R], VI, 189-201
Taxes on Knowledge, VI, 267-71
Sandown Bay, VI, 271-80
Exeter Hall Exhibition of Paintings . . . , VI, 338-45
The Leeds Controversy [R], VI, 345-49
The Recent Political Crisis, VI, 392-401
On the Parliamentary Pledges to be Required . . . , VI, 433-43
The Barons Bold on Runnymede [P], VI, 459
Miss Martineau's Prize Essays [R], VI, 475-84
The Village Poor House [R], VI, 536-44
Publications of the Polish Literary Society [R], VI, 587-95
Rajah Rammohun Roy on . . . India, VI, 615-17 [part of the article]
A Political and Social Anomaly, VI, 637-42
Autumn in London, VI, 660-67
On the Intellectual Character of Sir Walter Scott, VI, 721-28
Tagart's Memoir of Capt. Heywood [R], VI, 804-16
Whig Government, VI, 841-48
Tennyson's Poems [R], VII, 30-41
The Elections, VII, 41-49
? Channing's Sermons [R], VII, 132-36
The Dissenting Marriage Question, VII, 136-42
? On the Factory System, VII, 145-53

A Victim, VII, 164-77
The Poetical Works of Leigh Hunt [R], VII, 178-84
? Church Reform, VII, 207-11
? On the Conduct of Ministers since the Meeting of Parliament, VII, 243-51
Pauline; A Fragment of a Confession [R], VII, 252-62
? How to Play a Losing Game, VII, 285-87
Purcell's Sacred Music, VII, 289-97
A Letter to the Rev. ⸺ ⸺ . . . , VII, 347-54
Poor Laws and Paupers [R], VII, 361-81
? Silvio Pellico [R], VII, 403-12
Local Logic, VII, 413-26
? On Public Opinion as Shown by Petitions to Parliament, VII, 441-48
Rule Britannia, VII, 450-53
History of Priestcraft, [R], VII, 489-507
Caspar Hauser [R], VII, 517-25
? Aspland's Sermons [R], VII, 562-64
? The Schoolmaster Abroad, VII, 644-52
? On the Life and Character of the Late Mr. Roscoe, VII, 670-75
Utilitarian Reflections on the Norwich Musical Festival, VII, 751-60
? An Independent in Church and State [R], VII, 777-84
? Churchcraft [R], VII, 789-800
? Church Reform . . . , VII, 805-13
? Tales of the English [R], VII, 813-16
? Saint Monday [R], VII, 829-39
Note on Jewish Tithe, VII, 854-55
Postscript . . . for 1833, VII, 868-71
Forwards or Backwards, VIII, 1-7
The Story without an End [R], VIII, 70-76
Notes on the Newspapers
    Lady Hewley's Trust, VIII, 86-87
    Church Reform and the Dissenters; The War Cry, VIII, 155-57
    Commencement of the Session; Election Promises; Cross Voting; Constitutional Servility, IX, 204-8

Prospects of Reform; Dissenters' Marriage Bill, IX, 217-21
William Cobbett, IX, 486-87
The Indicator and the Companion [R], VIII, 101-3
Adam the Gardener [R], VIII, 139-55
On the Bishop of London's Defense of the Church Establishment [R], VIII, 249-63
"Mrs. Thomson, You are Wanted," VIII, 282-85
On the Separation of Church and State, VIII, 313-18
The Revolutionary Epick [R], VIII, 375-78
The Seven Temptations [R], VIII, 396-404
Campbell's Life of Mrs. Siddons [R], VIII, 533-50
Improvement of the Working People [R], VIII, 625-31
Retzsch's Fancies [R], VIII, 677-84
National Anniversaries, VIII, 749-55
The Wellington Dictatorship, VIII, 821-28
Autobiography of a Dissenting Minister [R], VIII, 868-76
The Amateur Music Festival, VIII, 883-84
The True Spirit of Reform, IX, 1-8
? The Elections, IX, 73-78
? The Riches of Chaucer [R], IX, 78-80
? Wordsworth's Poems [R], IX, 430-34
Mundi et Cordis Carmina [R], IX, 453-59
Warnings to the Tories . . . , IX, 501-8
The House of Lords—Reform or Abolition? IX, 565-71
Paracelsus [R], IX, 716-27
Political Gleanings, IX, 757-64
? Nicoll's Poems [R], IX, 764-70
New Year, X, 1-10
? Principles of Legislation for the Ensuing Session, X, 65-70
? Peerage Reform, X, 93-94
? Channing on Slavery [R], X, 193-203
? Mr. Spring Rice and the Newspaper Press, X, 278-80
? Letters of a Conservative on the English Church [R], X, 380-84
Politics of the Common Pleas, X, 393-400
? The Letters of Runnymede [R], X, 540-46
? The Rationale of Religious Inquiry [R], X, 554-57

? The Old World and the New [R], X, 597-607
? Mr. O'Connell and his Political Doctrine of Installment, X, 769-73
? Lisbon and Lord Palmerston, X, 780
? Foreign Policy, XI, 54-56

MARY LEMAN GRIMSTONE (later Mrs. Gillies) [M.L.G.]
The Spirit of an Infant to his Mother [P], VII, 724-26
A Mother to her First-Born [P], VII, 749-50
Pestalozzi [P], VII, 839-40
The True Diamond [P], VIII, 40
The Confessions of a Fag [P], VIII, 264-66
The Poor Woman's Appeal to her Husband [P], VIII, 351-52
The Apprentice Boy [P], VIII, 684-87
Human Animalculae, VIII, 714-16
Acephela, VIII, 771-77
The Last Scene of a Life [P], VIII, 853-54
Quaker Women, IX, 30-37
Female Education, IX, 106-12
Sketches of Domestic Life, IX, 145-53, 225-34, etc.; X, 14-25, etc.
Rich and Poor, IX, 342-47
Power and the People, IX, 489-98
Self-Dependence, IX, 595-604
The Protective System of Morals, IX, 683-88
Universal Co-operation, IX, 770-81
On Women of No Party, X, 79-80
Exclusiveness, X, 492-95
Political and Personal Discontent, X, 630-34
Example, X, 681-85
Amusements, X, 747-55
Occupation, XI, 91-96
On the Love of the Hideous; or, The Modern National Melodrama, XI, 357-60

MRS. CATHERINE HERING [Kathleen, K.T.]
Spring Song [P], VIII, 303
Song of the Month: June [P], VIII, 395-96
An Evening Reverie by the Sea-side, VIII, 842-44

The London Review versus the British Drama, X, 229-58
Spirit of Modern Publishers, X, 271-76
Indestructibility of the Drama, X, 329-38
Histories of China [R], X, 409-17
Sonnet to Wordsworth, X, 424
Critique on Six Pictures . . . , X, 440-42
Eminent British Statesmen [R], X, 461-68
Madrid in 1835 [R], 525-39
Chateaubriand's Sketches of English Literature [R], X, 589-96
Mexican Sketches, X, 608-16, 675-79, XI, 22-28
Journal of a Residence in Norway [R], X, 653-67
The Great Metropolis [R], X, 703-11
Our Representatives, XI, 1-12 [In.]
Dramatic Literature, [R], XI, 65-76 [In.]
Cosmo De'Medici. A Fragment from History, XI, 236-50 [In.]
Buckland's Geology [R], XI, 269-78 [In.]
The Innocent Debates on Spain, XI, 305-14 [In.]
Retrospective Glances, XI, 321-36 [In.]

ALEXANDER HUME [Daft Wattie]
An Auld Man's Song [P], VII, 229-30
Song of the Month. A May Day Memory. [P], VIII, 322

REV. HUGH HUTTON [H.H.]
The Mother [P], I, 569-70 [In.]
Withered Blossoms [P], I, 576 [In.]
The Sceptic and the Christian [P], I, 663 [In.]
Lines [P], II, 535 [In.]
Hebrew Lyric [P], IV, 768
A Meditation [P], V, 339
The Light of Nature [P], VI, 186-87 [In.]

REV. JOHN JOHNS [J., *locus* Crediton]
On the Prefaces to Matthew and Luke, I, 327-31 [In.]
Alexander at Paradise [P], I, 345-48 [In.]
Earth and Heaven [P], I, 655-56 [In.]
Lines to the Memory of a Young Friend [P], I, 733 [In.]
The Fall of the Leaf [P], I, 796-97
Naval Ode . . . [P], II, 21-22 [In.]
A Dream of Heaven [P], II, 89-90

Character of Napoleon Bonaparte [P], II, 766-68 [In.]

Song of Moses [P], IV, 297-300

Biblical Geography [Tr.] IV, 433-41

On Hearing the Call of the Cuckoo [P], IV, 458-59

An Autumnal Walk [P], IV, 760-63

Fanciful Wishes [P], IV, 820-21

Lines Suggested by Seeing an Infant on its Deathbed [P], V, 45-46

The Conversion of Abraham [P], V, 113-15

The Dreamer, V, 178-81

A Lay of Spring [P], V, 373-76

Psalm [P], V, 532

Lines Suggested by Moore's Life of Lord Edward Fitzgerald [P], V, 678-79

Autumnal Birds [P], V, 750-54

Devotional Thoughts on the New Year, VI, 11-15

On the Connexion between Poetry and Religion, VI, 485-91, 618-27, 817-24

On a Hawthorn in Bloom [P], IX, 341-42

SIR JOHN WILLIAM KAYE [Author of Jerningham]

Sheep-dog. A Sketch from Life, XI, 139-47 [In.]

Stephen Cameron . . . , XI, 368-76 [In.]

REV. JOHN KENTISH [N.]

Notes on Passages of Scripture, II, 668-69; III, 686-87, 844-46; IV, 518-21

Essay on Intellectual Vigour, II, 729-32

The Bishop of Lichfield's Charge [R], III, 7-14, 73-80

Bishop Marsh's Two Lectures [R], III, 245-53

Life of Professor Wodrow [R], III, 399-408

Sentiments of Certain Church-of-England Men on the Catholic Claims [R], III, 464-73

Hayley's Elegy on the Ancient Greek Model [Notes by Kentish], III, 618-28

Essay on the Passions, IV, 27-30

Memoirs of the Life and Writings of Frederick Hasselquist, IV, 217-21

The Protestant Controversy [R], IV, 363-67

Essay on the Preservation and Improvement of British Freedom . . . , IV, 665-69

On the Birmingham Free Grammar School Bill, V, 68-72

E. Whitfield's Poems [R], V, 200

Memoir of Henri Grégoire, Bishop of Blois [Tr.], V, 472-76

LETITIA KINDER (Mrs. Edwin Field)

Critical Notices

No. 6, IV, 123-24	No. 8, IV, 407-8
Nos. 7-9, IV, 187-94	Nos. 13-14, IV, 712-14
Nos. 6-7, IV, 258-61	Nos. 5-6, IV, 855-56
No. 10, IV, 330-32	No. 8, VI, 354-56
No. 3, IV, 467-68	

Hymns for Children [R], IV, 374-76

REV. W. LAMPORT [W.L.]

Tribute to the Memory of the late Rev. John Hincks [P], V, 223-24

REV. G. LEE

The History of the Jews [R], IV, 376-83

REV. BENJAMIN MARDON [M.]

Critical Notices

No. 1, IV, 181-82	Nos. 4-5, IV, 626-28
No. 3, IV, 256	Nos. 8, 10, IV, 707-9
No. 1, IV, 326-27	Nos. 6-7, V, 56-57
Nos. 1-2, IV, 465-67	No. 3, V, 279

Bishop Middleton on the Greek Article, IV, 268-69

Anonymous Inspiration, IV, 637

Sir W. Scott's Letters on Demonology and Witchcraft, V, 64-65

Mr. Tyrwhit and Dr. C. Lloyd, V, 350

HARRIET MARTINEAU [V., D.F., H.M.]

Peace and Hope and Rest [P], I, 331 [In.]

Sonnet ("The echoes of thy voice are heard afar"), I, 401 [In.]

On the Dangers of Adversity, I, 558-63 [In.]

On Dignity of Character, I, 785-91 [In.]

Address to the Avowed Arians of the Synod of Ulster [P], II, 79-80 [In.]

Sonnet ("Wearied with play, and sighing for repose"), II, 166 [In.]

On Country Burial Grounds, II, 230-33 [In.]
Ode to Religious Liberty, III, 41-44 [In.]
The Last Tree of the Forest [P], III, 80-81 [In.]
On the Agency of Feelings in the Formation of Habits . . . ,
    III, 102-6 [In.]
Obituary: Philip Meadows Martineau, III, 131-32 [In.]
On the Agency of Habits in the Regeneration of Feelings,
    III, 159-62 [In.]
Natural History of Enthusiasm [R], III, 417-25, 473-83 [In.]
Essays on the Art of Thinking, III, 521-26, 599-606, 707-12,
    745-57, 817-22 [In.]
Essays on the Pursuit of Truth [R], III, 545-51, 629-40 [In.]
The Survivor [P], III, 782-84 [In.]
Negro Slavery [R], IV, 4-9
Doddridge's Correspondence and Diary [R], IV, 15-26, 385-89;
    V, 321-25
Critical Notices
    Nos. 14-15, IV, 62   Nos. 2-3, V, 198-99
    Nos. 1, 2, 4, 7, IV, 115-28   Nos. 1-2, 5-7, V, 277-84
    Nos. 2, 3, 6, IV, 182-87   Nos. 1, 3-6, 8, 9, 11, V, 339-48
    Nos. 1, 2, 4, 5, 8, 9, IV, 254-62 Nos. 3-6, V, 489-91
    Nos. 3-9, 12, IV, 328-33   Nos. 2-4, V, 783-85
    Nos. 5-6, IV, 405-6   Nos. 11-13, V, 856
    Nos. 2-3, IV, 625-26
Calamy's Life [R], IV, 89-100
The Hope of the Hebrew, IV, 101-8
Crombie's Natural Theology [R], IV, 145-54, 223-30
Faith and Hope. A Parable, IV, 222-23
The Flower of the Desert [P], IV, 253
The Education of the Human Race, IV, 300-6, 367-73, 453-58,
    511-17
True Worshippers: a Tale, IV, 307-15
The Solitary: a Parable, IV, 361-62
The Forsaken Nest [P], IV, 383-84
Solitude and Society. A Tale, IV, 442-49
Tayler's Sermon [R], IV, 529-34
Hull's Discourses [R], IV, 590-94

Rajah Rammohun Roy on the Government and Religion of
India [R], VI, 609-15 [Part of the article]
Secondary Punishments [R], VI 667-69
National Education [R], VI, 689-94
The Main Principles of the Creed and Ethics of the Jews . . . ,
[R], VI, 717-18
A Parable, VI, 766-67
Some Autobiographical Particulars . . . , VII, 612-15
Songs of the Months, August, VIII, 533

REV. JAMES MARTINEAU

Irish Unitarian Christian Society, V, 356-60
On the Life, Character, and Works of Dr. Priestley, VII, 19-
30, 84-88, 231-41
Bentham's Deontology [R], VIII, 612-24 [In.]

JOHN STUART MILL [Antiquus, A, and φιλόμουσος]

The British Museum key's identification of Mill's contributions is incomplete and
in at least one instance seems to be inaccurate (see John H. Moggridge below).
Richard Garnett, who had access to Mill's correspondence with Fox in preparation of the *Life of W. J. Fox,* identified one article ("On the Defense of the
House and Window Tax") not included in the key. More recently, Professor
James McCrimmon's discovery, in the British Library of Political and Economic
Science, of Mill's manuscript bibliography of his writings, has made possible
identification of four more items. (See J. M. McCrimmon, "Studies Toward
a Biography of John Stuart Mill," unpublished Northwestern University doctoral
dissertation, 1937). These have been marked "McCrimmon" in the list below.
Mill's manuscript bibliography, which seems to have been compiled late in life,
does not, however, clear up all the difficulties: it does not include the above-
mentioned article identified by Garnett, nor does it include three other articles
listed in the British Museum key. They are: "Characteristics of English Aristocracy," a review of Bulwer's *England and the English;* "On the Application of
the Terms Poetry, Science, and Philosophy"; and one set of Mill's "Notes on
the Newspapers" (Oct., 1834). I believe that only the second can be safely attributed to Mill.

On Genius, VI, 649-59
What is Poetry? VII, 60-70
Writings of Junius Redivivus [R], VII, 262-70
Alison's History of the French Revolution [R], VII, 507-11,
513-16
On the Defense of the House and Window Tax, in the Edin-
burgh Review [R], VII, 575-82 [Garnett. Not in Mill's
bibliography]

? Characteristics of English Aristocracy [R], VII, 585-601
[Not in Mill's bibliography]
Views from the Pyrenees [R], VII, 660 [McCrimmon]
Blakey's History of Moral Science [R], VII, 661-69
The Two Kinds of Poetry, VII, 714-24
Comparison of the Tendencies of French and English Intel-
lect (Translated from Le Globe, journal of the Saint Si-
monians), VII, 800-4. Mill in his manuscript bibliography
says that this is the original of his letter to Charles Duvey-
rier, with a new heading. [McCrimmon]
Notes on Some of the More Popular Dialogues of Plato
    1. The Protagoras, VIII, 89-99, 203-11
    2. The Phaedrus, VIII, 404-20, 633-46
    3. The Gorgias, VIII, 691-710, 802-15, 829-42
    4. The Apology of Socrates, IX, 112-21, 169-78
Notes on the Newspapers
    The King's Speech; Mr. Shiel and Lord Althorp; The
Monopoly of the Post Office Clerks; Attendance in the
House; Lord Althorp's Budget; The Leeds Election; Mr.
O'Connell's Bill for the Liberty of the Press, VIII, 161-76
    The Ministerial Resolutions on Irish Tithe; The Debate
on Agricultural Distress; Mr. O'Connell's Declaration for
the Pillage of the National Creditor; Mr. Buckingham's
Motion on Impressment; The Dudley Election; The De-
bate on the Corn Laws; Political Oaths; The Trades'
Unions; The Solicitor General's Motion on the Law of
Libel; Sir Robert Peel on the Corn Laws; The Ministry
and the Dissenters, VIII, 233-48, 309-12
    The Tithe Bill; National Education; Mr. Roebuck and
the Times; The Proposed Reform of the Poor Laws; Gov-
ernment by Brute Force; The Church-rate Abortion; The
Beer-houses; Repeal of the Union, VIII, 354-75
    The Press and the Trades' Unions; Sir Robert Heron's
Motion; Loss of the Registration Bills; Lord Brougham's
Defense of the Church Establishment; Mr. William
Brougham's Bills for a Registry of Births, Deaths, and
Marriages; Sir Edward Knatchbull's Beer Bill; Death of

JOHN H. MOGGRIDGE
> Notices of France, VI, 635-36, 677-80, 729-33; VII, 14-19, 100-
> 11, 339-47 [Part of these are attributed in the British Mu-
> seum key to Mill, but internal evidence would seem to
> support the ascription of all of them to Moggridge.]

REV. R. MONTGOMERY
> On Irish Scriptural Education, VI, 308-14

DR. JOHN MORELL [J.M.].
> Conversion of a Catholic Priest, IV, 545-48
> On the State of Religious Opinon and Religious Liberty in
> Germany, IV, 585-89
> Letters from Germany, IV, 808-14; V, 30-34, 97-106, 174-78,
> 268-72, 289-98

T. N. NOEL [T.N.]
> Love [P], VI, 97-98
> The Spirit of Love [P], VI, 828
> The Beautiful [P], VII, 241-42
> Tokens [P], VII, 706-8

C. PARTRIDGE
> The Evils of Primogenitive Inheritance, VIII, 348-51

CHARLES REECE PEMBERTON [Pel. Verjuice, P.V.]
> The Autobiography of Pel. Verjuice, VII, 323-39, 392-403,
> 475-88, 529-45, 623-44, 691-705, 816-29; VIII, 21-39, 212-27,
> 666-75, 786-98; IX, 415-29
> The Dumb Orphan of the Prison of Santa Margherita [P],
> VII, 488-89
> The XV of August, MDCCCXXXIII, VII, 652-57
> John Bull, Esquire, of Wheedle-Hall, VII, 708-14
> Social Evils and their Remedy [R], VII, 733-43
> The Escape, VII, 772-77
> Notes on the Newspapers
> > Macready's Coriolanus, VIII, 76-81
> > The Birmingham Town Hall, and the Nomination Meet-
> > ing Therein, IX, 134-40
> Songs of the Months
> > February. St. Valentine's Day, VIII, 99
> > April. Tears and Smiles, VIII, 291
> > December, VIII, 828

Arithmetic for Young Children [R], IX, 284-87
Owen's Book of the New Moral World [R], X, 742-47
DR. SOUTHWOOD SMITH
On Cholera, V, 779-81
REV. WILLIAM STEVENS [S.]
Turkish Piety and Morality, V, 61-63
REV. EDWARD TAGART
Undesigned Coincidences in Scripture [R], IV, 613-15
REV. JOHN JAMES TAYLER [J.J.T., T., Philalethes Mancuniensis]
On the Spirit of Sects, II, 801-10 [In.]
Some Account of the Life and Writings of Herder, IV, 729-
38, 829-43
On the Evidence of the Resurrection, V, 145-53
Herder's Thoughts on the Philosophy and History of Man-
kind, VI, 34-42, 86-97, 165-78, 217-33
On the Studies and Ministry of F. V. Reinhard [R], VI, 734-
41, 797-804
On the Influence of the Spirit of Gnosticism, during the
First Centuries of the Christian Era, VII, 564-75, 602-12
EDGAR TAYLOR
Reformation in Spain [R], IV, 108-15
EMILY TAYLOR [E.T., K.]
New Year's Morning, IV, 1-4
Critical Notices

No. 3, IV, 119-20	Nos. 1-2, V, 52-54
No. 2, IV, 327-28	No. 4, V, 199-200
No. 4, IV, 403-5	No. 8, V, 542-45

On Love to God, IV, 159-62
On Public Worship, IV, 273-74
A Dialogue, IV, 451-52
Conscientious Deism, IV, 599-600
Sunday-School Hymns [R], IV, 826-29
Early Religious Instruction, V, 46-52
Midnight Lines [P], V, 584
? The Pestilence that Walketh at Noon Day [P], V, 690
The Visible and the Invisible, VI, 42-46
Maria Hack's Geological Sketches [R], VI, 213-14
The Bible Society Question [R], VI, 334-37

Weather [P], VIII, 352-53
The Golden Eagle [P], VIII, 353
HARRIET TAYLOR (in later life, Mrs. John Stuart Mill)
Critical Notices. No. 9, V, 58-59
The Snow-drop [P], VI, 266
Tour of a German Prince [R], VI, 353-54
Domestic Manners of the Americans [R], VI, 401-6
Hampden [R], VI, 443-50
Mirabeau's Letters [R], VI, 604-8
To the Summer Wind [P], VI, 617
Nature [P], VI, 636
The Mysticism of Plato [R], VI, 645-46
Sarrans on the French Revolution of 1830 [R], VI, 756-62
The Seasons, VI, 825-28
REV. WILLIAM TURNER, II [V.F.]
Signs of the Times, VI, 565-67
REV. WILLIAM TURNER, III [W.T., V.N.]
On the Controversial Character of Dr. Priestley, II, 152-54
[In.]
On Establishments, II, 161-63 [In.]
Reasons Why Christ Appeared after his Resurrection . . . ,
II, 236-39 [In.]
Remarks on Some Portions of Hartley's Rule of Life, II,
293-98, 595-601 [In.]
On the Locality of a Future State, II, 452-54 [In.]
Ordination Service, III, 409-16 [In.]
Notes on Dr. Bruce's Argument for the Pre-existence of
Christ, III, 772-77 [In.]
Thoughts on an Intermediate State, IV, 239-43
Congregational Magazine, IV, 473-74
On the Meaning of the Term Angel . . . , IV, 596-98
Limited Spread of Christianity No Objection to its Divine
Authority, IV, 657-61
On Future Punishment, IV, 801-8
Anderson's Historical Sketches of the Native Irish [R], V,
249-55
On the Parable of the Labourers in the Vineyard, V, 367-69

On Hearing Some Fine Music Ill-Played [P], X, 635
The Wedding Ring, [P], XI, 12-15
The Fallers-short [P], XI, 278
Sonnets, XI, 343-45

REV. ROBERT WALLACE

Biographical Notices of Eminent Continental Unitarians, V,
229-33, 326-31, 361-67, 445-49, 636-45, 741-49

REV. SAMUEL WOOD

The Pastors of Geneva and M. Gaussen [R], V, 607-15

REV. ISRAEL WORSLEY

On the State of Religion in France, VI, 124-29

ENLARGED SERIES, July, 1837-April, 1838

Identification of the unsigned or pseudonymous writings
which appeared during the ten months of the editorship of Leigh
Hunt is made possible by the existence of a presentation copy
in which Hunt indicated the authorship of most of such contributions. This volume was formerly in the valuable Leigh Hunt
collection of the late Luther A. Brewer; for an account of the
volume, cf. his *My Leigh Hunt Library* (Cedar Rapids, Iowa,
1932), pp. 174-78. After Mr. Brewer's death his collection was
purchased by the University of Iowa, and it is through the cour-
tesy of that institution's Library that the following compilation
has been made possible. Hunt's identifications do not continue
after the February, 1838, number. Several identifications not
made by Hunt have been included here on the basis of internal
evidence; these are indicated with a question mark. The list
does not, of course, include signed contributions by Hunt, such
as his "Blue-Stocking Revels," by G. H. Lewes, or by R. H.
Horne, such as his "Death of Marlowe." Since a new pagination
begins with the January, 1838, number, this and the three following numbers have been labeled as constituting Volume II of
the Enlarged Series.

THOMAS CARLYLE [T.C.]

Lilliputian [P], I, 85
Fortuna [P], II, 172

R. H. HORNE

Harefield Copper Works, I, 334-40

THOMAS WADE [*W*]
   The Curse of the Flowers [P], I, 107-8
   Three Sonnets [P], I, 390 [In.]
   Companionship [P], II, 88 [In.]
   Brain and Heart [P], II, 162-63 [In.]

Bibliography

The following are the works that have been chiefly useful in the preparation of this book. Standard reference works and many books which have been only incidentally useful have not been included. For the convenience of the reader interested in certain phases of the subject, the works consulted have been classified in four groups, even though the classifications cannot in all instances be mutually exclusive.

I. RELIGION

These works have been helpful in providing background for Chapter I and for the sections on religion elsewhere in the book.

Abbey, C. J. and J. H. Overton. *The English Church in the Eighteenth Century.* 2 vols. London, 1878.

Belsham, Thomas. *A Calm Inquiry into the Scripture Doctrine concerning the Person of Christ.* London, 1811.

Bogue, D. and J. Bennett. *History of the Protestant Dissenters.* 4 vols. London, 1808.

Bonet-Maury, G. *Early Sources of English Unitarian Christianity.* (Introduction by James Martineau.) London, 1884.

Carpenter, J. Estlin. *Unitarianism.* London, 1922.

Clark, H. W. *History of English Nonconformity.* London, 1913.

Coleridge, Samuel Taylor. *On the Constitution of Church and State.* Edited by H. N. Coleridge. London, 1839. [Contains the Lay Sermons.]

Colligan, J. H. *The Arian Movement in England.* Manchester, 1913.

Conway, Moncure D. *Centenary History of the South Place Society.* London, 1894.

Dale, H. W. *History of English Congregationalism.* New York, 1907.

Drysdale, A. H. *History of the Presbyterians in England.* London, 1889.

Elliott-Binns, L. E. *Religion in the Victorian Era.* London, 1936.

Gow, Henry. *The Unitarians.* London, 1928.

Griffiths, Olive M. *Religion and Learning.* Cambridge, 1935.

Holt, Raymond V. *The Unitarian Contribution to Social Progress in England.* London, 1938.

Hutton, W. H. *A History of the English Church: From the Accession of Charles I to the Death of Anne.* London, 1903.

Jones, Rufus M. *The Church's Debt to Heretics.* London, 1925.

McLachlan, Herbert. *The Religious Opinions of Milton, Locke, and Newton.* Manchester, 1941.

Milton, John. *De Doctrina Christiana.* In *Works,* Columbia University Edition (F. A. Patterson, General Editor). Vols. XIV-XVII. New York, 1931-1932.

Overton, J. H. and F. Relton. *A History of the English Church: From the Accession of George I to the End of the Eighteenth Century.* London, 1906.

Overton, J. H. *The English Church in the Nineteenth Century (1800-33).* London, 1894.

Priestley, Joseph. *The Use of Christianity, Especially in Difficult Times.* Farewell Discourse to his Congregation. 2d edition. London, 1794.

Stevens, Abel. *The History of the Religious Movement of the Eighteenth Century, called Methodism.* 3 vols. New York, 1858.

Stoughton, John. *Religion in England from 1800 to 1850.* 2 vols. London, 1884.

Tayler, J. J. *A Retrospect of the Religious Life of England.* 2d edition (with introductory chapter by James Martineau). London, 1876.

Tracy, Joseph. *A History of the Revival of Religion in the Times of Edwards and Whitefield.* Boston, 1842.

Warre-Cornish, Francis. *The English Church in the Nineteenth Century.* 2 vols. London, 1933.

Wilbur, E. M. *Our Unitarian Heritage.* Boston, 1925.

Wilson, Walter. *The History and Antiquities of Dissenting Churches. . . .* 4 vols. London, 1808-1814.

II. PERIODICALS

This section, in addition to works on the history and criticism of periodicals, includes biographies, denominational histories, and other studies which contain valuable material on the periodicals discussed and identifications of certain contributors. Periodicals as such have not been listed here, since the Index will be found to serve that purpose.

Andrews, Alexander. *The History of British Journalism*. 2 vols. London, 1859.

Ames, J. G. *The English Literary Periodical of Morals and Manners*. Mt. Vernon, Ohio, 1904.

Blunden, Edmund. *Leigh Hunt's "Examiner" Examined*. London, 1928.

Bourne, H. R. Fox. *English Newspapers*. 2 vols. London, 1887.

British Museum. *British Museum Catalogue of Printed Books: Periodical Publications*. London, 1899-1900.

Carlyle, Thomas. "Signs of the Times," *Edinburgh Review,* XLIX (1829), 439-59.

Churton, Edward. *Memoir of Joshua Watson,* 2 vols. Oxford, 1861.

"Contemporary Journals," *Monthly Repository,* XV (1820), 540-43, 601-2, 672-74.

Crane, R. S. and F. B. Kaye. *A Census of British Newspapers and Periodicals, 1620-1800*. Chapel Hill, N. C., 1927.

Dunton, John. *Life and Errors of John Dunton*. 2 vols. London, 1818.

Fletcher, J. R. "Early Catholic Periodicals in England," *Dublin Review,* CXCVIII (1936), 284-310.

G., C. "Cheap Periodical Literature," *Christian Reformer,* XVIII (1832), 219-27, 307-12, 369-73, 424-27.

Graham, Walter. *The Beginnings of English Literary Periodicals*. New York, 1926.

———. *English Literary Periodicals*. New York, 1930.

———. *Tory Criticism in the Quarterly Review*. New York, 1921.

[Grant, James.] *The Great Metropolis*. 2 vols. London, 1836-1837.

Gregory, Winifred. *Union List of Serials*. New York, 1927-1932.

Hainds, John R. John Stuart Mill's Views on Art. Unpublished doctoral dissertation, Northwestern University, 1939.

Hatfield, Theodore M. "John Dunton's Periodicals," *Journalism Quarterly,* X (1933), 209-25.

Herbert, Thomas W. *John Wesley as Editor and Author.* Princeton, 1940.

H[usenbeth], F. C. [Notes on early Catholic periodicals], *Notes and Queries,* 1867.

Gillow, Joseph. *Bibliographical Dictionary of the English Catholics.* 5 vols. London, 1885-1902.

Marr, G. S. *The Periodical Essayists of the Eighteenth Century.* London, 1923.

McCrimmon, James. Studies Towards a Biography of John Stuart Mill. Unpublished doctoral dissertation, Northwestern University, 1937.

McLachlan, Herbert. *A Nonconformist Library.* Manchester, 1923.

——. *The Unitarian Movement in the Religious Life of England.* London, 1934.

Mineka, Francis E. "The Critical Reception of Milton's *De Doctrina Christiana,*" *University of Texas Studies in English,* 1943.

More, Hannah. *Letters of Hannah More to Zachary Macaulay.* Edited by Arthur Roberts. London, 1860.

[Muddiman, J. G.]. *Tercentenary Handlist of English and Welsh Newspapers, Magazines, and Reviews.* The Times, London, 1920.

Nesbitt, George L. *Benthamite Reviewing: The First Twelve Years of the Westminster Review, 1824-36.* New York, 1934.

Peet, H. M. "The Religious Press," London *Times* (Supplement), Jan. 1, 1935, p. xxi.

Price, T. *Biographical, Literary, and Philosophical Essays Contributed to the Eclectic Review by John Foster.* New York, 1844.

Realey, C. B. "The London Journal and its Authors," *Bulletin of the University of Kansas, Humanistic Studies,* V, (1935).

"Revues Sommaires des recueils periodiques sur les sciences, les lettres et les arts, publiés dans la Grande-Bretagne," *Revue Encyclopédique,* tomes 27-32 (1825-1826). [14 articles]

Ryland, J. E. *Life and Correspondence of John Foster.* New York, 1846.

Shepherd, T. B. *Methodism and the Literature of the Eighteenth Century.* London, 1940.

Tayler, J. J. "On the Influences and Responsibilities of Periodical Literature," *Christian Teacher,* N.S., I (1839), 1-20.

Tyerman, Luke. *Life and Times of the Rev. John Wesley.* 3 vols. New York, 1872.

———. *Life of the Rev. George Whitefield.* 2 vols. London, 1877.

Warter, J. W. *Selections from the Letters of Robert Southey.* 4 vols. London, 1856.

Whitley, W. T. *A History of British Baptists.* 2d edition. London, 1932.

Wright, Thomas. *Life of Augustus M. Toplady.* London, 1911.

III. BIOGRAPHY

Aikin, Lucy. "Memoir of Anna L. Barbauld," in *Works of Anna L. Barbauld.* London, 1825.

Aspland, Robert Brooks. *Memoir of Robert Aspland.* London, 1850.

Bain, Alexander. *John Stuart Mill, a Criticism, with Personal Recollections.* New York, 1882.

Baker, J. M. *Henry Crabb Robinson.* London, 1937.

Belsham, Thomas. *Memoirs of the late Rev. Theophilus Lindsey.* London, 1812.

Benson, A. B. "Fourteen Unpublished Letters by Henry Crabb Robinson: A Chapter in his Appreciation of Goethe," *Publications of the Modern Language Association,* XXXI (1916), 395-420.

Blunden, Edmund. *Leigh Hunt, a Biography.* London, 1930.

Bosanquet, Theodora. *Harriet Martineau.* London, 1927.

Bowring, John. *Autobiographical Recollections of Sir John Bowring, with a Brief Memoir by Lewin Bowring.* London, 1877.

———. "W. J. Fox," *Theological Review,* III (1866), 413-48.

Briddell-Fox, Mrs. E. "Robert Browning," *Argosy,* XLIX (1890), 108-14.

Browning, Robert. *Letters of . . . , Collected by Thomas J. Wise.* Edited by Thurman L. Hood. London, 1933.

Carlyle, Thomas. *Reminiscences.* New York, 1881.

Carré, J. M. "Un ami et défenseur de Goethe en Angleterre, Henry Crabb Robinson . . . ," *Revue Germanique,* July-August, 1912, pp. 386-92.

Carpenter, J. E. *James Martineau: Theologian and Teacher.* London, 1905.

Chambers, E. K. *Samuel Taylor Coleridge, a Biographical Study.* Oxford, 1938.

Conway, Moncure D. *Autobiography.* 2 vols. Boston, 1904.

Fowler, John. *Life and Literary Remains of Charles Reece Pemberton.* London, 1843.

Fox, Franklin. *Memoir of Mrs. Eliza Fox.* London, 1869.

Garnett, Richard. *The Life of W. J. Fox, Public Teacher and Social Reformer, 1786-1864.* London and New York, 1910.

[Grant, James]. *Portraits of Public Characters.* 2 vols. London, 1841.

Griffin, H. W. and H. C. Minchin. *Life of Robert Browning.* 3d edition. London, 1938.

Hamilton, M. A. *John Stuart Mill.* London, 1933.

Holt, Anne. *A Life of Joseph Priestley.* London, 1931.

Hovelaque, H. L. *La Jeunesse de Robert Browning.* Paris, 1932.

Howe, P. P. *Life of William Hazlitt.* London, 1922.

Howitt, Mary. *Autobiography.* 2 vols. Boston, 1889.

Hunt, Leigh. *Autobiography.* Oxford, 1928.

———. *Correspondence.* Edited by Thornton Leigh Hunt. 2 vols. London, 1862.

Kenrick, John. *Memoir of the Rev. John Kentish.* Birmingham, 1854.

Kitchell, Anna T. *George Lewes and George Eliot.* New York, 1933.

Landré, Louis. *Leigh Hunt.* 2 vols. Paris, 1935-1936.

Linton, W. J. *Threescore and Ten Years.* New York, 1894.

McLachlan, Herbert. *The Letters of Theophilus Lindsey*. Manchester, 1920.

——. *Records of a Family*. Manchester, 1935.

Martineau, Harriet. *Autobiography*. With Memorials, edited by Maria Weston Chapman. 2 vols. Boston, 1877.

Mayer, S. R. Townshend, editor. *Letters of Elizabeth Barrett Browning Addressed to Richard Hengist Horne*. 2 vols. London, 1877.

Medway, John. *Memoir of the Life and Writings of John Pye Smith*. London, 1853.

Memoirs of the Rev. Augustus Toplady, in *Works of Augustus Toplady*. London, 1853.

Mill, John Stuart. *Autobiography*. Edited by J. J. Coss. Columbia University Press, New York, 1924.

——. *Letters of John Stuart Mill*. Edited by H. S. R. Elliot. London, 1910.

Morley, Edith. *Life and Times of Henry Crabb Robinson*. London, 1935.

Neff, Emery. *Carlyle*. New York, 1932.

Norton, C. E. *Correspondence of Thomas Carlyle and Ralph Waldo Emerson*. Boston, 1883.

Orr, Mrs. Sutherland. *Life and Letters of Robert Browning*. Revised edition by F. G. Kenyon. London, 1908.

Osborne, J. H. "Reminiscences of W. J. Fox . . . and of the Author of 'Nearer, My God, to Thee,' " *Universalist Quarterly*, N.S., IX (1872), 293-314.

Rivenburg, Narola E. *Harriet Martineau, An Example of Victorian Conflict*. Philadelphia, 1932.

Robinson, Crabb. Diary. In typescript. Dr. Williams' Library, London.

Rutt, John Towill. *Memoir of Joseph Priestley*, in *The Theological and Miscellaneous Works of Joseph Priestley*. 26 vols. London, 1817-1832.

[Saunders, John]. "W. J. Fox," *People's Journal*, III (1847), 69-73.

Shackford, M. H. *E. B. Browning; R. H. Horne. Two Studies*. Wellesley, Mass., 1935.

Spears, Robert. *Record of Unitarian Worthies.* London, 1876.

Stephenson, H. W. *The Author of Nearer, My God, to Thee.* London, 1922.

Taylor, Emily. *Memories of Some Contemporary Poets.* London, 1868.

Thirlwall, J. C. *Life of Connop Thirlwall.* London, 1936.

Turner, William. *Lives of Eminent Unitarians.* 2 vols. London, 1850.

Wallace, Robert. *Antitrinitarian Biography.* 3 vols. London, 1850.

Wallas, Graham. *Life of Francis Place.* London, 1918.

———. *William Johnson Fox.* Conway Memorial Lecture. London, 1924.

Wardle, A. C. *Benjamin Bowring and His Descendants.* London, 1938.

[Watkins, J. and F. Shoberl]. *A Biographical Dictionary of the Living Authors of Great Britain and Ireland.* London, 1816.

Williams, John. *Memoirs of the Rev. Thomas Belsham.* London, 1833.

IV. GENERAL

Brewer, Luther A. *My Leigh Hunt Library.* Cedar Rapids, Iowa, 1932.

Brown, P. A. *The French Revolution in English History.* London, 1918.

DeVane, William C. *A Browning Handbook.* New York, 1935.

Dobell, Bertram. *Sidelights on Charles Lamb.* London, 1903.

Elkin, Felice. *Walter Savage Landor's Studies of Italian Life and Literature.* Philadelphia, 1934.

Fox, W. J. *Memorial Edition of the Collected Works of W. J. Fox.* 12 vols. London, 1865-1868.

Halévy, Élie. *The Growth of Philosophic Radicalism.* Translated by Mary Morris. New York, 1928.

———. *A History of the English People.* Translated by E. I. Watkin and D. A. Barker. 4 vols. New York, 1924-1929.

Halkett, S. and J. Laing. *Dictionary of Anonymous and Pseudonymous Literature.* 6 vols. Edinburgh, 1927.

Hazlitt, William. *Collected Works.* Vol. III. London, 1902.

[Horne, Richard Henry]. *Exposition of the False Medium and Barriers Excluding Men of Genius from the Public.* London, 1833.

Kenwood, S. H. "Lessing in England," *Modern Language Review,* IX (1914), 197-212; 344-58.

Landor, Walter Savage. *Complete Works of Walter Savage Landor,* ed. by T. Earle Welby. Vol. XI. London, 1930.

Lincoln, Anthony. *Some Political and Social Ideas of English Dissent, 1763-1800.* London, 1938.

Locke, John. *Works.* 3 vols. London, 1727.

Lounsbury, Thomas R. *The Early Literary Career of Robert Browning.* New York, 1911.

Maccoby, Simon. *English Radicalism, 1832-52.* London, 1935.

Martineau, Harriet. *Five Years of Youth; or Sense and Sentiment.* Boston, 1832.

———. *Miscellanies.* 2 vols. Boston, 1836.

———. *Traditions of Palestine.* London, 1830.

Martineau, James. *Essays, Reviews, and Addresses.* 4 vols. London, 1890-1891.

McLachlan, Herbert. *English Education under the Test Acts.* Manchester, 1931.

Mill, John Stuart. *Dissertations and Discussions.* Vol. I. New York, 1873.

Neff, Emery. *Carlyle and Mill.* Revised edition. New York, 1926.

Neff, Wanda F. *Victorian Working Women.* New York, 1928.

Nicoll, W. R. and T. J. Wise. *Literary Anecdotes of the Nineteenth Century.* 2 vols. London, 1895.

Norman, F. *Henry Crabb Robinson and Goethe. Publications of the English Goethe Society,* Vols. VI, VIII (1930-1931).

Pemberton, Charles Reece. *Autobiography of Pel. Verjuice.* With an Introduction by Eric Partridge. London, 1929.

Price, Richard. *A Discourse on the Love of Our Country, November 4, 1789.* London, 1789.

Priestley, Joseph. *Essay on First Principles of Government.* 2d edition. London, 1771.

Quinlan, Maurice J. *Victorian Prelude.* New York, 1941.

Robertson, J. H. *History of Free Thought in the Nineteenth Century.* 2 vols. London, 1929.

[Scargill, W. P.]. *Autobiography of a Dissenting Minister.* London, 1834.

Stephen, Leslie. *The English Utilitarians.* 3 vols. London, 1900.

——. *History of English Thought in the Eighteenth Century.* 2 vols. London, 1881.

Stockley, V. *German Literature as Known in England, 1750-1830.* London, 1929.

Stokoe, F. W. *German Influence in the English Romantic Period, 1788-1818.* Cambridge, 1926.

Trevelyan, G. M. *British History in the Nineteenth Century.* London, 1922.

Veitch, G. S. *The Genesis of Parliamentary Reform.* London, 1913.

Walker, Hugh. *The Literature of the Victorian Era.* Cambridge, 1921.

White, Newman I. *The Unextinguished Hearth.* Durham, N. C., 1938.

Wordsworth, William. *Poems.* 2 vols. London, 1815.

Index